The Life and Political Economy of Lauchlin Currie

Lauchlin Currie in 1981.
Courtesy of Simon Fraser University.

The Life and Political Economy of Lauchlin Currie

New Dealer, Presidential Adviser, and Development Economist

ROGER J. SANDILANDS

Duke University Press
Durham and London 1990

Printed in the United States of America
on acid-free paper ∞
Library of Congress Cataloging-in-Publication Data
appear on the last page of this book.

Contents

Preface

Although this book is a biography, its main purpose is to offer a "Guide to Currie" similar in its aims to Alvin Hansen's *Guide to Keynes* (1953). But whereas Hansen's work attempted only to explain J. M. Keynes' *General Theory,* this book surveys the development of Lauchlin Currie's thinking and policy advice published over several decades in both English and Spanish in a wide variety of books, articles, and memoranda, not all of which are readily accessible to scholars today.

Currie's first published contributions to economics appeared in 1931 while he was teaching money and banking at Harvard. In these he attempted to explain the causes of the Great Depression. His writings on monetary and fiscal theory and policy in the early 1930s led Herbert Stein (*Fiscal Revolution in America,* p. 165) to describe Currie as the intellectual leader of the New Dealers who advocated compensatory fiscal and monetary policy. He was "the one most capable of independent analysis in the field of Keynesian economics" and came "closer than any other American economist to anticipating Keynes." Currie came to "Keynesian" conclusions by analyzing the expected value of savings (leakages) at a projected full employment level of national income relative to the current volume of offsets in the form of private investment and the so-called federal "net contribution." But when the *General Theory* appeared he was, and remained, skeptical of the value of many of the new concepts and terms introduced by Keynes.

Instead, Currie was able to arrive at independent explanations of inadequate effective demand relative to full employment potential by careful definition, analysis, and quantitative estimation of the supply of money and the motives affecting its demand, or the income velocity of money. He pioneered new quantitative series for these and related variables, and this was to be of great value for policy purposes. He exerted a significant influence on institutional development and macroeconomic policy in drafting the 1935 Banking Act and in shaping New Deal monetary and fiscal policies from his position as assistant director of research at the Federal Reserve Board, 1934–39 and later as an administrative assistant to President Franklin D. Roosevelt in the White House from 1939–45.

During the Second World War he directed lend-lease operations to China 1941–43, was acting director of the Foreign Economic Administration 1943–44, and headed the American delegation to Bern, Switzerland, to persuade the Swiss to cease wartime cooperation with Germany and recover looted gold. His involvement in U.S. policy in China was one of the reasons he was to be caught up in the hysteria surrounding the McCarthy trials in the early 1950s.

In 1949–50 he directed a comprehensive economic and social survey of Colombia as director of the first World Bank country mission. He was retained by the Colombian government to help implement the policy recommendations of the World Bank report and later became a Colombian citizen. He has been an important adviser to almost every Colombian government since that time. An exception was during a military government, 1953–58, when he turned to full-time dairy farming.

Influenced greatly by his Harvard teacher, Allyn Young, Currie has developed important new approaches to the theory of growth and development and these have shaped his policy advice. In particular, he has developed a "leading sector" theory of development based on a subtle blend of Sayian and Keynesian demand concepts, or of real and monetary demand. To escape the vicious circle of small market size and slow growth he has advocated policies to stimulate the construction sector and exports. This included a major institutional innovation, the constant-value, or indexed housing finance system that was introduced in 1972 as part of the Plan of the Four Strategies, written by Currie and implemented by the administration of President Misael Pastrana and which has sustained building throughout a long period of high inflation. He has also worked extensively on city planning.

My book was written during 1987–90 when Currie was still very active in policy advice, teaching, and writing. Thus the biography ends with a still evolving story of intellectual and policy contributions both in monetary and growth theory. My own association with Currie dates from the time he was my teacher and supervisor, in Canada and Scotland, between 1967 and 1970, and when his Colombian wife, Elvira Wiesner de Currie, taught me Spanish. Subsequently

I have worked extensively in Latin America, mainly Colombia, including periods as Currie's assistant at the Colombian National Planning Department and at the Colombian Savings and Housing Institute which commissioned me to write this biography.[1]

Professor Currie made available to me all his very extensive files that date from the early 1930s, together with some memoirs of his early life as a child in Nova Scotia and as a student at the London School of Economics and Harvard. I have been able to conduct extensive interviews with Professor Currie on every stage of his astonishingly varied career. His memory and analytical powers have remained extraordinarily clear and incisive even in his late eighties. Our discussions of his past and on-going work have for me, and I hope for him also, been immensely stimulating. Professor Currie has read my manuscript but, apart from correcting certain factual errors and mentioning certain gaps in coverage, has left me to make my own interpretations, appraisals, emphases, and organization of the material as I have found it in his files and published work. As will become clear, my assessment has, overall, been sympathetic; but Currie has encouraged and welcomed criticism and has himself drawn my attention to inconsistencies and weaknesses in his ideas and advice at various times.

One's overall impression is of a man forcefully driven since childhood not only to be right but to persuade others that he is right. Though often caught up in the heated fray, he has also tried to stand back from events of the moment to distinguish primary from secondary issues and convince policymakers to establish a rational set of priorities to achieve lasting results.

Though he has applied his penetrating mind and energy to identify fundamental principles and ideals he is also a pragmatist. A pragmatist, not in the sense that he will easily compromise with what seems easiest, most practical, most popular, or most "realistic," but in the sense that he has relentlessly promoted what he thinks needs to be done and what, given the will, could be done to put logical ideas rather than emotional gestures into practice. The will to act on principles in turn is subject to persuasion and Currie has, despite innumerable disappointments, never lost his faith or hope that, sooner or later, his powers of persuasion as a teacher, writer and policy adviser will pay dividends.

Apart from expressing my sincere gratitude to the Colombian Savings and Housing Institute, the Colombian Coffee Federation, and the University of Strathclyde (which gave me extended leaves of absence to write this book), I should also like to thank several individuals who have offered valuable comments on earlier drafts or in interviews, not least the publisher's anonymous readers. Byrd Jones of the University of Massachussetts was particularly helpful in making available to me his extensive notes on records in the U.S. National Archives and in suggesting additional insights into the New Deal era. Walter Salant of the Brookings Institution also made extensive comments on this period and on the later discussions on monetary and growth theory. Don Patinkin of the Israel Academy of Sciences and Humanities was very helpful on Currie, Keynes, and the Chicago School. Richard M. Goodwin of the University of Siena sent a fascinating letter on Currie, Schumpeter, and the Harvard of the early 1930s, which is reproduced in chapter 2.

On China, I am greatly indebted to Professor John Fairbank of Harvard, who read several drafts of chapters 4 and 5 and sent detailed and perceptive comments. My colleague David Williams at the University of Strathclyde and the late Washington-based journalist Joseph Alsop were also helpful on this episode.

On the general issues of growth and development I am indebted to my colleague Anthony Clunies-Ross. A. P. Thirlwall of the University of Kent gave valuable comments on an early draft of chapter 12, which caused me to extend greatly my discussion of the differences between Currie and Nicholas Kaldor in their very different interpretations of the ideas of their common mentor, Allyn Young, concerning the nature of "increasing returns and economic progress" and the policy implications. Professor Thirlwall, who recently produced a sympathetic and illuminating biography of Lord Kaldor, may not share my conclusions, though his earlier comments have, I believe, helped me to sharpen the issues.

On Colombia, I have benefited over the years from discussions with far more people than I can mention here. Recently I have been indebted to Luis Eduardo Rosas, Director of the Colombian Savings and Housing Institute, James Hanson of the World Bank, Alvaro Montenegro of New York University, Wilfred Owen of Brookings, Enrique Peñalosa, Colombian Ambassador to the United Nations in New York, and ex-President Misael Pastrana Borrero, who told me of his great sense of challenge and pleasure when Currie said, at their first meeting in the Presidential Palace in 1971, that his feelings then were the same as those he had on first entering the White House to serve President Roosevelt in 1939.

The entire first draft of my manuscript was typed in Bototá by Olga Lucía Gómez with extreme efficiency and cheerfulness, despite my scrappy writing in a language foreign to her. She also dealt with my extensive revisions, ably assisted by Alica de Tellez, to whom I am also most grateful.

Glasgow, February 1990

The Life and Political Economy of Lauchlin Currie

CHAPTER 1

The Early Years, 1902–25

Introduction

Lauchlin Currie's life (1902–) spans most of the twentieth century. He has been a student and top-level teacher and practitioner of economics and public administration for nearly seventy years. His professional work has carried him to many parts of the globe. Born a Canadian in Nova Scotia in 1902 he later assumed U.S. citizenship in 1934 in order to accept a government post in the U.S. Treasury; and then in 1958, at a time when a naturalized U.S. citizen could not reside outside the United States for more than five years without losing citizenship, he was invited personally by the President of the Republic of Colombia—where he had married and been settled for some years—to assume Colombian nationality. Aside from four or five years as a visiting professor at various American, Canadian, and British universities, he has lived and worked in Colombia for most of the period since 1949 when he was appointed as the director of the first World Bank mission to Colombia.

His first exposure to higher education was as a student at St. Francis Xavier University in Nova Scotia in 1920. Many years later the celebrated economist Harry G. Johnson was to obtain his first teaching appointment there, but in the early 1920s the college could offer relatively little instruction in the subjects that were beginning to arouse the interest of the young Lauchlin Currie and he moved on to the London School of Economics in 1922 without obtaining a degree from St. Francis Xavier's. Sixty-six years later, in May 1988, that was to be rectified when the university awarded him a Doctor of Laws, Honoris Causa.

After graduating from London in 1925 he attended graduate school at Harvard where he remained to teach until 1934 when Jacob Viner invited him to join his "Freshman Brain Trust" at the U.S. Treasury.

From there he moved with Marriner Eccles to the Federal Reserve Board where he was assistant director of research until his appointment in 1939 to the position of personal assistant to President Franklin Delano Roosevelt—thus becoming the first professional economist to work in the White House. During the 1930s he became, according to Herbert Stein's history of this period,[1] the intellectual leader of the New Deal economists, developing—independently of the Keynes of the *General Theory*—both the theoretical rationale for unbalanced budgets and extensive statistical support for macroeconomic policies to combat depression.

During the Second World War he directed the lend-lease program to China and made two important trips to Chungking in 1941 and 1942, meeting with leaders such as Chiang Kai-shek and Chou En-lai. He was also de facto director of the Foreign Economic Administration, 1943–44, and head of the American delegation to the Bern Conference in February 1945.

After a period as a private economic consultant in New York he was invited to direct the World Bank mission to Colombia in 1949–50. He has been a distinguished and often very controversial adviser, in a formal or informal capacity, to almost every Colombian administration since that time and is widely regarded as having done more than any other individual to promote serious thinking and policy on the economic development of that country. He has also written extensively for a wider, international audience on the theory and practice of growth and development and macroeconomics generally.

In the early 1950s he drafted some memoirs of his early life and work in the New Deal. However, these were never completed and never published, though copies were circulated and used by a few historians of the New Deal and wartime economic management such as Arthur Schlesinger and Herbert Stein. In drafting my own account and assessment of Currie's career after his arrival at Harvard in 1925 I deliberately ignored his memoirs, preferring to piece together first my own story from his published writings and unpublished speeches, memoranda, and correspondence in those years, together with contemporary records by other writers and the assessments of later historians. Only later did I check for consistency and completeness with the memoirs Currie wrote in 1952. I then incorporated a few passages into my own text.

For the early years, 1902–25, however, there can be no better record than the very personal account that Currie himself provided in his memoirs of the family and cultural influences on his early development as a child and student. I have, therefore, chosen to reproduce this material in its entirety. It is a revealing psychological self-portrait, and in 1952 Currie was reasonably well equipped to undertake an honest and objective analysis of self-development, having been closely associated for ten years after 1940 with some of America's leading psychoanalysts such as Harry Stack Sullivan, Erich Fromm, and Frieda von Reichman. Currie was for a time a member of the board of the William Alanson White Foundation (which established the famous Washington Institute of Psychiatry) in Washington and later was secretary of its New York branch. Also, he had himself undergone intensive and painfully revealing therapy for three or four months in 1945 with Benjamin Weiniger, on Harry Stack Sullivan's recommendation.

Currie's father had very successfully built up a fleet of merchant ships that sailed between Nova Scotia and the West Indies, South America, and Europe; but he had died when Lauchlin was only four. His mother was the greatest influence on his life, spurring him on to emulate his dead father, firing his ambition, and placing responsibilities on him as fast as he could handle them. She was an educated woman and, in a quiet way, strong and demanding. Years later, when her son informed her of his appointment as instructor at Harvard University, the news was greeted with characteristic nonchalance that indicated that she expected nothing less. Currie's life would, therefore, be an unending struggle to prove himself, to others but more especially to himself, and to fulfill his talents and the high expectations of those he himself held in high esteem. He would drive himself hard and expect the same of others. This is not always the recipe for harmonious relations but it is a necessary, if not a sufficient, condition for high achievement.

This biography is the story of those strivings and the results. It begins with Currie's own account, written in 1952, of the beginnings.

Currie's Memoirs: "The First Twenty Three Years"

Nova Scotia and California, 1902–22

I was born on October 8, 1902 on a cold foggy morning in a little fishing village called West Dublin on that side of Nova Scotia that fronts the Lab-

Currie's birthplace in West Dublin, a fishing village in Nova Scotia, 1904.

rador Current. I was the last of a family of five and was apparently not particularly welcomed. No name had been chosen in advance and my father lost interest in his hobby of selecting boys' names with a middle name beginning with V (Verne, Victor, Vincent). Perhaps to justify his suggestion that I be given his name, he said that I looked so small and puny I probably wouldn't live long anyway. In any case, my mother long afterward told me that I had cried continuously for 3 years and that she thought I would never learn to walk or talk,—hardly an auspicious start. In fact, when I finally did learn to walk, my career almost came to an abrupt end first by my setting myself on fire and again by my falling off the edge of a wharf into the ocean. In both cases I was saved by my father. It is fortunate I had no further misadventures as after the second one, when I repaid him on our cold wet trek back to the house by throwing stones at him and blubbering that I wanted "Ma" to rescue me, he swore that I could save myself the next time—a not unreasonable response under the circumstances.

He was in many respects a remarkable man. He was left at the age of sixteen by the drowning of his father in Halifax harbor, with his mother and a brother and many sisters to support. With little formal schooling and with few local opportunities, he supported the family, gradually acquired a substantial fleet of sailing vessels and left us reasonably well off by the time of his early death when he was only 44, on the income of which we lived very comfortably for the next twenty years. Unfortunately, I was only four when he died so I have few independent recollections of him. I have always liked my mother's story accounting for his success. After his father's drowning, a malicious neighbor said with ill concealed satisfaction that now young Lauch Currie would have to go to work like the rest of them. When this was reported to my father he said, "I'll be damned if I work" meaning, of course, manual work, and never did. He also, curiously enough, hated the sea from which he did so well and would never sail with any of his vessels on the trade of salt codfish to the West Indies, South America and even Spain, with return cargos of rum, salt, molasses and sugar. He combined the business acumen of the Scottish with a Scottish weakness,—fondness for hard liquor, and it was undoubtedly this latter that contributed to his early death. According to the family historian, a cousin by the same name as I who became prominent in Nova Scotian political life, the Curries had been the hereditary bards (poets and musicians) for many hundreds of years to the Clan Ranald MacDonald and had fallen on evil days after the Battle of Culloden Moor when they took refuge in South Uist in the Hebrides. From there my grandfather emigrated to Nova Scotia as a boy, running away, it is said, from an unsympathetic stepmother.

My mother, on the other hand, was of predominently German stock, bearing a name that was later to become very well known,—Eisenhauer—though with what she insisted was the correct German spelling. The first Eisenhauer, in a party of German emigrants, had been settled in 1755 by a British promoter in a cold, inhospitable part of Nova Scotia which they called Lunenburg.[2] When, in later life, I was much concerned with the problem of elevating standards of living, especially in lands more favored by Nature, I could not help marveling how my German forebears of two hundred years ago, in a land of rocks, hills and virgin forest where the efforts of three months a year must be devoted to the provision for the other nine, with little education or capital equipment, with primitive means of transport and harassed by the Indians, were able, in a very few years, to create for themselves a high standard of living in the essentials—health, food, shelter and clothing. It is certainly a tribute to the importance of the human factor in explaining a standard of living. With all this, they were able to maintain their religious fervor and a modicum of culture though they were almost entirely of peasant stock. My grandfather, for example, whose job was that of an expert sawyer—the man who hand sharpened all the various saws in a saw mill—, made and played a very fine violoncello in his spare time.

For better or for worse, my mother was unquestionably the dominant influence in my life. It was she who spurred me to emulate my dead father, who fired my ambition and placed responsibilities on me as rapidly as I could handle them. At the age of twelve I was harassing the very dear but not too practical executor of my father's estate (William E. Marshall) into raising interest rates on long outstanding mortgages and in checking on whether fire insurance policies on mortgaged properties had been kept up. I must have been quite a trial to the poor man, who actually had considerable renown as a poet.

It was also my mother who devised the system of providing me with pocket money. We had, shortly after my father's death, moved slightly inland and away from the fogs to the pleasant little town of Bridgewater, where I was to spend most of my boyhood. Everything that I could raise and sell from about an acre of ground was mine, even though my mother would, for example, buy the feed for the chickens. In this way, I had at least the illusion that I earned myself everything I spent.

My mother, a former schoolteacher, was an assiduous reader and I never lacked for books. For years I subscribed to The Boy's Own Paper—the beloved B.O.P.—and Chums from England, and to the Youth's Companion from the United States. I was probably of the last generation that read everything by G. A. Henty one could lay one's hands on. He was a prolific English boys' writer whose one hundred odd books covered practically every war in history. Although in reality they were rather tediously written, with long accounts of the disposition of forces in every battle, I have never been so enthralled by anything I read since. Even to-day, a mere memory of the titles—The Young Carthagenians, With Pike and Dyke, Under Drake's Flag and the others—still arouse a feeling of pleasureable excitement. The books were heavily moral in tone and invariably, in the case of the young hero, merit was richly awarded. After this rich fare, I found Horatio Alger and the Merriwell books rather tepid.

In view of my later and what most people may think my too facile changes in nationality, the influence of my early reading should not be overlooked. At that time, the paucity of strictly Canadian literature led me to read almost entirely English and American books and I was more familiar with those countries' histories than with that of my own. Thus, at a very early age, I felt almost as much at home in certain aspects of those two cultures as in Canadian. In the Maritime Provinces, again speaking of that time, we felt in many ways closer to New England than to the rest of English-speaking Canada, from whom we were separated by French-speaking Quebec. The movement between Massachusetts and Nova Scotia was sufficiently heavy to justify a steamship line and it was commonly said that there were more Nova Scotians living in Massachusetts than in Nova Scotia. I had an aunt and an uncle and numerous cousins living in Massachusetts and this was a common experience with many families. With my mother, I spent one winter in Worcester, and it was there, curiously enough, that I learned to do two things supremely important to me—to read and to skate. Later, at the age of sixteen, I was to spend a year in Redlands, California. Thus, by the time I went to study at Harvard and live in Cambridge, I went not as a stranger—an emigrant—but rather as a person returning to familiar surroundings. Similarly, when I went to study for three years in England I felt almost as much at home, although the marked difference in accents and little things like the different system of money will cause a Canadian, at least initially, to feel more a stranger in England than in the United States. In any case, it is apparent that at a young and impressionable age, I developed no excessively strong sense of nationality such as is normally experienced by, say, American children who share only unconsciously in the cultures of other nationalities. This is not to say that I was not a product of a particular culture at a particular time and will not remain so until my death but only that that culture did not happen to be very strongly nationalistic in tone.

In fact, I am still so much a child of a certain environment that I cannot conceive of better surroundings for a growing boy than a small town in the Maritime Provinces of Canada. The long winters were not a burden but a source of delight. The long winter nights, after the early supper at six o'clock, were a time to read near hot air registers. The woods came to the edge of town and continually beckoned a boy with a dog and a gun or a fishing rod or rabbit snares, depending on the season. One swam in the river and lakes in summer and skated on them in the winter. The exhilaration of a bobsled ride down a steep and often icy hillside can only be compared to skiing, which, unfortunately only came in after my boyhood. One knew everyone, young and old, and it is difficult to imagine how a child in a city can possibly have the same sense of "belonging"—of having one's roots firmly embedded in a particular place. When one went "downtown" to the Post Office, largely in the secret hope of catching a glimpse of a particular girl and maybe even speaking to her, one greeted and was greeted by everyone—one was Lauchlin Currie, the son of Alice Currie and the brother of Marguerite and Arthur Currie.

We were among the better-to-do, but there were few class lines. Nearly everybody was middle class, and although my mother did not invite workers or farmers to the house, we were friendly and I played with their children. It was not quite as idyllic as the condition described in Longfellow's Evangeline "where the rich were poor, and the poor had abundance" but almost. Two of my mother's closest friends were spinster sisters who had nothing. One was a dressmaker and one an expert cook. They both helped to prepare and then attended my mother's "parties" and no one thought anything of it. On Saturday mornings, market day, my mother would discuss many things with our particular farmer, with a complete absence of any condescension. In her eyes, a cardinal sin was "putting on airs" or snobbery of any sort. People were judged by their qualities, not by their money or social position. It was a sturdy, democratic community and the genesis of my later predilection for the New Deal and my indifference to social distinctions can probably be traced to this early environment.

I witnessed, in my youth, the passing of a particular type of social life. In the period before the First World War, social life was truly social. Whether it was a picnic, a motorboat trip down the river, a moon-light excursion, a sleigh ride in a big farm sleigh wagon, or a "party"—it was participated in by fifteen, twenty or more people and almost invariably included a long period of singing of old favorite songs. There was little occasion or opportunity for couples to go out alone. During and immediately after the First World War, all this changed, probably because of the coming of the automobile. Certainly couples preferred the new freedom, but there was a loss, especially in the group singing. We purchased our first car, a Chevrolet, in 1915 or 1916.

Both my elder brother, Arthur, and I were members of the Town Band. We played at garden parties, all winter at the Rink and, in the early days of the First World War, at recruiting rallies and at political functions. I was the youngest member of the Band for a time and I wore short pants. My uniform was a band cap. In the later days of the War, word would be telephoned before the arrival of the daily train from Halifax if a returning soldier was on board and a factory whistle would be blown. This entitled me to be excused from school to rush to the station. Sometimes only five or six of us would arrive in time but we did our best to give a welcome. Neither my brother nor I were very good musicians and my mother, who had a very true ear, used to suffer when she listened to the band.

My father was descended from those Highland Scots that had never been touched by the Reformation so that we were Catholics. There were very few Catholics in the town or indeed, in the country, and one priest had five parishes so that we could attend Mass only once a month. I acted as altar boy and my mother played the organ. It was a tolerant community and the Protestants always made a success of our annual Garden Party on which we relied heavily for funds for church repairs, furnishings and so forth. Through what I understood was a special dispensation, my father was a member of the Odd Fellows and I was always very much impressed when, on the annual grave decorating day, a group of Odd Fellows would wend their way to the Catholic Cemetery to decorate my father's grave. It was an early lesson in tolerance.

I mentioned spending one winter in Worcester, Mass. In addition we spent a winter in Sydney, Nova Scotia and another one in Halifax, both of which I recall with pleasure. My closest friend in the former ended up in a Reform School and in the latter became Vicar of St. Mary's Cathedral, Halifax. It was in Halifax, when I was thirteen or fourteen that I first began to take a serious interest in school, undoubtedly owing to a splendid teacher, Madam Sullivan of the Sacred Heart Convent. Her hold on her boys was such that we would often devote precious Saturday mornings waxing the floor of our school room. Upon my return to Bridgewater I was able to skip the Eighth Grade and so made up one of the years I had earlier lost through the frequent moves we made.

Despite those extended visits, Bridgewater was always home. But now occurred an event that was to mark my first loss of "roots"—of a sense of belonging. With rising prices and on a fixed income and the moving away of my brother and sister, we decided to sell our house. It was a sensible thing to do, but it meant that henceforth we visited in Bridgewater, rather than belonged there. Shortly after, we went to Southern California and from there I moved on to St. Francis Xavier College in Antigonish, Nova Scotia.

The year in Redlands, California, 1919–20, with my mother and sister, and where I was a junior in High School, was one long holiday. I received "credit" for music (band and orchestra), tennis (physical training) and debating. I recall representing Redlands in a debate with another high-school, taking the affirmative of the topic, "Resolved that the United States should intervene in Mexico with military forces!" I am glad to say we lost. It was also at Redlands that I recall an early example of my tendency to say and write unpopular things. The Human Fly climbed one of the higher buildings before a large and appreciative audience. I pointed out in the school paper that the only reason people went to see him was the morbid possibility that he would fall—that if he walked along a horizontal pole a foot above the ground, a feat requiring greater skill, nobody would bother to go to see him. As I might have expected, my classmates did not care for this analysis of their motivation.

We purchased a second hand Studebaker, a 1915 model, for weekend excursions in Southern California, as far as the Mexican border and the Imperial Valley and resolved to return to Nova Scotia in it. With a tent and cots strapped on the running board and a water bag dangling behind, we started out bravely enough, intending to follow more or less The Lincoln Highway. Unfortunately, that existed then only as a broad line on the maps. The trip was one long detour, with frequent breakdowns, one while crossing the Continental Divide, in Colorado, lasting the better part of a week. We holed up in an abandoned lumber camp and lived mainly on potatoes and dandelion greens. It was to be thirty years later, in Colombia, before I drove again on narrow dirt roads winding along the edge of canyons. After two months and many side excursions to various cities we arrived in Nova Scotia and my familiarity with the United States was further extended.

The two years I spent at St. Francis Xavier's University in a beautiful small town in northern Nova Scotia were strenuous and enjoyable. In one I completed my high school requirements and in the other I combined the Freshman and Sophomore Years by taking an impossible schedule of nine courses. The tone of the college was heavily religious and, in my time, about half the graduating class elected to study for the priesthood. Although there were some excellent teachers, both priests and laymen, the emphasis was on the classical and memory side, with textbooks and prescribed reading in all courses. Since at that time I had an excellent memory I had no difficulty in heading my class. Though I was very weak in mathematics, I got through my geometry and trigonometry by memorizing the solutions to all the problems listed at the end of each chapter from which the examination questions were invariably taken. In addition, I took private tutoring in Latin from the classics teacher, an Oxford man, and remember with a good deal of pleasure trying to produce elegant translations of Horace and Cicero. I won the prize in Church History, was on the orchestra and debating team and represented my class on the school paper.

Dr. Coady was just beginning his work in introducing Adult Education and Producer Cooperatives under the sponsorship of the Church, and which was later to become very well known. I acted as a sort of private secretary to him and he liked to dictate his speeches and sermons to me as I could take them down very rapidly in my kind of long shorthand and try to supply the elusive word. Although he didn't often accept my suggestion, it apparently helped him to find the word he wanted.

Under the influence of the environment, I had a rather intense religious experience, receiving communion daily and toying with the idea of the priesthood. My love of the things of the world and the flesh was too strong, however, and I realized that I had no vocation. I was probably the most consistent violator of the student imposed rule against "goofing" by a First Year man, i.e. engaging in the perfectly innocent and harmless practice of walking with a girl during our short free period from 3–4:45 every afternoon. The penalty was the painless but humiliating one of being seized by a group of upperclassmen, while the girl ran, and being tossed in the air half a dozen times. A more serious violation was attending, under pain of expulsion, the town skating rink at night. I did this so often that the school authorities must have known but I was never caught creeping into the school grounds long after lights were out and nothing was ever said to me. Maybe it was because I was, in every other respect, a model student. In any case, these two examples may indicate that I was not of the stuff that good priests are made.

In my second year, I began to get restless and feel that I should be getting more out of college. I pored over the catalogues of larger universities and eventually, under the influence of my classics professor, decided to try for Oxford. It was for this I took special tutoring in Latin and we actually began correspondence with University College, Oxford. About this time, I talked to the Vice Chancellor of the University, Father James Tompkins, who had one of the most active and enquiring minds on the campus. He shocked me, by saying in his high piping voice, "Don't go to Oxford. They're all dead there. If you want to go to England, go to the London School of Economics where they're alive. Laski, Webb, Hobhouse, Wallas and the others. Dangerous and irreligious men—but extremely able! Here, look over the catalogue". This was the end of Oxford for me. I wasn't sure what economics and political theory were about, but they sounded most exciting. Thus, at a certain moment, can offhand advice in a five minute talk change the course of one's life and work.

I immediately wrote to the London School and to my mother. The school replied that in lieu of the London Matriculation I could sit for a short general examination in four subjects, which I would have no difficulty in passing. My mother replied that she had always wanted to see England and would like to accompany me. So things were quickly decided and we sailed for England in the fall of 1922.

The London School of Economics, 1922–25

The impact of London and the London School of Economics on me, at that age, was tremendous. At one step I was translated from an intellectual backwater into one of the most intellectually stimulating spots in the world. I had read no modern literature and had no knowledge of nor interest in the great political controversies of our times. I had seen few plays, heard no first class music, and had come into contact with few, if any, first class minds or original thinkers.

At first, the impact was almost overpowering and I became very discouraged. Without the aid of a textbook, I failed in two of my four initial tests, French and English. I could not even identify the quotation "He maketh me to lie down in green pastures". They were, in reality, most easy tests and on the second try, with the aid of Hugo's Language School and poring over two little books on famous quotations, I passed them. The transition from being at the top of my class to failing in a specially devised easy examination for overseas students was only the first shock. The student speakers in the School's Union—a kind of debating society—filled me with awe with their easy improvised brilliance and wit and I sat silent and forlorn. My first friend seemed to have read everything and discoursed easily on any topic that came to hand while I felt an ignoramus.

However, after a bit, it became very exciting. After the talk by a great speaker at the Union—which could be Winston Churchill, Bertrand Russell; or another well-known figure—I would go home highly stimulated and write a long account of it in my diary, and discuss it at length with my friend the next day. New ideas and perspectives came so rapidly that I could not digest them. I was in an intellectual ferment and nothing seemed stable or fixed. My mother and I went to one or two plays or musical events every week and I made my first acquaintance with Shakespeare and Opera at the Old Vic. Also, I began to read furiously in modern literature, trying to make up for lost time.

I enjoyed being treated like a serious adult at the School. No attendance records, no textbooks, no hour or quarterly examination or tests—in fact no examinations at all except at the end of the first and third (last) years. Simply lectures and suggested books on collateral reading. In this way, one could arrange one's schedule rationally and devote an intensive period to one subject without interruption and begin to get some sense of getting inside of it and mastering it. The lectures, one a week in each subject, were repeated in the evening for the students who were working, and in my third year I made it a practice of reading all day at my desk in the reading room of the British Museum and catching up on the lectures from 6 to 8 o'clock in the evening. In this way, I would read an enormous amount on a subject in say a month. Although for my major subject, economic theory, I prepared papers and discussed and defended them in class, I feel in retrospect that there was not enough of this type of work and too much passive reading. It was probably assumed that one would discuss the subjects with one's classmates and it is true that a lot of this took place. With me, however, discussion could not take the place of writing as a means of developing one's ideas in an orderly fashion.

The School was undergoing a transition when I was there. The last of the founders, The Fabians, were passing from the scene and the School was feeling its way to a new orientation. Sidney Webb was giving a few lectures on municipal organization which I attended, more out of respect for the man than interest in the subject. Edwin Cannan was the Professor in Economic Theory. He had an acute and observing mind, was impatient of too elaborately evolved theories, and insisted on the down-to-earth, common-sense approach to economics. Although the School had a strong socialistic (in the British sense of the word) tinge, Cannan was mistrustful on the whole of State intervention and generally believed that things worked out "naturally" better than planned. He induced in us a superior attitude toward the great Cambridge economists, Marshall and Pigou, which was a little unfortunate since we were inclined to be critical without really knowing what we were criticizing. This same tendency existed in the courses on money and banking toward Keynes and I only came really to appreciate him much later. It was probably fortunate for my continuance in economics that I went to London instead of Cambridge as I could not have handled the amount of mathematical economics then stressed at Cambridge and would have been repelled by the subject. Cannan, on the other hand, gave the young student the comfortable, if somewhat misleading assurance that all that was needed for the solution of economic problems was the application of enlightened common sense.

Political theory was the domain of Harold Laski and he was easily the most brilliant and stimulating lecturer at the School. His hours would pass like five minutes and one had the illusion of how easily society could be organized on rational grounds. This illusion faded, however, when one came to re-read one's notes. The epigrams and wit were lacking and the bare skeleton of the argument frequently failed to carry conviction. It was my relatively poor showing in political theory that prevented me from receiving First Class Honors on my graduation and I had to be content with Second. Curiously enough, the only course in which I received a B instead of an A later at Harvard was in the same subject under Professor McIlwain. Obviously political theory was not my forte.

The most liked teacher at the School was Lillian Knowles, the economic historian. Her book was almost unreadable but she had a warm, kindly personality that endeared her to the students. Eileen Power, the historian, was the Glamor Girl on the faculty. In the course on logic, which I selected in place of mathematics, I gained what I never did from the latter. It was an excellent training in critical analysis and infinitely more useful for a person with my type of mind than mathematics. I struggled through Bowley's course in statistics. Hugh Dalton and Lees-Smith were later to become Labor Government Ministers. The former in public finance, was sardonic and amusing.

At this point it is worth pausing to consider an important influence on Currie at this time that is not brought out in his written memoirs. Currie had greatly enjoyed Dr. Wolf's course in formal logic which gave him powers of reasoning that he was never able to get from mathematics. He treasured "the six fallacies," especially the fallacy of composition. Thus he delighted in Keynes's exposure of this fallacy in ridiculing Dalton's proposal for a capital levy to pay off the national debt. Currie wrote later:[3]

Despite our rivalry with Cambridge I admired Keynes and I was considerably influenced by his early writings on the Economic Consequences of the Peace and his Economic Consequences of Mr. Churchill. The school was weak in monetary theory. So there were two supplementary influences, Cannan, in "getting behind the monetary veil to real things" and Keynes' insistence on the importance of the monetary veil! As brash young students we used to refer condescendingly to old Marshall and Pigou, for which I now blush. Remembering how critical students can be I look uneasily at my present classes and wonder how they refer to me.

In the early 1930s Currie applied Keynes's early insights on the difference between private and social accounting to justify unbalanced budgets as a remedy for the Great Depression. He thus felt a deep intellectual debt to the early Keynes but remained skeptical of the value of the later *General Theory*. As will be brought out in later chapters, Currie has applied the fallacy-of-composition test to a wide range of theoretical and policy issues and has found that the fallacy is pervasive, for example, in marginal productivity theory, in the "law" of diminishing returns, in the theory of declining marginal utility, in conclusions on the effect of productivity growth on farm incomes, in land use decisions in city planning, in social security schemes, and in the definition of money and the effect of changes in the demand for money.

However, returning to other influences from his London School of Economics days, Currie's 1952 memoirs continue:

> Curiously enough, I took no course with one of the professors at the School who influenced me most—J. H. Hobhouse. His two books—*Mind in Evolution* and *Morals in Evolution*—made a profound impression on me, as previously my world had been one of absolutes. For a time, I saw everything in comparative and relative terms—which was rather paralizing of enthusiams. I suppose it was a belated reproduction of the shock the Victorians experienced under the first impact of the idea of evolution. Another who influenced me greatly was R. H. Tawney. His *Acquisitive Society* and *Elements of Social Justice* I found exciting and they made me aware of the abuses of privilege much more than did Laski's lectures and books. Graham Wallas' explorations in *The Great Society* and *The Art of Thinking* helped to make me more aware of my mental processes and the always hidden motivations of convictions and views. Actually they were suggestive rather than profound books but they helped in the general ferment of ideas that was taking place. In one of his public lectures Graham Wallas said that in listening or reading we should always be alert to hear that thin small voice within us that cries "fiddlesticks." At the end of his lecture Tawney said that all throughout Professor Wallas' lecture he kept hearing that thin small voice. Wallas' sense of humor did not extend that far.
>
> Two younger teachers who had a great influence on me were Eve and Arthur R. Burns. She was Cannan's assistant and he a lecturer in Kings College and I passed many enjoyable and highly stimulating evenings at a kind of seminar they organized at their apartment. They later came to the United States where she became one of the outstanding authorities in social legislation and he, Chariman of the Department of Economics at Columbia University—both remaining excellent friends through the years. Lionel Robbins, who was shortly to play an important róle in changing the character of the School, was two years ahead of me and we never met. On the other hand I got to know well several graduate students, Talcott and Helen Parsons and Allen G.B. Fisher.
>
> My mother returned to Canada after a year and after we utilized my first vacation, having been joined by my sister Marguerite, to tour the British

Isles and Paris. I thereupon moved into a typical boarding house on Guilford Street, near the School and the British Museum. The landlady was a terror and the meals still a distasteful memory but the other boarders were interesting, one being the amateur ballroom dancing champion of England and another a highly intelligent woman from South Africa who made a precarious living by playing a cello in orchestras and writing pot-boilers for pulp magazines. I forgot about the meals in the flood of argument and anecdote that accompanied every meal. I also met there an English student, Burn Edgecombe, taking the commerce course at the School, and we shortly joined forces and roomed together for the next two years and I visited his home in Somerset many times. This association with hearty and simple middle-class people and my joining in the social life of their town did more than anaything else to make me feel at home in England.

Before that, I had been the recipient of many kindnesses from Lady Francis Ryder, who arranged for invitations for students from the Dominions to many country homes. Those visits were interesting and dispelled the loneliness of living in a great city, but I rarely felt completely comfortable or at home—the contrast was too great to my simple upbringing. I recall in particular an Easter visit to an enormous place near Bath. The interests of my host, a retired general, were limited to the army and sport, in neither of which I had the slightest interest. The going was difficult for both of us.

I was a member of the British-American Dance Club, which arranged dances every week or so during the season, and of something called The Empire Poetry League. The reading of poetry was a bit of a bore but the Sunday walking excursions along relatively unknown by-ways in the neighboring counties, ending at some country inn, were a joy.

To get around more, I purchased a motorcycle in my second year. It had only one recommendation,—it was cheap to operate. For the rest it was noisy, dirty, wet and exceedingly dangerous. My room mate and I, during the long vacation in 1924, toured the Continent with it and a sidecar. It was not a bad way to see Europe if you only have a couple of hundred dollars and don't mind sleeping in the fields, but I would recommend it only for the very young and very healthy. After our return I had a bad crash on a wet country road in which I broke my ankle and nearly lost my life. I sold the motorcycle with a great sigh of relief and nothing would ever persuade me to mount another.

I would not say that my three years in England were the happiest years of my life but they unquestionably were the most stimulating and intellectually exciting. I felt without moorings or anchor and religion did not give me the stable base it had before. The diary I kept at that time reflected many moods of depression and even despair. For a time, my favorite author was Hardy whose gloomy picture of the Universe was one dominated by blind forces and chance, and whose heroes were generally enmeshed in a series of cruel and unmerited frustrations. I remember starting Jude the Obscure late one evening and putting it down at four o'clock in the morning with a gasp. It ends with the completely frustrated and embittered Jude dying alone reciting aloud the psalm of Job "cursed be the day I was born" and so forth. Another favorite author was a brilliant young English naturalist who died young and who wrote under the name of N. P. Barbellion. My friend Reg Hinton and I would quote at great length passages to each other from his *Journal of a Disappointed Man.* I find that the copy which I still have is heavily underscored.

Despite all this activity and inner turmoil I accepted the Managership of the National Student Magazine of Great Britain and devoted a lot of time soliciting subscriptions and advertisements and putting it on its financial feet. It was my first experience in dictating to a secretary and as I suppose is a not unusual occurrence at the beginning, I wrote out completely first in long hand what I intended dictating.

Sometime during my third year at London I made an important decision on the choice of a career. My original intention had been to study law after I obtained my undergraduate degree and I still think it would have been a wise choice as I had the type of mind that would have been well suited for the law. However, I made what was probably the mistake of dropping occasionally into the Inns of Court, which were near the School, and listening to the cases being tried. The dreary formality of English law repelled me as did also the thought of spending my life being solely concerned with the mistakes, follies, and crimes of my fellow men. Naturally there are other and, to me, more interesting parts of the law in which one could concentrate, but I did not know about them or have anyone to advise me. On the other hand, I began to feel more interest and competence in economics and be attracted by the thought of studying and teaching it. It is perhaps not much of a science, but at least one could try to approach it in a scientific spirit and the thought of maybe being able to contribute something to raising the standard of living and hence presumably the happiness and well being of man, gave a content to the work of something more than merely earning a living. In the end, I applied for entrance to the Harvard Graduate School of Arts & Sciences rather than to the Law School.

On the advice of Professor Cannan I left London a week before the final exams for a rest at the little village of Alfriston, almost on the English Channel. It was a good rest but a bad mistake. The theory was that since there were no textbooks to be crammed, and the results would depend on all the work one had done in the previous two years, the important thing was to be fresh and alert mentally. Actually, however, I "cooled off" and the courses and exams began to seem remote and unimportant. It would have been better to have remained at least in the environment of work. Actually, however, I obtained Second Class Honors and in the long run it made no difference and I have my memory of wonderful June days on the English Channel.

After the exams I sailed for Canada, a very different person than the one who had left three years previously. It was a blessed relief, however, to plunge again into the summer social life of a small Canadian town with its daily round of tennis, canoeing, dances, and outings, with the knowledge that it would soon come to an end and I would start the grind again at Harvard.

CHAPTER 2

"Enter Here and Grow in Wisdom": The Harvard Years, 1925–34

The Student and Instructor

Currie registered at Harvard's graduate school in the fall of 1925. Study at Harvard was more highly organized than at the London School of Economics (LSE), with attendance records, a circumscribed choice of subjects, frequent hour tests, and mid-year examinations. He recalls that he had imbibed a little of the English feeling of superiority in educational matters and at first was inclined to be slightly contemptuous of the school. But he quickly found that there were some first-class brains among both professors and fellow students and that he could by no means coast along on his previous work. For two years he concentrated on intensive coursework, culminating in comprehensive written and oral examinations.

His most memorable teachers were Frank W. Taussig and Allyn A. Young. Taussig had a formidable reputation as the country's leading international trade theorist and Currie took his famous Ec 11 course in the development of economic theory, through which students came to have a fair working knowledge of Ricardo, J. S. Mill, Bohm-Bawerk, and Marshall.[1] Though Currie judged that Taussig had an orderly rather than a creative mind, he regarded him as a "truly great teacher in the sense that he aroused our intense interest in what were in reality relatively unimportant points in theory," and students gained a valuable training in critical analysis from the discussions among themselves that followed his classes. Taussig took an interest in distribution theory and still encouraged discussion of the wages-fund doctrine and the controversial ideas of Henry George, whom he had treated fairly sympathetically some years earlier in his *Wages and Capital* (1896). However, Taussig was generally more interested in pure theory and "equilibrium" than in policy. Discussions with Taussig were more in the nature of an intellectual game. Students had the impression that there was a definite answer to the problem under discussion, that he knew the answer and that it was up to the student to discover it. Currie later contributed to a volume of essays in his honor.[2]

Professor Allyn Young, however, was Currie's chief inspiration. He noted in his diary in 1927 that he "revered Young above all other men in the world. A minute with him sets me up for the rest of the day." In his memoirs Currie described him as "a true scientist with an enquiring, creative, and yet withal a humble mind." Young's most notable contribution, his presidential address to Section F of the British Association in Glasgow in September 1928,[3] was, with characteristic modesty, described by Young as a "mere variation on a theme" by the master, Adam Smith. His paper was, in fact, profoundly original, described by Nicholas Kaldor in 1975 as fifty years ahead of its time.[4] It was to influence greatly Currie's own perceptions and writings on the nature of the growth process, discussed in detail in chapters 12 and 13 below.

In contrast to Taussig, Young gave the impression in classes of thinking problems out as he went along. Currie wrote:

> He would frequently lapse into a brown study in the middle of a discussion and rouse himself with an obvious effort. He gave me the feeling that nothing was completely closed or decided—that monetary theory and business cycle theory were open fields in which it was still possible to make significant contributions. He had a trick or habit that I tried to imitate when I became a teacher. In the discussions in his class, one of us would timidly offer a suggestion, or make an observation which, naturally, was frequently half-baked or beside the point. He would usually gaze intently at the speaker for a few moments and then say, "That is an extraordinarily interesting point. What Mr. X. is suggesting [or alternatively: has in mind] is . . ." and he would proceed to attribute relevant and profound thoughts to you that you never dreamed of, and to which you listened with a surprised and pleased glow. In this way he avoided hurt feelings and yet kept the discussion going along relevant and significant lines.
>
> I had a typical experience with him in an examination. The whole examination consisted of an essay on a theoretical topic. After I had written for almost three quarters of the allotted time, I suddenly decided that I had the wrong slant and thought of a better way to handle the theme. I skipped several lines and explained my dilemma and gave an outline of how I would have developed the matter if time had permitted. He wrote on my paper that he liked both my attitude and my second suggested approach and was giving me an A for it. [*Memoirs*, pp. 24–25.]

Allyn A. Young (1876–1929). Currie dedicated his *Supply and Control of Money in the United States* (1934) to Young's memory. *Courtesy of the London School of Economics.*

In 1927, at the end of Currie's second year in the graduate school, he was selected by Young to be his assistant for the following school year—a very high honor and one which could have assured his career at Harvard. Unfortunately, however, shortly afterward Young was invited to occupy the chair of political economy at the London School of Economics for three years, the chair of Currie's old teacher, Professor Edwin Cannan. With his deep respect for English economics, he could not resist this honor. Late in 1928 the University of Chicago invited Young to be the new chairman of their department. He declined the offer but felt that, out of courtesy, he ought to go to Chicago to explain personally his decision to stay at Harvard. During his return to London in early 1929 Young contracted pneumonia and died in a London hospital at the age of only fifty-two. The sudden death of his mentor and patron was a deep personal shock and loss to Currie. He tells how his complete absorption in his work was revealed by Mrs. Young's unutterably sad account of his death when, in his delirium, he lectured for hours and hours on end.

In his *Autobiography of an Economist* (London: Macmillan, 1971), Lionel (Lord) Robbins, who returned to the LSE from Oxford to take up a chair in economics upon the death of Allyn Young, pays tribute to Young as an economist of "massive erudition" (p. 120). However, at the same time he suggested that Young's appointment at the LSE was not a great success because "he was not generally a good lecturer" and was a poor administrator. He gave Robbins the impression he was a profoundly unhappy man with a tortured temperament, ill at ease in his surroundings, distracted by his duties and difficult to talk to.

This view surprised Currie, who, commenting on Robbins's autobiography and on a copy of Nicholas Kaldor's notes on Young's LSE lectures[5]—which had just been obtained for him by the present writer—wrote him in reply, January 2, 1989:

> . . . . I did get to read more carefully the Young lectures as reported by Kaldor. . . .They make a fascinating document even though only the notes of a student. What Robbins criticised—the slowness of delivery—bore out what I think I told you was my impression—that he *thought* them out as he went along. What I recalled most was missing—the dialogue with the students and his care to make something worthwhile of points raised by students (including me). Even 60 years later they make the treatment of many texts appear superficial. I was surprised he resorted to diagrams as much as Kaldor reported.
>
> . . . I agree that it is probably better to stick to Young's verbal formulation than his own uses of curves—which can't express the "togetherness" of economic phenomena.
>
> . . . What mattered to Robbins was verbal facility (which he had) and administrative detail (Beveridge had Mrs. Mair for that). He wrote as though Young had left Harvard for good which I don't think was true. His post at Harvard was filled only on a temporary basis by Hawtrey and Schumpeter until after his death, when the latter was appointed to fill it. . . . He asked me to be his assistant on his return. What apparently weighed with him was the income—which I never appreciated. He never for a moment gave me the impression of being an unhappy man. I remember his bright smile and eager interest in the subject at hand—which he apparently didn't have with Robbins!

In a memorial tribute (*Economica,* April 1929) the director of the LSE, Sir William Beveridge, also gave an account of Young's work in

London that differed from Robbins's. He spoke of Young as "a main pillar of our School," a great teacher, venerated by his students, and happy in his work in London. "He came to us promised for three years; we were gladly bound to him for life if he would stay." Likewise, a long obituary in the London Times:

> A profound scholar, Young possessed also the charm of personality. Of imposing stature, with a noble head and kind and penetrating eyes, he won his way to the hearts of students not by any of the gifts of the orator, but by the sense that he gave of a complete command of his subject and by a kindliness of disposition which made him take endless pains on their behalf. No man was more ready to see all the sides of an argument; he had none of the intellectual arrogance which sometimes accompanies great mental gifts; and if ever he felt anger it was with those who refused to acknowledge merit in the work of other schools or of modern writers of a tendency opposite to the received tradition. These qualities of mind and character, which made him a great teacher, made him also the most sympathetic and helpful of colleagues. No one could go to Young without receiving enlightenment, and, since his range of knowledge was extraordinary, without the impression that here was a man who was an absolute master in his chosen field.

Currie's other teachers at Harvard included the following: Charles McIlwain, in political theory; Thomas Nixon Carver, W. Z. Ripley, Edwin Gay, C. J. Bullock, John H. Williams, and Harold Burbank in various fields of economics and economic history; and W. L. Crum in statistics. Currie regretted that the department was so poorly represented in the field of public finance, a field closely related to monetary and business cycle theory in which Currie was to specialize and teach. Bullock, records Currie, "was a violent reactionary, really, I believe, mentally unbalanced, and Burbank was exceedingly mediocre."

Burbank, because of the reluctance of the more able members to take on adminstrative responsibilities, was the chairman of the department. He has been credited with having created the best economics department in the United States—that of MIT—by deciding that Paul Samuelson was not good enough for Harvard. When, as early as 1930 or 1931 Currie began to feel that self-accelerating deflationary forces were too strong to be checked by easy money and other conventional measures and to suggest, in his classes, that the government should embark on a large-scale public works spending program and not try to cover the current cost by taxation—i.e., deliberately incur a deficit—Burbank called him in and warned that he should stop talking such nonsense and stick to his subject of money and banking.

Currie's class, which entered in 1925, was an exceptionally good one and many of his classmates, such as Douglas Brown, Edward Beach, Donald Wallace, Theodore Yntema, and Tony Monteros, later occupied leading posts in important universities and corporations. But Currie records that "the one who was destined to become the best known, and who was also perhaps the most brilliant, was Harry Dexter White. We were, from the first, friendly rivals and remained on this basis for the next ten years." In White's papers in Princeton University Library there is a "Memorandum Prepared by L. B. Currie, P. T. Ellsworth, and H. D. White," dated January 1932, which outlined remedial measures to combat the Depression, "which had cost more than the Great War," by canceling all debts and reparations, by creating an administration of public works, by reducing tariffs, and by the purchase by the reserve banks of $1 billion of securities to increase liquidity.[6]

Currie's friendship with White was to continue until White's death in 1948. For several years White occupied key posts in the U.S. Treasury and there kept in close contact with Currie who likewise occupied influential positions in the Federal Reserve Board and later the White House.

They entered their Ph.D. theses in the same year for the Wells Prize, which, if won, meant publication in the Harvard Economic Series. White, the protégé of Taussig, submitted his thesis on the French international accounts, 1880–1913. Currie's was on bank assets and banking policy. Accoring to Currie "it was a close race and the judges disagreed as to which of us should receive the prize. Finally, the theses were given to a faculty member for final decision. He confessed later that he disapproved so strongly of certain ideas I had expressed in another and completely different article that he awarded the prize to White." So Currie's Ph.D. thesis was not published, but shortly afterward Harvard did publish his *Supply and Control of Money in the United States* (1934).

Currie's Ph.D. thesis included a chapter that condemned in forthright terms recent Federal Reserve monetary policy as primarily responsible for precipitating and then deepening the Great Depression during and after 1929. This chapter was later published under the title "The Failure of Monetary Policy to Prevent the Depression of 1929–32," in the *Journal of Political Economy,* April 1934. Years later, Earl Hamilton, Harry G. Johnson, and Albert Rees were to select that article for inclusion in *Landmarks in Political Economy* (University of Chicago Press, 1962), a volume that collected together what were judged to be the twenty-four most significant papers published by the *Journal of Political Economy* in its first seventy-five years. In that volume Currie's penetrating exposure of misguided monetary theory and management stands alongside contributions by, for example, Veblen, Pareto, J. M. Clark, Viner, Knight, Henry Simons, Paul Sweezy, Samuelson, Friedman, Metzler, and Lerner.

Another of Currie's group was A. G. Silverman who, though an instructor at MIT, was completing his requirements for the Ph.D. degree at Harvard. Currie recalls his "brilliant and unusual mind. He especially delighted in the more abstract problems of economics and philosophy." Currie found Silverman and White both very stimulating in different ways, but later, during the McCarthy period, his friendship with them was to have serious consequences because of an alleged involvement in a communist spy ring.

When Allyn Young left for London in 1927, John H. Williams was asked to give his course on money and banking, the course in which Currie had been appointed as assistant. Currie's memoirs record:

> It was the first time he had taught the subject and, of course, it was my first teaching assignment, so we started fresh together. It became a large and popular undergraduate course. He lectured twice a week and I broke the class up into five sections of some thirty to thirty-five boys in each one for an hour each week. It was a happy combination that lasted for some years. He was an excellent and popular lecturer. My job was to establish closer contact with the members of the class, develop the themes of the lectures through the Socratic method, grade all papers and the course theses—which was an important element of the course, accounting for about one-third of the final grade. Fortunately Williams and I shared the same general approach to the subject and we became warm personal friends.
>
> I particularly enjoyed teaching by the Socratic method, which, to be successful, requires the active participation of the classes and is suitable only for theoretical topics. Usually it is best to confine the discussion to one point. The basic objective was by skilful questioning and guidance of the discussion to have the class, or the bulk of it, arrive itself at the point you want to make, just at the end of the hour. One must keep alert, modify the questions as required, and accelerate or decelerate the development of the topic, depending on the time element. It was much more strenuous than lecturing but the compensation was that it was infinitely more stimulating for both the students and the teacher.
>
> The course in money and banking became too popular for my comfort.

> It invariably received favorable ratings in the Harvard Crimson's Confidential Guide to Courses. In one year there were some one hundred and eighty enrollees and the sections became too big and the chore of grading papers a really onerous one. That year I had a pile of course theses about four feet high, on all of which I tried to make suitable written comment as I went along. I was referred to in the Crimson as a driver, but a just and reasonable fellow (a regular guy), which description pleased me very much. (*Memoirs*, pp. 27–28)

Among the many hundreds of students who attended Currie's classes in the years between 1927–34, some were to become prominent economists, including Paul Sweezy, Wilfred Owen, Walter and William Salant, Richard Goodwin, Moses Abramovitz, A. G. Hart, Martin Krost, and Emile Despres. Paul Sweezy's brother Alan was a fellow instructor who later worked for Currie for a while at the Federal Reserve Board.

For a while Currie also assisted Ralph Hawtrey, who was a visitor for a year, and Joseph Schumpeter. Some of the young instructors were later to claim rather contemptuously that Schumpeter's main credentials were that in the early 1920s he had, as Austrian minister of finance, presided over the wildest inflation his country had ever known. Perhaps chastened by the Austrian inflation, Schumpeter was at this time extremely conservative on monetary matters, siding with Hayek and Robbins in a "neutral money" theory of inflation. In this theory, which Currie believed showed no sense of practical realities, the money supply is said to be rising excessively fast, causing inflation, if, despite falling prices, the fall in prices is less than the fall in unit costs brought about by rising productivity. (A modern variant on this theory is that monetary conditions in 1929–32 were "easy" because, while the nominal money supply fell sharply, prices were falling even faster so the "real" money supply increased.)

John Kenneth Galbraith has remarked that Schumpeter's "political and business misfortunes had left him with a deep distaste for practical affairs, and he condemned as intellectually debased economists who presumed to advise on practical questions."[7] However, he did use his influence to comment on policy in the Depression, usually to encourage further depression as "salutory." Currie recalls that he occasionally put his theories into practice. He believed in wage flexibility as a cure for depression. Hence he supported Harvard's decision to cut the wages of the support staff. Professors' salaries, of course, were not changed and as prices fell Schumpeter enjoyed a rising real income. This accorded with his pronouncement that "a gentleman cannot live on less than $50,000 a year."

Richard Goodwin, one of Currie's students at Harvard, and later a distinguished Cambridge economist, now at the University of Siena, recently wrote an article highly critical of the Harvard economics faculty at this time.[8] In response to the present writer's inquiry about whether he would include Currie in his censure, he sent the following very revealing letter:

Siena, 30 Oct. 1989

Dear Roger Sandilands,

I have just read with fascination your very informative letter and the excerpt from your forthcoming book.

Indeed I thought the faculty at Harvard were a bunch of whited sepulchres; and I still think so. While I was there seven professors published a book about the Great Depression—a book of concentrated mumbo-jumbo that has been rightly totally forgotten; they were labelled the 7 Wise Men. And it included Schumpeter, whom I admire enormously, but who talked the most unutterable rubbish at the time.

I was very pleased to read the table of contents, which gave me an outline of Lauchlin Currie's career, about which I have heard little. My dismissal of Harvard did not include Currie, and I was saddened to read that he would like to have had a job there; he would have improved it.

I did my degree in history, government and economics, with mainly the politics part, but with economics as of increasing interest and the second part. Fortunately I took Currie's course and it was more or less the only good thing I found in the economics faculty. He was spendid; each lecture he would bring the latest data from the Fed. and say how unsatisfactory and tell us why. That I am not just being friendly about him will be established by the fact that, after doing my degree in Oxford (this time concentrating on economics), I decided to do a B. Litt and which I later turned into a Ph.D. at Harvard. It took 4 years of my life and in imitation of Currie, I attempted (for the first time in England), to construct monthly time series for the quantity of money. The title may well have been literally copied—the Supply and Control of Money in the UK; there is a copy in the Widener Library and in the National Institute, London. After a century of talk about money, no one had ever actually tried to count it!!! Alas for me, Phelps-Brown published a parallel series in the Journal of the Royal Statistical Society, so, miserably, I abandoned my intention of publishing the thesis, which was literally inspired by Currie's work.

When I returned to Harvard just before the war, I got, on the basis of the thesis, the job of being John Williams's assistant. I was enchanted to learn that Currie had been the same. I enjoyed the work and think I did it well but not as well as Currie. The thing was that Keynes had happened and I became increasingly concerned with the determination of output, not solely through the banking system.

About Schumpeter: Currie was wrong, though he had good grounds. As an undergraduate, I was a member of a discussion group and for one meeting we asked the newly arrived Schumpeter to explain Marx to us. He told us that his economics was all wrong, though he had some good ideas. As a youthful radical I was furious with him and returned, some years later, full of hostility to him. After one year's contact I began to soften and ended up being a friend and great admirer. He was a real continental intellectual; he loved discussion and would give any amount of time to anyone who, he thought, had anything to say. He was a snob and a reactionary, but Paul Sweezy and myself were two of his best friends, and he knew we were both hopeless reds. For him, in fact, since we both came from banking families, we simply illustrated how capitalism would end, not the way Marx said. Like you, I hope to publish a book next year (on Chaos [OUP]), and in it one section demonstrates how wrong Schumpeter was with his (to me profound remark) that the cycle is simply the form growth takes—that was of course why he was talking such nonsense about the 1930's. And yet, as I grow older and more senile, the more I am impressed with him; I think he plays as large or larger role than Keynes! and yet the idiot dismissed the G.T. as rubbish!

I was also very interested to find out that Currie had studied with Allyn Young; Nicky Kaldor always talked so much about him (calling him Aline Young) that I often wondered what was so good about him—also it shows what an ass Lionel Robbins was. Tragic that he died so young! he would have left a legacy.

Incidentally, Schumpeter was not only Finance minister but after, as a private banker, lost his family fortune! He was a curious man, in some ways vain, but for example, in his lectures he never mentioned his own work and in his great work on history of theory, he never mentions his own work.

Well I must thank you for your generosity in sending me the letter and the photocopy, both have given much pleasure and made me think.

Sincerely,
Richard M. Goodwin

The Coming of the Great Depression

As soon as his first job was secured, in 1927 Currie was married, in a civil ceremony, to Dorothy York Bacon, a landscape architect who continued working in Boston until the arrival of Morgan, their first child, in 1929. A second boy, Roderick, was born in 1934.[9]

In 1928, having chosen a Ph.D. topic on bank assets in the United States and Britain, he sailed to England with his wife to spend a few weeks in London collecting data on British bank assets.[10] His topic was of profound contemporary significance, for his work coincided with the fateful Federal Reserve policy of 1928 and 1929 in the lead-up to the Great Depression that began around July 1929. By October the U.S. industrial production had already fallen by more than 2.5 percent.

Meanwhile, however, Currie has recalled:

> I had the tremendous satisfaction of feeling that I was doing my job adequately and of having a growing mastery of my subject. Finally, I was being very successful in the stock market.
>
> I had started in a small way at the end of 1927 investing my share of the family estate and contracted in addition a small loan. Unfortunately, since I was very successful, my friends and relatives asked me to invest sums for them. By the middle of 1929 my original stake of $15,000 had been run up to $150,000 and the money of my mother and brother was also in the market. The accounts of the various friends were pooled in a single account which was doing very well. When I left for a vacation at Nantucket in early September I felt my economic future was assured. It is true I had a loan of $100,000 but it was secured by stocks worth $250,000, which was, as things were then considered, very conservative. Unfortunately however, I had invested in stocks that had experienced the most spectacular rise and which, quite naturally, later experienced the most spectacular falls. During that fateful October of 1929 the equity shrank so rapidly I began to receive margin calls, all of which I met by selling stocks. By the beginning of November, I was out of debt, but with less net worth than I had started with two years previously.
>
> It was a not uncommon experience and one which, even to-day, can arouse little sympathy. And yet it was a terrible blow to me, both financially and emotionally. On the whole, my friends took their losses philosophically, though there were some reproaches. The worst was the loss of a good part of the inheritance of my mother and brother. He had died in early 1929 and I had been responsible for persuading his widow to bring her three young sons to Cambridge and send them to a good private boy's school. At the same time I had started a family and my wife had given up her job. I suddenly found myself the main support of nine people on an instructor's salary of $2,700 a year, and without any life insurance.
>
> The first thing I did was to call an insurance company and take out a $20,000 policy. It was a prudent thing to do, but it did increase my ex-

penses. I then cast about for ways and means of increasing my income by taking on additional teaching assignments, monitoring examinations, private tutoring and even acting as Chief Usher at the football games. In these various ways, and by carrying a terrific schedule of work, I was able to increase my income every year of the Depression, which must have been something of a record. After the first year, my nephews won scholarships, which were a help, and eventually the family returned to Nova Scotia where living expenses were much less.

In the years 1930–33, in addition to my regular Harvard schedule, I gave courses at Radcliffe, gave two courses at Miss McClintock's School for Girls in Boston, was a professor at the Fletcher Graduate School of Law and Diplomacy, completed my thesis and was awarded my Ph.D. degree, wrote various articles for Economic Journals and completed my book on the Control and Supply of Money in the United States. My teaching load alone was twenty-three hours a week (six to nine hours was considered a full schedule at Harvard).

Unquestionably, the hardest work was my two years teaching assignment at Miss McClintock's School. This was a "finishing" school for well-to-do girls of sixteen to seventeen who could not or did not care to go to college. To hold the interest of a class of forty to forty-five of such girls in economics for an hour was a real challenge which used to leave me exhausted. I used an uncompromising text, Schlicter, and the Socratic method, and did not fare too badly. At least some of the girls were sufficiently interested to devote part of their summer vacation to auditing my course in the Harvard Summer School.

Fortunately, although my health was not too good, I enjoyed most of the work. Actually, I derived considerable satisfaction in finding that I possessed sufficient resiliency and toughness to withstand the reverses and carry the load. One who always had to make his own way in the world would probably have said I was very fortunate. However, I had hitherto had a sheltered and secure life and mistrusted my ability to cope with reverses. (*Memoirs,* pp. 29–32)

The stock market crash of October 1929 was so dramatic and occurred so close to the beginning of the Great Depression that there is a widespread feeling, amongst the general public and professional economists alike, that the main blame lay with greedy, irrational speculators, aided and abetted by bankers' loans. John Kenneth Galbraith's entertaining best-seller, *The Great Crash* is perhaps the best known and most forceful exposition of this view. Charles Kindleberger,[11] despite acknowledging that the Dow Jones index of stock prices at its peak in 1929 was not very different, after allowing for inflation, from its peaks in 1970 and 1983–84, nevertheless concluded:

> In the light of the sudden collapse of business, commodity prices and imports at the end of 1929, it is difficult to maintain that the stock market was a superficial phenomenon, a signal or a trigger, rather than part of the deflationary mechanism. One should not be dogmatic about it, but it is hard to avoid the conclusion that there is something to the conventional wisdom which characterized the crash as the start of a process. The stock market crash is less interesting for the irony it permits the historian, bemused by the foibles of greedy men, than for starting a process which took on a dynamic of its own. (p. 116)

In fact, however, the collapse of stock prices halted in December 1929 and prices rose for the next six months. The New York index of stock prices in April 1930 stood at 171, compared with 166 in October 1928 and 216 in September 1929.[12] The real collapse of stock prices occurred after May 1930 when prices slid almost continuously to a low of 34 in June 1932. After President Roosevelt assumed office in March 1933 business began to revive and, with business, stock prices rose fairly steadily from 42 in March 1933 to 154 in March 1937, declining thereafter as a new business recession set in.

Since 1929 there have been several periods when stock prices have risen as fast as in 1929 and other times when they have fallen more sharply than between October and December 1929, notably in October 1987, without precipitating a depression of the depth and duration of that in the 1930s. Kindleberger asserts that "the danger posed by the market was not inherent in the level of prices and turnover so much as in the precarious credit mechanism which supported it, and the pressure which it exerted on credit throughout the United States and the world" (p. 109).

Similar views were echoed in high places in 1929. When Herbert Hoover took over from Calvin Coolidge as President in March 1929 he spoke of the dangers inherent in the stock market. Grave concern was also expressed by Governor Roy Young, chairman of the Federal Reserve Board, by Adolph Miller, an influential board member, and by Senator Carter Glass, who, having chaired the committee that drafted the 1913 Federal Reserve Act, regarded himself as the father of the Federal Reserve System. All stressed the need to control stock market speculation and curb banks' security loans to brokers and others. Throughout 1928 and 1929 the Federal Reserve had been tightening monetary conditions by forcing member banks into debt with the reserve banks through open market sales of government bonds and the raising of the discount rate. So, when the stock market crashed and output and employment fell disastrously thereafter, those who had advocated and implemented a tight monetary squeeze—with the biggest turn of the screw in August when the discount rate was raised to 6 percent—felt their consciences were clear.

They believed that if any blame attached to the monetary authorities, as opposed to hysterical speculators who were diverting the nation's credit into unproductive stock market transactions, it lay with the decision in the autumn of 1927, in the light of business recession that year, to ease credit conditions by open market purchases of $200 million and a lowering of the discount rate to 3.5 percent at the Federal Reserve Bank of New York, where the stock market was located. Adolph Miller later described this action as "one of the most costly errors committed by any banking system in the last 75 years,"[13] because it was followed by a sustained growth of stock prices. These prices increased by about 33 percent between September 1927 and September 1928, followed by a further 33 percent rise to September 1929. Miller's view was endorsed by Professor Lionel Robbins in London who stated that it was from this date, when the Federal Reserve Board let its concern with deflationary pressures in Europe override domestic considerations, that "the situation got completely out of control."[14]

Having made this grave inflationary "blunder" in late 1927 A. C. Miller and other key officials in the Federal Reserve—such as E. A. Goldenweiser, its director of research, and his deputy, Woodlief Thomas—became increasingly obsessed with the course of stock prices.[15] In their retrospective assessments of this period Goldenweiser and Thomas agreed that, despite successive increments in interest rates and open market selling that put member banks heavily into debt with the reserve banks during 1928 and 1929, policy had erred only in being insufficiently restrictive.[16]

Currie's Diagnosis of the Causes of the Depression

These views were subjected to searching theoretical and empirical scrutiny by Lauchlin Currie during 1929 and 1930 in preparing his Ph.D. dissertation. This was originally submitted in January 1931 and subsequently revised and extended[17] for the Wells prize competition in October 1932. There followed a series of articles in the *Quar-*

terly Journal of Economics, the *Journal of Political Economy,* and the *American Economic Review* that were highly critical of Federal Reserve policy and the American banking structure.

From the outset Currie's writings have been characterized by the importance he attaches firstly to a clear statement of the nature of the problem at hand, and secondly to the need for clear definitions of basic concepts followed by an uncompromising acceptance of all the logical consequences that stem from those definitions.

Stating the nature of the problem in this way has invariably oriented Currie's interests toward policy issues for which he has invoked or developed relevant theories. He has had little interest in "ideas to play with rather than to use." Only by subjecting theories to quantitative and qualitative tests can their validity or usefulness for policy purposes be assessed. Likewise, only through clear definitions can policy confusion and conflict be avoided. In his early work on money and banking nowhere was this confusion more evident, or more calamitous in its consequences, than in the vagueness and semantic confusions surrounding the concepts of "money," "velocity," "credit," and "speculation." After these basic concepts had been carefully defined and measured, in some cases for the first time, Currie was ready to use them to evaluate monetary and fiscal policy in the late 1920s and early 1930s, and thereafter to exert his own direct influence on policy.

In his dissertation and the published articles that arose directly from it Currie began by remarking how pervasive, especially in America, was the theory of the Banking School.[18] This was despite the apparent intellectual victory of the ideas of the Currency School in the first half of the nineteenth century. In 1810 the famous report of the Bullion Committee passed judgment on the banking principle, or "real bills" doctrine, "that there can be no excess in the issue of Bank of England paper, so long as the . . . discount of mercantile Bills is confined to paper of undoubted solidity, arising out of real commercial transactions, and payable at short or fixed periods." The committee declared: "That the doctrine is a very fallacious one, your Committee cannot entertain a doubt. The fallacy upon which it is founded, lies in not distinguishing between an advance of capital of Merchants, and an additional supply of currency to the general mass of the circulating medium."[19]

The currency principle theorists were mainly concerned with ensuring that the note issue would remain fully convertible with gold.

The banking or commercial loan principle threatened an excessive expansion of the note issue and increase in prices because in practice it was not possible to ensure that the new money was used only once—on the real production being financed by the loan—and because the new money would anyway bid resources from other uses on which the existing stock of money was being expended.

Currie restated this refutation in modern terms, for a fractional-reserve, deposit-banking system. He emphasized that the "circuit velocity of money" was greater than unity so that incomes and expenditures would be increased by more than the initial increase in bank loans and the new bank deposits created thereby. When the commercial loan is spent on raw materials or the wages of labor, the recipients will spend this new money on other goods and services before the commercial loan is repaid. Even when the loan is repaid the banker will usually be able to relend the deposit, so the new money remains in circulation. So long as banks have no difficulty lending their deposits, the only limit on deposit creation is the availability of legal reserves. If the central bank is guided by the demand by businessmen to borrow against "real bills" then there is potential for an expansion of reserves and hence deposits which, multiplied by their circuit velocity, will determine a multiple expansion of incomes and expenditures that would soon outstrip real production and so force prices to rise. The rise in prices would encourage an even greater demand for loans for commercial purposes which, if accommodated, would expand money incomes and expenditures even more rapidly.

In practice the central bank does not create reserves solely or mainly by rediscounting commercial paper because commercial banks are unwilling or unable to become indebted to the reserve banks except for emergency purposes. Currie's studies showed that banks had a profound "repugnance to indebtedness" even when such indebtedness was not unprofitable. If commercial banks borrowed from reserve banks in order to expand all commercial loan opportunities that presented themselves the system would soon break down. Nevertheless, the Federal Reserve Act of 1913 was framed largely according to the commercial banking principle so that only commercial bills were eligible for rediscount at the reserve banks. In a characteristic statement in 1923 the Board asserted its belief "that there will be little danger that the credit created and contributed by the Federal Reserve banks will be in excessive volume if restricted to productive uses."[20]

Thus the guiding principle behind Federal Reserve policy in the

1920s was mainly to ensure, or encourage, member banks to make productive rather than unproductive, and liquid (short-term) rather than illiquid (long-term) loans. For this the ideal was the short-term commercial loan.

This approach to central banking Currie considered totally misguided in principle and in practice disastrous. In the first place, he showed that paradoxically the *least* liquid of bank assets were their short-term commercial loans. This was because these were the least marketable (since liquidation required sale of inventories or semifinished products). Furthermore, he showed that commercial loans were most popular at that time with the less successful, smaller-scale merchants and farmers with close ties to smaller country banks. There were, therefore, strong local pressures making it much more difficult to call in these loans prematurely or, indeed, not to renew them. This, incidentally, was an important reason for a weak and vulnerable banking structure that later helped cause thousands of small unit banks to fail, with profound deflationary implications that aggravated the depression after 1930.[21]

During the prosperous years of the 1920s the larger, more profitable corporations increasingly liquidated their commercial debts with banks and relied more on their own profits to finance inventories. Thus, commercial loans were increasingly directed to smaller, less profitable firms and industries. The overall proportion of bank assets accounted for by commercial loans declined progressively from 21.2 percent in 1923 to 13.9 percent in 1929.[22] These trends were viewed with increasing alarm by the Federal Reserve Board.

Currie pointed out that the most liquid of banks' assets were their security loans and investments because these were the most marketable. The rapid growth and sophistication of the New York Stock Exchange he saw as a generally benign development because it increased the marketability of these assets, enabling individual banks to liquidate rapidly whenever they were faced with excessive withdrawals. On the other hand, Currie strongly emphasized the different economic and practical implications of individual bank liquidations compared with liquidation *en masse* by the entire system. The need for a general liquidation may arise either because the public is switching deposits into cash or because of an open market selling policy by the central bank.

In such circumstances he insisted that it was inappropriate for the reserve banks to confine their rediscounting facilities to a narrowly defined set of eligible commercial bills. This could force mass liquidation of security loans and investments and of commercial loans to smaller customers whose bills were not eligible. This carried the danger of precipitous price falls, foreclosures, and declining incomes.

As for the criterion of "productiveness" in the commercial loan theory, its refutation was again linked with the recognition that the initial ostensible purpose of a loan did not determine its final use. Depending on the reserves-deposit ratio and the income velocity of circulation, incomes and expenditures would expand by a multiple of the initial loan and in directions difficult to determine a priori. Thus the main criterion for central bank reserve policy should be the relationship between global expenditures and the overall productive capacity of the economy, together with some attempt to monitor and guide the character of spending within this overall income-expenditure framework.

According to the commercial loan theory, security loans were the most unproductive type of loan and absorbed credit from more productive uses, thereby denying the "legitimate needs of industry." Currie insisted that this claim had little substance. He examined the relationship between changes in the rate of interest and security loans and found that this relationship was much weaker than that between the interest rate and restrictive policies pursued by the Federal Reserve Board. Bank security loans represented only a very small portion of all security loans. The majority of stock purchases and sales were effected via brokers in the stock market clearing house, thus requiring little *net* use of bank deposits. A detailed examination of the movement of individual stock prices revealed that throughout the "speculative orgy" of 1929 investors displayed a considerable degree of rational selectivity based on different earnings records and potential.[23] Thus it was hard to sustain the view that the stock market generally channeled funds to the least profitable or productive sectors, though, or course, abuses existed and mistakes were made. In other words, security loans may help to sustain stock prices but the main reasons for stock price movements lay elsewhere—in general market conditions, profits, and nonbank loans.

Excessive bursts of bullish optimism in the market could carry the general level of stock prices above that justified by sustainable real market conditions. So speculators certainly do risk losses. Furthermore, Currie acknowledged that stock market prices could have various effects on the relation between saving and investment.

The relation between saving and investment was the crucial guide for Currie as to the appropriate direction of monetary policy, though the effect of the stock market on this relation was for him only one—and probably a relatively minor—effect among many that had to be monitored by the authorities as an indicator of overall business conditions and prospects. Currie acknowledges the influence of the pre-*General Theory* Keynes in his attention to this relation. As explained in later chapters, Currie was, and remains, highly skeptical of the usefulness of the new ex post definitions of savings that Keynes advanced in the *General Theory* and of the operation of a predictable Keynesian multiplier to bring about an equilibrium between savings and investment via multiple expansion and contraction of income, except insofar as such changes can be traced to expected changes in money and its income velocity.

Rising stock prices have an ambiguous net effect on savings. Some speculators may cash their paper profits by selling and using the proceeds to increase current consumption. This effect, however, is offset by increased saving by those who will have purchased those same shares. More commonly, paper profits will not be realized in cash and some shareholders may save less than they otherwise would have done. Others, however, watching the rise in stock prices may increase their savings out of current income to acquire new stock. Speculators, being wealthier, may also carry larger demand deposits, thereby reducing the average velocity of circulation of the money stock.[24]

As for the effect of rising and falling stock prices on investment, Currie was skeptical that there was a significant independent effect. In the absence of rising prospective earnings, due largely to other considerations, it was doubtful if rising stock prices alone would induce significantly more real investment than would have been undertaken for other reasons. On balance Currie believed that rising stock prices would be more likely to contribute to a boom by decreasing savings than by increasing investment.

Nevertheless, he strenuously criticized the Federal Reserve Board for basing its policy solely or primarily on the single relatively minor influence of stock prices on the balance between savings and investment. He did not go so far as Milton Friedman and Anna Schwartz who believe the authorities should have ignored the stock market. Nevertheless, Friedman and Schwartz are very close to Currie's diagnosis of the conditions leading up to the 1929 crash and the failure of the monetary authorities to focus primarily on real business conditions.

Many commentators are inclined to believe that because there was a great slump after 1929 this must have been preceded by a great boom.[25] Winch states: "In the seven year period to the summer of 1929 American capitalism assumed its most triumphant and reckless form. Industrial productivity and national income both rose by over 40 percent in this period."[26] However, this period included recovery from the war and the sharp recession of 1919–21, and growth averaged less than 5 percent a year.[27] Despite secular expansion, only seven out of sixteen industrial groups recorded maximum profits in 1927–29 while eight of them recorded larger profits in the 1923–25 period.[28] Moreover, prices were constant or even tending to decline.[29] D. H. Robertson, in reviewing Currie's 1934 book on the supply and control of money characterized Currie's description of the period as one of "sloom followed by a bump."[30] However, Currie went on to show that the monetary authorities allowed the bump to develop into a drastic slump, for the contraction after 1930 was of truly calamitous proportions. Up to 15 million were unemployed (between 25 and 30 percent of the work force) and millions more were on abbreviated working hours, at a time when there was no cushion of social security.

Friedman and Schwartz lay the blame for precipitating the depression squarely on Federal Reserve Board policy and, to a lesser extent, on the particular monetary arrangements then in existence. They also blame the pernicious influence of the real bills doctrine held by influential figures such as Senator Carter Glass, an "undeviating follower" of the doctrine who, even after 1930, condemned the "extraordinary policies" of the New York Reserve Bank in failing to restrict loans to real bills only. "In his eyes, the failure was responsible for the boom and the bust" (p. 388). Friedman and Schwartz also condemn the unhelpful propaganda of H. Parker Willis (who helped Carter Glass frame the 1913 Federal Reserve Act) against "inflationary" policies in 1932, by which time the money supply had collapsed to less than 80 percent of its 1929 level. Willis had been a student of J. Lawrence Laughlin, another prominent exponent of the real bills doctrine.

In view of Currie's trenchant criticism of the banking principle and real bills doctrine in several important publications between 1931–35 it can surely be no mere oversight on the part of Friedman and Schwartz that they do not once mention Currie's work in their detailed survey of the monetary policies and ideas of that period. Instead, Friedman and Schwartz note that, apart from the "important exceptions" of Harold Reed, Irving Fisher, J. W. Angell, and Karl Bopp, "the literature, and particularly the academic literature on the banking and liquidity cirsis is almost as depressing as that on the contraction in general."[31] Harold Reed, incidentally, was the same person whom Currie, in reviewing his *Federal Reserve Policy, 1921–30,* had criticized at the time for his contradictory views on the appropriate aims of monetary policy and, in particular, for claiming that speculation threatened runaway credit.[32] Reed, therefore, had concluded that restrictive Federal Reserve policy in 1929 was justified.

Friedman and Schwartz were later criticized, in particular by Thomas Humphrey and Don Patinkin, for ignoring the contributions of non-Chicago economists, especially Currie, to monetary theory and statistics.[33] A clue to this neglect may also be found in John Kenneth Galbraith's discussion of the advice later given to Roosevelt by George F. Warren to raise the price of gold in 1933 and thereby increase the money stock. Galbraith emphasized that Warren regarded this as a conservative proposal and noted that "Warren's reference to conservatism . . . was not casual. By manipulating the gold price he believed that a great deal of other public and reformist action, including most of the New Deal farm program, could be avoided. He was one of the first in a long line of monetary reformers extending to Professor Milton Friedman . . . who have hoped that their changes would make other and more comprehensive government action unnecessary. They are monetary radicals because they are political conservatives."[34] (In the margin of his copy of Galbraith's text Currie has noted in pencil "and Fisher too.") There is a suggestion that in Friedman's view one cannot be a bona fide monetarist if one is also a New Dealer and so need not be given serious consideration, even when, as stated by Thomas Humphrey, "Currie was the *only* American monetary theorist in the early 1930s to hold the Federal Reserve authorities responsible for precipitating the Great Depression."[35] Fairly typical of contemporary opinion was the view of W. E. Spahr, who complained in his review of Currie's 1934 book that "he seems to take for granted that our money and banking structure is largely at fault in the difficulties of 1929–33 without considering whether the chief trouble might not have been the World War and the attendant maladjustments."[36]

Empirical Studies of Income, Money, and Velocity

In addition to Reed and Fisher, another of the "important exceptions" mentioned by Friedman and Schwartz was James Angell. It is worth pausing to consider Angell's work at this point because Currie had reviewed one of Angell's books in 1936,[37] and had been involved in an exchange with him earlier (1934) over their simultaneous but independent and differing estimates of the income velocity of money.[38]

National income estimates did not become available for the United States until the early 1930s (and *current* estimates not until the mid-1930s) and so the concept of the *income* velocity of money was at that time relatively novel.[39] The chief focus of early discussions of velocity was in terms of the *transactions* velocity, most notably in the well-known writings of Irving Fisher. Total transactions included intermediate payments as well as an enormous volume of transfer payments, especially the sale and purchase of financial claims. But the early statements of the quantity theory were formulated in terms of the postulated stable transactions velocity which, it was believed, preserved a fairly constant relation to final output. Currie already called these assumptions into question in a February 1933 article[40] in which he had criticized the proposal advanced in 1931 by the official Committee on Bank Reserves to impose an *automatic* increase in bank reserves whenever bank debits increased, on the grounds that an increase in debits reflected an increase in the activity (velocity) of deposits. Currie argued that there can be a huge increase in transactions velocity with no increase in the income velocity.

Given the increase in bank debits at the height of stock market activity in 1929, the principle advocated by the Committee on Bank Reserves would have meant a further rise in reserve requirements at a time when monetary conditions were already very tight and the real economy already declining. Currie argued instead that central bankers needed greater *discretionary* control over reserves, with an eye to general business conditions, to offset the business cycle. He also pointed out that time deposits and other financial transactions were secularly increasing in importance. Thus, this would effectively involve a secular increase in reserves against demand deposits and discriminate unfairly against member banks relative to nonmembers. Agreeing with proposals in Keynes's *Treatise on Money* (1930), Currie urged reform in terms of greater discretionary power to alter reserves.[41] Unlike the Chicago monetary theorist Henry Simons, he argued that automatic rules make more difficult the task of central bankers and could render monetary policy pro-cyclical rather than counter-cyclical.

Ironically, however, Keynes himself had published a short paper in 1932 endorsing the views of the Committee on Bank Reserves.[42] In particular, he agreed that a policy that increased reserve requirements automatically in line with the volume of bank debits would have been appropriate in 1929. Keynes was swayed by the committee's argument that the turnover of bank deposits had risen very rapidly between 1925 and 1929. In contrast, Currie argued that the *income* velocity of money had risen only slowly over this period, though his November 1933 paper in the *Quarterly Journal of Economics* did show some acceleration in 1929 and a fall thereafter.

Currie's views on reserves and bank debits were also sharply at variance with those of Joseph Schumpeter who persisted in a focus on bank debits and a related transactions version of velocity.[43] Schumpeter criticized Currie's series on the money supply because it failed to correlate well with bank debits. He claimed to find a closer relationship between debits and the strange series he preferred of total deposits less bank investments. He also arrived at opposite conclusions from Currie regarding different reserve requirements against demand and time deposits (p. 853). He claimed that the shift from demand deposits (with higher reserve requirements) to time deposits was an instrument of monetary *expansion* in the 1920s. Throughout this period Schumpeter was worrying about "inflationary" monetary policies, even when the price level was falling. In fact, Currie has claimed that in the early 1930s he was the only person on the Harvard faculty who regarded monetary policy as deflationary—though some, like Seymour Harris, later became prominent "Keynesians" when it became fashionable so to be, having earlier disdained Currie's views and sought to block his promotion. This long rankled Currie since he would dearly have loved to remain at Harvard, from which prestigious vantage point he believed it would be easier to achieve a more pervasive and permanent influence on his profession both in terms of economic theory and, indirectly, policy than was possible when working inside the machinery of government itself.

In deriving his 1933 estimates of income velocity Currie drew on the recent pioneering work of Simon Kuznets, Wilfred King, and Morris Copeland in estimating national income.[44] He and James Angell published, in the same November 1933 issue of the *Quarterly Journal of Economics,* the first estimates of income velocity of money for the United States. These two estimates differed considerably, however, partly because of differing definitions and sources of income, but much more importantly because of differing definitions of "money."

As has already been indicated, Currie had early come to the conclusion that one of the most important sources of error and confusion in monetary theory and policy rested on the definition of the term "credit," which at one moment is identified with total loans, at another with bank deposits of different types, and sometimes simply with qualitative measures of creditworthiness.[45]

Because of their adherence to the commercial loan theory of central banking, the Federal Reserve Board focused on "credit conditions" in the sense of loans. It was the type and quantity of loans that the authorities sought to control. Consequently the growth of money in the sense of the nation's means of payment (currency plus demand deposits subject to transfer by check) had been largely a matter of accident. Indeed the FRB published data on loans but not on money. Therefore, Currie had to calculate for himself a monetary series for the period 1921–31. This was actually the first means of payment series worked out for the United States.

In commenting on Currie's contribution to monetary theory, Karl Brunner wrote: "Currie was among the pioneers in our field assembling and assessing data on the money stock. He fully appreciated that meaningful analysis cannot proceed in the absence of reliable data. This pioneering work eventually forced the Federal Reserve Authorities to develop suitable monetary data on a broader scale, and particularly collect and publish data bearing on the nation's money stock."[46]

The task was a difficult one because many banks did not publish separate figures for demand and time deposits. He thus had to partition the series according to the typical proportions of each type of deposit in banks that did publish separate series. Adjustments were also made to avoid the double-counting of interbank deposits and the "float."

James Angell avoided these difficulties in his 1933 paper (as did Friedman and Schwartz later) by simply taking *all* bank deposits plus currency as the definition of money for the purpose of calculating income velocity. Perhaps this would not matter if both definitions of money moved in exactly the same way. But this was then, and still is now, not the case.[47] In the United States in 1928 "credit" in the sense of loans increased by 8 percent and such credit expansion continued into 1929. This led to calls for a more restrictive policy. Credit conditions clearly appeared very lax. Yet demand deposits actually contracted in 1928. Between 1925–29 demand deposits increased by an average of only 0.8 percent a year. The faster growth of incomes and expenditures during this period was, therefore, made possible by an increase in velocity. Currie's November 1933 article showed this in quantitative terms. Income velocity rose fairly steadily from 2.82 in 1921 to 3.48 in 1929 and fell thereafter.[48] James Angell, meanwhile, using currency plus *total* bank deposits as his definition of money, presented estimates of 1.53 for 1921 and very similar figures for the years to 1928, the last year estimated, when it stood at 1.51.[49] Friedman and Schwartz's figures, based on a similar definition of money, also show a slight fall in velocity over this period.[50]

Currie's figures for velocity were consistent with his a priori expectations that velocity could vary pro-cyclically, rising in the upswing and declining in the downswing, which, incidentally, cast further doubt on the appropriateness of a nondiscretionary money rule.

Currie was much more interested in empirical verification of his monetary theories than was true of contemporaries at Chicago, notably Simons and Mints. Don Patinkin has noted that these latter "were so convinced on *a priori* grounds of the validity of their analysis and consequent policy proposals that they saw no need to subject these proposals to empirical study."[51] He noted that this attitude is strikingly revealed in the following paragraph from Simons's 1935 review of Currie's book, *The Supply and Control of Money in The United States* (1934):

> The study reflects a rare combination of penetrating theoretical insights and patient competence in the analysis of banking statistics. The highly realistic treatment will make the author's argument convincing, or at least disturbing, to many readers who would be unimpressed by "mere theory." For critical students, however, Dr. Currie's inductive verifications will be largely gratuitous—although everyone will be grateful for the excellent statistical compilation and analysis. In general, the author's fundamental insights are so sound that failure of statistical confirmation would only indicate error or inadequacy in the statistics. (*Journal of Political Economy*, 1935, p. 556)

Despite these laudatory comments, Simons rejected Currie's focus on the means of payment as the appropriate object of control and expressed concern that control over demand deposits would lead to significant conversions into savings deposits – a proposition that Currie denied. In Simons's 1936 paper on rules versus authorities in monetary policy he claimed that velocity was too variable, and that fixing the supply of money might merely serve to increase the perverse variability in the amounts of "near moneys" and in the degree of their general acceptability.[52] Consequently, he advocated a policy rule of keeping the price level constant rather than an alternative rule of keeping the quantity of money constant. Friedman contended that had the facts been available to Simons he would not have interpreted the Great Depression in terms of such an instability of velocity, and so would have chosen instead a policy rule stated in terms of the quantity of money.[53] Patinkin takes issue with Friedman on this, for he notes that Currie's empirical studies were available to Simons and, since Simons reviewed his book in 1935, he should have been less concerned about the possibility of extreme variations in velocity in normal times. Nevertheless, Currie's studies did show some procyclical variation in velocity and this weakens the case for a nondiscretionary money rule such as advocated later by, for example, Clark Warburton and Milton Friedman.[54]

It is significant that Currie partly explained the observed procyclical variations in income velocity of the means of payment with reference to the rate of interest, insofar as this also tends to move procyclically. (This pro-cyclical movement in velocity greatly aggravated the effects of the fall in the money supply after 1929.) According to Patinkin, "the failure even to mention the rate of interest as a possible explanation of the observed variations in the velocity of circulation" characterized the earlier writings of Irving Fisher, Carl Snyder, James Angell, and Clark Warburton.[55] Patinkin does not mention Currie in this context, but actually Currie did consider this relationship, albeit without the emphasis or elaboration that is required if a new idea is to attract attention. Commenting on monetary policy in the period leading up to the 1929 crash, he wrote:

> . . . far from speculation absorbing funds, it actually operated to increase the effective purchasing power of the community. From the beginning of 1928 to the middle of 1929 the volume of means of payment declined. In spite of this, monetary incomes increased sufficiently to take off a considerably increased flow of goods at stable prices. The income velocity of money increased by 1.3 percent in 1928 and by 4.5 percent in 1929. It seems reasonable to suppose that an important factor contributing to this

> increased velocity was the drawing-down of large inactive corporation deposits attracted by the high call-money rates. A more conservative statement would be that although the requirements of the financial circulation may have increased, still this did not lead to a decrease in the industrial circulation. The latter, on the contrary, actually increased.[56]

Also in his 1934 book he complained that the "needs of business" criterion for monetary policy would involve an expansion of money during the upswing and a contraction during the downswing of the cycle. However,

> if stable business conditions were the objective of monetary policy the needs of the community for money would frequently dictate a contrary movement. In other words the demand for loans and the demand for money vary inversely. In the upswing of the cycle the disutility of holding idle money balances increases owing to the greater opportunities for profitable investment; but, for the same reason, there is also an increased demand for loans. On the downswing the lack of opportunities for profitable investment leads to a decreased demand for loans and an increased demand for money to hold.[57]

The estimates of income velocity made by James Angell in 1933 and by Friedman and Schwartz in their 1963 study actually failed to reveal any pro-cyclical variation in velocity. Friedman and Schwartz themselves argued that velocity may be expected to vary pro-cyclically but they glossed over the way this expectation is contradicted by their evidence for the 1920s based on the use of a broad definition of money.[58]

Angell explained the tendency he found for velocity to decline (slightly) during the 1920s in terms of structural changes in payments practices and geographical distribution of business. Currie offered a different explanation for Angell's results by compiling his separate series for demand and time deposits and comparing their growth. Time deposits exhibited strong growth relative to means of payment and increased slightly faster than incomes.

Currie regretted Angell's emphasis on the movement of total bank deposits because these were very likely to give misleading signals to the monetary authorities. If there is a secular tendency for time deposits to increase relatively fast then this would impart a deflationary bias to monetary policy. However, the community's savings can move erratically between different types of interest-bearing financial assets, dependent on small differences between the interest rates offered by banks and nonbank financial intermediaries. There exists a much smaller interest elasticity of substitution between money proper (currency and demand deposits) and nonmoney assets. If one does not draw the line between those noninterest-bearing assets that are actually used as means of payment (in the settlement of debts) and all other financial assets then there is no logical place at which to stop. If one includes bank time deposits why not also deposits in nonbank financial institutions? Many assets (including marketable securities and call loans) are almost as "liquid," in the sense of being readily convertible into money proper, as bank time deposits.

This focus on liquidity rather than money for many years dominated British thinking on monetary theory and practice, due largely to the influence of Keynes's liquidity preference theory. It was not until around 1970 that the British authorities bothered to publish an official series on money! Currie's contributions to monetary theory and monetary statistics in the United States may be a significant reason for the sharp difference between U.S. and British approaches to the importance of monetary policy in macroeconomic management.

The Distinction Between the Primary and Secondary Functions of Banks, and Implications for Monetary Control

Currie preferred to draw a sharp distinction between banks' primary function as the supplier and administrator of a substantial part of the nation's means of payment, and their secondary function as middlemen or intermediaries for investing part of the nation's savings. He noted that the secondary function had become more important in the period 1920–32 but that by focusing on this the monetary authorities had been misled into pursuing a disastrously restrictive policy in 1929.

In his 1934 book Currie was also to show that the practice of requiring reserves against bank time deposits (but not the time deposits of nonbanks), and the differing requirements against different kinds of banks, led to automatic but unpredictable and often undesired changes in overall reserve requirements and, hence, in demand deposits. This greatly complicated the attempts of the Federal Reserve Board to control reserves and deposits in the degree most appropriate for countercyclical economic management.

From the point of view of monetary control, focus on adjusted demand deposits was most helpful because this aggregate could be controlled by the authorities most easily through more active open market policies and variations in reserve requirements.[59] Currie insisted on the practical importance of working with the bank reserves-deposits ratio instead of the relation between the money base (including cash in circulation) and the total money supply. (Fifty years later, in other contexts, he was still insisting on this point.)

Control over the currency portion of total means of payment can only be effected indirectly, through control over demand deposits which, by altering the flow of incomes and expenditures, also changes the desired volume of cash holdings. Independent movements in the cash to deposits ratio, however, have to be monitored by the authorities and, when appropriate, offset by policies to vary demand deposits. But this first required that the authorities switch their attention to money rather than credit and the composition of banks' earning assets. Instead, Currie flatly asserted in 1933 that

> the reserve administration is not in the slightest degree interested in credit in the sense of means of payment. Hence, it cannot be expected to be aware of the necessity of permitting expansion of demand deposits to prevent a downward secular trend of prices. Probably the reason why the banking authorities have always been reluctant to concede that there is any connection between "credit" and prices is because it is difficult to see any relation between loans and the value of money.[60]

Another issue of vital importance that Currie stressed in various publications between 1932–34 concerned the degree of "repugnance to indebtedness" by different classes of borrowers and at different phases of the business cycle.[61] In 1928 and 1929 member banks were forced into their highest ever level of indebtedness with reserve banks, at the same time as the rediscount rate was raised significantly. This conjunction led to a contraction of demand deposits in 1928 because member banks disliked indebtedness, even when it was profitable. Country banks were somewhat less sensitive, and speculators least sensitive of all. When the New York rediscount rate was raised to 6 percent on August 9, 1929, stock speculation actually increased. Higher interest rates mainly served only to squeeze monetary conditions further at a time when business conditions were already turning down at home and abroad. This was just one example of what Currie called the "perverse elasticity" of the U.S. money supply, thanks to a "banking school" approach to monetary control.

Although the Federal Reserve Board relaxed its stance after the stock market broke at the end of October, its actions were timid and late. More reserves became available for a few months but only enough to reduce member bank indebtedness; the Board did not engineer any significant *net* increase in reserves, even though the banks did not face a shortage of potential borrowers. Brokers' loans increased in the first months of 1930 and there was a $4.5 billion increase in banks' holdings of bonds.[62] Member banks lacked reserves so that further lending could have required that the banks take the initiative in remaining in, or reverting to, indebtedness with the reserve banks. But, as Currie's studies had shown, the repugnance to indebtedness is even greater in a depression than in an upswing. As a result of the banks' unwillingness to remain in debt, and the failure of the reserve authorities energetically to expand reserves, the money supply contracted by 3.7 percent in the year to June 1930.

The fact that interest rates declined in late 1929 and early 1930 has been taken by some writers, notably Peter Temin recently,[63] as an indication that monetary policy was not to blame for the depression. Temin attributed the depression to autonomous declines in private spending. He argued that if there had been adequate demand for loanable funds, and desire to spend, interest rates would not have fallen. Temin also claims that since prices started to fall faster than the nominal money supply in 1930 the real money supply was expanding; therefore monetary conditions were not restrictive.

Currie's view, however, was that the monetary authorities should have made adequate reserves available both to get banks out of debt and to satisfy the natural desire, mainly on the part of business, to build up liquid cash balances at a time when sales and prices were declining. Instead, a drastic decline in velocity aggravated the fall in the money supply and the authorities passively acquiesced to the decline in incomes and expenditures that this implied. The Federal Reserve Board believed that lower interest rates demonstrated the appropriateness of their response. They failed to appreciate that banks' repugnance to indebtedness at any price, especially in a recession, required that monetary expansion be accomplished not by lower interest rates alone but by active open market operations. Reserves had to be created by purchasing bills and securities, not by expecting member banks voluntarily to borrow reserves.

This approach of Currie's foreshadows recent controversies in monetary theory as to whether the "real balance effect," especially as analyzed by Don Patinkin, can be invoked to reconcile classical (Walrasian) value theory—in which real resource allocation is determined solely by the structure of relative prices—and classical monetary theory (the quantity theory of money) in which the absolute price level is dependent solely on the quantity of money relative to goods, so that money and the general level of prices have no real effects.[64] Money is "neutral," or a veil.

One assumption of this theory is that there are no "expectations effects."[65] But in the context of the early 1930s Currie insisted on the importance of price expectations. If a fall in the money supply reduces prices people may be led to expect *further* price reductions. This may motivate an increase in the demand for real money balances, hence further reductions in the demand for goods and services. A perverse real balance effect sets in and money is not "neutral," at least not in the short run, which may in practice mean not for some years. An active policy is called for, to increase the supply of real money balances (M/P) via a rise in the nominal money supply (M) rather than passively waiting for a fall in the price level (P) to bring recovery.

Likewise, Currie emphasized that a fall in the interest rate would be insufficient in such circumstances to arrest economic decline. With a reduction in monetary expenditures and falling prices businessmen defer their production plans, fearing that eventual sale prices will not cover current costs. Hence decline sets in motion forces tending to reinforce it. Falling interest rates do not reflect loose monetary policy, nor do they represent a sufficiently strong stimulus to counter the forces of decline. They are simply one of the symptoms or consequences of depression brought on and perpetuated by a disastrously restrictive monetary policy.

During the wave of bank failures in the autumn of 1930 and in 1931 the Federal Reserve adopted a basically passive stance. Recalling the monetary-banking panics preceding 1913, experts thought a real panic would lead almost at once to bank failures—the long delay before Kreditanstalt or the Bank of the United States failed was treated by contemporary bankers as a sign the Federal Reserve and/or Hoover's exhortations were working.[66] The bank failures, brought on by excessive, unrelieved indebtedness, destroyed more and more of the nation's money stock, velocity continued to decline, and the result was one of the deepest and most prolonged business slumps ever known.

Temin (1976, 1981) insists that the creation of new reserves would simply have caused the banks to build up excess reserves. Commenting on Temin's 1981 paper, Peter Lindert endorses Currie's view that increased reserves would have prevented banks from failing and would have kept up the money supply. He refers to the ample evidence now available on the money-income relation that indicates that a greater money stock would sustain higher incomes and expenditures.[67] Likewise, Karl Brunner (1968) writes:

> Currie's systematic discussion of policy issues considers also some notions often repeated by the Federal Reserve authorities . . . Many believed that the Federal Reserve had tried to stem the deflationary tide of the preceding years by means of an expansionary policy. The experience was interpreted as a demonstration that monetary policy was useless . . . Currie shows that this belief is a myth . . . The examination reveals not inability to exert influence but a persistent inactivity and drift. Open market policy and acceptance policy were not systematically used to raise the monetary base. His analysis shows that the Federal Reserve authorities could have effectively prevented the collapse in the monetary stock during the Great Depression. Currie's explicit challenge to the ruling myth has been thoroughly vindicated in recent research bearing on our monetary policy.[68]

Currie acknowledged that after the latter part of 1932 excess reserves did start to build up. However, he insisted that although this did indicate that expansionary monetary policy would be much less effective on its own after that time, it was illegitimate to conclude that monetary policy would have been ineffective earlier. The degree of depression and the abnormal loss of confidence in 1932 were quite different from conditions in 1930 and 1931. "If we are to argue on the basis of similarities, 1924 offers a better basis for comparison with 1930 than does 1932, and in 1924 banks utilized a considerable increase in reserves (much greater than in 1932) to bring about an expansion of adjusted demand deposits in member banks of over 10 percent."[69]

In a chapter of his 1934 book devoted to the question of excess reserves, Currie noted that in normal depressions investments (long-term business loans) increase most rapidly, enabling banks to remain fully loaned up. Thus he rejected the arguments of Taussig and Wesley Mitchell (prominently repeated by Nicholas Kaldor in modern times) that the ability of the banking system to expand deposits depends mainly on business conditions and the demand for loans. "Unless the depression is abnormally severe banks can offset the decline in their commercial loans by increasing their investment portfolios, and our greatest hope in promoting business stability through monetary means lies in action taken before a depression becomes a disaster."[70]

Thus the following remarks by Paul Samuelson are hardly fair: "Lauchlin Currie wrote a book . . . when I was a student. The ink was hardly dry before he had repudiated all its contents, but nobody told me that; and when I received the book with the ink dried, I had to wrestle with the question whether after all it was not M that had really caused the change [in activity and prices], since allegedly without the change in M there would not have been the change in interest rates to produce the first effect."[71]

Currie merely pointed out that if an abnormally severe depression is allowed to develop then supplementary measures would be more necessary than usual. He did not repudiate the analysis of his book for less abnormal conditions or for preventing an abnormally severe depression from arising in the first place.

Throughout this period there were those who continued to insist that the Great Depression was the fault of a "speculative orgy" and that deflation was a necessary purgative. In Schumpeter's words, "any revival which is merely due to artificial stimulus leaves part of the work of depressions undone, and adds . . . new adjustments of its own which have to be liquidated in turn, thus threatening business with another crisis ahead."[72]

Meanwhile, on the fiscal front, as private expenditures, especially construction, were plummeting, President Hoover announced some very modest public expenditure increases and tax cuts in 1930, but mostly he relied on exhortations to private businessmen to cooperate in promoting recovery. As the economy slumped tax revenues slumped too and the budget deficit widened. This offended the conservative instincts and private accountancy perspectives of the majority of politicians and economists, not least Hoover, and at the end of 1931 a large tax increase was announced in a vain effort to balance the budget as the depression deepened.[73] Some economists, notably a group at Chicago, including Jacob Viner, protested at this and endorsed a mild dose of deficit finance as helpful to recovery.[74] But Viner felt constrained in his endorsement of deficits because he could not consider or endorse a deliberate abandonment of the gold standard.[75]

During the 1932 election campaign both Hoover and Roosevelt were insisting on the need to balance the budget as economic conditions worsened. The Glass-Steagall Act and the Securities Act were passed in 1932 and 1933. Currie declared that this legislation, still bearing all the hallmarks of the commercial loan theory of central banking and stock market speculation, showed that the wrong lessons had been learned from the wave of bank failures and the 1929 stock market crash.[76] This legislation focused primarily on the quality rather than the quantity of bank assets, though in 1932 Senator Glass had reluctantly accepted a temporary relaxation of his cherished "eligibility" rules for rediscounting commercial paper. Nonetheless, the main concern was to prevent banks from making loans for speculative purposes, or, indeed, for the purchase of any securities at all, and the act separated banks from security affiliates and brokers. It extended branch banking to a limited degree but prohibited nationwide branch banking. The reasoning behind this legislation was that bankruptcies had been caused by bank ownership of stocks whose values had plummeted in 1929. It ignored the way that the reserve banks had failed to provide adequate lender-of-last-resort support to prevent mass liquidations of debt.

Prior to Roosevelt's inauguration on March 4, 1933, a crisis developed. The resources of the Reconstruction Finance Corporation, established in 1932, were inadequate to prevent more and more bank failures in the absence of more vigorous open market purchases by the reserve banks. A prolonged nationwide bank holiday was declared. Currie recalls telling his Harvard classes that this was nothing to worry about. "You close the banks and then you re-open them and nothing of consequence has happened." To his consternation and embarrassment, however, several hundred banks never opened their doors again and, while their reserves remained frozen, yet more of the nation's money supply, and hence monetary expenditure, was extinguished.[77]

It has been claimed that many of the bank failures reflected the overextended position of small, mainly rural banks with long histories of failures. Nevertheless, there is a big difference between isolated cases of failure due to poor management on the part of individual banks, and a simultaneous wave of failures when reserve banks fail to provide additional reserves to prevent *mass* liquidations following a *general* loss of confidence among depositors that causes a significant fall in the overall stock of money and monetary expenditures. Currie, incidentally, favored an extension of branch banking on the grounds that this would lessen the risk of small rural bank failures.

Reform Proposals

We have already indicated the main arguments of Currie's 1934 book, which drew together the various aspects of monetary theory and policy that he had discussed in various articles published in the preceding years. He concluded his book with several important suggestions for enhancing the effectiveness of control. The first requirement was a sound understanding of the main purposes of central bank control by those in authority, this being the control of the nation's money supply rather than the character of bank lending. This, in turn, required that the government should concentrate on supplying the appropriate quantity of money while banks and other financial institutions concentrated on lending the predetermined money stock. Ideally this would involve 100 percent reserves against all demand deposits.

As Currie's book was going to press he learned that a group of economists at the University of Chicago, led by Henry Simons, had put out a mimeographed report on banking and currency reform that contained a proposal for a 100 percent reserve against all bank deposits. Aside from possible differences in definitions of money, Henry Simons was interested in the way such an arrangement could facilitate the operation of an automatic "money rule," while Currie saw it as a way to enhance discretionary management of the supply of money at different phases of the business cycle.[78]

Even if the 100 percent reserve proposal were unacceptable, Currie urged that at least the reserve requirements should be uniform against all demand deposits, regardless of class of bank. This would enhance control because there would be no automatic (and often pro-cyclical) change in the money supply arising solely from shifts in deposits from one class of bank to another. Likewise, he urged the abolition of reserve requirements against time deposits so that shifts between demand and time deposits would have no effect on the money supply. He also urged a tax on excess reserves so that banks could not independently increase the money supply by accommodating an increase in the demand for loans, which often moves pro-cyclically and hence represents a destabilizing potential. This was to become an issue of increasing importance in the coming years.

In general he favored greater discretionary power to manage the economy, and distrusted changes in the money supply that arose automatically. This included mistrust of the automatic gold standard with fixed ratios of gold to deposits and currency.[79] Gold movements do not necessarily move in sympathy with the needs of a stable economy, being sensitive to interest rates and confidence factors that also move pro-cyclically.[80]

Lastly, he urged a revision of the way in which the reserve banks presented their weekly statements.[81] Their balance sheets arranged items in a way that focused attention on their loans and investments which have no predictable relation to monetary supply and control. More germane to supply and control was the way in which the various balance sheet items affected member bank indebtedness, or reserve balances. Depending on the time and type of bank contracting the indebtedness this was a crucial determinant of the expansion or contraction of deposits. Control over the supply of money, or the nation's purchasing power, depended on the degree to which the authorities could control those items affecting reserves and bank indebtedness.

Within a few months of the publication of this book Currie was to be pitched into the center of decisionmaking in Washington, D.C., on monetary and fiscal matters, first at the U.S. Treasury and then at the Federal Reserve Board, where he would have the opportunity to turn his academic work to practical account.

CHAPTER 3

The Treasury and Federal Reserve Board, 1934–39

Viner's "Freshman Brain Trust" at the U.S. Treasury, 1934

Currie's controversial views on deficit financing did not endear him to some of the senior professors at Harvard. He propounded his heresies not only in the classroom and in academic publications, but also sought to influence current policy through appeals to a wider audience. In January 1934 he was intrigued by President Roosevelt's budget message in which he declared, with some reluctance, that he would be violating the budget-balancing philosophy to which ideally he would have preferred to adhere. Currie persuaded five of his fellow instructors at Harvard to join him in sending a letter to the President endorsing the main features of the New Deal recovery program, including deliberate departure from the gold standard.

Currie's attitude was that if the choice was between the gold standard or the needs of sixteen million unemployed, then so much the worse for the gold standard. He stuck two cartoons on his study door, one showing South Africans digging up gold from the mines, the other showing Americans digging holes under Fort Knox to bury it again. The President was apparently pleased by the show of support from the Harvard instructors, for their letter was released by the White House to the *New York Times* and given considerable prominence. The senior professors at Harvard were less pleased by the publicity and none of the six signatories was given tenure.[1]

Later Currie elaborated his views on adjustment under the gold standard and under floating exchange rates in a paper entitled "Domestic Stability and the Mechanism of Trade Adjustments to International Capital Movements," published in 1936 in a volume honoring F. W. Taussig, his old teacher.[2] Here he explained the need to establish domestic stability as the primary goal of monetary policy and to subordinate international gold and capital flows to that end.

He explained the different ways in which gold flows could enhance or obstruct the attainment of full employment and price stability under different types of exchange regimes and different degrees of slack in the domestic economy. This paper included an early explanation of how the adjustment mechanism would work under a flexible exchange regime which, to the intense displeasure of some influential officials in the Federal Reserve Board where he was then working, called into question the beneficence of the automatic gold standard system.

Currie's main complaint concerned the way that international lending necessitated disruptive adjustments to prices and wages, output and employment out of all proportion to the potential benefits of the lending. A capital inflow, for example, required a trade deficit, or excess of imports over exports. Given the relatively small size of the trade sector in the United States a large disruptive change in national income and expenditure was required to bring about a small increase in imports. Though this paper was not novel in explaining the adjustment mechanism under the gold standard its focus on "possible losses incident to the mechanism of adjustment itself" had perhaps not been stressed in this way before. Nor had there previously been much analysis of the adjustment mechanism, and its costs, to capital flows under flexible exchange rates, and his analysis anticipates by some fifty years the problems that capital flows posed for stability in the 1970s and 1980s.

Characteristically, Currie was less interested in analyzing the adjustment process for its own sake as for its real-world significance and policy implications:

> If capital movements entail a departure from internal stability, the resulting loss to the community should, of course, be offset against any gains that may later arise from such movements. While such losses may be dismissed as transitional difficulties, the transition may be so long and entail such disturbances as to dwarf the gains after adjustment has occurred. Monetary authorities can have little assurance that capital movements will continue at a steady rate and for a long period and, therefore, must weight heavily the transitional disturbances entailed by such movements. . . . It offers support for the development and use of controls to reduce the magnitude of capital movements and to prevent the adjustment of trade to such movements.

In November 1932 Jacob Viner, then at the University of Chicago, visited Harvard to give a series of lectures to staff and graduate stu-

Jacob Viner (1892–1970). He recruited Currie for the U.S. Treasury in 1934. Currie dedicated his *Accelerating Development* (1966) to him. *Courtesy of Princeton University Library.*

dents. This marked the beginning of a lifelong friendship and voluminous correspondence between Viner and Currie.[3] Currie was the only person at Harvard at that time upholding that university's prestige vis-à-vis Chicago in the field of monetary theory and statistics. The compensation was that as he fell into disfavor at Harvard he gained favor in Chicago and this, curiously, led to his leaving Harvard at the instigation of Viner.

In November 1933 President Roosevelt appointed Henry Morgenthau, Jr., as acting Treasury secretary. The appointment was confirmed in January 1934. Soon afterward Morgenthau suggested to Professor Viner that he assemble the best young brains he could find in the fields of monetary theory, public finance, and banking legislation, give them an absolutely free rein and see what they could come up with. One bright suggestion or idea, it was thought, would justify the whole effort. Thus the Freshman Brain Trust was born. It was after Currie's first class in the Harvard summer school toward the end of June 1934 that he received a wire from Viner in Washington asking him to join the Brain Trust for the summer months.[4] Currie hastily secured a substitute for his Harvard course and left for Washington "for three months." When at the end of this period Viner asked him to stay on at the Treasury, Currie requested a further leave of absence from Harvard but this request was denied. With some bitterness, Currie therefore resigned his Harvard post. His three-month stint in Washington would eventually stretch into eleven years.

A fellow instructor at Harvard at the time was Edward S. Mason. He wrote later: "The attitude of the Harvard Economics Department toward the New Deal in the early years was critical rather than cooperative or constructive. The economists who flocked to Washington in the early 1930s were mainly from Columbia, Cornell and Wisconsin. Harvard contributed a number from its younger staff, notably Lauchlin Currie and Harry White, whom Viner pronounced to be too good for Harvard."[5]

Currie's brief at the Treasury was to develop the embryo plan he had presented in *The Supply and Control of Money in the United States* for 100 percent reserves against demand deposits. The object was to outline what would be an ideal monetary system for the United States in the absence of any need for compromise or gradualism. Currie started work at the Treasury on July 1, 1934.

As we have seen, Currie was thoroughly dissatisfied with the existing banking structure and with the powers and theoretical approach to monetary control of the Federal Reserve System as established by the 1913 Federal Reserve Act and the confused amendments of the 1932 Glass-Steagall Act. "The truth is," he had written, "that the whole modern conception of the function of a central bank of controlling the community's money is lacking in the Federal Reserve Act. The reserve banks were set up mainly to provide an elastic currency (cash) and to 'accommodate legitimate business' with short-term loans."[6]

Currie's *Proposed Revision of the Monetary System of the United States* was submitted to Secretary Morgenthau in September.[7] Characteristically, he began his report by setting out a clear statement of the nature of the problem and the consequences of conflicting or vague objectives and ambiguous definitions in monetary or credit policy. The present system, "instead of operating as a maladjustment-compensating factor has, for the most part, operated as a maladjustment-intensifying factor. Fundamentally the faulty working of our monetary system may be attributed to the unsatisfactory nature of the compromise of private creation of money with governmental control" (p. 197).

Even if the authorities were interested in controlling the supply of money rather than the quality of bank assets, this task was rendered unduly difficult by the system of unit banks, differing degrees of sensitivity to indebtedness to the reserve banks, and reserve requirements that differed between class of bank and type of deposit. Furthermore, there was enormous diffusion of responsibility for the control of deposits, and conflict of interests and objectives.

Control depended on a sharp distinction between the supply of money and the lending of money. Banks performed two important but distinct functions: they supplied and administered an important part of the nation's money stock and, along with other institutions, they acted as intermediaries between lenders and borrowers. Under a fractional reserve banking system these two functions are intertwined and often confused. Effective control over the money supply depended on the ability to force banks into debt with reserve banks, on banks' unwillingness to remain in debt, and on their willingness or ability to make loans.

The observed perverse elasticity of the U. S. monetary system could be avoided, Currie insisted, if control over the money supply was exercised by a small committee of technically qualified, disinterested members of the Federal Reserve Board centered in Washington, responsible to the President and Congress, and charged with the specific objective of formulating monetary and, where necessary, other policies for maintaining general business stability. Such a "mandate" was more in accord with the duties of a central bank than the vague, almost meaningless objectives set out in the 1913 Federal Reserve Act to "accommodate commerce and business."

If 100 percent reserves were required against all demand deposits subject to checking and if zero reserves were set against all other kinds of bank deposit, the authorities would have direct and speedy, rather than indirect and delayed, control over the money supply through its direct control over reserves. Reserves can be varied via open market operations and gold flows (though these in turn can and should be subject to offset by open market operations when the criterion of business stability dictates this). Switching between bank deposits and cash would no longer affect the total money supply, only its composition. The change would nationalize the nation's money supply but would not nationalize the banks' assets. Indeed it would reduce interference in the banks' increasingly important lending functions.

Since there would be zero reserve against time deposits, switching between nonbank financial assets and bank time deposits would not affect reserve requirements and so would leave deposits unchanged. Currie's plan also minimized any new incentive for banks to encourage switching between demand and time deposits. This would be accomplished by measures to ensure that banks' earnings would not be affected by the need to hold 100 percent reserves against demand deposits. They would thus be adequately compensated for the significant costs involved in handling and clearing checks.[8] Also, the monetary authorities would have the power to fix maximum rates of interest on time deposits, insist on a minimum period of six months' deposit before interest could be paid on them.[9] and prohibit checking against time deposits.

Among the qualities Currie listed as essential for his proposed small policymaking committee, to be composed of not more than five members, were: an ability to think in terms of general, community interests rather than sectional and regional interests, and an ability to see through the fallacy of composition as applied for example to savings, inventories, bank liquidations, and tariffs; the ability to think in terms of the relative quantitative magnitudes of things and skepticism of ceteris paribus assumptions; the ability to understand the interrelations of economic phenomena; and flexibility of mind and willingness to publish and explain the theory of and empirical basis for their policy recommendations. Signed reports of committee proceedings were to be published.

The duties and powers of the committee were to include open market operations, international capital controls, variations in the price of gold, recommendations regarding interest paid on time deposits, and data collection. If these monetary powers were deemed inadequate to the task of controlling general business activity the committee was to be empowered to make recommendations on taxation and government spending.

Although these measures would obviate the need for branch banking, nevertheless the plan recommended this as a means of spreading risks and reducing the need for local liquidations. Currie also noted that the plan would help solve the problem of excess reserves. He noted that a major constraint on government spending of $3 billion of Treasury "profits" from gold revaluation in 1934 was that this would not only increase deposits currently but would also increase excess reserves and hence limit effective control of possible inflation in the future.

Although Currie believed that the 100 percent reserve requirement was the ideal instrument for effective control over money, his main concern was to establish a proper central banking authority, with power vested in "a small, politically responsible and expert body of persons feeling a keen sense of responsibility for the behavior of the monetary mechanism."[10] Without this body, "under the present system of in part private and in part governmental creation of money, of diffusion of authority and responsibility, of uncertainty as to objectives . . . the prospect of securing skilful monetary administration is almost hopeless."[11]

In other words, even if it were not possible to move immediately to a 100 percent reserve system, the existence of a proper central bank—with centralized powers over the nation's money supply and dedicated to the task of stabilizing overall effective demand for goods and services—would be the best guarantee against the type of monetary mismanagement that had brought such ruin to the nation in the early 1930s.

Marriner Eccles Meets Currie

Earlier in 1934 Marriner S. Eccles, an unorthodox, millionaire Mormon banker from Utah had been persuaded by Henry Morgenthau to assist him at the U.S. Treasury. Eccles has described the unlikely sequence of events that brought him to Washington, beginning with a chance meeting in February 1933 in Salt Lake City with Stuart Chase who was impressed by his bold advocacy of deficit spending to get the nation's money to work. Most bankers were vehemently committed to "fiscal responsibility" without which, they claimed, there could be no business confidence, hence no business recovery. Eccles was completely untrained in economics but was a very successful practical banker and businessman who took pride in the fact that none of his bank's depositors had lost a cent, despite the wave of failures affecting other banks in the early 1930s. His ideas on under-consumption probably came from Foster and Catchings (and, through them, from Marx).[12] They did not come from Keynes, whom he had never read. He wrote proudly: "My conceptions were based on naked-eye observation and experience in the intermountain region. Moreover, I have never read Keynes' writings except in small extracts up to this day."[13] Foster's and Catchings's ideas on underconsumption were closer to Hansen's "secular stagnation thesis" than to a business cycle theory of periodic excess saving of the type stressed by Currie and the earlier, but not so much the later, writings of Keynes.[14]

Stuart Chase introduced Eccles to Rexford Tugwell, one of Roosevelt's original "brain trusters," and in November 1933 Tugwell in turn introduced him to several other New Dealers, including Mordecai Ezekiel and Henry Wallace at the Department of Agriculture and Harry Hopkins, Harold Ickes, and Jerome Frank. This same month Will Woodin, the treasury secretary, retired through ill health and Henry Morgenthau, an old family friend and neighbor of Roosevelt, succeeded him. Morgenthau was an ultraconservative on fiscal matters and known as Henry the Morgue because of his intense gloominess. In his early days at the Treasury he was feeling his way around and nervously awaiting congressional approval of his appointment.

He was persuaded by Tugwell to call Eccles for a meeting in January 1934 and, despite the evident clash of temperament that was to worsen over the coming years, later invited him to assist him for a year in reorganizing the Treasury Department. In March Eccles joined, as the Treasury's representative, the President's Emergency Committee on Housing, chaired by Frank Walker. Winfield Riefler of the Federal Reserve Board was economic adviser and secretary. The committee's work resulted in federally guaranteed private mortgages, with house buyers able to obtain mortgage loans for a greatly increased fraction of the purchase price. These measures for reviving a badly depressed construction industry were later to help shape Lauchlin Currie's ideas for housing as an "independent" or "leading" sector in recovery programs for the United States and more especially Colombia.

In July Currie arrived at the Treasury and there in September was introduced to Eccles. They found they shared a common enthusiasm for bold, unorthodox fiscal and monetary programs. In other ways they were very different, but the differences were highly complementary so they made a good team. Referring to the move they were shortly to make together to the Federal Reserve Board, Currie has remarked: "Rarely have two people with such different judgements or aptitudes which complemented each other so well been so suddenly catapulted into a strategic spot at a critical moment which enabled them to make an impact."[15]

Eccles had a lively, enquiring, imaginative mind and he loved to talk. Rich and self-confident, he was accustomed to power, though he was not always sufficiently diplomatic and was unfamiliar with the workings of Washington politics. He had never been to college and found it difficult to formalize his ideas in writing. He was, up to a point, respected by bankers and businessmen for his experience and success in these fields, but his lack of formal training made it more difficult for him to command respect in academic circles when he advanced his unorthodox ideas in bold but relatively unsophisticated terms. Currie, on the other hand, had impeccable academic qualifications and wrote impressively both for academic and non-academic audiences. Thus later he could be used as a brilliant speech writer. He provided the more technical arguments for an expansion program and could support these by quantitative research on the appropriate magnitudes, types, and channels of expenditures.

In June 1934 Eugene Black resigned as governor of the Federal Reserve Board and the affairs of the Board were directed by its vice-governor, J. J. Thomas, until a permanent successor to Black could be chosen.[16] In August Secretary Morgenthau told Eccles that he had been discussing the possibility that he fill the position, and in September Roosevelt himself informed Eccles that he was being considered. Eccles replied that "the post would be an appealing one only if fundamental changes were made in the Federal Reserve System."[17] He explained that the Board was hamstrung in its defense of the public interest by the power of the men who ran the reserve banks throughout the country. He asked the President for time to put into shape the specific changes he had in mind.

The Currie-Eccles Proposals for a Reformed Federal Reserve System

Congressional elections intervened and it was not until November 4 that Eccles had another meeting with the President. He took with him an eight-point memorandum on "Desirable Changes in the

Administration of the Federal Reserve System."[18] It was Currie who drafted this memorandum, though in his memoirs Eccles reveals that he emphasized an additional point, not in the memorandum, that he thought vital, namely an extension of the types of paper eligible for rediscount at the reserve banks to include any "sound asset."[19] Eccles thought that if long-term bank loans were also eligible then banks would lend more aggressively and profitably to the private sector, so reducing the need to lend to government. Thus Eccles retained several of the characteristics of the conservative banker. Currie, by contrast, was much less interested in the nature of banks' assets (loans) as in ways to vary the *aggregate* of bank assets and their counterpart deposit liabilities. If anything, in Currie's view a widening of the elegibility provisions endangered control over the aggregate of demand deposits by weakening the banks' "repugnance to indebtedness," especially during an upswing of the business cycle. Control over aggregate assets and liabilities was the central concern of the memorandum proper. This Eccles only summarizes in his memoirs, but it was, in fact, the essence of the Banking Bill which Eccles subsequently battled fiercely to get accepted by the Senate and House of Representatives.[20]

The memorandum began by explaining that without conscious control the supply of money had a tendency to move pro-cyclically. "If the monetary mechanism is to be used as an instrument for the promotion of business stability conscious control and management are essential." It stressed that at that time "main reliance must be placed upon increased governmental and private expenditures to bring about a rise in national income." This was very much in line with Eccles's own thinking for some years, and Currie too had already initiated studies in the Treasury (with a brilliant young student, Martin Krost, whom he had brought with him from Harvard), on "pump priming" and the "net income-creating federal expenditures" series. Thus, the memorandum continued, "the most important role of monetary control at the moment is assuring that adequate support is available whenever needed for the emergency financing involved in the recovery program."

The rest of the memorandum stressed ways and means of strengthening central control of open market operations as the main instrument of reserve policy. In line with the diagnosis and recommendations in Currie's Treasury report to Morgenthau, it was explained how disastrous was the existing diffusion of power and responsibilities over reserve policy and how reform must be in the direction of concentrating authority in the hands of a small policy-formulating body. The Federal Reserve Board in Washington should have the power of approval over appointments and the power to *initiate* reserve policy. This way a true central bank for the United States would be created.

A few days later Roosevelt announced Eccles's appointment as governor of the Federal Reserve Board. Currie moved with him as an assistant, with the nominal post of deputy director of research and statistics, and set to work drafting the main lines of what was to be the 1935 Banking Act which established the Board of Governors of the Federal Reserve system in Washington as the definite center of power over U.S. monetary policy.

The 1935 Banking Act

There followed an acrimonious battle between Eccles and the regional bankers (especially Governor George Harrison of the New York Federal Reserve Bank) who saw their power about to be diminished dramatically. Senator Carter Glass was upset because he had not been consulted by Roosevelt over Eccles's appointment, and sought to block and delay the ratification of his name by Congress. He was also violently opposed to the legislative changes which overhauled the system he had put in place in 1913. Professor H. Parker Willis of Columbia, who had helped Senator Glass draft the original Federal Reserve Act, denounced Eccles's bill as the most dangerous and unwarranted measure of the entire New Deal. His view was endorsed by Joseph Schumpeter and James W. Angell, among others, who declared, "The passage of such a measure will invite ultimate disaster."[21] Eccles did too little to flatter or consult with Glass who succeeded in watering down the proposed legislation, though not disastrously. Eccles cleverly linked the bill dealing with the change to the Federal Reserve System with sweeteners concerned with the Federal Deposit Insurance Corporation (FDIC)[22] and the delayed repayment of loans by bank officials. Leo Crowley, head of FDIC, was unsuccessful in his opposition to the tying provision; and as July 1, 1935, approached, the date on which bank officials would be obliged to repay loans or resign, the opposition began to crumble.

President Roosevelt signing the Banking Act of 1935. With him in the Oval Office are, *left to right:* Senator Carter Glass, J. F. T. Connor, Senator Duncan Fletcher, Secretary of the Treasury Henry Morgenthau, Jesse Jones (head of the RFC), Representative Henry B. Steagall, Marriner Eccles, and Leo Crowley (FDIC). *Courtesy of the Federal Reserve Board.*

Recalling his own role in the passage of the Banking Bill, Currie's unpublished memoirs (p. 44) record:

> For the first six months in my new post I was completely immersed in the legislative struggle that preceded the passage of the Banking Act of 1935. I was privy to all the political manoeuvering. It was a liberal education for an academician and valuable experience for my later years in Washington. An adviser in Washington is of limited usefulness unless he acquires some sense of what is feasible and how projects and policies should be presented to have the best chance of being adopted. I would not say, however, that I ever became an expert in that side of Washington. My academic habits of mind were too deeply ingrained and I quickly became impatient with subterfuges, circumlocutions and compromises. I was always very happy to leave the handling of the "Hill" to others, and had as little contact as I could with Congress. While working on the Banking Bill, therefore, I did not lose sight of longer range problems and the need for more basic research.

The 1935 Banking Act changed the name of the Federal Reserve Board to the Board of Governors of the Federal Reserve System, to reflect the shift of real power away from New York to Washington. Though Currie and Eccles had orignally wanted a small board of five technically qualified members,[23] eventually it comprised seven members, better paid than before but with no insistence on technical qualifications, appointed by the President and confirmed by the Senate. The previous Board had eight appointive members plus two ex officio members, the secretary of the Treasury and the comptroller of the currency. In the final version these ex officio members were, to Eccles's relief, removed.

It established a new Federal Open Market Committee (FOMC) consisting of the seven Board members plus five representatives of the twelve Federal Reserve banks. The constitutionality of privately elected representatives on the FOMC, helping to decide the nation's money supply, has recently been challenged in the United States. Paul Volcker, on a visit to Bogotá in 1986, asked Currie whether this had been considered at the time. Currie did not remember it being an issue, though he himself was opposed, on other grounds, to the inclusion of private and regional interests in this national body.

The Board in Washington was empowered to initiate and prescribe open-market policies to be pursued by the Federal Reserve banks. The Board and the FOMC were to keep and publish a complete record of their deliberations and actions taken. In practice, as Currie had hoped, this has greatly improved the quality of the officials taking up appointment on the Board and the quality of open market policy.

It had been Currie's intention to give the Board unlimited powers to alter reserve requirements, with a view eventually to achieving the 100 percent reserve system.[24] Carter Glass, however, succeeded in circumscribing reserve changes to a maximum of twice the minimum percentage prescribed in existing laws. The opportunity for more radical reforms was thereby ruled out and over the years the distinction between demand and time deposits has become more blurred, probably to the detriment of effective monetary control.

Eccles successfully broadened the lending powers of reserve banks. Further, the Board could set a maximum limit to interest rates paid by member banks on time deposits and regulate security loans and margin requirements. This was a hangover from the concern with security loans in 1928–29.[25]

One important provision in the bill that was lost was a new mandate to replace the existing one which called on the Board to accommodate the credit needs of commerce, agriculture, and industry. The new mandate would have required the Board "to exercise such powers as it possesses in such manner as to promote conditions conducive to business stability and to mitigate by its influence unstabilizing fluctuations in the general level of production, trade, prices and employment so far as may be possible within the scope of monetary action and credit administration.[26]

One of Currie's critics during the passage of the Banking Act was Benjamin M. Anderson, chief economist at the Chase Manhattan Bank, who, in testimony before the Senate Committee on Banking and Currency in May 1935, subjected Currie's *Supply and Control of Money in the United States* to a comprehensive attack that ran to twenty-eight printed pages. The Chase National Bank distributed over 100,000 copies of this testimony.[27] In his reply in the *Quarterly Journal of Economics* Currie wrote:

> My main criticism of commercial loans was that, from the viewpoint of monetary control, they expand on the upswing and contract on the downswing of business. Dr. Anderson does not deny that this is the characteristic behaviour of commercial loans. In his view, this is as it should be. The clue, I think, to Dr. Anderson's violent antipathy to my book is that he is opposed to the whole idea of conscious monetary control for the attainment of any objective. . . .
>
> Dr. Anderson objects to the objective of business stability on the grounds that "it says nothing about the more fundamental function of the Federal Reserve System, which is to protect the soundness of the economy and to protect the quality of credit in the country, to provide additional currency for seasonal needs and for emergencies, and to expand credit as needed for the accommodation of commerce, industry and agriculture. That is their first job. For control we are apparently to place our faith in "the bank credit men of the United States, who have done outside of academic walls an altogether superior piece of scientific work in studying the conditions under which commercial loans may properly be extended," and in the "careful and exact and fine calculation" that results when the business men come and sit with the banker once a year or more, to discuss their plans, and especially to consider how much money they may safely use." In this way, "credit" will be kept "sweet and clean." It is a pretty picture and undeniably is much easier to understand than "the vague speculations of the 'modern monetary theorists.'"
>
> The main issue between Dr. Anderson and myself is a fundamental one that represents a cleavage between the monetary and banking writers in

this country. One of the aims of my book was to call attention to this issue and to attempt to expose the theoretical weaknesses of the Commercial Loan Theory of Banking as contrasted with the Monetary Theory of Banking. Adherents of the Commercial Loan Theory, who include many of our prominent writers on banking, would seek to lessen maladjustments by restricting, so far as possible, banking assets to commercial loans. Monetary writers, on the other hand, stress the money-supplying function of banks and would seek to lessen maladjustments through monetary control. The long continuance of this unfortunate cleavage is largely attributable, I think, to the failure to state the issues clearly. I am grateful that he has afforded me the opportunity to call attention again to the fundamental character of the issues. It is not too much to say that upon a student's attitude toward it will depend the whole character of his work in the field of money and banking.

During the turbulent months when the Banking Act was passing through Congress the economy was beginning to recover from the depths of the Depression but there was a long way to go before output and employment could regain their 1928–29 levels. Shell-shocked from earlier failures, banks accumulated excess reserves rather than seeking potential borrowers. Under these circumstances Currie realized that greater emphasis would need to be placed on measures to stimulate public and private spending directly.

The Federal "Net Contribution" Series

While working on the 100 percent reserve plan at the Treasury in 1934, Currie became more involved in statistical research and advice on direct measures to stimulate public and private expenditures. This too was very much Eccles's view of priorities, though any change in, for example, the size of the federal budget deficit would call, of course, for complementary monetary policy.

In a letter to Eccles on November 17, 1934, Currie discussed their impending move to the Federal Reserve. Currie warned Eccles that the director of the research division, E. A. Goldenweiser, constituted a bottleneck for research staff, preventing alternative views from reaching the Board. In the past the advice of the research division left much to be desired. Currie wrote:

The practically unanimous view in the Division is that Federal Reserve has never been too restrictive (G. even defends or has defended the '31 policy) but has, on the contrary, erred on the inflationary side. They are, so far as I can gather, not interested in money and have never compiled a series of money. They have done little work on velocity and none on income. . . .

. . . I think I am a better monetary theorist than anyone on the staff and that my attitude and objectives are closer to yours. Hence my chief usefulness would be in business trend analysis, in developing statistical data of a forecasting nature, in work on the technique of monetary control, in making the analysis in the Annual Reports and monthly Bulletins more respectable, and finally in being of assistance to you in the preparation of speeches and statements and in aiding you in keeping up with the advances in business cycle theory and business trend analysis. I think I could get along *personally* with G. all right but I am under no illusions concerning the wide divergences in our theoretical approach.

In fact, personal relations between Goldenweiser and Currie, who ran his own small independent research unit and reported directly to Eccles, were always strained. Though nominally Currie was Goldenweiser's deputy, the latter was resentful of the way that Currie could undercut his authority because of his closer ties with Eccles.[28] Also the longtime research director deeply resented Currie's trenchant criticism of Federal Reserve policy in 1929–32 and often blocked his publications. But Eccles—surprisingly in view of his willingness to take on the power of the private bankers—was anxious to make as few changes of personnel at the Federal Reserve as possible.

In a series of memoranda on *Confidence,* 1934, *Comments on Pump Priming,* February 1935,[29] *A Suggested Works Program,* March 6, 1935, and *Recovery,* April 13, 1935, Currie sought to provide Eccles and the growing band of New Dealers in Washington with a coherent justification for unbalanced budgets financed through borrowing. Hitherto the New Deal had no coherent theory or plan to raise production and restore full employment. The trials and errors of the period 1933 and 1934, with their curious mixture of expansive and deflationary measures, was past. The annual struggles over the budget were between the "humanitarians" (mostly noneconomists) on the one hand and the "restoration of business confidence" adherents (most of the banking, business, and economics establishment) on the other.

There was a vacuum to be filled—a sound theory of expansion of employment and production that would allow both for the economic necessities called for by the situation and for the aspirations of the socially minded New Dealers. The task that Currie set himself was no less than to fill that vacuum, not just in general theoretical terms as Keynes was to do later,[30] but also in terms of the quantitative magnitudes needed for policy.

In his 1934 memorandum he had subjected the slogan of "business confidence" to careful analysis and had concluded that in a profit economy business would only expand when it paid to do so. In conditions of universal excess capacity, and with building costs high in relation to rents, profitability waited upon an increase in effective demand by final consumers and home buyers. Relief expenditures were too small to accomplish this.[31] A greatly increased federal expenditure on construction would have a much bigger impact.

When it became clear that Roosevelt was prepared to allocate only $4 billion to public works programs, Currie's subsequent memoranda were devoted to assessing the different impact that different types of public expenditures would have on overall incomes and expenditures.

In *Comments on Pump Priming,* February 1935, Currie implicitly advanced an early version of the full-employment budget concept. Using the output achieved in 1928 as a benchmark, but making allowances for subsequent price and productivity changes, he calculated the gap between 1934–35 actual levels of private expenditures on producers' and consumers' goods and the level of total expenditures required for reasonably full employment. He distinguished the expenditures which would be expected to respond first to a recovery in sales, namely inventories. Only when excess capacity had been eliminated could this be expected to be followed by expenditures on machinery and equipment, followed later by factory construction, and then, as increasing incomes forced up rents in relation to costs, by residential and commercial construction. A recovery based on increasing inventories alone was a precarious one which could quickly evaporate. Not until there were signs of a recovery in private construction—and so far there were not—would there be assurance of income-producing expenditure continuing for a sustained period. "It is essential, therefore, that pump priming be continued until there is evidence of a real spurt in privately financed construction," he wrote.

Currie estimated that the monthly pump-priming deficit needed to fill the gap in the meantime should range between $400–500 million, or about double its actual level. As he said later: "Considering that total federal expenditures had fallen to $2 billions in 1932, the preference expressed in the paper for a *deficit* of between $5 and $6 billions in a year indicates my willingness, for policy purposes, to accept the implications of the theory."[32]

He recognized the possibility of secondary (or multiplier) effects arising from these expenditures but was extremely unwilling to generalize about the magnitude of these effects which in some circumstances could be completely absent. The effect depended on the income velocity of new money, which could differ greatly from the average velocity of all money. In later Keynesian jargon we could express this in terms of the marginal propensity to spend. However, Currie's focus on velocity of money differs from conventional Keynesian analysis in that Currie's approach allows us to consider expenditure changes as the composite effect of changes in money and velocity. Keynes's income-expenditure approach obscures these effects since we are often not told whether, for example, an increase in permanent spending is financed with existing or new money, though John Hick's famous 1937 paper, "Mr. Keynes and the Classics," did much to integrate the income-expenditure approach with analysis of money flows. Nevertheless, for various reasons Currie still believes that the Keynes of the *General Theory,* in contrast to the Keynes of the *Treatise,* was neither necessary nor altogether helpful to the advance of the New Deal and counter-cyclical macroeconomic management in the United States.

This February 1935 memorandum again revealed Currie's pragmatic approach and his focus, for policy purposes, not on *general* theory and ceteris paribus assumptions but on the relative magnitudes of different forces operating simultaneously and on how the effect of these different forces changes through time. Currie listed seven different ways in which a deficit may be obtained. He arranged them in order of their effectiveness for stimulating income-creating expenditures, from governmental refinancing of private debts (most of which would probably be saved) to subsidies on private expenditures, especially housing. This last relied on the "leverage" principle, explained in detail in *A Suggested Works Program,* March 6, 1935.

The leverage effect was quite different from a Keynesian multiplier. It was the extra private spending induced by, say, a 20 percent subsidy on housing. Currie did not consider Keynesian-type secondary or multiplier effects because he analyzed fiscal and monetary effects separately. An increase in government spending is analyzed on the assumption that it is financed by borrowing part of the existing money supply. In these circumstances secondary effects depend on an increase in velocity. The leverage principle may increase velocity by inducing people to spend existing excess cash balances for the specific purpose of taking advantage of the subsidy. But in conditions of depression Currie doubted whether any further secondary effects, or increases in velocity, could be expected.

If a fiscal expansion was accompanied by an expansion of the money supply then there could be a greater effect on expenditures and income. Currie analyzed these effects with the classical (or pre-*General Theory* Keynesian) tools of the quantity theory, carefully distinguishing, however, the average velocity of the existing money supply from the velocity of new money. It depended on business conditions, the degree of excess capacity, and expectations.

But to return to the 1935 "pump-priming" memorandum, Currie called for the use of the leverage principle to derive maximum total expenditure increases because the government seemed adamant in refusing to increase expenditures beyond $4 billion a year. His approach emphasized that it was not merely the *size* but the *character* of the deficit that mattered for recovery. This analysis, incidentally, anticipated modern discussions on the relative effectiveness of expenditure increases compared with tax reductions in controlling aggregate demand and acting on motivations.

It cannot be stressed too strongly how controversial and offensive were such views at that time. Currie passed these memoranda directly to Eccles and to a small circle of his New Deal friends outside the Federal Reserve. Harry White at the Treasury was sympathetic but could not push very far his conservative boss, Secretary Morgenthau, who came to dislike Eccles intensely. Jacob Viner at Chicago was sympathetic toward Currie's work and was urging him to submit a version of the pump-priming article for publication in the *Journal of Political Economy.* Unfortunately, however, along with the important, related article on federal income-increasing expenditures prepared with Martin Krost later in 1935, publication was vetoed by the Reserve Board's director of research, E. A. Goldenweiser, on the grounds that "it might cause trouble."[33]

In the April 15 memorandum on recovery Currie again reviewed and rejected the arguments in favor of a "natural" recovery unaided by pump-priming deficits. He noted that, unlike the nineteenth century, expenditures on durable goods—the most variable part of expenditures—were now a large proportion of the total and so required more active public expenditure-offsetting in both the upswing and the downswing.[34] He also examined further the differing impacts of different types of public expenditures, distinguishing between those that competed with and those that complemented private expenditures.

Thus from an early date Currie appreciated the deficiencies of the official, accountants' measure of the federal cash deficit for purposes of recovery policy. From early 1935 he was working with Martin Krost on the quantitative estimation of his heretical measure of the deficit. Because of the passion aroused at that time by the very word deficit, he used various names for his new series that he hoped would make clearer not only its quantitative but also its conceptual significance and its usefulness as a policy tool. Thus he moved from the "pump-priming deficit" to "Federal Net Income-Increasing Expenditures," the "Government Net Contribution," "Income-Increasing Deficit," and, in his paper at the American Economic Association meetings in Chicago, December 1936, "The Net Activity-Stimulating Expenditures of the Government."

Currie quickly abandoned the pump-priming analogy because it suggested to some that one short dose of government spending would be sufficient to get the economic machine moving ahead without further help. Depending on circumstances (in particular, on how private-sector offsets to saving were moving) Currie recognized that the government might have to keep pumping and pumping for some time. Thus Currie did not advance the simple pump-priming theory, described by Herbert Stein and Alan Sweezy, that leads to the conclusion that income would always expand as long as the government's contribution is positive.[35] However, according to Joseph Lash, citing interviews with Leon Keyserling and Joseph Pechman, by 1936 Currie's "economic ideas began to influence the whole inner group [of the New Deal] and he became known throughout the government as the leading advocate of 'pump priming.'"[36] This suggests that the pump-priming analogy, though in Currie's view misleading and simplistic, did have a strong and lasting semantic appeal.

In their memorandum *Federal Income-Increasing Expenditures, 1932–35,* written in late 1935, Currie and Krost examined all the main items of government receipts and expenditures and tried to decide the extent to which these affected expenditures on currently produced goods and services, which of them were merely transfers, and which merely changed savings. They concluded that any similarity between the "net contribution" and the reported cash deficit was purely coincidental. The reported budget position could be in balance while the net contribution was in heavy deficit. Thus there was no necessary conflict between those who wanted a balanced budget in the official sense and those who wanted the federal government to provide a big stimulus to business: "By selecting income-increasing types of expenditures and non-income decreasing methods of raising revenue, it is conceivable that a balanced budget could be maintained and at the same time a considerable stimulus given to business" (p. 30).

Deficit Spending Versus Balanced-Budget Expansion

Although it is not stated in a rigorous theoretical form, this is, nonetheless, a fairly sophisticated statement, possibly the original statement, of the famous balanced-budget multiplier theorem. The conventional mathematical formulation of the balanced-budget multiplier theorem, based on very restrictive assumptions, was first advanced by William Salant in July 1942.[37] Currie, however, has always been skeptical of the usefulness of this formulation. In fact, his 1935 memorandum explicitly rejects any net stimulus arising from an equal increase in government spending and income taxes, since at that time he believed these latter revenues would be paid from income that would all have been spent. He modified that extreme position later in his paper to the American Economic Association in December 1936.[38] By deducting the extent by which incomes are decreased by taxes from the extent to which government expenditures are directed on current production Currie and Krost arrived at their "net contribution." This is a direct measure of the impact on national income of a balanced expansion of the official Treasury measure of government receipts and expenditures.

Contrary to assertions by Walter Salant and Paul Samuelson,[39] the Currie-Krost net contribution is not a multiplicand (that is, does not induce further increases in incomes and expenditures) except in special circumstances. And Samuelson is wrong to assert that "it was the government deficit, $G - T$ (or, in those early days, $G + T_r - T$), that was thought [by Currie, Krost, and Henry Villard] to constitute the government stimulus. Hence a high balanced budget could still represent a zero stimulus!" (p. 45). As we have seen, that depended on the nature of the cash items on the expenditure and revenue sides of the government budget, and an accounting balance would not always be a balance in economic terms.

If, in economic terms, there was a net contribution, despite a cash balance on the official Treasury budget, so that no new money was being created, there would only be further multiplier effects (making the net contribution a multiplicand) if there are accelerator effects on investment that induce businessmen to draw down their existing cash balances, thereby increasing the income velocity of money.[40] In the condition of 1935 it was unwise to rely much on these effects as there was widespread excess capacity in industry. For similar reasons, in such conditions there may only be weak multiplier effects even when there is a deficit accompanied by an expansion of money. The velocity of new money may be very low.

In the case where there is no accompanying increase in the money supply (the usual assumption in the conventional balanced-budget theorem) the Currie-Krost "net contribution" represents the relatively small first round of the conventional balanced-budget multiplier series. To finance this first round expansion taxpaying households and businesses have to run down their cash balances or borrow.

If households and businesses are currently holding their optimum levels of cash balances and debt relative to incomes, then the depletion of these balances, or increased debts, to pay for a sudden increase in tax obligations can only be a temporary expedient. As soon as (gross) incomes are restored through government spending of tax revenues taxpayers will replenish their balances and repay debts. Thus it is not logical to accept the theorem's assumption that the marginal propensity to save (MPS)—or marginal demand for money, as Currie would prefer to regard it—is identical and unchanging throughout the sequence of events. As velocity and MPS return to their previous levels in the second round, the expansionary effects are reversed unless there is another subsequent increase in the net contribution. Thus in general a balanced-budget expansion would have no more than a small ephemeral impact on activity if it is not accompanied by an expansion of the money supply.

In the conditions of the 1930s the size of the increase in a balanced budget required to stimulate recovery by effecting a permanent change in the propensity to save or demand for money to hold (velocity) would be enormous and politically unimaginable. More feasible and effective would be a relatively much smaller increase in an unbalanced budget (that is, deficit spending) accompanied by expansion of the money supply until such time as households and businesses once again had a sufficient motive to reduce their cash balances (relative to incomes) toward the levels of the 1920s.

Returning to the text of the Currie-Krost memorandum itself, it is interesting to note that the derivation of the statistical series and its use for policy purposes were possible without recourse to the Keynesian identity of savings and investment. Although Currie and Krost treated savings as resulting from the difference between the aggregate money income and expenditures on consumers' goods and services, and hence as "leakages" or reductions from the demand for goods that were restored by expenditures on nonconsumers' goods, nevertheless, it was stated that savings could exceed or fall short of investment. (But this is also true in Keynesian analysis if involuntary saving and forced inventory investment are excluded.) In any case, the memorandum states quite clearly that "at every stage of the production-consumption cycle there are leakages, or rather savings. An initial expansion of income due to investment [either public or private] must, if it is to be maintained, be fed continuously by new investment to offset the steady succession of savings" (p. 9). The arguments for and against an induced recovery versus a natural recovery (the type generally favored) were treated from the point of view of "expectations." On this basis it was suggested that an excess of investment brought about by government spending was not only subject to control but was equally efficacious in bringing about recovery. There was further criticism of the prevailing and predominant view that deficits undermine confidence and tend to reduce private investment.

While the argument lacks the analytical rigor of the *General Theory,* for policy purposes it stressed the key role of expectations; that business expectations depend on demand; that demand requires (and results in) an increase in income; and that this, in turn, requires that investment exceeds voluntary saving. It postulated a multiplier (secondary spending) but professed to see no way of predicting its magnitude. The pump-priming analogy was dropped, with a general caution against the use of mechanical analogies in economic analysis, and, instead, stress was laid on the phrase "income-increasing expenditures." The continued rise in national income from a constant deficit was defended, not too clearly, by postulating rising secondary expenditures. But a caution was introduced that the budget could be balanced without harmful repercussions only if secondary spending and private investment exceeded saving (including the decline in the deficit). The memorandum concluded with a presentation of the monthly figures since 1932 and a clear implication that the magnitudes indicated were helpful but inadequate to the circumstances.

The reported Treasury deficit of nearly $4 billion for fiscal 1934, for example, exceeded the Currie-Krost deficit by nearly $2.5 billion, or by over 60 percent.

The series was not exactly in accord with the definitions later used, as some transfer payments like the veterans' bonus and social security disbursements (but not appropriation to the Social Security Reserve Fund) were included while social security collections were deducted.[41] Double counting was eliminated by working out a consolidated statement including all government agencies.

As a result of this work, after 1935 the New Deal had both a sound theoretical case for deficit spending as a recovery measure, and a monthly series for the express purpose of measuring the federal income-increasing expenditures or net contribution. The combination of theory and quantitative measurements was a formidable one and effectively filled the vacuum mentioned earlier, though strong opposition remained in the government and, of course, outside.

Goldenweiser blocked publication of the series and memoranda in the *Federal Reserve Bulletin,* and Eccles was reluctant to override his objections in the face of the continuing orthodoxy of the system. But the series, which differed widely from the accounting Treasury deficit, was maintained by Krost for some years. It circulated privately, marked "not for publication," but attributed to the division of research of the Board, with the methodology available in mimeographed form. However, it was widely used in the government and Currie referred to it continually in subsequent memoranda and articles. The series was maintained for a while after Krost's premature death and Currie's departure for the White House, but was discontinued in the spring of 1942.[42]

The period from 1935 to 1940 was spent by Currie in elaborating the theory, in persuasion, in filling statistical gaps and in attempting to apply the theory in policies adapted to the changing business situation. An example was an August 1936 memorandum, *Public Spending as a Means to Recovery,* in which Currie acknowledged that "in the past six months there have been encouraging signs that the recovery movement is beginning to progress to a point where it can proceed under its own momentum." (p. 19). However, he warned that the magnitude of private "savings-offsetting" expenditures "is as yet comparatively small, both in relation to such expenditures in the twenties and in relation to the current volume of saving. While the need for the Government's net contribution to the increase in the national income is diminishing, there is no assurance that it can be dispensed with entirely at this time. It would, in other words, entail grave risks of imperilling the progress of the recovery movement either to cut expenditures abruptly or to impose heavy taxes of a kind that decrease the buying power of the low income groups" (p. 20).

This memorandum clearly indicated that a positive net contribution was needed for as long as private expenditures remained inadequate to sustain recovery. It was not simply a question of an initial pump-priming operation that could very soon thereafter be stopped, although at this time Currie was guardedly optimistic about the future course of private expenditures and, hence, of the possibility of reducing the government's net contribution without damaging recovery. Events were to shatter this optimism, mainly because the net contribution in 1937 was to fall far more drastically than Currie envisaged or thought appropriate when he prepared this August 1936 memorandum.

The "Large Deposit Study" and "Closed Banks Study"

In the latter part of 1935 and early 1936 Currie directed a pioneering study of the distribution and activity of demand deposits. This "Large Deposit Study" sought to discover who owned the nation's money supply, as a first approach in treating changes in money flows in terms of changes in the demand for money or velocity. Banks were asked to reply to a questionnaire on the ownership of large deposits on two dates, October 1933 and November 1935, classified by economic types: business, government, financial institutions, consumers, and foreigners.

This was perhaps the first time anyone had attempted a serious empircal examination of the significance of the distribution of the nation's money supply among different groups. If different groups have different motives or propensities for holding money the distribution can affect the overall demand for money and the flow of monetary expenditures on goods and services. Traditional monetary theory ignores the question or assumes it away, for distributional effects would undermine the "classical postulate," in its strict theoretical form, that "money is neutral."[43] As will be seen in chapter 12 below Currie made further contributions in the 1980s to this important but neglected aspect of monetary theory and policy.

The information obtained on changes in deposit holdings helped Currie identify the causes of business developments in the recovery period after October 1933. He noted that business raised no new money from bank borrowing or from capital markets. Thus business was not borrowing and spending the current savings of the community. However, their holdings of demand deposits increased substantially. From this he deduced that the causal sequence of events must have run from an increase in the government's net contribution, followed by increased expenditures by consumers of their new incomes, followed by the retention of part of these receipts of business as expanded business deposits. Increased deposit holdings reduced velocity and acted as a depressive influence. But fortunately, Currie noted, government continued their activity-stimulating expenditures to offset this. The general conclusion was that government, not business, had initiated and sustained recovery over this period, and that the study of the distribution of demand deposits represented a significant advance in the understanding of the factors behind changes in income velocity.[44]

In a letter to Currie on June 18, 1936, Jacob Viner wrote: "I have already read—and completely and closely—your revised report on the large deposit study. I think it is a grand job, and that the results are significant, at least in the sense that they would have to be dealt with in any genuinely penetrating statistical study of the cycle problem. I agree absolutely with your main finding that the recovery has taken the form of an excess in governmental expenditures over governmental current revenues, accompanied by an excess of business receipts over business expenditures."

But again Goldenweiser disagreed. In a letter to Viner on July 20, 1936, Currie reports that "Goldenweiser said that it was didactic and controversial, full of my own pet theories, and that it was evident I had not the slightest conception how to handle a statistical subject . . . [he] has laid down a rule that nothing can be published by the division which he does not understand, which limits the possibilities seriously."

In the middle of 1936, however, Currie was able to conduct another bank study, this time of the proximate causes of bank closures in 1931 to 1933. There were problems in getting the Federal Reserve Board to sponsor this study but the Works Progress Administration (WPA) was casting around for statistical projects to provide jobs for unemployed white-collar workers. So Currie had himself appointed a WPA deputy administrator for the purpose of directing the Closed Bank Study, and his assistant Martin Krost and other Federal Reserve Bank officials, notably Roland Robinson, organized a few hundred white-collar workers, including several former bank presidents (of failed banks), to sift through the records of over a hundred closed banks.

The results revealed that the loss of deposits attributable to the panic withdrawals of small depositors was a negligible factor in causing bank suspensions. Before lines formed outside banks it was typically the large depositors, well connected with and informed by bank directors, who accounted for the bulk of withdrawals. The conclusion was drawn for national policy that while the results gave support to the principle of deposit insurance to protect small savers, they raised serious questions as to the effectiveness of deposit insurance alone in preventing bank suspensions brought about by loss of confidence. Much more generous support was needed from the reserve banks to save banks faced with sudden and large deposit withdrawals when the value and liquidity of their assets were only temporarily impaired. In many instances, if allowed to go through a recovery period, many of the closed banks would have been solvent.[45]

The Undistributed Profits Tax and the New Dealers

Another issue that had occupied Currie's attention in 1936 was the bitterly fought legislation over the undistributed profits tax.[46] This was basically a Treasury proposal, with much of the work done by Herman Oliphant. Morgenthau (though not Oliphant) favored the measure mainly as a tax-raising measure. Eccles and Currie at the Federal Reserve favored it mainly for its potential in stimulating recovery by encouraging large businesses to make their profits available for spending by others instead of accumulating large excess, unspent business balances. Eccles and Currie also wanted to exempt the first $15,000 of profits so that small companies, short of capital and hav-

The Treasury team for the 1936 Tripartite Agreement. *Seated:* third and fourth from left, Secretary Morgenthau, Herman Oliphant; *standing:* second from left, J. H. Williams; third from right, H. D. White; far right, Jacob Viner. *Courtesy of the Princeton University Library.*

ing less recourse to outside funds, would not be hindered in their expansion plans. This exemption would apply to 90 percent of profits. The Treasury resisted these changes, however, because they would reduce revenues, and Morgenthau was furious with Eccles for his interference in tax matters. A much watered-down version of the legislation, excluding most of the Federal Reserve proposals, was later passed.[47]

1936 was an election year and for the first time an economist, Leon Henderson, had been appointed to the National Democratic Committee. Currie's memoirs (pp. 55–56) record:

> Leon had no staff and had not specialized in monetary policy so he appealed for help to Eccles. The Chairman, in his position as head of an independent technical agency, did not feel that he should participate in an election but he asked me to be as helpful as I could. Thus began my long and close friendship with Leon which in turn led to my close association with Ben Cohen, Tom Corcoran, Jerome Frank, Isidor Lubin and, to a less degree, with Harry Hopkins, William Douglas and Henry Wallace. Henceforth, what I had to say and write influenced to a greater or less extent not only Eccles but the whole inner New Deal group. Both through my contacts with Harry White and directly, my views reached Henry Morgenthau,

though I had less influence with him, in part, I suspect, because although I think he liked me personally he regarded me as an "Eccles man". A little later, I was appointed a member of a committee of the National Resources Board and got to know well "Uncle" Fred Delano (uncle of the President), Harry Dennison and Beardsly Ruml and their economists Gardiner Means and Tom Blaisdell. Others I saw frequently included "Beany" Baldwin of Farm Security, Aubrey Williams of the National Youth Administration, Bob Nathan, Louis Bean and Paul Appleby. For a time Mordecai Ezekiel held regular meetings at his home for the discussion of current problems and programs and those offered still another forum for the dissemination of ideas. Thus in the years 1937–39, as the research I had initiated began to bear fruit and while the New Dealers were still a compact, and, on the whole, united group, I was in a position to exert an appreciable influence on governmental thinking, particularly as it related to recovery problems. Eccles interposed no objection to these wider contacts and I was careful to keep him fully informed and he was interested in what was being thought and said around Washington. His own position was a little peculiar. Generally he was "with" the New Dealers but not "of" them.

Statistical Series on Expenditures

In 1936 and 1937 Currie succeeded in expanding his research unit's staff to fill important statistical gaps that were hindering his analysis of the government's net contribution and other expenditure offsets to savings. Work at the Commerce Department on national income measurement, initiated in 1933 under the direction of Simon Kuznets, was of little help to Currie for purposes of current analysis and policy. Among other deficiencies, national income measures excluded the federal budget deficit.[48]

In 1936 Currie hired George Terborgh from Brookings and, for a short period, Arthur Gayer from Columbia. Terborgh prepared current statistical series on different types of durable goods, including producers' plant and equipment, residential construction, and government investment. Terborgh, however, strongly disapproved of the use made of his work by Currie. Later, in 1937, Currie recruited V. Lewis Bassie from Chicago, on Viner's recommendation, and he prepared the important series on current inventory changes derived indirectly or by inference from the series on changes in production and consumption. The work of Terborgh and Bassie also served as a basis for constructing a current overall index of degree of plant utilization that appeared to be the single most important determinant of new capital investment. Other recruits were Malcolm Bryan, Alan Sweezy, and, for a time, Emile Despres (whom Currie later nominated as his successor at the Board when he moved to the White House).[49]

Currie was anxious to have these statistical series because they could be used as leading indicators of business trends. He was to make use of them in identifying independent and dependent sectors or, to use the terminology he adopted in later years, "leading" and "following" or "exogenous" and "endogenous" sectors.

In this connection it is interesting to quote from a 1935 memorandum: "In certain types of business, interest charges are a negligible factor. . . . In others, such as residential and office building, they are extremely important. A classification of business according to the importance of interest costs might be significant for the purpose of testing the current effectiveness of monetary policy."[50]

Appraising the work of Currie and his assistants, Carol S. Carson has noted that

> in the process of calculating these "offsets to saving" and relating them to national income aggregates, the economists at the Federal Reserve moved deeper into product component estimation. They developed, by original estimation or by adjustment and combination of data from other sources, the following major offsets to gross saving: expenditure on plant and equipment charged to capital account; private housing expenditures; value of the changes in inventories; net addition to disposable cash income attributable to public bodies; net foreign balance on current account; and net change in consumer credit.[51]

The TNEC Hearings and Currie's Assessment of the New Keynesian Theory

Currie's analysis of independent and dependent sectors, with accompanying statistical support, culminated in the testimony he and Alvin Hansen were to give before the Temporary National Economic Committee (TNEC) in 1939.[52] Currie's tables and charts presented the historical magnitudes of these various offsets to savings and then related them to movements in national income. The message was that only if offsets are made to equal the "full employment" level of savings can full employment national income be achieved.

Herbert Stein noted that early in 1938 there had been two contending New Deal views about strategy for getting out of the Depression—the antimonopoly view and the spending view. The TNEC was established at the instigation of the SEC, headed by Leon Henderson and Jerome Frank, to investigate the concentration of economic power. However, on Currie's initiative macroeconomic policy was added.[53] He had always believed that overall monetary and fiscal policy was a far more important explanation of inflation and depression than questions of monopoly and the structure of industry, and believed that some of the interventions on prices and wages during the period of the National Recovery Administration (NRA) did little or nothing to aid recovery. Stein notes that the hearings turned out to be mainly a showcase for Keynesian economics. Hansen and Currie, "by then well converted, were the star witnesses."[54]

It is a moot point how far it is accurate to describe Currie as a convert to Keynes in the same sense that the term does apply in the case of Alvin Hansen. We have seen that Currie was influenced by Keynes's earlier writings but was lukewarm to the *General Theory.* Hansen, by contrast, was for many years very hostile to the Keynes of the *Treatise* and, indeed, until early 1938 was also hostile to the *General Theory.*[55] While a professor at Minnesota he had written a very critical review of that book for the *Journal of Political Economy.*[56] In the fall of 1937 he moved to Harvard. There, in his famous fiscal policy seminar, conducted jointly with John H. Williams, and in discussion with graduate students and young instructors—including R. B. Bryce, Walter Salant (a former student of Currie's), Lorie Tarshis, Paul Samuelson, Emile Despres (later to accompany Currie on an official wartime mission to China), and Richard Musgrave (later to be the tax expert on Currie's 1949 World Bank mission to Colombia)—he became an enthusiastic defender of Keynes' new theories. In particular, Hansen used the analysis of the *General Theory* to support and develop his controversial theory of secular stagnation: that private investment could not be relied on to keep pace with a growing propensity to save, and that technology might produce chronic unemployment.

But by this time (1938) the main lines of the New Deal had already been drawn. Leon Keyserling probably goes too far when he remarked that he had "been unable to discover much reasonable evidence that the New Deal would have been greatly different if he [Keynes] had never lived, and if a so-called school of economics had not taken on his name."[57] Nevertheless, it may well be true that had the *General Theory* never appeared the New Deal itself would not have been very different. For policy purposes Currie had, by 1935, already filled the theoretical vacuum, thanks partly to the influence of the earlier Keynes, and was well advanced in providing the supporting quantitative series required by policymakers to indicate current economic trends and the magnitudes of appropriate compensatory monetary and fiscal adjustments. He rather resented the implication made by Alan Sweezy (1971), referred to above, that his position was based on a primitive pump-priming analogy, whereas after the failure of 1937 Hansen came along with a truly scientific explanation.

Actually Currie was quite critical of some of the interpretations and uses made of the *General Theory* by Alvin Hansen and in a May 1938 paper presented at the University of Chicago, "Some Problems in Connection with a Compensatory Fiscal Policy," he took issue with his "mature economy" thesis as an explanation of the 1937 recession. However, for current policy purposes during the recession, when increased government spending was needed for recovery, Currie welcomed Hansen as a valuable and articulate ally. In an October 1936 memorandum to the Federal Reserve Board and at a meeting in Morgenthau's house attended by high government officials, he presented a straight exposition of the main strands of Keynes's *General Theory.* But after some empirical investigation of some of Keynes's ideas, in a paper presented to the National Industrial Conference Board in April 1937,[58] he criticized Keynes's new schema and terminology. He was skeptical of the ability of a general theory to explain individual business cycles and was especially critical of Keynes's "fundamental psychological law" that the marginal propensity to save would rise over time. Following Frank Knight, whose writings he greatly admired, Currie insisted on the insatiability of wants and potential demand. This was important, for it differed from Hansen's later "mature economy" approach in which private demand was deemed to be satiable. Nor was Currie impressed by Keynes's awkward definition of involuntary unemployment, preferring, as a practical matter, to focus on "normal" employment levels and compare current levels with that norm.

He was one of the first economists to subject Keynes's investment multiplier to empirical tests,[59] finding that its value ranged from twenty to a negative number. Nor was the stability of the multiplier enhanced by experimenting with lags. The marginal propensity to consume was also highly variable, though here Currie was probably thinking more of the absolute variation in consumption rather than the change in consumption relative to change in income.

He also felt that Keynes tended to confuse money and savings and disliked the use Keynes made of the concept of liquidity preference as a "demand for money." Nowhere did Keynes precisely define money. Currie preferred to distinguish the demand for money proper, as a demand for command over goods and services, from the demand for command over interest-bearing assets, or the demand for (interest) income. The former demand, together with money supply, determined the price level; the latter the interest rate. Currie felt that there was no reason why the demand for *liquidity* could not be satisfied by holding interest-bearing assets, albeit at shorter rather than longer term. There was no need to hold money itself.

Lastly, Currie was skeptical of what he saw—perhaps wrongly—as Keynes's emphasis on the interest rate as a major influence on the marginal efficiency of investment and the decision to invest. Business was much more influenced by the state of effective demand, sales, and prices than by the interest rate. If prices and sales are falling, then a policy to reduce the interest rate may be completely ineffectual by itself in reversing the trend of investment. But nor was a secular decline in the interest rate necessary to induce sufficient private investment to absorb full employment savings as national income rose over time. The insatiability of wants would take care of secular growth. The main problem for macroeconomic policy was not secular stagnation but cyclical instability.

Thus Currie did not feel that the *General Theory* was especially helpful in explaining cyclical instability. His own thinking, influenced by Keynes's earlier work, had already provided him with what he regarded as more satisfactory explanations of cyclical instability, which in turn offered a rationale for counter-cyclical monetary and fiscal policy. His analysis and policy conclusions were based on an examination of movements in the money supply and the determinants of its demand (velocity), and of the relationship between an estimated full employment national income potential, the expected full employment level of savings (leakages), and the corresponding combined total of private investment and government net contribution required to offset those leakages. He had worked out these ideas fairly fully, together with the quantitative magnitudes needed for policy purposes, well in advance of the publication of the *General Theory.*

The Causes of the 1937 Recession

This problem of instability became acute once more in the latter part of 1937 and in 1938 when the U.S. economy suddenly fell into another severe recession after three or fours years of recovery. Opponents of government spending were quick to blame the recession on deficits and the associated loss of business confidence, and Morgenthau called for reliance on the driving force of private enterprise. Eccles was, for the moment, in the doghouse. It was then that the Currie-Krost deficit series proved its worth.

In a long memorandum, *The Causes of the Recession of 1937,* April 1, 1938,[60] which was privately circulated within the government, Currie demonstrated that there had occurred at the end of 1936 and early 1937 a very sharp transition from a relatively high monthly deficit to almost a zero net contribution, and that it was this transition rather than the preceding deficits that had checked the growth in consumer buying power and led to a sharp increase in inventories in the first half of 1937. In short, far from the theory being discredited by the recession, it was vindicated and reinforced by the experience. As Byrd Jones commented later: "By providing a coherent account of the recession, this essay brought fresh spirit to those who viewed government policy as a potent means to attain and maintain full employment."[61]

In late 1936 and early 1937 there were conflicting signals about the state of the economy but the general mood was optimistic. Federal net income-producing expenditures began to turn down sharply in the last quarter of 1936 but, so far as it was possible to tell with the available, inadequate statistics, all other offsets to savings were continuing to increase until well into 1937. Currie later regretted that he did not stand up more resolutely against the prevailing tide of opinion and warn more forcefully of the danger of the sharp decline in the government contribution as it occurred.

Nevertheless, in a memorandum dated 16 December, 1936, he had warned that the inventory boom posed a danger that a recession would follow as excess stocks were worked off. An unhealthy development was the growing tendency to mark up commodity prices following increased unionization and associated wage increases; and this, in turn, was encouraging an unhealthy degree of stock-building that could not last. He ended the memorandum by stating that "there is not much we can do in the near future about this movement except possibly by warnings and the psychological effect of raising reserve requirements."

Currie had in any case been unhappy for some time about the level of excess reserves held by banks.[62] These potentially frustrated the effectiveness of monetary control, which depended crucially upon the ability of the reserve banks to force member banks into debt. In the light of rising prices and business activity Currie believed there was a danger that the money supply could expand too rapidly on the basis of excess bank reserves, especially if accompanied by an increase in the velocity of business deposits.

The first increase in reserve requirements was effected in August 1936 as a precautionary measure,[63] reducing excess reserves by $1.5 billion, which still left nearly $2 billion excess. This had no adverse effect on interest rates, the money supply continued to increase, and inflationary pressures actually built up after that date.

On January 30 the Federal Reserve Board announced a second increase in reserve requirements, effective March 1, in light of the steady inflow of gold that had swelled excess reserves to over $2 billion. It is interesting, however, that in a memorandum to Eccles dated January 25, 1937, Currie warned of the long-run restrictive effects of reserve requirements against time deposits. He warned that these requirements were inconsistent with other measures directed to maintaining a steady flow of purchasing power. His memorandum emphasized "the practical importance of the theoretical distinction between time and demand deposits." Also on January 25, 1937, Currie submitted a twelve-page memorandum, *Would a Further Expansion of Money be "Injurious"?* in which he argued that the present volume of money, at a "normal" velocity of circulation, was adequate to finance full recovery and that further expansion entailed some risk. However, he did warn (p. 11) that federal revenues and expenditures may be moving in such a way as to offset the expansion of other earning assets of banks.[64] "The balance of probabilities, however, appears to favor a further expansion of money," he judged, and so recommended action to offset this.

The money supply continued to increase to the end of March and only began to decline in April. The Board was concerned that, with the money supply now some 15 percent higher than in 1929, if velocity were to recover to its 1920s level spending could increase alarmingly. However, the reserve increases were still designed as precautionary rather than restrictive measures, and as a way to make open market operations more effective.[65] Open market purchases were, in fact, made in April and November which, along with the desterilization of some inactive gold, increased bank reserves, though not by enough to arrest the decline in the money supply that continued to the end of the year.[66]

Friedman and Schwartz attribute most of the responsibility for the 1937–38 recession to the FRB's reserve policy and the decline in money stock. They pour scorn on explanations based on the fiscal record.[67] But real incomes turned down in April 1937,[68] and in the preceding six months (September 1936–March 1937) the money supply had been increasing at an annualized rate of 5.9 percent, though it is true that the increase had been reduced from the high annualized rate of 19.9 percent recorded in the six months before that. Though a case can be made for the contention that monetary contraction between April and December 1937 and again, briefly, between April and July 1938 aggravated the recession, it is very hard to accept Friedman and Schwartz's claim that monetary policy was the main cause of the recession. Banks and businesses remained highly liquid and there was little movement in interest rates. Few theorists would expect an immediate impact on incomes and sales to result from the small decline in deposits that were taking place at this time.

Currie's explanation, based on the sharp fall in the government's net contribution to incomes after August 1936,[69] is more consistent with the timing of the recession. The federal net contribution declined drastically from $4.3 billion in 1936 to $1.1 billion in 1937, partially recovering in 1938 to $2.4 billion.[70] In the crucial period March to September 1937 the net contribution fell to only $60 million a month compared with an average of $335 million a month in 1936. This change was largely due first to the $1.4 billion of veterans' bonus bonds cashed in 1936 (half of which was assumed to affect the net contribution estimates, though the impact might well have been much more than half), which was passed over the President's veto and which contributed to a perhaps excessive government net contribution in 1936. Then, by contrast, in 1937 there were no bonus payments and instead substantial new tax collections were made, starting in February under the 1937 Social Security Act. In a memorandum to Eccles,

Analysis of Mr. Altmeyer's Statement . . . on the Old-Age Reserve, February 25, 1937, Currie angrily pointed out the deflationary implications of building up a large social security reserve fund.

In a recent paper Walter Salant has also expressed some skepticism on Currie's defense of the raising of reserve requirements in 1936–37 to mop up a portion of the high excess and forestall a possible excessive expansion of aggregate monetary demand as conditions of full employment were resumed.[71] Salant maintained that the Keynesian lessons about the "demand for liquidity" had still not been absorbed by Federal Reserve officials at that time. Although reserves were excessive in the legal sense, they were not excessive in the economic sense because the banks themselves at that time had a high demand for liquidity and so sought to restore excess reserves to their previous level.

This interpretation overlooks the fact that with the drastic decline in the government's net contribution after March 1937, by about $275 million a month, the commercial banks lost one of their major low-risk lending opportunities—the opportunity to buy a large volume of government bonds which were being sold to cover the government's cash deficit. A portion of these bonds had been purchased by the commercial banks. These now had to turn to the private sector if they were to avoid an increase in excess reserve holdings, and the adjustment would naturally take time. Meanwhile, the private sector was less willing to borrow to expand plant capacity or increase voluntary inventory holdings in the face of a leveling off in consumer sales. The latter, in turn, could be explained largely by the big decline in government expenditures accompanied by a big increase in government tax receipts. Banks' holdings of excess reserves could be explained, therefore, as a development that was difficult for them to avoid since the sharp fiscal change caught them off balance and they needed time to adjust, resulting in some diminution in demand deposits and increase in the excess of reserves. These developments are unlikely to have arisen if the government's monthly net contribution to spending had been maintained at 1936 levels.

Currie's memorandum, *An Appraisal of Current Prospects and a Tentative Program,* May 18, 1937, noted the prospect of a substantial decline in the federal net contribution over the coming year and predicted a considerable slackening in the growth rate during the rest of 1937. He was hopeful that private expenditures would be sufficient to maintain a modest advance in production. However, this would depend greatly on the uncertain picture on inventories. He warned that if inventories delined a minor recession could ensue.

In fact, it soon became clear that the economy had gone into decline. By October 1937 Currie was sending much more forceful and anxious memoranda to Eccles. One of these, *The Decline in the Federal Contribution to the Growth in Community Expenditures,* October 19, 1937, included a table showing the drastic decline in the monthly net contribution after January 1937. He explained that private expenditures and production were stagnating and were an inadequate offset. In another memorandum, *A Tentative Program to Meet the Business Recession,* October 13, he told Eccles: "I have a strong feeling that the President has not grasped the seriousness of the situation. I should like to suggest that you see him and point out the possibilities and outline a possible program designed to moderate and shorten the recession."[72] He urged expansionist open market operations to offset the decline in the money supply. He also urged measures to increase the net contribution, especially increased WPA relief expenditures since "expenditures of this type are most effective in maintaining consumer buying power and helping inventories to be moved." Lastly, he stressed building:

> The importance of securing a building revival next year cannot be overstressed. The continuance of recovery depends on it. Certain types of increasing expenditures are primary and certain types are secondary or derivative. For example, plant and equipment expenditures are derivative in the sense of depending on a growth in demand and production—we cannot expect them to *initiate* an upward movement. This is the basic weakness of the position of those who are merely content to make a large volume of capital funds available. . . .
>
> More generally the impetus to increasing expenditures must come from buildings, as in 1922 and 1924, or from an excess of government expenditures over receipts, as in 1934–1936. Since there will be an excess of tax collections in the near future, we are by a process of elimination forced back to building as being the primary source on which we must depend for a reversal of the downward trend in incomes, demands and production.

President Roosevelt was greatly alarmed as the recession gathered steam in 1937. On the urging of Harry Hopkins, the President, in an unprecedented occasion on November 8, 1937, met directly with three key technicians, Leon Henderson (working for Hopkins), Isador Lubin (commissioner of labor statistics), and Lauchlin Currie, for a four-hour session for which Currie prepared a short memorandum, *The Causes of the Recession,* which argued along the lines of the longer memorandum referred to above. As well as emphasizing the alarming decline in the government net contribution, the memorandum explained how financing charges for housing could be reduced to stimulate the independent building sector.[73] The group took direct issue with Treasury Secretary Morgenthau who was at that time still urging a balanced budget on the President.[74] Morgenthau blamed the slump on a "loss of confidence" due to the failure to balance the budget.

What influence the group may have had on the President is uncertain, but in any case he abandoned his flirtation with the balanced-budget policy and, despite the grave misgivings of Henry Morgenthau, who threatened to resign, gave his wholehearted support to new legislation designed to increase expenditures and to stimulate expenditures outside the budget, which by 1938 had become the unquestioned recovery program of the New Deal wing of the administration, though not pursued with the vigor and flexibility that Currie would have liked.[75]

Commenting on the "struggle for the soul of FDR" during this period, Herbert Stein wrote:

> The big fiscal decision made in Washington between the publication of the *General Theory* and the absorption of the American economy in the war was the decision to embark on a spending program in the spring of 1938. The assimilation of the *General Theory* into American thinking and the formulation of a Keynesian school came too late to be of much influence in that decision. Of course, there was in this period a considerable group of "spenders" in Washington, including Eccles and Currie at the Federal Reserve, Hopkins at WPA, and Wallace, Ezekiel and Bean at Agriculture. Their ideas were of pre-Keynesian origin and did not respond quickly, if ever, to what was new in the *General Theory.*
>
> Currie was probably the intellectual leader of this group, the one most capable of independent analysis in the field of Keynesian economics. Ezekiel describes him as having come closer than any other American economist to anticipating Keynes.[76]

The 1939 Lend-Spend Bill

Toward the end of 1938 the President was persuaded by Frederic A. Delano, chairman of the National Resources Committee (NRC), to appoint a fiscal and monetary advisory board that would include Treasury Secretary Morgenthau, Federal Reserve Board chairman Eccles, director of the budget Daniel Bell, and the NRC chairman. It was to have its own technical staff drawn from these agencies. Roosevelt announced that the Board was to study "the whole range of a great many problems that relate to fiscal and monetary policies in respect of sound and orderly recovery, and conditions necessary to avoiding the peaks and valleys of booms and recessions."

Morgenthau was the Board's nominal chairman but, according to Dean L. May:[77]

> It became clear, as the board began its meetings, that the point of view of those dominating the discussions was most uncongenial to that of Morgenthau. Lauchlin Currie, who became a leading figure in the technical staff, prepared a memo for Eccles during the early life of the board which showed the direction of its studies. He wrote that a proposed program of research would "pretty well boil down to: (a) What caused the downturn in 1937? (b) How can we get a high level of national income? (c) What should be done to prevent a recurrence of developments of 1937?" Currie emphasised the point that the board was "vitally interested" in these three questions and has "something to contribute to them" but should be alert to "a danger that the outside experts that might be selected may be heavily committed already on the wrong side (from our point of view)."

The work of the committee had an influence on the President's budget statement in January 1939, and he was persuaded by Eccles to give greater publicity to the concept of compensatory fiscal policy in answering the critics of the New Deal's various lending and spending programs that it was hoped could be launched in the spring and summer of 1939.

Thus, by 1939 the "fiscal revolution" in America was well advanced, and the battle between those who advocated "natural" recovery and those who maintained, as Currie put it, that "it is the proper role and responsibility of the State to insure that the economic machine functions at more or less full capacity," was moving perceptibly in favor of the latter group.

Nevertheless, there were setbacks even at this stage of the revolution. In early 1939 Currie drafted the Works Financing Bill which Eccles passed to Senator Barkley to sponsor before Congress in July.[78] Ben Cohen and Tom Corcoran helped in the task of assembling the program and preparing the bill and the accompanying message of the

President to Congress. The bill was framed in such a way that a major spending program "outside the budget" could be approved. It was hoped that the budget balancers would be appeased in this way. It provided for "the construction and financing of self-liquidating projects," and would authorize the Reconstruction Finance Corporation to borrow funds guaranteed by the government to spend or lend or make available to other government agencies to spend or lend. Hence, the proposed legislation became known as the "Lend-Spend Bill" and met with fierce opposition from Congress. Congress saw through the balanced budget ruse and eventually killed the bill.

One of the bill's main provisions involved leases to railroad companies so they could acquire new rolling stock without themselves initially incurring large expenditures or debts that they were reluctant to incur at that time. Currie saw this proposal as a potentially very effective way to stimulate demand exogenously, not unlike his earlier proposals to stimulate housing demand by reducing current financing costs.[79] Initially the railroad companies were very favorable to the idea in discussions with Currie but later they grew suspicious that it was a disguised path to nationalization. They preferred autonomy over a smaller railroad than a large railroad with interference from government. When shortly afterward war came, the war effort was hampered by inadequate railroads, power, and other infrastructure projects that were to have been expanded under the Works Financing Act.

In his memoirs (p. 85) Currie wrote:

> I still feel that it was a pity this bill was defeated as in my judgement it was the most soundly conceived of all the recovery measures. As it turned out, spending on munitions first by the Allies and then by the United States Government made it unnecessary as a recovery measure although the advance addition to railroad and electric generating capacity and the betterment of the highway network would have been of inestimable value in lessening the pressure on manufacturing capacity and labor in the war years. The real importance of the bill, however, was in giving the Government a permanent means, *outside the budget,* of varying highly desirable expenditure to compensate for excessive variations in private expenditures—another built-in stabilizer. It is almost impossible to conduct proper compensatory policy in timing and volume through the regular routine of new legislation and appropriations.

Despite this setback Roosevelt was by now less reticent about spending a way out of recession and the federal net contribution nearly doubled in 1939 to around $3.6 billion.

When six posts of administrative assistant to the President were created under the Government Reorganization Act of July 1939, Lauchlin Currie, at the age of thirty-six, was the candidate of the New Deal spending wing for one of these posts. Thus came to him the opportunity to exert a direct influence on the President from inside the White House itself where he would remain for the next six years.

CHAPTER 4

In the White House: Peace and War, 1939–45

Economic Advice to President Roosevelt, 1939–41

In June 1939 President Roosevelt called the chairman of the Federal Reserve Board on the phone. Marriner Eccles records the conversation as follows:[1]

> "Marriner, I guess you are going to give me hell."
>
> Without knowing what he had in mind, I replied: "Mr. President, I do not know what good it would do me to give you hell, even if I wanted to."
>
> "Well," he explained, "I am going to steal Lauch Currie from you. I need him here as one of my assistants." He quickly baited the hook.
>
> "I am sure you will realize," he continued, "that it is not such a bad thing after all as far as the Board and you are concerned. You, of course, see the advantages at once of having a friend in court who can represent and speak for *your* point of view."

Needless to say, records Eccles, Currie changed jobs without further argument. In July 1939 he thus became the first economist to hold an official post in the White House, as adviser to the President. The Employment Act of 1946 established a permanent place for professional economists in the Executive Office of the President. The statutory advisory responsibilities of the President's Council of Ecoomic Advisers are similar to those Currie carried out informally from 1939 to 1945.

One of the chief qualifications for the six posts of administrative assistant as laid down by Charles Merriam and Louis Brownlow in drafting the 1939 Government Reorganization Act was that they should possess a "passion for anonymity." Thus as presidential adviser Currie had more influence but less liberty to express his views publicly. In this he differed from the more independent chairmen and members of the postwar councils of economic advisers. One or two of these chairmen, notably Leon Keyserling under the Truman administration and Martin Feldstein under the Reagan administration, have been quite outspoken in public, and the council's signed assessments and recommendations are published in the annual *Economic Report of the President.*

Arthur Schlesinger has commented that "for Roosevelt, the techique of liberal government was pragmatism. . . . Nothing attracted Roosevelt less than rigid intellectual systems. . . . His attitude toward economists was typical. Though he acknowledged their necessity he stood in little awe of them. . . . Roosevelt dealt proficiently with practical questions of government finance, as he showed in his press conferences on the budget; but abstract theory left him cold."[2]

The famous meeting between Roosevelt and Keynes in June 1934, for example, left both men skeptical. Currie, however, seems to have made a more favorable impression on the President in their long session in November 1937. Roosevelt liked the way that Currie was able to present a dissenting opinion forcibly but without getting steamed up and red in the face. Currie too, like the President, was pragmatic and policy oriented. He used theory, of course, but not in a dry, abstract way. He seldom resorted to equilibrium theory and ceteris paribus assumptions. What was *appropriate* depended on circumstances; what was *feasible* depended not only on purely economic possibilities but on political and administrative considerations, which Currie keenly understood.[3] When he was drafting the 1935 Banking Act, for example, Currie had long struggles with Eccles to convince him that the Federal Reserve Board had to be ultimately responsible to the President. Eccles wanted complete independence. Currie argued that Federal Reserve policy could make or break a President, depending on its results, so it was unreasonable to deny him and Congress a role in shaping monetary policy.

In his work at the Federal Reserve, Currie understood the need for diplomacy and coordination with key officials in the various agencies whose cooperation was vital if New Deal policies were to be understood and made to work. He often acted as go-between or peacemaker with Eccles and Morgenthau, as he had been a long-time friend of Harry White who enjoyed Morgenthau's confidence.

A long letter marked "very confidential" sent to Eccles, December 12, 1936, illustrates his role very well. The occasion was the bitter row that had blown up between Morgenthau and Eccles over the respective responsibilities of the Treasury and FRB for gold sterilization policy. After urging Eccles to make soothing overtures to Morgenthau, he concludes: "Since the contribution you can make rests in the final analysis on the degree of cooperation you can obtain from the Secretary, I think you will be prepared to make real sacrifices for the sake of the wider objectives. It is this knowledge which has emboldened me to express myself so strongly and to run the risk of incurring your displeasure."

Currie has recorded his role in recruiting and working with New Dealers throughout Washington:

> By 1939 I had become the first economist in the White House and we were becoming a formidable group. I had recruited Dick Gilbert and his group—V. L Bassie, Rod Riley, and the rest—for Harry Hopkins at Commerce, which gave support to Bob Nathan, long a lone outpost in hostile territory. I had turned my post at the Federal Reserve over to Emile Depres. I was, I am happy to say, responsibile for bringing Ken Galbraith to Washington and for getting Gerhard Colm placed in the Bureau of the Budget, now moved to the Executive Office of the President. Walter and Bill Salant, Griff Johnson, Alan Sweezy, Arthur Gayer, Malcolm Bryan, George Eddy, Albert Hart and Martin Krost were my former students or associates and were occupying key posts. Our position in the Treasury was getting stronger as Harry White gained influence, and we had close working relationships with Gardiner Means and Tom Blaisdell in the NRPB and the members of the Board, and with Ezekiel and Louis Bean in Agriculture, with Isador Lubin in Labor and, of course, with Leon Henderson and Jerome Frank in the SEC. Hansen was winning converts outside. We did not sleep much, but when we did the *General Theory* kept working. With the Works Financing Act of 1939 and our long discussions on a major revision of the Social Security System, Roosevelt finally acquired a firm grasp of the theory.[4]

Many of the officials who dealt with Roosevelt were exasperated by his pragmatism and apparent willingness to listen respectfully to a host of opposing views, and even to appoint people with opposing views to work uneasily with each other. But Currie admired this approach. If it often caused confusion and conflict it also had great potential advantages. It might cause many small errors, but if handled shrewdly it could minimize the chance of major blunders. The grave charges leveled by David Halberstam against President Lyndon B. Johnson over his policy on Vietnam—that he listened only to his supporters and the bearers of good news—could not be applied to Roosevelt.[5]

Nevertheless, Currie would no doubt endorse Schlesinger's view that

> without some critical vision, pragmatism could be a meaningless technique. . . . For some politicians, such an approach meant nothing more than splitting the difference between extremes; the middle of the road was thus determined by the clamour from each side. At times it appeared to mean little more than this to Roosevelt. But at bottom he had a guiding vision with substantive content of its own. The content was not, however, intellectual . . . it was rather a human content . . . the people mattered . . . his philosophy of compassion had a particular bias toward the idea of security.[6]

And so it was that the two main issues that Currie dealt with in his meetings with Roosevelt before the United States entered the war were the continuing problem of heavy unemployment (around nine million were still unemployed) and the need to revise the Social Security Act.

Currie has recalled[7] that working with Roosevelt had similarities and dissimilarities to working with Eccles. Like Eccles, Roosevelt felt no particular need of advice. An enormous amount flowed on him gratuitously and he had fairly definite ideas on most subjects. Most people who wanted to see him wanted something and in the course of a lifetime in politics he had selected a number of devices to protect himself from importunities. One was to do all the talking himself.[8] He rarely asked questions, but in talking he would keep an eye on his listener to gauge the reaction.

Currie saw the President for about half an hour twice a week, after press conferences. He usually had a list of eight to ten things to take up with him. He counted himself lucky if he was able to touch on half of them before his time was up. His opening remark was a crucial one as the President would pick it up and off they would go on that. Currie's task then was to get him around to the other points. He was amiable and would agree to most of the things that Currie proposed if they would not encounter too much opposition. Currie learned to rely usually on one-page memoranda that could be disposed of by him with a "yes" or "no" or "OK" or "go ahead" or "talk to me" scrawled by him in the narrow margin.

Currie's work during 1939 and 1940 covered a bewildering variety of subjects ranging from plans for boosting power supplies, transport and defense equipment in preparation for "defense" (war), social security legislation, banking matters, the budget, political matters in the run-up to the 1940 presidential election, farm security, housing, a national program for youth, and foreign economic relations.

In his first months in the White House Currie's main preoccupation was defense preparations. With so much slack existing in the economy, a greatly expanded production program was feasible but Currie was anxious to make recovery as orderly as possible. The slack in the system was very unevenly distributed and, after the defeat of the Works Financing Bill, Currie continued to call attention to the alarming deficiencies in railroad equipment, power capacity, and skilled labor.

His attempts in September and October 1939 to work up the story on possible electric power shortages resulted in his first brush with the War Department, in particular the assistant secretary, Louis Johnson. The President had authorized Currie to examine material in the War Department on the probable war demands for transportation, power, and various types of industrial products. It soon became apparent to Currie that very great power shortages were in prospect, that the industry's plans to meet these were quite inadequate, and that the War Department was being too complacent and obstructive in releasing detailed information. Currie returned to the President with a draft of instructions to Assistant Secretary Johnson, including the removal of one of his key officials. Despite some bitter resistance this was done. In his unpublished memoirs (p. 118) Currie records:

> The President seemed amused by my indignation and zeal and signed the instructions without changing a word. I was so new and green to my job that I did not then realise how unprecedented it was for the President to do such a thing. He had long become inured to the sabotage that took the form of passive resistance on the part of people down along the line of government. About this time he referred, still in an amused fashion to, as I recall, Ickes, that "Lauch Currie is trying to buck the War Department but I don't think he'll get very far".
>
> . . . A few days later the President signed an order making the civilian headed National Power Policy Committee responsible for the work of increasing preparations in this field and it had some degree of success in alerting the industry to the probable future needs and in getting more work initiated earlier than would otherwise have been the case. I was quite happy with the outcome, though Johnson and the power industry undoubtedly regarded me as a troublemaker.

There were a number of similar confrontations with the officials of various agencies, including the Army and Navy, for example over requests to alter the timing of expenditures and the placing of orders, designed to fit better with compensatory aggregate expenditure objectives. Jurisdictional disputes were particularly acute with respect to the Treasury and the Budget Bureau.

In helping to draft the President's January 1940 budget message, one of Currie's early suggestions was for a number of government corporations to repay to the federal government that part of their capital that was in excess of normal working requirements. This, in government accounting, would appear as a revenue and reduce the deficit projected in the President's January 1940 budget statement by $700 million, without affecting income-producing expenditures or receipts.[9] Roosevelt liked that suggestion very much and with modifications the proposal was incorporated into the budget. However, the director of the Bureau of the Budget, Harold Smith, was much less happy, mainly, Currie believed, because he had not first thought of the idea himself. Smith bluntly told Currie that this was none of his business and that he was responsible for the budget. As Eccles had done for many years, Currie was often to experience the unpleasant consequences of stepping into the jurisdiction of a jealous secretary of the treasury[10] and director of the budget. Currie's description of the difficulties he faced are of general interest:

> . . . Morgenthau made it abundantly clear that he did not appreciate my interest in matters of taxation and Treasury financing. Hence, after six months in my new job, I found myself confronted with the alternative of dropping work in some of the main fields of my interest and competence, or of suffering very bad relations with two of the most powerful agencies of the government. In the course of time I worked out a modus vivendi with Morgenthau whereby I participated in Treasury policy-forming conferences but with the implicit understanding that I would work *with* the Treasury and make my suggestions there and not directly to the President—not very satisfactory from my point of view. On the other hand I could appreciate that it could be most trying for Morgenthau to have a relative junior in the Government hierarchy giving contrary advice or criticism directly to the President on matters for which in the last analysis the Secretary of the Treasury was responsible. Smith was a tough jurisdictional man—for him it was the Budget Bureau against the field—and I never could establish very amiable relations with him. He was later to block me off from other activities. I do not think my problem was a personal one but would have confronted (and will confront) any economist on the personal staff of the President. (Memoirs, pp. 124–25)

On March 18, 1940, Currie prepared an uncharacteristically long *Memorandum on Full Employment* for the President.[11] By this time, although the United States had not entered the war, defense expenditures and war exports were expanding. Currie had for some time been looking at the problem of strategic bottlenecks but, looking ahead, Roosevelt had asked him also to do some work on the problem of postwar reconstruction and to handle unofficially any planning to meet economic problems caused by defense programs.[12] Currie replied that this problem was but one special case of the overall problem of securing and maintaining full employment that he and Alvin Hansen had explained in their testimony before the TNEC in 1939.

War exports, by providing an offset to saving, were a temporary aid. Their disappearance would intensify the problem. What was required was a continuing program of public investment providing an outlet for savings, developed, so far as possible, outside the budget, and to remove obstacles and provide incentives for private investment, particularly in the housing field.

Currie remarked: "I have come to suspect that you are somewhat bothered by the apparent conflict between the humanitarian and social aims of the New Deal and the dictates of 'sound economics'. I feel convinced that in place of conflict there is really complete harmony and for that reason only the New Deal can solve the economic problem."

The memorandum included proposals on pensions and unemployment insurance, both of which operated at that time as large deflationary forces in the economy. It appeared probable that in 1940 tax accruals in these two systems would exceed benefit payments by over $1 billion, thus nullifying the effect of deficit spending. Roosevelt was very interested in these ideas, so Currie worked up a proposal that he and Eccles had been interested in for some years, to convert the present social security system into a pay-as-you-go system and avoid building up the giant reserve fund that was favored by Arthur Altmeyer, chairman of the Social Security Board.[13] Currie's scheme would permit universal coverage of old-age pensions immediately, with regional differentials. This was a major, complicated reform and required a number of meetings and discussions—with the President including several days at Warm Springs in April. The scheme was worked out in considerable detail but no word of what was being proposed ever leaked out until it was included in the President's first campaign speech later that year before the Teamsters Union. However, by that time mounting interest and alarms over the war in Europe dominated public interest and the social security proposal was shelved.

Nevertheless, Currie insists that these discussions made an impression on Roosevelt and, as a result, by this time he had a firm grasp of the theory. In particular he came to understand the fallacy of composition and could see, for example, that a national social security system differed from a private insurance company and did not need an excess of contributions in order to build up a reserve fund to earn interest to pay benefits years later. By contrast, a national system permitted withdrawals (benefits) to be financed from the *current* contributions of the present-day work force. These ideas could only be grasped, as they were by the President, by someone who clearly understood the distinction between private and social accounting.

Earlier, on March 27, 1940, the President had sent Currie an unusually long memorandum in which he disputed the official unemployment estimates of between 8.5 and 11.2 million. Roosevelt listed a number of people he knew personally who, though unemployed on a particular date, were not continuously unemployed nor destitute. Reasoning from the particular to the general he then concluded that there were no more than six million unemployed people "who are eager to work and who really need work in order to feed, clothe and house themselves and their families. . . . Your figures show that slightly over four million of them are receiving aid from Federal and State Governments. That means that there are less than two million who ought to have work provided for them in some way as a social and economic need. That's not bad at all. It is nearly accounted for by the number on the WPA waiting lists."

Currie's memoirs (p. 157) record: "Needless to say I guarded this memorandum carefully as a mere intimation of its contents at that time would have been a political bombshell." In reply, Currie defended the official estimates but heard no further on the matter. "I don't imagine that my reasoning carried conviction," he wrote, "as it was probably too abstract for the President, but at least it intimidated him so that he never expressed his heretical views in public. The President's memorandum illustrates both his down-to-earth practical type of thinking, and also the weakness of this method to solve certain types of economic problems."

As 1940 progressed defense and stockpiling expenditures increased significantly. Specific bottlenecks and price increases were of growing concern and Currie was engaged in various activities to alleviate and penalize these.[14] After the fall of France and Belgium in May 1940 Leon Henderson was appointed to the National Defence Advisory Commission, with responsibility for monitoring and advising action on price increases. On Currie's recommendation John Kenneth Galbraith was appointed Henderson's deputy.

Despite these specific and strategic bottlenecks, in his fiscal policy memorandum dated June 4, Currie insisted that "a fundamental fact at the moment is that America possesses an overall great excess of unutilized material and human productive resources. Hence, the financing of national defence should be directed at taking up this slack rather than toward the diversion of resources from the making of consumer goods to the manufacture of armaments. This latter course is proper only when the economic machine is already working at capacity."

On economic grounds he favored a postponement of the consumption taxes being proposed by the Treasury until the economy was more nearly providing full employment. Currie argued these points even more forcibly, with detailed figures on employment and the potential national income at full employment, with some lightening of the average work week, in *Expansion Possibilities of Our System*, December 2, 1940. Of particular interest is his estimate that 2.5 million people could be withdrawn from agriculture who had remained on the farms because of inability to secure good jobs in cities. He also emphasized that several million other "marginal" workers were available for more productive employement. Twenty years later, in 1960, Currie was to adapt and develop these ideas for application to the conditions facing Colombia, where he was then a citizen, in an important development program known as "Operation Colombia."

Even as late as April 4, 1941, in a tax program memorandum to the President, Currie was still impressed by the large amount of slack and excess capacity in the system generally. Though specific bottlenecks existed, these called for specific measures—the setting of priorities, state allocation, and direct price controls—rather than general deflationary measures. General taxes, he noted, were not an effective means of controlling such situations; these operate through depressing the level of *total* demand for goods. Total demand and, in consequence, total employment, would have to be curtailed to an exorbitant degree if the troublesome prices were to be affected significantly.

A week later, on April 11, 1941, Roosevelt established the Office of Price Administration and Civilian Supply with Leon Henderson its director. John Kenneth Galbraith became the "czar" of prices. But, as Galbraith himself has recalled, during the war so much slack was mobilized into productive use that despite the massive military requirements the supply of civilian consumer goods rose from $230 billion in 1940 to $255 billion in 1944 (constant 1972 prices).[15] In this, U.S. experience and policy differed significantly from the British, which was guided by greater military requirements and the prescriptions of Keynes's *How to Pay for the War* (1940).[16]

In 1940 the issue of an excess profits tax had arisen. In a November 13 memorandum, *New Tax Legislation,* Currie ironically noted how the various inequities and inconsistencies of the proposed legislation contrasted with the advantages of the undistributed profits tax, an unsatisfactory version of which, as we saw in chapter 3, was passed in 1936. This was repealed in 1938. "If we had a progressive personal income tax," he noted, "and if all earnings were distributed, there would be no particular point in having a corporate excess profits tax." The inequity arose from the fact that some shareholders in a highly profitable company may be a lot poorer than some shareholders of less profitable companies not subject to the tax. If an undistributed profits tax encouraged dividend payments then shareholders could be taxed according to their own ability to pay.

During the course of 1940 Currie also found time for foreign economic relations, in particular with the U.S. neighbors Canada and Mexico. At Warm Springs in April Roosevelt had suggested that Currie, an ex-Canadian, examine aspects of U.S. relations with Canada. In August Currie visited Ottawa and discussed the likely reorientation of Canada away from traditional economic and political ties with Britain and closer ties with the United States, whatever the result of the war in Europe. Roosevelt was delighted with Currie's report and urged him to talk with Mackenzie King and maintain his contacts with Ottawa, which he did—finding the Canadians very helpful in subsequent lend-lease operations, including C. D. Howe, the minister for munitions, Lester B. Pearson at the Canadian legation in Washington, and the economist Lorie Tarshis.

On one occasion the Prime Minister, Mackenzie King, invited him to his home on a Saturday afternoon. He wanted to talk of his relations with F.D.R. and especially on the relation of Harry Hopkins to F.D.R. He seemed to regret that he had no such confidant himself and was envious of the President. On another occasion Currie introduced T. V. Soong, brother-in-law of Chiang Kai-shek, to Ottawa for discussions on Canadian supplies to China. He was given a red carpet welcome dinner with the Governor-General and a meeting with the Prime Minister, culminating in a ball at the country club with the Prime

Minister (who had once lived in China) leading a serpentine dance. The P.M. obviously enjoyed himself and in driving the Curries back to the Chateau Laurier he directed the chauffeur to drive around in order to show them the notable features of Ottawa. To those who have known the reserved nature of Mackenzie King, says Currie, this may not be believable, but he insists it happened.

On Currie's recommendation in December 1941 President Roosevelt set up the Joint War Production Committee, to which Currie devoted much time, making frequent visits to Ottawa. This led to a greatly increased flow of orders for military equipment placed by the United States in Canada, which had ample spare capacity.[17] Progress was also made in standardization of products in the two countries and in exchange of information on best production techniques. This played a lasting role in converting Canada into an industrial country.

On relations with Mexico, Currie had various meetings in 1940 with Sumner Welles at the State Department over the oil crisis and over measures to persuade Mexico, through various soft loan arrangements, not to cooperate with the attempt by Japan to purchase scrap from her. These and other measures taken were designed to further America's "Good Neighbor Policy" and cooperation on national defense. Currie was instrumental in involving James Forrestal, another administrative assistant to the President, in Latin American affairs. Shortly afterward Forrestal was appointed assistant secretary of the navy, and Roosevelt appointed Nelson Rockefeller to succeed him in the office for Latin American affairs in the White House.

Currie's incursion into Mexican and Latin American affairs was initially prompted by his Harvard classmate Antonio Monteros, who had become a prominent investment banker in Mexico (and later Mexican ambassador to Washington) and who, in May 1940, asked Currie to intercede over the appropriation of foreign (mostly British) oil companies. When Roosevelt referred him to Sumner Welles, the assistant secretary of state, Currie was somewhat nervous. In his memoirs (pp. 152–53) he recalled:

> Up to that time, the State Department had been an unknown and hostile territory and having in mind my other jurisdictional troubles, I expected a stony reception from Welles, whom I did not then know. Although Welles could have easily and quite properly brushed me off, he was cordial, "welcomed my interest" and explained in some detail the status of negotiations and his ideas and plans with respect to Mexico. I came away very much impressed with his grasp and understanding of the issues involved and ap-

preciative of his attitude. I saw him on many occasions afterwards and never had cause to modify my original impression. He was unquestionably one of the most competent persons I encountered in Government and his decisions and grasp were in marked contrast to the uncertainty and indecisiveness that prevailed around the Secretary's office. I could understand why the President always preferred to deal with Welles when he could and also how much of our highly successful Latin American policy was owing to the smooth working understanding of the President and Welles. To my mind, it was a great loss to the country that circumstances were such that Welles could not have been Roosevelt's Secretary of State. Actually, he functioned as such, but under enormous difficulties.

Subsequent to this interview, Larry Duggan came to see me at Welles' suggestion, and we became very good friends. He later appealed to me on several occasions for the President's intervention to smooth the periodic crises that arose between Hull and Welles, and I did what I could. The basic conditions that gave rise to these crises, however,—Welles' competence and forcefulness and Hull's jealousy and vindictiveness—did not permit any permanent solution except separation.

Currie's Role in China Before Pearl Harbor, 1941

These foreign initiatives, together with Currie's frequent contact with the military over defense spending, strategic stock piling, and so on, admirably equipped him for the role that he was to play in January 1941 when Generalissimo Chiang Kai-shek invited him, at the Chinese government's expense, to investigate the grave problems of inflation and foreign exchange in war-torn China. The suggestion probably came from Chiang's brother-in-law, T. V. Soong. He, with the help of the former New Deal lawyer Tom Corcoran, was in Washington promoting Chinese interests. In China, Chiang Kai-shek's Nationalist Kuomintang forces and Mao Tse-tung's Communist army had established an uneasy armed truce during the occupation of parts of China by Japanese invaders. The Generalissimo was now appealing to the United States for further material assistance, ostensibly to defend Chinese territory from further Japanese encroachments, but also to strengthen his position against the Communists.

T. V. Soong had already been negotiating some loans from the U.S. Treasury. He was probably now looking for someone who could speak for the Chinese in court (the White House). It was an opportune time, for President Roosevelt had announced in December 1940 his plans for lend-lease to Britain and her allies. He agreed that Currie's mission to China would be useful in assessing China's needs and reporting on the confused situation there.[18]

Thinking that his mission was to be concerned with purely technical economic issues, especially inflation, Currie took with him Emile Despres from the Federal Reserve. However, when he arrived in Chungking, via the Philippines and Hong Kong, it became clear that his visit was being used for broader political purposes, in particular to demonstrate to the world that the United States supported the Nationalist government and that China was a "Great Power." For this reason Currie was greeted and treated as the personal representative of the President which on this occasion he was not (though this was his status on his second mission to China the following year).

President Roosevelt did, however, ask Currie to convey a verbal message to the Generalissimo expressing the hope that civil war would not break out to the prejudice of the united resistance to the Japanese, which was the administration's policy at that time and appeared to be obviously in the interests of the United States. This was the policy that Currie did his best to further in the next couple of years when he was intimately involved in the execution of the administration's China policy. No doubt Currie was being used by Chiang and other Chinese leaders on this and subsequent occasions, but not in the sense that he was led to do anything contrary to the policy of the U.S. government. Any private reservations he had regarding corruption and brutality in the Nationalist government were kept in the perspective of U.S. policy to maintain that government as its ally in the war against the Japanese. This is forgotten or ignored by those commentators who have criticized Currie's cordial relations with the Chiang family and his work in expediting the military and civilian lend-lease programs to China. It is indeed ironic that, as Michael Schaller has noted, Currie was later to be caught up in the hysteria surrounding the "loss" of China and accused of being a communist agent.[19]

In Chungking Currie found that the Chinese leaders were mainly interested in military assistance and not much interested in the inflation survey. Military assistance was desired by Chiang at least as much for its importance in attacking, then or later, the Communist threat in northern China as to combat the Japanese.

President Roosevelt's view of China was a romantic one, inherited from his grandfather, Amaso Delano and uncle, Frederic Delano, who had lived there. Amaso Delano remarked that China was "the first for greatness, riches and grandeur, of any country ever known." According to Michael Schaller,[20] "he passed down the family fortune and fascination with China to his grandson." Thus Roosevelt was predisposed to look sympathetically on Chinese requests for aid and was encouraging the adulation of Chiang Kai-shek and the Kuomintang (KMT) in the American press. As mentioned, T. V. Soong, Mme. Chiang's brother and later China's foreign minister, was assiduously promoting Chinese interests in Washington and was treated respectfully until Treasury Secretary Morgenthau uncovered evidence of massive embezzlement by Chiang's family.[21]

Currie left on the hazardous week-long journey to Chungking in late January, arriving back in Washington in early March. He was feted by the Chinese leaders who tried to persuade him, with some success, that they really were committed to economic reforms as well as to their war against Japan. Currie also met the Communist leader Chou En-lai. This meeting took place with the knowledge and approval of the U.S. ambassador, but took place at the home of the British ambassador, Sir Archibald Clerk-Kerr, who knew Chou En-lai well, because the Generalissimo, though he gave his permission for the meeting, requested that it be given no publicity. Currie's purpose was to express to Chou the hope that civil war would not break out and that the united resistance would continue. The meeting occurred shortly after the "New Fourth Army incident" in which there had been a bloody confrontation between Nationalist and Communist troops after the latter had crossed into Nationalist territory. Nevertheless, an uneasy united front existed and Chou was resident Communist representative in Chungking.

Chou insisted that the Communists were not hostile to the United States or to U.S. aid to China.[22] He only hoped that it would not be turned against the Communists rather than the Japanese. The Communists wanted to preserve unity in the fight against Japan. He wanted more democracy but acknowledged the wartime need of strong central leadership. Without being asked, he volunteered the view that Chiang was the only man who could preserve some sort of national unity despite various disaffected groups, including some pro-Japanese elements. He was, not surprisingly, unimpressed by government "reforms."

With or without the illusion that his words would be heeded, Currie recommended that Chiang's best strategy to undercut support for

Currie with Madame Chiang Kai-shek, Chungking, February 1941. Photo by Carl Mydans. *Life Magazine,* © Time Inc.

the Communists would be to follow Roosevelt's example of promoting liberal economic and political reforms.[23] He recommended that China be treated as a great power, given additional economic and military support, and encouraged to reform. A political compromise should also be encouraged in order to avert both civil war and a Communist victory.

The most important reform that Currie urged on the Generalissimo was a land tax.[24] The government, which had no revenue other than printing paper money, adopted the recommendation to take over the collection of the land tax from the provincial governments, and in kind rather than in rapidly depreciating currency. This not only strengthened the position of the Nationalist government vis-à-vis the provincial governments, but also provided the only genuine revenue of the government for the duration of the war. "This reform is not only desirable on budgetary grounds," Currie told the Generalissimo, "but it would also serve to emphasize to the people that this government was determined to proceed along the lines of social justice and equality laid down by Dr. Sun. It would cut the ground out from under the Communists and they should be forced to applaud it. The tax would fall largely on the well-to-do land owners who are now profiting by the inflation." Sadly, it was reported later that in practice the tax was imposed more ruthlessly on poorer peasants than on the large landlords.

Currie's proposal was hardly novel, since in such an agricultural economy the land tax was an obvious suggestion as an alternative to the inflation tax. It has been suggested that Currie was being used by Chiang in this. John Fairbank, for example, writes: "Chiang Kai-shek was growing steadily weaker but had to maintain his claim to power and use the Americans. He had wanted for a long time to take over the land tax from the provincial authorities and by getting Currie to recommend it, since it was such an obvious thing, he succeeded in getting an American sanction for it to make it more feasible. . . . As I believe he suspected at the time, he was chiefly being used."[25] Currie himself insists that the suggestion was his own and did not come at the Nationalist leaders' prompting. In fact he believes that Chiang was not in the slightest bit interested in his views on economic matters and was interested only in U.S. military assistance.

Currie was certainly aware of the underlying brutality and corruption of the regime. After all, his briefings in Washington had included talks with people with quite left-wing views, such as Harry White and Sol Adler at the U.S. Treasury. In Chungking he had heard the views of Chou En-lai and, of course, those of U.S. foreign service officers who, as noted by Fairbank, "because they spoke Chinese and travelled around so much, were the chief people who knew the score in popular discontent."[26] Currie came to rely particularly on briefings given by John Carter Vincent who, in Currie's view, was more willing than many of his fellow officers to separate his personal views on the Chiang regime from his duty to carry out U.S. policy. This was to support the Nationalist struggle against the Japanese and not to weaken Chiang's government by furthering the Communists' ambition. (Currie's official relations with Vincent are discussed further in chapter 5.)

Michael Schaller has argued that Currie was the first person to draw up a coherent policy on China for the Roosevelt administration, but criticized him for being "completely unaware of the fundamental class and land struggle which underlay China's crisis. He possessed no sense of what forces the KMT represented, or why the Communists could successfully appeal to the peasantry."[27] But Schaller erroneously stated that Currie made no report to Roosevelt on his meeting with Chou En-lai and that instead he only reported the views of Chiang Kai-shek and those such as Colonel James McHugh, at the military mission, who was sympathetic to Chiang. Actually Currie presented a separate three-page report on his meeting with Chou (referred to above), and also mentioned the meeting in his report on talks with the Generalissimo.

On his return to Washington in March, the lend-lease bill was being passed through Congress and Currie suggested that Roosevelt add China to the list of potential beneficiaries. This Roosevelt was happay to do and over the coming months he stepped up his aid to China and imposed further trade and oil embargoes on Japan as Japan advanced south into French Indo-China. A group of financial, transport, and political advisers was sent to Chungking but their influence on Chiang's reform programs was small. Among other things, Currie was responsible for sending Owen Lattimore as political adviser to Chiang Kai-shek in April 1941; for promoting civilian and military aircraft programs (including the expansion of the American Volunteer Group, AVG), which he saw as the most effective way that China could be aided; and for sending a group of New York trucking experts, recommended by Harry Hopkins, who tried to improve the organization of supplies across the rugged mountains to Burma along the narrow Burma Road, but who could not stop the corruption. In April Hopkins officially appointed Currie as administrator in charge of lend-lease for China.[28] The British were so entrenched in the lend-lease and planning machinery that a special pleader for China, with direct access to the President—as the British had through Hopkins—was essential if China was to get anything.

Currie thus became immersed in the administration of lend-lease supplies, displaying considerable initiative in tracking down materiel that could be used by the Chinese, sometimes diverting supplies destined for other theaters when he could persuade the President and others they were less needed there. This brought him into sharp conflict at one point with Britain's Air Marshall Harris who, according to Currie, barked at him down the telephone: "See here, you can't do this. We bought those planes with our own money." One can imagine his exasperation, but the British had been consulted on the matter and were persuaded that the defense of Singapore would be helped by a strengthened Chinese air force that could harry the Japanese, bomb their supplies in central China as they passed along the exposed artery of the Yangtze, and even bomb industrial targets inside Japan. Currie asked Harry Hopkins to cable Averell Harriman in London to clear the matter with Sir Archibald Sinclair, the secretary of state for air, and this was done. But there were many other frustrating delays, broken promises, and bottlenecks. Some of these bottlenecks were alleviated by placing orders in Canada, which had greater spare capacity, and this did much to spur that country's industrial development.

Securing ordnance proved especially difficult. At first, the army could spare only pack howitzers. However, Currie was able to secure machine guns and ammunition from Canada with lend-lease funds. C. D. Howe, accepting Currie's personal guarantee that payment would be made, arranged for these to be shipped by Canada to Rangoon even before the orders were formally placed with the War Department. They were the first munitions China was to receive under the lend-lease program and were used in the defense of Burma. This diversion of ordnance from Canada exposed Currie to severe criticism from Lord Beaverbrook, British supply minister. These Canadian orders were later arranged by the Joint War Production Committee that Currie helped set up in December 1941 after the United States had formally entered the war.

The supply program to Claire Chennault's American Volunteer Group, or "Flying Tigers," was one of Currie's major preoccupations. Chennault enjoyed the confidence of the Chiang family, who favored the air force, and in Washington Currie was asked to support a supply program for Chennault and also to organize a training program in Arizona for thousands of Chinese pilots. Currie had mixed feelings about Chennault's mercenaries; personally he did not much approve of them, but helped them anyway because that was official policy and he was asked to do it. He was, however, very enthusiastic in his support for the expansion of the civilian passenger and cargo operations of W. L. Bond's China National Aviation Corporation (CNAC) with whom he had flown on the treacherous nighttime flights between Hong Kong and Chungking.[29]

Michael Schaller's account of events leading up to Pearl Harbor attaches great significance to Joint Board Paper 355 (JB 355) entitled *Chinese Aircraft Requirements,* which Currie prepared for the Joint Aircraft Committee on May 10, 1941, and which was passed to General Marshall and the Joint Board for consideration.[30] This document stressed the role an air force in China could play in defending

Singapore, the Burma Road, and the Philippines against Japanese attack, but also recommended strategic bombing of targets in Japan itself. Use of the AVG and, later, Chinese pilots trained in the United States, would avoid direct involvement by the U.S. military.

A modified proposal which, for the shorter run, scaled down the aircraft requirements to a little more than half the original five hundred, but which repeated the proposal that these be used for incendiary bombing of Japan, was submitted to General Marshall and the Joint Board later in May. It should be noted that similar proposals that stressed the need to expand the air force in China under Chennault's command, and its possible use for offensive as well as defensive missions, had been endorsed by President Roosevelt in December 1940 after meetings with Treasury Secretary Henry Morgenthau, Secretary of State Cordell Hull, Secretary of War Henry Stimson, and Secretary of the Navy Frank Knox.[31] Thus Currie's proposals were in general in line with existing policy, though General Marshall had expressed strong opposition, which Stimson came to share.[32]

On July 18, 1941, Secretary Knox and acting Secretary of War Robert Patterson formally notified the President of their endorsement of Currie's JB 355 plan. Schaller noted:

> Undoubtedly influenced by Currie, Roosevelt affixed his initials to the Secretaries' letter on July 23. The President included the notation, "but restudy military mission versus the attaché method." He perhaps referred to a related aid mission concurrently being despatched to China by the War Department. Still extremely wary of air strategies, General Marshall had moved to send an army group to China under General John Magruder; its job would be to study the organisation and supply requirements of the Chinese army.
>
> Here again was an example of both clandestine military operation and the opposition of the regular army to the air strategy being pushed by "outsiders" like Currie and Chennault. Chennault himself saw Magruder's mission as a tool of Marshall and the "regular" War Department planners who hoped to push a ground strategy in China, undercutting plans for offensive strategic bombing of Japan. Magruder allegedly warned Marshall that Chennault's proposed attack might lead to a rapid Japanese response directly against the United States.[33]

Actually, at the end of October 1941 Magruder reported his grave concern over an "imminent" Japanese drive on Kunming, aimed at cutting off the Burma Road, and urged support for Chiang's request for significant air reinforcements.[34] Marshall was very irritated by Magruder's nervousness. Stanley Hornbeck of the State Department agreed. He told Marshall that Magruder was causing his department "more worry than there was actual need for" and requested that his department be sent messages from the military mission in Chungking directly, rather than indirectly via Currie.

Marshall was evidently unsympathetic to Currie's determined efforts to acquire for China the aircraft and supplies that had been promised earlier, as he now preferred to build up the air forces in the Philippines.[35] He told Roosevelt (letter, November 5, 1941) that "the best deterrent to Japan was a strong position in the Philippines. The US would not be at its full projected strength in the Philippines until February or March 1942. Until that time war in the Far East has to be avoided."

Actually, Currie's personal recollection was that President Roosevelt was frustrated by domestic political opposition to direct involvement by the United States in the war against fascism. Thus it is possible that Roosevelt was quite willing to risk full-scale war in this way, though for a short while some consideration was given to the possibility of seeking a modus vivendi with Japan. When rumors of this reached Chiang Kai-shek he was greatly agitated. Owen Lattimore and Colonel McHugh cabled Currie from Chungking to plead against any such agreement. In a memorandum to the President on September 13, 1941, Currie argued that an American agreement with Japan "would do irreparable damage to the goodwill we have built up in China . . . and would nullify the effect of lend-lease aid to China."[36] Toward the end of November Roosevelt killed the plan for a possible truce and a few days later the attack on Pearl Harbor dissolved isolationism and provided the occasion for bringing the United States into the war, solidly backed by public opinion.

Referring to Currie's earlier JB 355 proposals, Schaller commented that the plan to bomb Japan's cities "raises questions as to the extent, if any, of Japanese foreknowledge. Granted that the larger causes of the war lay in the overall incompatibility of Japanese and American interests in the Pacific and that the de facto American oil embargo of July 26, 1941, provided an immediate cause, the secret American air strategy may still have influenced the course of events. Certainly the information which the Japanese government did possess about Chennault's activities was a source of great concern in Tokyo."[37]

Schaller evinces disapproval of the AVG on the grounds that it violated American neutrality and may have provoked Pearl Harbor, which he regards as a disaster. But in the absence of Pearl Harbor the United States may not have been directly involved either in the war with Japan or the war against Hitler, which many people—certainly Currie—believe would have been an even greater disaster. However, Schaller considers that the clandestine plans for secret air warfare in 1941 set a major precedent for U.S. military and political planning that would be invoked in later years. He noted that the AVG was resurrected after the war as a force known as Civil Air Transport and played an active combat role in Vietnam as a para-military arm of the Central Intelligence Agency. Schaller continued:

> The long-term implications of Chennault's AVG were of course imagined only dimly, if at all, in December 1941. But in the context of America's China policy at that time, these plans evidenced a much deeper involvement with the Nationalist regime than is usually imagined. Given the willingness to sponsor a covert attack upon Japanese forces and Japan itself, it is increasingly difficult to believe that anything short of general war could have emerged from the Japanese-American confrontation of 1941. The necessary political, military and economic sinews of an alliance had been stretched between Washington and Chungking. It only awaited a catalyst to emerge. Tokyo itself dramatically provided this on December 7, 1941.[38]

When word reached Washington on Sunday morning, December 7, 1941, of the bombing of Pearl Harbor, Currie hurried to his office and, with the help of John Fairbank, prepared a complete up-to-the-minute inventory of all the war materiel en route or on order from the Chinese. Supplies were strung across the Pacific. There was even a chartered Pan Am amphibian plane loaded with supplies for Chennault, in the charge of a mercenary pilot recruit who had just resigned from the U.S. air force under the arrangements Currie had made for the setting up of the AVG. The plane had reached Midway Island. The local commander there had more planes than pilots so he pressed the recruit into service. But then the Japanese bombed his airfield and he then found he had more pilots than planes. So Pan Am flew the recruit back to Pearl Harbor where he was inducted back into the U.S. Air Force.

Role in China after Pearl Harbor, 1942–44

Two days after Pearl Harbor Currie submitted a memorandum to the President calling attention to China's great danger if the Japanese invaded Burma, where lend-lease supplies were awaiting shipment to China, and suggesting the desirability of getting the agreement of the British and the Chinese to a joint defense of Burma. In response to Currie's enquiry, the Generalissimo stated that he was willing to dispatch immediately the AVG and three army divisions (each with a nominal strength of around 9,000 men).[39]

The British, however, through General Wavell, rejected Chiang's offer and this deeply offended the Chinese leader. Wavell was reluctant to use Chinese troops, fearing they might later challenge Britain's colonial claims on Burma and never leave. Furthermore, Wavell had a poor opinion of Chinese troops as a fighting force, partly because they had been unable to push the Japanese out of China. He was forced to revise his opinion when the British fared even more disastrously in the face of the Japanese, but by then valuable time had been lost.

In the following months Currie exerted through every channel as much pressure as he could to get a coordinated command and adequate forces and supplies in Burma. If he had been successful soon enough it is possible that China's lifeline could have been kept open. But by May Burma had fallen to the Japanese. This was a major catastrophe for China, and a serious blow to the Generalissimo's prestige in China.

After the United States had formally entered the war Claire Chennault continued his maverick command of military aircraft operations. But the man chosen by General Marshall and Secretary Stimson to be Chiang Kai-shek's chief-of-staff and commander of U.S. forces in China, Burma, and India was General Joseph W. Stilwell, who arrived in India in late February. Stilwell first visited China in 1911, had distinguished himself in the First World War in France, and then, after learning Chinese, returned to China in 1920 where he spent most of the next two decades. Thus he acquired an unrivaled knowledge of Chinese geography, history, and culture, and of the roots of the vicious power struggles between rival Communist and Nationalist factions and against the Japanese invaders. He felt a deep attachment to China and in many ways, therefore, he was the natural choice. He was, however, described by Forrest Pogue, the biographer of Stilwell's close friend General Marshall, in the following way:

> Lean to the point of guantness, perpetually squinting through steel-rimmed glasses as a result of a near-blinded eye injured in a World War I explosion, profane, irascible, well disciplined in body, undisciplined in tongue, Stilwell was totally lacking in the art of diplomatic finesse. A man with a compulsion to speak and damn the consequences, he sounded off against colleagues and superiors with a zest that caused momentary amusement but ultimate dislike. The nickname "Vinegar Joe," applied in affection, became a damaging trademark. As a safety valve for his temper he poured part of his bile into his diary and personal letters. Unintended for publication and unedited by him, they appeared in the postwar years as the work of an amusing but temperamental officer, bedevilled by poor digestion and Job-like afflictions, who took peevish and childish revenge upon his contemporaries by characterizing them with ludicrous names and rude remarks.[40]

John Paton Davies, who later served as Stilwell's political adviser has also described Stilwell's characteristically contemptuous feelings for President Roosevelt and Harry Hopkins in Washington as he left in February.[41] On arrival in Chungking he was soon to develop far worse animosity for Generalissimo Chiang and anyone who tolerated him, not least Claire Chennault and his fighter pilots. Stilwell saw the air force mainly as a diversion of resources from his army which he wanted to use to defend (and later to win back) Burma from the Japanese.

He demanded, but was not given, complete and unambiguous command over Chiang's army in Burma and over all lend-lease supplies. He was angry and frustrated when this was denied him. Shortly afterward the American and Chinese troops were routed by the Japanese in Burma and Stilwell placed the blame on Chiang for issuing contradictory orders to his Chinese generals instead of leaving everything to himself. Since his return to Chungking in May he and Chiang had not been on speaking terms. Relations between Stilwell and Ambassador Gauss were also very strained.

Against this background Lauchlin Currie arrived on his second mission to Chungking, as the President's personal representative, on July 21, 1942. His assignment was to get Stilwell and Chiang working together again and meanwhile to act as a go-between. Currie also found that Ambassador Gauss shared Stilwell's antipathy for the Chinese leaders, toward whom his manner was very perfunctory, and Gauss's disdainful attitude appeared to Currie to extend to the Chinese people in general. He thus made few concessions to Chinese sensibilities and culture. He had not seen H. H. Kung, the minister of finance and Chiang's brother-in-law, for eight months.

In his August 24 report to the President, Currie noted:

> Probably from the best of motives Chinese propagandists and various American friends of China have built up in most Americans' minds a completely erroneous picture of the progress that has been made toward a modern state and a modern army. Consequently many American officers became disillusioned when they discovered the degree of waste, inefficiency and corruption that pervades Chinese affairs, ignoring the relatively great strides that have actually been made and judging China by American standards. Instead, therefore, of keeping their eyes on the main chance and of doing what actually can be done to sustain and aid the Chinese, they are inclined to be impatient at not being able to do what they would like to do and end up by believing that nothing can be done.

Currie reported a strong anti-British feeling among the Chinese due to their neglect of China and reluctance to mount a joint offensive against Burma. Earlier that year Currie had spoken about China to Churchill during his visit to Washington. In Roosevelt's presence Churchill told Currie, probably with some impish skepticism, that he had not realized the importance of China before coming to Washington.[42] Churchill's implied message was that China was important only because Americans thought it was important, but he did then speak of planning a Burma offensive later that year. However, in June 1942 Tobruk fell to Rommel, so Churchill diverted supplies (especially aircraft) destined for China, in order to meet the urgent crisis facing Egypt and North Africa. This incensed Chiang Kai-shek who threatened to discontinue his war with Japan unless certain demands—the famous "Three Demands"—were met. He wanted three U.S. divisions in India to help the Chinese efforts to reopen communications with India, 500 aircraft, and 5,000 tons of supplies per month. It was part of Currie's mission to explain the difficulties the United States faced in supplying China and to smooth things over with the Generalissimo by convincing him of America's basic goodwill.

Stilwell, meanwhile, had been hoping to persuade Chiang to mount a major joint offensive against the Japanese to recover Burma. He thought that if Chiang would agree to this campaign then the Americans would meet his Three Demands ultimatum. Hence, when Currie arrived in Chungking to report that no American divisions would be assigned, Stilwell was naturally very frustrated. Contemptuously he recorded in his diary that although this was one of the Three Demands, Currie, whom he referred to as "Cutie Currie," was, nevertheless, "all pepped up" after initial talks with the Generalissimo, and "thinks he smoothed it all out."[43] Later, when Marshall informed Stilwell of the efforts through Currie and McHugh to have him recalled, he assured him of his support and advised him "to develop more of patience and tolerance than is ordinarily expected of a man, and much more than is your constituent portion."[44]

Currie's general appraisal of the situation in his August 24 report to the President was that the Generalissimo was "in large part a prisoner of the cliques and factions that surround him. He has staked his position and prestige very largely on his pro-American position. . . . His presitige, however, has suffered severely by the allied reverses, and by what is generally felt to be American neglect."

Currie concluded:

> . . . . If this appraisal is correct I am convinced that we have a unique opportunity to exert a profound influence on the development of China and hence of India. It appears to me to be profoundly in our national interest to give full support to the Generalissimo, both military and diplomatic. I do not think we need to lay down any conditions nor tie any strings to this support. If our dealings with him are conducted on a high moral plane and if he is convinced of our friendly attitude, I think we can rely upon him so far as lies within his power to go in the direction of our wishes in prosecuting a vigorous war policy and in creating a modern democratic and peaceful state.

With the benefit of hindsight Currie's "no conditions" approach has been criticized, but his attitude at the time was influenced by the fact that U.S. aid to Britain and Russia had also been without strings in order not to offend allies but instead to create maximum goodwill. This, as Tuchman has written, was in tune with the President's way of thinking: "Temperamentally Roosevelt was predisposed against the quid pro quo management of Lend-Lease although the War Department, at Stilwell's urging, favored it. Roosevelt did not like haggling and thought it would be ungenerous to exact terms from a beleaguered ally."[45] Although Currie was later to modify his own position on conditionality, at this time he believed it inconsistent that China, as an ally, should be treated differently from Russia. This is revealed in a memorandum to Winston Churchill, drawn up at the latter's request in June 1942, in which Currie put forward various suggestions for improving Sino-British relations.[46]

The memorandum began:

> The most frequent and vehement charge made by the Chinese against Britain is that China is not treated as an equal ally, but rather as a semi-colonial country. The Chinese do not feel that they are a party to the close relations that prevail between Britain, the United States, and Russia, and are therefore not satisfied with the status as one of the United Nations. The single most effective stroke that could be made to combat this feeling would be to conclude a Sino-British pact as similar as possible to the Russo-British pact.

British policy over the internal affairs of India was another source of friction with the Chinese. Currie returned from Chungking via New Delhi on August 9, expecting to have an interview with Nehru. This proved impossible as that was the day on which all the Congress leaders were imprisoned. Watching the disturbances in Delhi and fearful of the involvement of U.S. troops in these disturbances, he dispatched an urgent wire to Washington suggesting that the United States avoid identification with British policy. He feared that anti-British feeling in China could easily spill over into anti-American feeling, thus impeding the war effort and jeopardizing America's postwar influence in China as well as India.[47] He had told Chiang of Roosevelt's growing dissatisfaction with the old colonial system and his plans for promoting the economic development of the colonies into modern democratic states, stressing that "any tendency in China toward militant chauvinism, toward a growth of reaction and a failure to make progress in a democratic direction, the weakening of power of the central government, and the strengthening of military commanders and various groups, cliques and factions, would all tend to chill American interest in the economic development of China."

Although Currie succeeded in his main diplomatic mission to get Stilwell and Chiang on speaking terms again, he did not think this could last and this would not help the war effort. In his report, therefore, he recommended that General Stilwell be withdrawn, along with Ambassador Gauss, and that there be a real attempt to change the contemptuous attitudes displayed by Americans in China, no matter how much, from their personal and American perspectives or from the point of view of peacetime ideals, these may have been justified. Currie's "no conditions" approach to relations with Chiang was partly predicated on the assumption that Stilwell and Gauss would be soon replaced by individuals with more tact, though Currie was under no illusions about how much could be accomplished even then.

He recommended that Stilwell be replaced by General Raymond Wheeler, currently serving in India and generally held in very high regard as an able administrator with an engaging and sympathetic personality.[48] Back in Washington President Roosevelt was sympathetic but preferred not to put the idea himself to General Marshall. Instead he delegated the task to Currie who told the present writer that the President felt somewhat intimidated by the general. In any event Marshall intimidated and was dismissive of Currie, bluntly rejecting the suggestion that Stilwell be replaced by Wheeler. "Wheeler is not a line officer, he's only an engineer," he told Currie. Stilwell, by contrast, was a fellow officer from West Point and a regular military man.

Years later, the incident still rankled with Marshall who, in an interview with the official war historians, recalled that "a gnome-like man came into his office, curled one leg under him and said the President wanted Stilwell relieved. 'He does, does he?' said Marshall. Currie replied yes, he did. Marshall asked how long Currie had been in China. 'Three weeks, Sir,' replied Currie, and, facing the bleak silence of the Chief-of-Staff, departed."

But Currie did not give up. In early September a reply to the Generalissimo's Three Demands had been readied by the War Department for the President's signature. Marshall told the President that the proposed message included definite conditions that Stilwell had "repeatedly advised" should be met by the Chinese government to make American aid effective. Pogue has stated that the message was promptly referred to Currie, who strongly objected to Stilwell's advice that Chiang be requested to train and reorganize thirty Chinese divisions in the province of Yunnan.[49] This was not the time to press this program, for "after all we are not going very far to meet his request." Pogue noted that Currie was also fearful of the effect of Marshall's recommendation that Chiang be asked to use Stilwell as his adviser in the reorganization. In the light of the Generalissimo's state of mind, made so clear to him, Currie was afraid this suggestion would be taken as a deliberate affront. Currie told Marshall frankly (letter, September 14, 1942): "At the risk of being tiresomely insistent, I would again in all earnestness ask you to consider a shift in command. I am certain that the present arrangements cannot work."

President Roosevelt again suggested to General Marshall on October 3 that Stilwell be replaced, but Marshall stood firmly behind his friend. Tang Tsou has written:

> Although Currie's recommendation for Stilwell's recall was not adopted, his general approach was followed by the President and contributed to the weakening of Stilwell's position in his dealing with the Nationalist government. Currie's view on the proper method of dealing with Chiang Kai-shek was in harmony with the President's temperament. As Stimpson and Bundy observed in connection with dealing with the Russians, "Small-minded haggling was no part of Mr. Roosevelt's nature, and in the larger sense this was most fortunate, but it left lesser officials at a considerable disadvantage in trying to make cooperation mutual."[50]

In this same connection Tang Tsou also reproduced part of the revealing letter that Roosevelt sent to Marshall in March 1943 when the President overruled Marshall and Stilwell, and granted Chiang's request to give Chennault command of his own U.S. air force in China and to place air power above the army reform program:

> . . . . Stilwell has exactly the wrong approach in dealing with Generalissimo Chiang who, after all, cannot be expected, as a Chinese, to use the same methods that we do. When Stilwell speaks about the fact that the Generalissimo is very irritable and hard to handle, upping his demands, etc., he is, of course correct; but when he speaks of talking to him in sterner tones, he goes about it just the wrong way.
>
> All of us must remember that the Generalissimo came up the hard way to become the undisputed leader of four hundred million people—an enormously difficult job to attain any kind of unity from a diverse group of all kinds of leaders—military men, educators, scientists, public health people, engineers, all of them struggling for power and mastery, local or national, and to create in a very short time throughout China what it took us a couple of centuries to attain.
>
> Besides that the Generalissimo finds it necessary to maintain his position of supremacy. You and I would do the same thing under the circumstances. He is the Chief Executive as well as the Commander-in-Chief, and one cannot speak sternly to a man like that or exact commitments from him in the way we might from the Sultan of Morocco.

Christopher Thorne also discusses this memorandum and describes Roosevelt's portrayal of Chiang here as "pure fantasy."[51] He also criticizes Currie for helping to build up an idealized portrait of Chiang for display to the American public while others "were endeavouring to bring about a more realistic attitude." However, as Currie remarked later: "So far as I was able I alerted FDR to the inefficiency, curruption and completely authoritarian character of the Chiang regime but Chiang *was* the head of the Government just as Stalin was."[52]

Roosevelt's rebuffs on these occasions offended Marshall deeply. A sympathetic account of Marshall's position is given by Eric Larrabee: "Chiang constantly threatened to 'leave the war' against the Japanese, a war which he was not fighting anyway. This blackmail astonishingly persuaded numbers of Americans (Marshall and Morgenthau were honorable exceptions) to go on urging that money and munitions be poured down the rathole for the purpose of 'keeping China in the war.'"[53]

Larrabee also refers (p. 568) to the "needless indignity" suffered by Marshall because President Roosevelt chose to tell him of a decision that had gone against him and in favor of Currie, while Currie himself was "sprawled in an armchair" in a corner of the President's room. (Currie himself, however, has no recollection of ever having met with Marshall and Roosevelt together.) Larrabee says that Marshall was bitter for years after at the treatment he received at the White House on matters pertaining to China, and apparently reserved a special scorn for Currie.

Though Currie was overruled on the replacement of Stilwell, he remained convinced that the situation called mainly for an able supplies administrator and someone who could smooth relations rather than a swashbuckling general bent on usurping the ultimate authority of the Chinese leader and himself lead the Chinese armies into battle. He felt it was a pity that Stilwell's talents as a top combat commander could not have been put to better use in a different theater. Currie later wrote: "I recommended displacing Stilwell because I felt the truce I had fixed up was temporary and could not last. The recommendation of Wheeler was merely to smooth relations—not to get China to fight. It was Marshall who was naive on this point."[54]

Currie had also recommended the replacement of Ambassador Gauss but the State Department similarly resisted Currie's suggested alternatives, namely John Carter Vincent, Ben Cohen, or Owen Lattimore. Currie himself was suggested but, with the refusal to replace Stilwell, it was decided that Currie would not be a good choice either. Currie came to regard that as a narrow escape because he later considered that the fall of China to the Communists was inevitable. Those American diplomats and military advisers in the Chunking embassy, such as John Service, John Paton Davies, and John Carter Vincent, especially those who visited Mao Tse-tung and Chou En-lai in Yenan in 1944 and who, noting the high morale and organization they found there, urged that the United States and KMT forces cooperate more closely with the Communists, later suffered badly in the McCarthy witch-hunt for scapegoats to blame for the "loss" of China. Currie, despite having urged support for Chiang, was not immune. He was under a cloud of suspicion for some time, but no charges were ever brought against him.[55]

Nevertheless, with Stilwell remaining in China, hating Chiang, hating Chennault, hating Roosevelt, and hating the British for neglecting China and Burma, nothing improved in China and Currie grew increasingly disillusioned himself. In May 1943 he wrote to the President that Chiang's "position as probably the only leader of the various groups and cliques, both in and outside the army, is believed to be secure. His power to command and secure obedience, on the other hand, is severely circumscribed."[56]

The last part of this May 1943 memorandum is worth quoting in full for it reflects Currie's growing disenchantment with prospects for reform in China or for effective, coordinated operations against the Japanese. Also, however, he felt increasingly that the defeat of Japan did not depend crucially on American efforts from mainland China and, therefore, that America was in a strong bargaining position vis-à-vis the Nationalist government and should make its own, unpressured decisions as to what level of support was appropriate. The memorandum may have influenced Roosevelt's coolness toward Chiang when they met at the important Cairo Conference a few months later, in November.

> The men surrounding the Generalissimo and the groups in turn surrounding them are with few exceptions men jockeying and maneuvering for position, power and privileges. Many can hardly be characterized as honest, efficient or patriotic men. They are distrustful of Western democratic influence as tending to threaten their privileges. They want American military and financial aid but not American culture or ideas. On the other hand, they are even more distrustful of Russia, whom they accuse of giving moral support to the Chinese communists and whom they fear will give physical support in the future. These considerations give some clue to the current dominant anti-foreign, anti-communist lines in Chungking policy. The disproportionate amount of emphasis placed on the abolition of the unequal treaties arises partly out of a desire to conceal the absence of any posi-

Franklin D. Roosevelt with Chiang Kai-shek and Madame Chiang at the Cairo Conference, November 25, 1943. *Courtesy of the Franklin D. Roosevelt Library.*

tive reform program and partly out of a desire to stir up and keep alive the distrust of the Western powers and discredit their democratic pretensions.

Men like the Minister of War, the Minister of Education and the Head of the Secret Police must necessarily feel profound distrust of our policy and influence. It would be most unrealistic to expect their actions to be motivated in the slightest by any feelings of friendship for us or gratitude for what we may do. We do have genuine and admiring friends in China. These, however, are largely in the university faculties and lower ranks of the Bureaucracy, and the former are being gradually starved and demoralized.

The conclusion appears inescapable, therefore, that we are dealing with a large group of men who have definite interests with which they fear we may interfere, who have no particular affection for us, and who are determined to secure as much from us as possible while parting with as little as possible. If it were possible for us to win the war with no help from China and with no prejudice to China's ability to secure its war aims, and at the same time, strengthen the ability of the Kuomintang to perpetuate its power, resist reforms and suppress the Communists, this would constitute the ideal outcome from the Chinese Government's point of view.

Our national interest, on the other hand, would best be served by the maximum use of a united Chinese Army and people, by progress toward a more efficient, honest, democratic state, and by the avoidance of civil war.

Our Bargaining Position—The Chinese have in every way sought to create the impression that our bargaining position is weak. Basically this rests on the thesis, constantly repeated, that the Japs can be defeated only from operations from the mainland of Asia. We must, therefore, the argument runs, at any costs keep China in the war. From time to time the threat or warning of "collapse" or, in more veiled terms, the "defection of important elements to Wang Ching-wei" is made.

Actually the Chinese Government's bargaining position is quite weak and ours is strong. Chiang and the various party leaders have time and again and in numberless ways, shown that they share in our complete conviction of ultimate victory over Japan. To go over to the Japs would merely mean, in their eyes, going over to the losing side and leaving the future of China to the Chinese communists. In addition, of course, Kuomintang leaders look to America for billions of dollars in the post-war period while the Army, in particular, look to us for the airforce and industrial underpinning of an ordnance industry that will permit the suppression of the communists and will provide the requisite strength for the eventual clash with Russia they all expect. Moreover, both Chinese governmental and private cash balances (including those of Ministers) are in this country and would presumably be forfeit under certain conditions. Finally, it is not inconceivable that Japan can be defeated otherwise than from the mainland of Asia and it would do no harm to drop hints to this effect. It is inconceivable that Japan would be unbeatable if we had no allies on the mainland.

Some Possibilities.—The underlying factors sketched above obviously must enter into the determination of our Far Eastern military and political policies. Before, for example, completely committing ourselves to a defeat of Japan through China policy, we must assess the amount of help we may realistically expect from China (a) in retaking Burma, (b) in offensive action against Japanese forces, (c) in defensive action against Japanese attacks, (d) in organizing transportation in China. These, in turn, depend upon the full exploitation of our bargaining position in securing a revolutionary change in the will and ability of Chinese armies to fight. The dangers that must be faced are that certain elements in China will seek to secure the maximum in supplies while refraining from combat with the Japs; and that the building up of a powerful American airforce in China will induce the Japs to attack before a sufficiently strong ground force to defend airbases can be built up and trained. So long as advanced airbases and land forces

> have to be supplied from India, logistics will favor the Japanese. It may be taken for granted that before we are in a position to threaten Japan seriously from China the Japanese will make a supreme effort to destroy our base of operations.
>
> Another direction in which our bargaining position must be exploited fully is in the political and economic field.
>
> Neither the Government nor the Communist forces can be expected to make their full contribution to the war against Japan when they expect to have to engage in a war of extermination against each other. Moreover, such a war following or just preceding the defeat of Japan would be prejudicial if not for the preservation of the peace of the world certainly for the atmosphere in which a good peace can be contrived. There is grave danger that another Spain is in the making, where great powers line up in support of the different factions.
>
> The solution of these problems requires statesmanship of a high order on the part of America. No occasion should be lost to demonstrate our friendship for the Chinese people: with the Government, however, the efficacy of sentiment and friendship is limited. We must insist on certain things being done and, assured that our diagnosis of the situation is correct, be prepared to disregard threats and reproaches in the realistic pursuit of our interests. It will, in the long run, cost us little more to defeat Japan from the islands and sea than from the mainland. It will cost us nothing to withold financial aid in the post-war period. Our task will be enormously facilitated if the Chinese Government learns that we view the situation in this light and that our military and financial aid has a price. Unless we stick to that price, our aid will not serve the cause of the United Nations but will, on the contrary, be definitely harmful.

Meanwhile, Chennault, after much wrangling, agreed to serve under overall military command, was made a brigadier-general, and took command of the Fourteenth U.S. Air Force in China. His attacks on Japanese-held bases in the summer of 1943, however, resulted in heavy losses. Chennault blamed the inadequte ground defense of his air bases and insufficient planes. Chiang met Roosevelt at the Cairo Conference in November and angered the President by requesting an enormous increase in U.S. aid while again refusing to commit his forces to the Burma campaign.

Early in 1944 Roosevelt asked Currie to arrange for Vice President Henry Wallace, a good friend of Currie's, to make a trip to China. It seems that this suggestion was made by Roosevelt partly with domestic political considerations in mind in the run-up to the November presidential elections. Wallace needed a higher profile than he had

had recently if Roosevelt was to keep him as his running mate in the elections. Currie arranged for Owen Lattimore and John Carter Vincent, also good friends of Currie's and both brilliantly informed on Chinese affairs, to accompany Wallace.[57] Unfortunately, Wallace omitted to take a team of reporters with him, so for five crucial weeks he was out of the domestic limelight. There was even stronger political opposition to Wallace's nomination as running mate than there had been in 1940. Wallace did not return from China until just a few days before the Democratic Convention in July and Roosevelt was forced to agree to a new candidate.[58] The President's health was giving rise to concern and so the choice for Vice President was more than usually critical. It was Harry Truman who gained the nomination.

There has been considerable speculation as to Roosevelt's true attitude toward Wallace at this time. Currie recently sent the following recollections on the episode to the present writer in a memorandum dated February 16, 1989:

> One day, in early 1944, the President called me to his office to discuss an important matter. It concerned Vice-President Wallace. I was rarely consulted on political matters but this was an exception for two reasons. It was because I was on friendly terms with Wallace and I was supposed to be "an expert on China," and it concerned China. The President opened the conversation by saying that in the forthcoming Democratic Convention it was by no means certain that "Henry" would be renominated as Vice-President and that he (the President) was not in a position to insist on it. In a somewhat similar situation, a few years previously, Henry had made a trip through Latin America and had received much favorable publicity. The President was thinking that Wallace might do something similar with similar results by making, at this time, a trip to China where the political and military situation was very difficult. The President would like me to discuss the matter with Wallace and help him in any way I could in arrangements for the visit. I, of course, said I would be delighted to do so.
>
> In talking with Wallace, I found that he was very keen on the visit but wished to inclue Mongolia. If I had been more politically minded I would have said that nothing, politically, could be gained from Mongolia. Instead, I said that the best informed man I knew on Mongolia was Owen Lattimore, whom, in 1941, I had recommended as a "political" adviser to Chiang Kai-shek (but his was not the "political" advice that Chiang wanted). For the visit to Chungking I recommended John Carter Vincent as the most knowledgeable and objective person.
>
> I did not know that Wallace intended to make a lengthy visit unaccompanied by pressmen so that the President's purpose, at least ostensible pur-

> pose as stated to me, was ignored. At a highly critical point for Wallace's career (and for the country) Wallace disappeared completely from the public eye. As told in the biography of Vincent,[59] Wallace got an excellent grasp of the situation in China and insisted strongly to Chiang on the necessity of coming to some arrangement with the Chinese Communists, all of which might have served a highly useful purpose if Wallace became President, but helped him in no way to be nominated as Vice-President.
>
> It is possible, of course, that the President did not wish him to be his running mate again and was using me to get Wallace out of the way. But at least he did stress the possible publicity ends that might be served and it is a well established political observation that a Vice-President has difficulty building up favorable publicity. But again it can be said that if the President was concerned with the domestic political aspects of Wallace's trip, I was the wrong person to advise and help Wallace. The weight of opinion is that Roosevelt did not wish Wallace to be renominated but this is not what he indicated to me.
>
> Wallace's renomination and subsequent Presidency would have changed the course of history. Most probably the atomic bomb would not have been dropped on Japan and the Cold War would not have been so cold, at least in its earlier stages.

Wallace used his visit to China to urge Chiang to seek a negotiated settlement with the Communists and to insist that a team of American observers be allowed passage to Yenan. He reported to Roosevelt that "Chiang, at best, is a short-term investment. It is not believed that he has the intelligence or political strength to run post-war China. The leaders of post-war China will be brought forward by evolution or revolution and it now seems more like the latter."[60]

In July 1944 General Marshall was still determined to retain Stilwell and give him more authority. With the help of Secretary Stimson at the War Department he drafted a strong message to Chiang which Roosevelt was persuaded to sign—though he first moderated some of the language—asking that Stilwell be given command of all forces in China and press them into a major offensive against the Japanese.[61] This was followed by an even stronger message in September which particularly offended the Generalissimo because of the way that Stilwell chose to deliver it to him personally with undisguised pleasure.

In his diaries Stilwell wrote: "I handed this bundle of paprika to the Peanut and then sank back with a sigh. A harpoon hit the little bugger right in the solar plexus and went right through him . . . Beyond turning green and losing the power of speech he did not bat an eye. He said, "I understand," and put the cover on the teacup upside down to indicate the conversation was at an end." However, Pogue (1987, p. 46) noted: "Stilwell did not sense that more was ended than a meeting. He had miscalculated badly. It would be difficult for his friends in Washington to save him again. His diary entries, admittedly written only for the delight of his family and close friends, reveal not only the depths of his injured feelings but also an amazing insensitivity, which later made it almost impossible for his supporters to mount an effective defence of his actions."

Chiang was left with no alternative but to demand his withdrawal or lose all face. Events appeared to vindicate Currie's appraisal of two years earlier, that the peace he had patched up between Stilwell and Chiang could not last and that he should have been removed then to a different theater where his talents as a command officer could have been better deployed.

Meanwhile, Marshall and Stimson had also persuaded a reluctant President Roosevelt to appoint the Oklahoma Republican Major General Patrick Hurley as special envoy to smooth relations between Stilwell and the Generalissimo and, soon after, to replace Clarence Gauss as ambassador. According to Pogue (1987, p. 40), "Marshall was equally wrong in his appraisal of the new Ambassador when he told Stilwell, 'I am inclined to think that he could pour more oil on the troubled waters out there to your advantage than any other individual that may be selected.'" Hurley was present when Stilwell delivered Roosevelt's letter to the Generalissimo on September 19 and initially did all he could to support Stilwell. Though Chiang told him that same evening that he wanted Stilwell removed, Hurley's message to the President four days later concealed the true situation and spoke instead of Stilwell's willingness to compromise and of the Generalissimo's willingness to give him "field command of Ground and Air Forces and with it his complete confidence," indicating that "while the situation is difficult harmonious solution is possible."

Hurley also spoke of indications leading "toward harmony with the so-called Communist troops." He believed he could patch up differences between the Nationalist and Communist leaders and soon after flew to Yenan to seek an agreement with Mao. John Paton Davies records how Hurley astonished everyone when he emerged from his plane on landing in Yenan to meet the Communist leader. Standing stiffly to attention in his major general's uniform, a tall, six-foot-three figure with a bushy white moustache glistening in the sun, he gave forth a bloodcurdling Choctaw Indian war whoop.[62] After concluding an agreement with Mao he promptly reneged on it when the Nationalists protested at the relatively minor concessions Hurley had made. The career diplomats tried to send a message to Roosevelt to protest at Hurley's behavior. Enraged by this show of "disloyalty" the ambassador "Hurleyed" many of them out of China. By this time Roosevelt was too ill and preoccupied with the war in Europe to take much interest in China and Hurley remained there after Roosevelt's death in April 1945.

Notable among those who have criticized Currie for recommending continued support for Chiang and for recommending Stilwell's transfer are Barbara Tuchman and John Paton Davies. However, Tuchman eventually concluded that Stilwell's mission, supported by General Marshall, "failed in its ultimate purpose because the goal was unachievable. . . . The Kuomintang military structure could not be reformed without reform of the system from which it sprang and . . . to reform such a system 'it must be torn to pieces' . . . China was a problem for which there was no American solution."[63] Likewise, Davies concluded his story on Stilwell by conceding that

> the command crisis over Stilwell may be said to have been the inevitable result of two illusions. One was a romantic image of China. The second was an assumption that the United States could pretty much work its will on China. . . . Americans assumed in early 1942 that the Chinese would, in a spirit of cooperation and eagerness to learn, welcome tutelage, even though by a nation which until then had undergone nothing but humiliation in fighting the Japanese. Within the government it was realized that intrusion of American authority into Chinese internal affairs could be an exceedingly touchy business with a people who, for good reason, were hypersensitive about foreign intervention. But this was slighted because, after all, we were allies and the American Government could therefore take liberties with a wartime partner which in other circumstances would be impossible. Although Stalin quickly disposed of this assumption with regard to the Soviet Union, Washington persisted in it toward China.
>
> . . . The American people and government, with their fiery vision of Chiang and China, expected aggressive, can-do American military leadership in China. They got it in Stilwell. . . . The pity of it all was the waste.[64]

But these were precisely the attitudes that Currie had been so severely criticizing at the time and which motivated his much censured recommendation that Stilwell be withdrawn and replaced not by a man who would rage and fume at the Generalissimo for refusing to commit his armies to a major offensive, but by someone who could smooth relations and administer supplies efficiently, presumably because this would be the surest way of ensuring cooperation in tying down the Japanese, influencing the Chinese toward "a more efficient, honest, and democratic state," avoiding civil war, and preserving goodwill toward the United States in postwar China.

John Fairbank, after offering a sympathetic view of Stilwell as a top American combat commander who also knew China well, spoke the language and "got below the surface, as other Americans found it difficult to do," similarly conceded: "Stilwell's taking on the assignment to put a road and pipeline across northern Burma was a desperate attempt to accomplish something through American logistics which strategically turned out to be no use whatever since the war ended as the pipeline began to operate. The idea that Stilwell could command Chiang Kai-shek's armies was absolute moonshine and could only have led to multiple disaster if anyone had attempted to carry it out."[65]

But this is why Currie wanted Stilwell removed at an early stage. Joseph Alsop, a well-known journalist, friend of Chennault, and outspoken critic of Stilwell writes: "Currie was one of the enormous group of sensible persons who recommended the dismissal of General Stilwell. The truth is that hardly anyone failed to recommend the dismissal of General Stilwell—and here you may include President Roosevelt himself—except for General Stilwell's patron, General Marshall, General Stilwell himself, and the young Foreign Service officers whose program depended heavily on General Stilwell's authority."[66]

In the end Currie's involvement, or, indeed, that of other Americans in China probably made little difference to the course of Chinese history. It probably did little to shorten the war against Japan and may have diverted some resources from more important theaters. The Communists would in any event almost certainly have overthrown the Nationalists by 1949, if not sooner.

By 1943 Currie had come to agree with Churchill's view that China was now a relatively unimportant theater and became increasingly engaged in other concerns.

The Foreign Economic Administration, 1943–44

In July 1943 the Foreign Economic Administration, (FEA), nominally under the direction of Leo Crowley, was created to coordinate the activities of various disparate agencies operating in the foreign field. The FEA absorbed the work previously handled by the Board of Economic Warfare and also took over the civilian side of the lend-lease program.

Though nominally the head of FEA, Leo Crowley remained in his office at the Federal Deposit Insurance Corporation (FDIC) which he had previously directed. Currie was appointed deputy administrator of FEA in charge of policy matters and until the end of 1944 spent most of his time in the new FEA offices. He retained his office in the White House, however.[67] His initial tasks were to ensure unified and consistent policies of the agencies merged into the FEA and to work out a basis of proper working relationships with the State Department, so that foreign economic policy was conducted smoothly within the framework of overall foreign policy for which State was responsible.[68]

Civilian lend-lease occupied much time. Currie handled the negotiations that resulted in arresting the growth of British dollar reserves, at which some American opponents of lend-lease were protesting. This was achieved by strengthening the "reverse lend-lease" program so that the United States could acquire food and raw materials from the British Commonwealth without immediate dollar payments. This in turn made possible an increase in lend-lease supplies of greater use to the Allies and strengthened the overall lend-lease program.

Lord Keynes was the chief British negotiator on lend-lease as well as on plans for the post war stabilization fund that eventually emerged as the International Monetary Fund (IMF). In a letter to Sir Wilfred Eady, October 3, 1943, Keynes wrote:

> Under Crowley Lauchlin Currie is Administrator, which means that he is, so to speak, the senior civil servant in charge of all the operations of the Department under Crowley, who has what we should regard as Ministerial responsibility. The staff of OLLA under Knollenberg is undisturbed and it is not yet clear to me which of the various matters in which he might take a preliminary interest Currie will in fact concentrate on. Conceivably he will be content to leave OLLA mainly to Knollenberg. But conceivably he may not. If he does interest himself in it difficulties are likely to arise. Currie is an old friend of mine and I know him well, but there is no one more difficult to handle. He is extremely suspicious and jealous, very anti-British on such issues as India, and always inclined to assume the worst. He is not fundamentally unfriendly or unreasonable. But he is certainly one of the most difficult to be sure of. For example, if he were to take a strong line about the balances we might have a lot of trouble before he could be persuaded otherwise.[69]

Keynes was a doughty defender of British interests, but likewise Currie sought to negotiate agreements that were equitable to both sides without undermining U.S. interests unduly, for example, with respect to U.S. exports to commonwealth countries after the war.[70] Keynes, however, was exasperated whenever Currie put difficulties in his way, both in 1943 and again in late 1944 over Stage II negotiations. He was pleased when Oscar Cox took over lend-lease negotiations from Currie because Cox "is surely very much easier to deal with."[71] At one point, in November 1943, Keynes referred to Currie as a "small-minded official, decidedly of the second class" though "by no means without capacity."[72]

Part of Currie's brief, however, was to defend the controversial lend-lease program from scandal and political attack, which could soon have had an even more serious effect on Britain's interests. Keynes himself, in a letter to Sir John Anderson dated December 12, 1944, recorded:

> On my last day Lauchlin Currie, the civil service head of lend-lease, sought to explain and justify to me the difficulties he had been putting in our way, some of which he knew I had thought unnecessary, by showing me an issue of *The American*, a weekly of Mr Hearst's, about to appear with numerous charges of alleged lend-lease abuses without a vestige of foundation, of a character which we should no more ask than the Americans would concede. This only shows, I replied, how vain it is to protect yourself by refusing reasonable measures when the grounds on which you are attacked invariably relate to alleged crude acts of quite a different order which neither you nor we have ever contemplated; to which he rejoined that the Lend-lease Administration had survived unscathed so far precisely because it had been able to show that every plausible charge made against it was based on falsehood. Shortly before, I may add, in a nation-wide radio address during the campaign, Mr Dewey himself had gone out of his way to denounce Mr Currie by name as a cryptocommunist who had been investigated by the Dies Committee, contrary to the facts and without a vestige of evidence, on no better ground than that he had been one of the original group of New Dealers, whose services the President had always retained, and was also believed to be an intimate of the Vice-President, Mr Wallace. I often had to complain, as a consequence of all this, that I was turned down not only when there was a good reason, but also, just as likely, for a reason which everyone admitted to be bad; and that it was hard luck to be caught both ways.[73]

The Phase II lend-lease agreements were to have provided for continuance of lend-lease to Britain after the war, in the form of substantial credits from the Export-Import Bank, sufficient to maintain U.S. exports at their wartime level and thus maintain output and employment. To Currie's great disappointment, however, Leo Crowley and Secretary Morgenthau, anxious as ever to uphold the virtues of sound finance, supported Secretary of State James Byrnes's decision to terminate the lend-lease program as soon as Germany surrendered. It was also disappointing that the postwar Marshall Plan for Europe was least generous in its treatment of Britain.

As the tide of war turned decisively in favor of the Allies, areas of Italy, Greece, Yugoslavia, and France were liberated. Ensuring that certain essential civilian requirements were made available for these liberated areas became another important task for the FEA.

U.S. aid to liberated Italy was a particularly controversial subject. Currie was one of the leading advocates of greater assistance and the entension of the lend-lease program for the immediate reconstruction of the Italian economy. He told Treasury Secretary Morgenthau and Under-secretary Daniel Bell: "I think it is in our interests . . . to get that economy self-sufficing and operating again as soon as possible, otherwise we will have to carry those people indefinitely."[74]

There was much opposition in America and Britain to helping the Italians but Currie's approach was in line with Roosevelt's instincts. Also, Roosevelt was anxious to win Italian votes in the forthcoming Presidential elections. Nevertheless, according to Miller, the belief that America could limit its aid to short-term humanitarian relief dominated policymaking until late 1946, "with results that were nearly disastrous for American interests" because of the growing Communist threat in Italy.[75] In October 1944 Hopkins and Currie were again "twisting many arms" in the War Department and the War Shipping Administration to ensure that the bureaucracy delivered on the President's commitments.[76]

At the FEA Currie was also involved in the preparation of plans for economic controls to be imposed later on Germany by the Allied Occupation Forces (though he was not involved in the policies actually adopted later at the instigation of Secretary Morgenthau and others, which Currie opposed). Much preparatory work was also done in planning how German assets concealed abroad might be ascertained and secured. This was one of the subjects negotiated by Currie with the Swiss government in Bern in early 1945.

Other work concerned export licensing and import procurement (preclusive buying) policy. At one time Currie was the largest purchaser of duck feathers in the world (from China); and he took the initiative in clearing up a long-standing problem with the importation of crystal quartz (mica, a highly strategic material) from Brazil. The FEA also worked with General William Donovan, head of the Office of Strategic Services, in helping select strategic targets for bombing raids.[77]

Lastly, but very importantly, another aspect of economic warfare involved increasing pressure on the neutral countries as the allied military position improved. Under Currie's direction the FEA took the lead in exacting important concessions from Sweden in first reducing substantially and later eliminating completely the shipment of ball-bearings to Germany.[78] The FEA pressed consistently for a more stringent policy with regard to Argentina, and by late 1944 was also advocating a hard line on Switzerland. In general the FEA, supported strongly by the under-secretary of war, Judge Robert P. Patterson, naturally urged a harder line toward the neutrals than did State Department officials concerned with the broader foreign policy picture.

The Bern Conference, February–March 1945

After November 1942, with France completely occupied by German troops, Switzerland was surrounded by Axis forces and so had little choice but to obtain basic supplies, especially coal, from Axis sources. In exchange Switzerland supplied electricity, gave safe haven to German deposits in Swiss banks, and allowed transshipments of goods (but not troops or military stores) by rail between Germany, Italy, and France across Swiss territory.

Generally the British had been more sympathetic than the Americans toward the difficulties the Swiss faced and toward their traditional position on neutrality. In America, however, the State Department tended to prefer a softer approach than that adopted by the War Department, the FEA, and the Treasury—which had frozen Swiss assets in the United States when the Swiss refused to identify their owners.[79] Switzerland resisted many of the demands made on them to reduce their relations with the Axis powers.

By late 1944, however, with France liberated Switzerland was no longer so dependent on Germany for supplies and the Allies' bargaining power increased as it became evident they would win the war. This would put them in a position to impose postwar economic sanctions on the Swiss if they failed to cooperate now. Furthermore, at Bretton Woods in July the Allies had adopted Resolution VI which called on the governments of neutral countries to uncover and hold all assets owned or looted by the enemy and eventually to surrender them to the post-liberation authorities.

In January 1945 President Roosevelt appointed Currie to head the U.S. delegation to negotiate with the Swiss government in Bern. He took with him Orvis Schmidt, a U.S. Treasury official (for whose work in Bern Currie had the highest praise[80]), John Lovitt of the State Department who had been working in London with the British on policy toward the Swiss, and David L. Gordon.[81] British and French representatives, led by Dingle Foot and M. Chargucread, also joined the mission to Switzerland.[82]

Currie carried with him to the President of the Swiss Confederation, Eduard von Steiger, a letter from President Roosevelt that Currie had drafted. It stated succinctly the issues for negotiation:

> We have respected the traditional neutrality of your country and have sympathized with the past difficulties of your position. We forebore pressing our demands when you were isolated by our enemy and were in no position to do other than carry on a large trade with him. We are now in a better position to meet your most urgent needs and defend your liberties if they are threatened. I know in these circumstances that you will be eager to deprive the Nazis of any further assistance. It would indeed be a trial to any freedom-loving Swiss to feel that he had in any way impeded the efforts of other freedom-loving countries to rid the world of a ruthless tyrant. . . .
>
> I hope also that you will lend every assistance to our efforts in the postwar period to track down and seize the property of our foe.

Currie told the Swiss that the U.S. government was prepared to be very liberal toward Swiss requests for supplies through France, especially coal, if the Swiss would drastically curtail their cooperation with Germany and northern Italy.

Faced with a mixture of threats and promises, the Swiss agreed to most of the Allies' demands. If the Allies would provide coal this would greatly lessen Switzerland's dependence on Germany. In the middle of the negotiations, however, General Bedell Smith, chief-of-staff to General Eisenhower, suddenly canceled a previous offer to cooperate on coal shipments to Switzerland. Bedell Smith was furious at the idea of helping the Swiss because of their collaboration with the Germans. Currie immediately rushed by train from Bern to Versailles to get the offer restored, emphasizing the importance of the concessions the Swiss were making and reminding the general of the refuge enjoyed by American airmen who had parachuted into Switzerland and of the support of the Red Cross to prisoners in Germany.

Another embarrassment that threatened the progress of the negotiations arose when some stray Allied bombs fell on Swiss territory, with loss of Swiss lives and property. Currie sent an urgent wire to Roosevelt, then in Yalta, to appeal for a halt to bombing operations near the Swiss border. There were no further incidents.

Apart from coal the only other important commodity the Germans could offer Switzerland was gold. Currie was most insistent that Switzerland should stop accepting gold from Germany. Perhaps not surprisingly, from a nation of bankers, he encountered greatest resistance to this suggestion. He did eventually secure agreement, but the problem of holdings in Switzerland of looted gold was to involve difficult negotiations long after the war was over, when the Swiss were able to secure an agreement very favorable to themselves.[83]

On his return to Washington, Secretary Morgenthau congratulated Currie: ". . . you have not only thwarted the Nazis' plan for using Switzerland as a financial hideout, but also have laid the basis for the Allied Military Government in Germany to take control of German assets in Switzerland. Of all the wartime negotiations with neutral countries with which I am familiar, I consider that this one has been conducted most ably and has yielded the largest wartime and postwar results."[84]

Peace Terms

Related issues concerning postwar dealings with Germany may be noted in connection with Currie's active interest during and after the war in the work of the Council on Foreign Relations. In 1943 he had debated the question of postwar reparations with Alvin Hansen who, with Jacob Viner, had shared the chairmanship of the council's economic and financial group. Hansen "thought it was generally agreed that the experience of the last war was conclusive and that reparations were an impossible and harmful device." He worried that the demand for reparations would buoy up the German economy, expand its plant capacity and sustain its exports while depressing the economies of the countries taking reparations. Currie, however, "thought this argument should not be pushed too far. After all, if one believes that there is some good to be had from importing foreign products in the course of international trade, there is surely some benefit in importing the same goods without charge."[85]

Nevertheless, toward the end of the war, in meetings chaired by Larry Duggan in the State Department to draft possible peace terms, Currie very much supported a plan under which Germany would be admitted to the family of nations in good standing after a relatively short period of five to seven years of reparation payments. It was aimed at avoiding revanche and the mistakes of the Versailles Treaty so that democratic forces in Germany would be strengthened and nazism repudiated. Incidentally, in March 1945, while the guest of John Maynard Keynes in Cambridge, England, Currie had been urged by Keynes to impress on Roosevelt the dangers for Britain's competitive position in the world if the Soviet Union first stripped Germany of its manufacturing equipment and then the United States replaced it with new and modern equipment.

In the event Currie was unable to have any influence on U.S. policy toward either Britain or Germany when the war ended. He was disappointed at the way that Leo Crowley and Oscar Cox (who had replaced Currie at FEA in November 1944) appeared to support Secretary Byrnes's proposal for immediate termination of lend-lease to Britain. As for Germany, the preliminary plan drawn up by Duggan's committee was overtaken by the extremely harsh Morgenthau Plan for the "pastoralization" of Germany. At Yalta, Roosevelt supported Morgenthau's views which on this occasion fatefully coincided with those of Stalin. After Roosevelt's death, however, Truman adopted a different approach, that of the cold war, in which Germany was seen as a bulwark against communism. Thus, under the Marshall Plan Germany would be treated much more generously than Britain, and the fear that Keynes had expressed proved well founded.

CHAPTER 5

Postwar America and the McCarthy Period, 1945–54

The War Ends

On April 12, 1945, Franklin Delano Roosevelt died in Warm Springs and the presidency passed to Harry Truman. The war in Europe ended a few days later and in August the war against Japan was also over. Currie remained at the White House for a few weeks until Truman had selected his own candidates for administrative assistants.

With the Japanese removed from China civil war had flared up between the Nationalists and the Communists. As the Communists swept to their inevitable victory the ugly witch-hunt for scapegoats began in the United States. A purge of suspected communists and "fellow-travelers," often identified on the flimsiest of evidence or the flimsiest of association, was launched, first by Patrick Hurley and later by Senator Joseph McCarthy. Life was particularly unpleasant for those blamed for having "lost" China. Finding posts in government or in good universities was not easy for Currie and he moved to New York to establish Lauchlin Currie and Co., engaged in consultancy and the export-import business. Over the next three years he nearly made a fortune several times. But each time the fortune slipped from his grasp at the last moment. Among numerous projects he negotiated—some successfully, others falling through because of a failure to secure an export license or for other reasons—were the planning and supply of equipment for a bicycle plant in Shanghai (stopped by Mao's Communists when they took over), low-cost housing and a match factory in Argentina, a tire plant in Czechoslovakia (stopped by the Russians), and oxygen tanks for Mexico. He traveled widely to Europe and South America in connection with this business.

However, his heart was never fully in the business or in New York. He maintained his contacts in Washington, mainly through the National Planning Association, a private body established in the early

1940s to promote acceptance of Keynesian fiscal policies. Its members included many of Currie's friends such as Gerhard Colm, Robert Nathan, Isador Lubin, Leon Henderson, Mordecai Ezekiel, and Thomas Blaisdell. He also kept in touch with the Council on Foreign Relations, whose meetings he had attended during the war.

He was also on the board of the Council for Italian American Affairs, which was organized in 1945 to inform Americans about Italy's desperate economic and political plight and lobby for action to meet the crisis. The board's executive director was Alan Cranston and other members included Allen W. Dulles, Sumner Welles, and New York's new mayor, William O'Dwyer. The council tried, initially with little success, to persuade the Truman administration to conclude a nonpunitive peace treaty with the Italians and to increase U.S. aid substantially. The lobby worked closely with Ambassador Tarchiani, generally supported the political and economic objectives of the Italian government and, despite much friction with the Truman administration, later threw its weight behind the administration's interventions in Italy to support de Gasperi's fight against the threatened Communist takeover in 1947–48.[1]

Another interest outside of the business of making a living from exporting and importing was his association with the William Alanson White Institute of Psychiatry whose headquarters were in Washington. Currie had met America's leading psychoanalyst, Harry Stack Sullivan, during the war when Sullivan requested (unsuccessfully) Currie's support for his proposal to visit England to study the psychological effects of the blitz on Londoners.[2] They developed a friendship and Currie attended the meetings of the Institute of Psychiatry, later becoming a member of the Board of Trustees. Later he also attended the meetings of the institute's New York branch, where he was acquainted with Erich Fromm.

Toward the end of the war, when Currie was serving on a State Department committee drawing up recommendations for peace terms to be imposed on the Germans, Currie invited Harry Stack Sullivan to offer his suggestions. He thought it would help to have the views of a leading psychiatrist, who may have been capable of a relatively dispassionate approach to the issues, to counterbalance the extremely hard line being pushed by Henry Morgenthau and Harry White. Currie was looking for support for his own view that it was important to keep separate one's hatred of Nazism from one's attitude to the Germans as a people. However, to his consternation he found that

Sullivan's response was as bitterly emotional as Morgenthau's; and so ended that little overture.

Harry Dexter White, Owen Lattimore, and the McCarthy Era

In 1946 the International Monetary Fund and the International Bank for Reconstruction and Development opened their doors to business. These institutions had emerged from the 1944 Bretton Woods Conference that had been so brilliantly organized by Currie's friend at the Treasury, Harry Dexter White. In 1949 Currie was to be appointed by the World Bank to organize and direct a comprehensive economic and social survey of Colombia. In separate sessions held on August 13, however, both Currie and White had made voluntary appearances, at their own request, before the House Committee on Un-American Activities (HUAC) to testify their loyalty to the United States and strenuously to deny the sensational allegations or insinuations made by Miss Elizabeth Bentley and Whittaker Chambers before that same committee some days earlier, that they had been sources of information for a Communist spy ring working for the Soviets.

Bentley and Chambers were both self-confessed former agents for the Soviets and they produced independently two lists of names of persons they knew or believed were Communists, Communist sympathizers or, in Currie's case, as asserted by Elizabeth Bentley, as someone who, perhaps unwittingly—she did not know—had passed on information to Soviet agents, but who was not a Communist himself. (Later she testified that she thought he was a Communist.[3])

Unlike many of the persons named, Currie and White volunteered to appear before HUAC and did not plead the Fifth Amendment. White's testimony before the committee began with a denial that he had ever been a Communist and with the presentation of an eloquent defense of democratic, pluralist ideals. The statement of his creed and the celebrated series of blunt exchanges between him and Congressman Richard Nixon drew applause from the audience.[4] As is well known, HUAC hearings were conducted in an extremely belligerent and prejudicial manner, particularly during the period from 1948 through 1954 when the air was heavy with suspicion and fear.

The chief protagonist, Senator Joseph McCarthy, was to become notorious for his smear tactics and blunderbuss approach to the Communist menace, relying heavily on hearsay, guilt by association, the "evidence" of anonymous accusers, the technique of the "big lie," and extraordinary bullying. Equally notorious, however, was J. Parnell Thomas, chairman of HUAC in 1948. Robert Carr has graphically described the extreme vulgarity of his character: "Again and again Thomas conducted committee hearings as though he were a cheap comedian or a participant in a street-corner political harangue. . . . It is clear that he hated the New Deal and all its works with every fiber of his being and that he welcomed every opportunity that came to the committee to discredit the Roosevelt-Truman program by discrediting its supporters."[5] When Harry White was giving evidence Chairman Thomas interrupted to make gratuitous remarks about how, for a man who was supposed to be suffering from a heart condition (White had earlier given him a note requesting a short break at the end of each hour of the proceedings), he seemed to be very fond of playing sports. Three days later White's heart condition killed him.

A few months later, on December 20, 1948, another committee member, Karl E. Mundt, caused embarrassment even to his own supporters, including Congressman Nixon, with the remarks he made immediately following the mysterious death of Larry Duggan, former high official at the State Department and now director of the Institute of International Education and a friend of Currie's, who had fallen from the sixteenth floor of his office building in New York ten days after the FBI had been questioning him on his loyalty.[6]

Mundt revealed that Isaac Donald Levine (Whittaker Chambers's nephew, in whose house Chambers claimed he had hidden the famous documents that were to lead to the conviction of Alger Hiss for perjury) had testified in a closed hearing two weeks earlier that Duggan was a member of a six-man Communist conspiracy whose names had been given by Chambers in 1939 to Adolph Berle, assistant secretary of state, in the hope of gaining immunity from prosecution for his previous activities. Levine had been present at the meeting with Berle and had later made a note of the names from memory. They included that of "Lockwood Curry."[7] However, at that time Mundt released to the press only that part of the transcript in which Levine had revealed Duggan's name. When asked when he would reveal the other five names, Mundt quipped, "We will give them out as they jump out of windows." Following a heated public controversy over the manner in which the FBI had intervened in the case, on December 24 the U.S. attorney general announced: "The FBI investigation has produced no evidence of Mr. Duggan's connection with the Communist Party or with any other espionage activity. On the contrary, the evidence discloses that Mr. Duggan was a loyal employee of the United States Government." Whittaker Chambers himself also issued a statement denying he had named Duggan as one of those who had passed State Department papers to him in the 1930s, but he did not repudiate all of his insinuations.

Regarding another committee member, John Rankin, Carr remarked that it was difficult to know whether to dismiss him as a cruel but meaningless joke in the annals of the committee, or to take him seriously. He was "incredibly prejudiced" and "capable of flying into towering rages in which he bullied witnesses and made dire threats against them."[8] However, Carr (p. 224) also recorded that Rankin seemed to have a tender spot for Scotchmen and grew angry at the attack upon Lauchlin Currie by Elizabeth Bentley:

> You certainly have an unlimited credibility. If you would take the word of any Communist, Silverman or Silvermaster, or both of them, and I believe you named another one, whom you relayed it through, who was also a Communist, if you take that testimony as to what this man Currie, as I said, a Scotchman, has said about the Communists—it just looks to me as if we have gone pretty far afield here to smear this man by remote control, instead of getting someone who heard him or who knew that he had made any statement.

Elizabeth Bentley had claimed that Currie was connected in some way with one of two alleged espionage rings in Washington, headed by Victor Perlo and Nathan Gregory Silvermaster, both economists working in the government during the war. Currie had known Silvermaster since 1940, initially in connection with a request by President Roosevelt that Currie investigate an alleged mutiny on an American merchant ship (which actually turned out to be a peaceful one-day strike in port). Silvermaster was director of research at the Maritime Labor Board and was sent by the chairman of the board to hand relevant material to Currie at the White House. Currie in his unpublished memoirs (1953, p. 151) noted: "Silvermaster appeared to be an ardent New Dealer and we found that we had some mutual friends. I had no further official contact with him but we saw something of each other socially."

When the Office of Naval Intelligence objected to Silvermaster taking up a new post at the Board of Economic Warfare (BEW) in 1942 on the grounds he was a Communist, the board asked Currie, who was acting as liaison between the White House and BEW, to intervene in the matter. Currie referred it to the under-secretary of war, Judge Robert Patterson, for his review. The subsequent investigations carried out by Judge Patterson and Major General Strong of military intelligence resulted in the charges being withdrawn. According to Elizabeth Bentley's hearsay testimony it was Silvermaster, not the BEW, who asked Currie "to intervene in his behalf."[9] Later Currie's version of events was supported by the letter that came to light addressed by Judge Patterson directly to Milo Perkins of BEW, and this was inserted in the records.

Both Currie and Harry White knew Silvermaster socially and both were asked whether they had been in the famous basement where Silvermaster was alleged to have kept equipment for making photographic copies of secret documents to be passed to Soviet agents. It was White's admission that he had played ping-pong there that provoked Chairman Thomas's deprecatory remarks about the fondness for sports of a supposedly ill person.

Among the other persons named by Bentley and Chambers the most prominent was Alger Hiss. Hiss did not invoke the Fifth Amendment when he appeared before the committee, but the statements he made under oath were eventually to lead to a five-year jail sentence for perjury after Chambers's sensational revelation, in December 1948, of copies of government documents, typed on Hiss's typewriter, that were held to demonstrate that Hiss had been meeting Chambers as late as 1938, which Hiss had denied, presumably to pass on these papers.

At the same time, three months after White's death, Chambers also produced a four-page penciled memorandum in White's handwriting which, he claimed, was passed to him by White in 1938 as part of a regular stream of such documents containing sensitive material to be passed to the Russians. This was the first time that it had been suggested that White had been a spy. The evidence in White's case was far from conclusive, there being no proof that Chambers obtained this memorandum from White himself, and questions were raised as to why Chambers had not revealed White's involvement years earlier when, having broken with the Communists, he first gave names to Adolph Berle.

The Hiss case breathed life into HUAC and Senator McCarthy pursued his investigations with increasing vigor. In February 1950 the

Tydings Committee (a subcommittee of the Senate Committee on Foreign Relations) was set up to investigate disloyalty in the State Department. McCarthy, protected by legal immunity on the floor of the Senate, accused Owen Lattimore of being "the top Soviet espionage agent." Lattimore immediately returned from Afghanistan to fight these charges and was cleared by the Tydings Committee.[10] But McCarthy sustained his attack, eventually securing formal charges against Lattimore on various perjury counts (including one relating to his use of Currie's office in the White House upon his return from China in 1942) through another body, the McCarran Committee, which was set up by the Senate in December 1950 to investigate internal security and in particular the affairs of the Institute of Pacific Relations with which Lattimore had been connected for many years. Lattimore appealed and in 1955 was cleared on all counts.

These proceedings brought Currie's name back into the limelight in connection with allegations of disloyalty and espionage that he thought had been disposed of in 1948. The atmosphere in 1950 was even more charged than in 1948 because of the Communist victory in China in 1949 and the onset of the Korean War. The "China Lobby," led by Alfred Kohlberg, was placing the blame on errors made by State Department officials and others concerned with China policy in the past decade, notably Currie's friend John Carter Vincent,[11] and many were accused of disloyalty and with promoting the cause of Chinese Communists.

Currie, as a major player in Chinese affairs during the war against Japan, was a prime target and he appeared before another grand jury in Washington in 1953—where he faced rough questioning from the notoriously rough Roy Cohn—to deny all charges. The purpose of such juries is to determine whether the prosecution (or the FBI) has sufficient evidence on which to justify a trial. Though his name had cropped up many times, mainly because he had known several people who were being accused of communism or espionage, in both cases the jury declared there was no case for a trial. Nevertheless, it was a bitterly painful period, at a time when he was carrying a heavy load of work and responsibility in Colombia in connection with his World Bank mission (which presented its report in September 1950) and the subsequent implementation of its recommendations. His first marriage was also breaking up at this time, and one of his main anxieties was the effect that the damage to his own reputation might have on the careers of his two sons in the United States.

He was forced to clear up a number of questions. Firstly, why did he recommend Owen Lattimore to be Chiang Kai-shek's political adviser in 1941? His answer was that he had not known Lattimore previously and could not recall who first suggested his name, though he had himself first written to Ambassador Messersmith in Cuba enquiring of Messersmith's interest and availability for the post.[12] It is possible that the suggestion of Lattimore's name first came to Currie from the President himself,[13] who in any case asked Currie to get the reaction to Lattimore from Admiral Yarnell and President Isaiah Bowman of Johns Hopkins, a personal friend of the President. Their reactions, conveyed to the President on May 6, were both very favorable. Currie himself interviewed Lattimore around the same time and reported favorably to the effect that he thought Lattimore shared the broad political philosophy of the President.

Roosevelt decided to nominate Lattimore and asked Currie to clear it with Secretary Hull. Currie's recollection was that Hull did not relish the idea of an American political adviser to Chiang Kai-shek but did not feel strongly enough about it to raise objections. Stanley Hornbeck of the State Department later testified (McCarran Committee Hearings, p. 3209) that Hull did object but Currie's recollection differs from Hornbeck's. He and Hornbeck together drafted the cable that was sent to the Generalissimo on May 29, as being from Currie. Hornbeck told the McCarran Committee (p. 3210) that he "expressed doubt whether the nomination of Mr. Lattimore was a suitable nomination," but that Currie had replied that "there could be no reconsideration inasmuch as the nomination had already been sent to Chiang Kai-shek." Currie stated in a letter to Sumner Welles, January 7, 1953, that Hornbeck's memory was at fault here as the record shows that he participated in the drafting of the cable of notification to Chiang sent May 29, 1941, and that the State Department did have ample opportunity to object to the President, something which Hornbeck seems to have been denying before the McCarran Committee.[14]

At these hearings it was suggested that Lattimore's cable to Currie on November 25, 1941, conveying Chiang Kai-shek's fierce opposition to a modus vivendi with Japan, may have been intercepted by the Japanese and so may have precipitated Pearl Harbor, a result fervently desired by the Russians. Hence, evidence of pro-Soviet activity on Lattimore's part, hence maybe on Currie's part also. That the Japanese fleet had by then already set sail for Pearl Harbor, and that America's entry into the war was also fervently desired by Chiang Kai-shek and Churchill, was conveniently ignored by Lattimore's detractors.

Such, generally, was the nature of the allegations or innuendos leveled against Currie: guilt by association with a small number of persons who were either shown to be Communists or alleged to be sympathizers and fellow travelers, without taking Currie's record as a whole. It was Currie's contention, expressed in his statement to Senator McCarran, that to "concentrate attention on one or two incidents or relationships may easily lead to a totally wrong impression of my work, interests and motivations. When such incidents or relationships are brought into focus by relating them to my total work, there is less danger of drawing misleading inferences."

Nevertheless, Goodman, for example, may be justified in his critical judgment that Currie had a "sneaking respect for the Communists around him" that was inappropriate for a person in his position, though Goodman here uses the term "Communist" rather loosely and prejudicially.[15] In a letter to a lawyer friend, Richard H. Wels, February 14, 1951, Currie admitted: "In view of the current atmosphere, I was probably too accessible and not sufficiently circumspect. However, I certainly had no idea then of what the world would be like today. As you remember, in the early days the New Deal was in the nature of a Crusade and New Dealers felt a strong sense of comraderie. Later we were all united in pushing along with the War. The atmosphere of suspicion and caution only arose after I left the Government."

Some of the allegations raised against Currie at this time seem merely preposterous, such as that by Freda Utley that after VE Day Currie had overruled the joint chiefs-of-staff and turned back a boatload of captured German munitions destined for China, and that the guns instead ended up with the Russians.[16] At that time Currie was not in the government, and was never in a position to overrule the joint chiefs-of-staff.

Likewise, another ex-Communist, Louis Budenz, told the McCarran Committee (p. 594) that Earl Browder, the secretary-general of the Communist Party of the United States, had told him (Budenz) that Currie had helped him (Browder) prepare a statement in 1942 that attacked "very sharply the reactionary clique in the State Department which was favoring Chiang Kai-shek and injuring the Chinese Communists." In his personal notes prepared for the committee Currie responded angrily:

This monstrous story is patently false. Here is a charge of the gravest kind of a conspiracy between the head of the Communist Party in the United States and an Administrative Assistant to President Roosevelt never before mentioned by Budenz in his thousands of hours of testimony to the F.B.I., to Congressional Committees or in his publications. Such a relationship was presumably of so little importance that Budenz says that Browder remarked of it "incidentally"! May we now expect Budenz to "remember" other conspiracies between Browder and Currie? Surely, there could not have been just this one!

The actual facts of the case, and my sole connection with it, are as follows: In early October of 1942 I was present when Mr. Sumner Welles called on President Roosevelt. . . . I remember very well Mr. Welles telling the President that Browder had publicly accused the State Department of advising Chiang Kai-shek to keep some 1,000,000 of troops to blockade the Communists and prevent them from fighting the Japs. This was the first I had heard of the charge. In view of the Administration's policy of encouraging a united resistance to Japan in China, Mr. Welles felt that it was worth while to attempt to secure a public retraction from Mr. Browder. President Roosevelt concurred. Mr. Welles then asked the President if I might be present as I had recently returned from China and could attest to the Department's policy there. The President also agreed to this request.

Mr. Welles thereupon asked Mr. Browder to come to see him in Washington and when he did so asked me to attend a meeting in his office. We had no prior consultation on this meeting and I had no part in the preparation of a statement Mr. Welles read to Messrs. Browder and Minor. My part in the meeting was confined to a few remarks to the effect that I could attest that the Department's policy was one of encouraging united resistance in China to Japan. Mr. Browder then confessed that he had no specific information and would accept our word. He further agreed, in answer to a specific request by Mr. Welles, to retract his charges publicly, which he subsequently did. This was the first and last occasion I met Mr. Browder. It was the only time I ever consciously met a member of the American Communist Party. I am confident that Mr. Welles will recall that I took no initiative of any kind in the episode.

In a letter to Currie dated January 24, 1953, Sumner Welles affirmed Currie's recollections of this incident, except that Welles stated that he believed it was someone else in the White House who initiated the meeting, not Currie or Welles.

Budenz had made similar grave accusations against John Carter Vincent to the McCarran Committee in August 1951. Budenz, who began his "revelations" to the FBI in 1946, now "remembered" that he had "heard in official Communist Party circles that John Carter Vincent and Owen Lattimore were members of the Communist Party traveling with Henry Wallace" to China in 1944 and that they could be relied on to guide Wallace along Communist Party lines.[17]

Such allegations were damaging also to Currie as he had been responsible for arranging the Wallace trip and had recommended that Vincent and Lattimore accompany the Vice President. In writing of this episode Gary May has noted that "the more Budenz accused, the more popular and wealthy a public figure he became: By 1953, his activities as anti-government polemicist, lecturer and congressional witness were earning him seventy thousand dollars a year," thanks partly to the patronage of Alfred Kohlberg, millionaire businessman and publisher.[18]

Joseph Alsop, by now one of America's most respected journalists, examined Budenz's charges in his syndicated newspaper columns. Referring to the "K'un-ming cable" which Wallace had drafted in 1944 with the help of Vincent and Alsop, and which recommended the replacement of General Stilwell by Albert C. Wedermeyer, an officer more acceptable to Chiang Kai-shek (and later a prominent Republican ally of Kohlberg and McCarthy), Alsop argued that since Stilwell despised the Nationalists and admired the martial skills of the Communists, his removal was "one of the really striking and decisive anti-Communist acts of the war." Alsop asked why Budenz had refused to state in 1950 before the Tydings Committee that Vincent was a Communist whereas now he was confidently doing so, and on this basis concluded that he should be brought to trial for perjury.

Wallace came to the support of Alsop and Vincent by asking President Truman to release the text of the K'un-ming cable and claimed that "if my recommendation had been followed when made, the generalissimo would have avoided the disasters resulting from the Japanese offensive in East China later that summer. And if Chiang's government had thus been spared the terrible enfeeblement resulting from these disasters, the chances are good the generalissimo would have been ruling China today."[19]

However, Vincent's own view of developments—and Currie has expressed a similar opinion—was that "there never was a time when we could have saved China for Chiang Kai-shek without going into the country with a large army and literally establishing a protectorate. The historical tragedy is that the rise of Communism coincided with the complete deterioration of the Nationalist Government. Revolution there would have been. We tried to make it a liberal one, but the odds were against it."

There was little the United States could do to promote reform if the Kuomintang leaders were themselves unwilling to make the changes that might have boosted their popularity vis-à-vis the Communists. Currie's official involvement was confined to the war years, including the period leading up to Pearl Harbor. During the war Roosevelt's policy—to promote which was the responsibilty of the State Department, the foreign service officers in Chungking, and Lauchlin Currie in his capacity as lend-lease administrator—was naturally based mainly on what was in the best interests of the United States and the Allied war effort. This meant doing whatever would keep the Chinese in the war against the common enemy.

The promotion of internal reform would no doubt have been useful in accomplishing these ends, since reform could have helped avert civil war and brought the Nationalists and Communists into closer collaboration in fighting the Japanese. But for the United States these domestic reform objectives were secondary. If Chiang was unwilling or unable to achieve these reforms then, nevertheless, so long as he remained the undisputed leader of the bulk of the Chinese people—and in 1941 even Chou En-lai told Currie that this was the case—it still made sense for the United States to support him for as long as the joint war effort against the Japanese was vital to U.S. interests.

After the war General Marshall came to share the view of John Carter Vincent and others that there was relatively little the United States could do to force reform on the Kuomintang regime. When he was first sent to China as President Truman's special envoy in December 1945 he was confident he could exert an influence, prevent civil war, and strengthen the Nationalists against the Communists. But when finally he left China in January 1947 he left "tired, angry and frustrated but more knowledgeable about Chiang Kai-shek and the Kuomintang than when he had first arrived. . . . (His) effort to end the Chinese civil war failed, but in the process the general attained something more important than success: an understanding of Chinese politics and an appreciation of America's limited ability to resolve China's complex economic and political problems. This was the great achievement of the Marshall mission."[20]

Other Americans who had reached this conclusion rather earlier than the general were made scapegoats for the "loss" of China. Marshall himself was not immune from attack. In June 1950 Senator

McCarthy insinuated in a Senate speech that Marshall was part of "a conspiracy so immense and an infamy so black as to dwarf any previous such adventure in the history of man."[21] However, the attack on Marshall was not sustained and McCarthy shrewdly concentrated on easier targets.

For Currie there were many other questions to face pertaining to his relations with people connected with Chinese affairs. Why, for example, had he been friendly with Edward C. Carter, secretary-general of the Institute of Pacific Relations (IPR) which was alleged to have been a front for Communist propaganda? And why had he attended two IPR conferences, helping to select speakers at one of them?

The letter, already cited, from Currie to his lawyer friend Richard H. Wels in New York, dated February 14, 1951, is worth reproducing in full, as it summarizes the main issues and conveys eloquently the atmosphere of the times and the personal effect it all had on Currie.

February 14, 1951

Mr. Richard H. Wels
551 Fifth Avenue
New York 17, New York

Dear Dick:

I was distressed to learn from your letter of February 9th that there is a possibility that Victor Lasky may do another piece on me. As you know, Seeds of Treason not only caused me a great deal of mental distress but also seriously jeopardized my present work. I have been so completely absorbed in Colombia for the past eight months that the thing had receded a bit in my mind until your letter revived it.

I have a rather baffled and helpless feeling as to what to do. I had, of course, hoped that my voluntary appearance before the House Un-American Affairs Committee and my willingness to answer all questions would have settled the matter, but apparently it hasn't. One difficulty, I suppose, is that there is some truth in most of the statements of fact. It is the *inferences* drawn from these allegations that are all wrong.

For example, I did make a contribution to the Washington Committee on Aid to China of $2.50 in 1939. I did know White, Silvermaster, Silverman and several of the others mentioned both professionally and socially. I was once at least partially instrumental in helping Silvermaster. I did once entertain the First Secretary of the Russian Embassy, who was later alleged to be the head of the Russian espionage. I did once meet Earl Browder.

If one selects out these particular acquaintances and episodes over a period of ten years and ignores everybody else I knew and everything else I was doing, one could build up a sinister and certainly misleading picture. I suppose the only thing one can do is to explain as fully as possible the nature of these relationships and acquaintances, as I tried to do in my testimony. Even that, however, still tends to concentrate attention upon what are really isolated and unrelated phenomena.

For example, the contribution to the Washington Committee was solicited by young Art Hersey, who was under me in the Research Division of the Federal Reserve Board, who had been a missionary's son in China and who, I am convinced, was completely ignorant of any Communist associations of the Washington Committee. White and Silverman I had known at Harvard and I had the highest regard for their abilities, which were outstanding. From time to time in Washington, our work crossed and I saw a good deal of them, particularly of White when we occupied similar positions at the Treasury and Federal Reserve Board. Our contacts were almost exclusively concerned with current problems of the day. Our families entertained back and forth probably once a year.

On two jobs for the President, I consulted Silverman frequently. One was on a scheme for a national old-age pension program which was originally planned to be an issue in the 1940 election. The other was an abortive Maritime Labor Unemployment Compensation Program which was to be tacked on to the Railway Retirement Board. He was one of the ablest people in these fields in Washington.

Silvermaster I had again met quite independently through some work that I had done at the President's request that involved the Maritime Labor Board. I found him able, well-read, and an ardent New Dealer. Consequently, I had no hesitation in accepting invitations to his house. I believe we entertained them also several times. On the episode of "intervention" on his behalf, the request actually came from the Board of Economic Warfare since the charge against Silvermaster jeopardized its whole relationship with G-2 and the Army. In view of the fact that this was a question of relationships between Government agencies, it still seems to me to be the most natural thing in the world for me to have called Judge Patterson to ask him to review the documents in question. The whole episode consisted of two telephone calls, probably taking five minutes of a very busy day, as I was preparing for my second Mission to China at that time. I would probably have forgotten the whole matter had not Silvermaster been so grateful and referred to it on several occasions and had not Judge Patterson called me about a month or so later and thanked me for calling the matter to his attention and to tell me that the charges, in his judgment, were not supported by adequate evidence and were being withdrawn. If I had had any question about Silvermaster up to that point, which I cannot now recall, they would probably have been erased by Patterson's remarks.

The episode of Browder was again completely unrelated to the others. Sumner Welles raised with the President the matter of Browder's charges that the State Department had egged on Chiang Kai Chek to attack the 4th Army Group. He felt that in view of our interests in having all Chinese fight the Japanese, the charge should be nailed and he wanted to try to get a retraction from Browder. The President assented, as I recall, without much interest and Welles asked if I might be present at the interview because I had been to China and could support his position. At the interview, Browder acknowledged that he had no inside information, accepted Welles assurances, and agreed to retract the charges, which I believe he did. My only contribution was a statement that at no time had I seen or heard anything that would substantiate Browder's charges. Although this was Sumner Welles' affair, not mine, I cannot see how asking Browder to retract charges would "reinstate him in the good graces of the Government." I am sure that Welles' only concern was in preserving the precarious United Front in China.

Again in the case of the Russian Secretary, I met him through Luther Gulick and found him exceptionally well read and intelligent. If you can think back that far, you will remember that we were all most curious about the Russians and, at that time, admiring of the fight they were making. Contacts with the Russians were always good subjects of after-dinner conversation and, as you remember, their receptions were the most crowded in Washington.

Doubtless if one went back over all my activities in the crowded eleven years I spent in Washington, one could find other contacts with people who have since been charged or figured in the news in some way, for example, Owen Lattimore. The damnable part of this method of selection, however, is that it gives a completely wrong impression of my activities and interests. I suppose I knew and met thousands of people, particularly those in my profession, and we entertained or were entertained, I imagine, on the average of two or three times a week. I was used as a reference by most of the economists in Washington and I either recommended or, when I was at the Foreign Economic Administration, hired a great number of people. The ones I particularly remember were people like Bill O'Dwyer, Adlai Stevenson, Parker McCollester, Stanton Griffis, and people of that standard. If any of the people in those years I saw or worked with were Communists, they certainly gave no indication of it, as, of course, may have been natural. Actually, of course, in those years the Communists took the New Deal line and I don't think it occurred to any of us to probe beneath that, particularly as a lot of people used to call the New Dealers Socialists and Communists anyway.

In view of the current atmosphere, I was probably too accessible and not sufficiently circumspect. However, I certainly had no idea then of what the world would be like today. As you remember, in the early days the New Deal was in the nature of a Crusade and New Dealers felt a strong sense of comraderie. Later we were all united in pushing along with the War. The atmosphere of suspicion and caution only arose after I left the Government.

The saddest part of the business is that it has clouded the only thing I left Washington with—a good name. Otherwise I imagine I now would be back in Washington. In the present atmosphere, I suppose I shall have to remain in the sidelines, which isn't a pleasant prospect. I only hope the sorry business will not prejudice my sons' careers, as it has mine.

Anyway, I am glad that you had an opportunity to talk to Lasky. I most certainly hope that before he writes anything more, I will have an opportunity to go over the whole story with him. It is possible that I may get back in a month or so and I'll give you a ring to see what can be fixed up.

Sincerely,
Lauchlin Currie

LC:ds

The taint did not easily fade. The John Birch Society kept up the pressure on those whose names were raised by McCarthy, though the suspicion and fear diminished perceptibly after the Senate's successful censure motion on McCarthy in December 1954. In July 1954, however, the U.S. government refused to renew Currie's passport, ostensibly on the grounds that he had resided, apart from brief periods, outside the United States for more than five years. At that time this meant loss of citizenship for a naturalized citizen, a rule that later was declared unconstitutional.

Currie was in a most difficult position at that time. He had not "fled" the United States. The sponsor of his original visit to Colombia in 1949 was the highly respectable World Bank and Currie was closely connected with Truman's Point Four program in Colombia in 1950 and 1951 and also the UN Technical Assistance Program. His work in Colombia was fruitful and satisfying and in April 1954 he married Elvira Wiesner, a Colombian interior designer. But if he remained in Colombia and sacrificed his U.S. citizenship, he knew this would be interpreted by many as a confession of guilt. His decision was so interpreted by many people, including, for example, John Stormer, who, as late as 1964 in his best-selling book *None Dare Call It Treason* (Florissant, Missouri: Liberty Bell Press, p. 72), of which over a million copies were printed, wrote:

In 1949 Currie fled the United States and relinquished his citizenship to avoid testifying about his participation in a Soviet spy ring while on the White House staff. In 1961 the *Chicago Tribune* revealed that Currie was in South America administering the Alliance for Progress dollars the U.S. was providing to help "fight communism" in Columbia (*sic*). The *Chicago Tribune* after detailing Currie's participation in the World War II Soviet spy ring, said "This is the man who is planning how the dollars provided by a country which has stripped him of citizenship are to be employed in Columbia. It will be surprising if President Kennedy doesn't find out he has made an alliance for Communist progress in that country."

The reference to the Chicago press recalls an incident from 1966. At that time Currie was visiting professor for a term in Michigan and was sitting in the office of Karl Brunner, who was editing a new edition of Currie's 1934 book on the supply and control of money in the United States. The phone rang and at the other end was a prominent Chicago economist. Brunner told him of his work with Currie. "Impossible," exclaimed his friend, "Currie is a fugitive from justice somewhere in South America." "No, I assure you he is not," Brunner insisted. "He's sitting right here in my office."

An ironic episode occurred in 1961 when Currie was returning to the United States for the first time for several years to seek support from leading academics and international agency officials for a new development program he had devised for Colombia. He was accompanied by his friend Virgilio Barco (later to be President of Colombia, 1986–90). Barco took him straight from the airport in Washington to the White House for an unscheduled and unpublicized luncheon with Walt Rostow, a friend of Barco's and at that time President Kennedy's National Security Adviser (see chapter 8). Fortunately no word of this meeting reached the John Birch Society.

In the circumstances of the early 1950s, however, Currie did choose to remain in Colombia, sacrifice his U.S. citizenship, and later become a Colombian citizen. To escape completely from the atmosphere of fear and amorphous charges and a state of mental bitterness, and also because it was impossible for him to work usefully as an economist during the time of the military junta that seized power in Colombia in June 1953, he chose to use the savings he had accumulated to purchase a farm in a beautiful area in the mountains twenty miles from Bogotá and devote his entire time to it until the return of civilian rule in 1958. In retrospect he has had no regrets. He thoroughly enjoyed the new problems and achievements of a dairy farmer (see chapter 7) and later could return to the economic work he enjoyed.

For this he has been grateful to Colombia, and when later he was a resident in Canada (1967–71) and had the opportunity to resume his Canadian citizenship, with a good job (see chapter 9), he chose to retain his citizenship of Colombia which President Alberto Lleras Camargo had personally conferred upon him in 1958.

CHAPTER 6

The World Bank Mission to Colombia and Its Follow-Up, 1949–53

Recruiting the World Bank Team

The International Bank for Reconstruction and Development (IBRD) opened its doors for business in June 1946. Its main concern in its first years of operation was with the postwar reconstruction of Europe. After 1948 it gradually turned its attention to the development of poorer countries. In July 1948 Colombia submitted an application for a loan of $78 million to finance unspecified projects within a list of broad investment categories such as railroads, highways, power plants, agricultural equipment, and ports.[1] The World Bank president, John McCloy, discussed this "shopping list" with Emilio Toro, Colombia's executive director of the Bank, and suggested that the Bank could not be sure this loan would be financing the country's most urgent needs.[2] Toro replied that the Bank should send a study group to Colombia to find out for itself what these needs were. The matter was passed to the Bank's vice president, Robert Garner, and, through Toro, he established that President Mariano Ospina Pérez was enthusiastic about the idea. This led to the formation of a fourteen-man mission in 1949 to make the first comprehensive country survey made by any international agency.

Early in 1949 Robert Garner called Currie for an interview at the Bank in Washington to assess his suitability as head of the mission. Having satisfied himself that despite his New Deal associations, then increasingly under attack by conservative senators, Currie was not in favor of state corporations to the detriment of private enterprise, Garner offered him the job.

In May 1949 no precedent existed for such a mission or study. The Kemmerer missions of the 1920s to a number of Latin American countries, including Colombia, were limited to the setting up of central banks, budgets, and accounting systems and putting countries on

Currie's arrival in Colombia as director of the World Bank mission. *From left to right:* Gordon Grayson, Currie, Robert Garner (vice president of the World Bank), and Martin del Corral.

the gold standard. The World Bank in 1948 had sent teams to investigate individual projects in various countries, but none had attempted an overall survey of economic and social conditions with a view to establishing priorities within a broad-based development program. Thus little was known in the 1940s about less developed countries and their needs. The underlying hypothesis at Bretton Woods was that they were capital-poor and needed loans for development.

Garner originally envisaged a four- or five-man general survey to take approximately three months. However, he agreed to Currie's suggestion that the terms of reference be very broad: to formulate a development program to raise the standard of living of the mass of the Colombian people. To fulfil this assignment Garner agreed to extend the size of the mission to include experts in a wide range of fields including health, education, and community facilities. It was also agreed that Currie himself would handle the general field of public administration. Thus from an early date the Bank extended its interests beyond traditional bankable industrial, agricultural, transport, and public utility projects, though Currie was later to encounter considerable resistance to bank financing of social projects. "Damn it, Lauch," Garner was to tell Currie in 1951, "we can't go messing around with education and health. We're a *bank*!"[3]

Another innovation was the recruitment of an expert in foreign exchange, Roger Anderson, who was loaned to the mission by the International Monetary Fund (IMF). However, both the IBRD and the IMF had misgivings about this collaboration as they were anxious at that time to establish their respective jurisdictions, and Currie had great difficulty incorporating recommendations on exchange in his report because the Fund was unhappy about such recommendations appearing in a Bank publication. However, a third innovation was the acceptance of Currie's recommendations that he be personally responsible for the report of the mission—which permitted more freedom to make evaluations.

The Bank nominated three of its own junior officials: Gordon Grayson as general assistant to the mission, Jacques Torfs, an economist who covered a variety of fields, and David Gordon (one of the American delegates who had accompanied Currie to Switzerland in 1945) who advised on municipal facilities. Richard Musgrave, then at the University of Michigan, was the chief economist and adviser on public finance and banking.

The bulk of the financing of the mission was carried by the IBRD but with contributions of personnel from the IMF and the U.S. Public Health Service, and the Colombian government covered local costs and half of the fee of the independent consultants. Currie was retained in his capacity as an independent consultant so that he, rather than the Bank, would carry full responsibility for the recommendations contained in the mission report. He was given complete discretion over the planning of the mission and much of the recruitment. From the beginning he planned the study to be comprehensive and quantitative, with some indication of priorities. He wanted to avoid a report that consisted of a collection of disconnected monographs or of a rambling, inconclusive discussion of pros and cons in qualitative terms, such as had characterized recent reports on Haiti and Brazil. (These Missions were initiated after the Colombian mission but the reports appeared before Currie's.) Having little idea of the problems he would encounter he attempted to recruit experts who were generalists in their fields and whom he hoped, therefore, would be flexible and imaginative in their approach, thus making it easier to produce an integrated and internally consistent report based on feasible quantitative magnitudes.

First Impressions of Colombia

The first members of the mission arrived in Bogotá on July 10, 1949, and the last left on November 5. Emilio Toro suggested that Robert Garner accompany the mission for the first few days to add to its prestige, but in the end he stayed for ten days, traveling extensively and somewhat frivolously around Colombia with Currie in tow. This made it difficult for the mission chief to get his team quickly organized for the serious work at hand and he was relieved when Garner returned to Washington, but was appreciative of the added prestige the Vice President's presence gave to the mission.

The mission arrived in Colombia at a time of great political tension and communal violence. Many of the buildings in the center of Bogotá were still burnt-out shells from the "Bogotazo" of the previous year that followed the assassination of the popular political figure Jorge Eliécer Gaitán. Presidential elections were due in a few weeks and the two main parties, the Liberals and Conservatives, were bitterly disputing the way the prospective elections were to be handled. After interviewing most of the leading political personalities in Washington and Bogotá, including Mariano Ospina Pérez, Eduardo Santos, Alberto Lleras Camargo, Laureano Gómez, Roberto Urdaneta Arbelaez, and Carlos Lleras Restrepo, all of whom had been or were to become presidents of Colombia, Currie concluded that the divisions between the parties had little to do with ideology or principle, but more with constitutional issues and powers, and with personality differences.

The aspects of Colombian economy and society that most impressed Currie during his first four months in the country were the general poverty, coupled with the great richness of natural resources. In Nariño, the spectacular volcanic region in the south of Colombia, he commented that he had never seen such rich-looking land inhabited by such miserably poor, superstition-bound and wretchedly educated people. Every young woman carried a small child on her back and another inside her. Currie was to persuade the public health expert on his team, Dr. Joseph Mountin, assistant surgeon-general of the

U.S. Public Health Service, to change his views on birth control. Later Dr. Mountin initiated work in the National Health Service in Washington that led eventually to the pill.

Currie quickly became aware of the low level of public administration and the lawlessness that had extended to government officials in many areas. This led him to stress the need to minimize government controls and direct state operations while at the same time strengthening economic planning, in the sense of establishing priorities for social infrastructure and community facilities, coordinating and rationalizing fiscal, monetary, and exchange policies, and improving the data base. In these ways he hoped to lessen the danger of inflation, reduce bureaucracy, improve the social yield of scarce capital, and influence the actions of private individuals and groups through the provision of a favorable economic environment and a system of incentives and deterrents.

Colombia in 1949 was predominantly an agricultural country, with coffee the main source of foreign exchange earnings, followed by oil and gold mining. Out of the total labor force 63 percent was engaged in agriculture, using very primitive techniques. Most farm families worked fragmented parcels of land in difficult and remote terrain, producing subsistence crops. The more fertile and accessible flatlands were owned by a relatively small number of wealthy landlords who cultivated commercial crops or, more commonly, devoted these lands to extensive cattle grazing. At the time Currie saw this as a most uneconomic and suboptimal use of the best land, and one of the main proposals in his report was a graduated land tax to force underutilized agricultural land into use. This was to encounter greater resistence than any other proposal and was not implemented. Over the ensuing decades natural economic forces and the inheritance laws brought about a major transformation in the distribution and use of these agricultural lands so that less was heard of the need for an agricultural land tax and more of the need to capture the more important increment in urban land values.

With agricultural techniques so primitive, productivity per farm worker was extremely low in 1949. Despite protests from some members of the World Bank as they discussed the mission's work and Currie's compilation and interpretation of the results, Currie insisted on the relevance of comparisons between conditions in Colombia and those in the United States and other economically advanced countries. In particular, he contrasted the 63 percent working in Colombian agriculture with the 14 percent in the United States and insisted on the need to plan for and create the conditions that would effect a rapid expansion in Colombia's urban population relative to the rural. This would be achieved by increasing productivity in all sectors, not least agriculture, by drawing on the nearly two centuries of development of machines and techniques abroad, by improving the organization and efficient use of existing capital in agriculture, and by achieving an integrated national transport system.

Currie was convinced that agricultural output could be increased with little or no additional labor. In the face of rapid population growth this meant that labor from the overpopulated regions of Boyacá, Nariño, Santander, and the Atlantic coast could be recruited for work in urban industries, services, and construction, which thus could expand without excessive wage increases. In this way an increase in the standard of living of the masses would be expected to come about mainly through increasing general productivity and a redistributed work force that would expand the supply of wage goods. Total production was so low in relation to population that greater equality of income, while doubtless desirable, could not be the main way to increase significantly the standard of living for the majority of the population. Thus correction of income inequality was not to be allowed to divert attention away from efficiency or productivity.

As the work of the mission proceeded, attention focused increasingly on two problems that had a major bearing on the efficient functioning of the economic system as a whole: inflation and transportation.

The problem of inflation was tackled from various angles. First, the mission had to make statistical estimates for each of the major economic sectors and use these to compute national income and its uses, especially the division between consumption and investment.[4] This helped to ensure that the mission's recommendations on a public investment program, and its projections of private capital formation over a five-year plan period, 1951–55, would be consistent with projected fiscal revenues and private savings.

Second, the whole field of money and banking required careful study and reorientation. Currie was highly critical of the influence of the Kemmerer approach to central banking, with its emphasis on short-term, "self-liquidating" loans and the quality rather than the quantity of bank assets. This approach focused on the liquidity of individual banks rather than the system as a whole and imparted an inflationary bias since the Banco de la República was only too ready to accommodate "productive" government investments without fully understanding the effect of this on commercial bank reserves and hence on total bank lending and the overall money supply and monetary spending.

Monetary inflation in turn distorted the pattern of investment in favor of short-term and speculative projects, tended to worsen income distribution, and reduce the competitiveness of Colombian products in world markets. This reduced international reserves. This in turn induced the government to support the reserves by imposing an enormously complex multiple exchange rate structure, together with tariffs and quantitative controls on imports. Price inflation also was tackled directly through official price controls rather than indirectly through appropriate monetary and fiscal policy. The results again were disincentives, distortions, bureaucracy, and corruption.

The second area on which the mission increasingly focused attention was transportation. Because of Colombia's dramatic topography and neglect of its highways and railroads, the country could be classified into at least four main economic zones with wretched communications and transport between them. Apart from some city streets, there were only thirty-five kilometers of paved roads in the whole country, built by the United Fruit Company to connect Sevilla with Santa Marta. This considerably reduced the effective market size for most products, severely limiting the opportunities to exploit economies of scale and the division of labor and, hence, productivity. Colombia's total population then was 11 million with an average income in 1947 of only $176. The report therefore stressed the need to provide a highway network that would connect the main cities and ports with paved roads built to modern grade and curve specifications, a single-gauge interconnected national railroad system, improved ports and waterways, and a modern air transport organization. While the main cities were being interconnected they were to be supplied with larger electric generating systems, telephones, water, sewers, and intracity transport.

In the face of the enormity of the challenge posed by such dire poverty, political strife, and administrative inefficiency it would have been easy for Currie to have succumbed to the sense of defeatism and cynicism that he commonly encountered. In view of the fact that most people then believed fatalistically that poverty was inevitable, the mission's broad terms of reference—to produce a program to raise the living standards of the masses—did not seem so banal. But it did require vision, tenacity, positive thinking and supreme self-confidence in the rightness and efficacy of his diagnoses and prescriptions.

In an address given by Currie on the occasion of a farewell luncheon tendered the mission by their hosts at the Banco de la República, October 28, 1949, he praised the Colombians for the warm hospitality, cooperation, and help they had given the mission. The task now was to return to Washington to integrate and coordinate the various studies and produce a consistent and feasible program of action, though he noted that a prerequisite for agreement between the IBRD and the Colombian government would doubtless be political stability and the rule of law. He warned that some of the things the report would say would not please everyone; "but a diagnosis pleasing to all would be meaningless." He believed that clashes with members of his own mission, with IBRD officials, and with individuals and organizations in Colombia were inevitable if he was to do a good job, and he never courted popularity for its own sake. He constantly reminded his IBRD chiefs Robert Garner and Richard Demuth, when they accused him of creating antagonisms, that there was a trade-off between being popular and accomplishing something. He was gratified by a letter from Richard Musgrave (June 18, 1950) in which Musgrave attributed the great success of the mission to Currie's "proper combination of long-run patience with short-run impatience." In any case the successful outcome of the Currie mission, which resulted in significant reforms and a steady flow of loans, can be contrasted with the disastrous relations emanating from similar missions to Brazil shortly afterward, and the almost complete freezing, after 1954, of bank lending to Brazil for over ten years.[5]

Several months were spent in Washington completing and refining the various reports, arguing with the IMF over what could be included, and integrating everything into a consistent overall report. The bulk of the writing was completed by March 1950 and the resulting book, with over 600 pages of text, excluding the technical appendices, was published simultaneously in English and Spanish in September that year. The first sixteen chapters were devoted to a "Diagnosis of the Problem," followed by fourteen chapters devoted to "The Program," or prescriptions. This led one Colombian columnist to declare that in this the Currie report differed from the usual report which first presents the program and then lets the problems follow.[6]

Implementing the Report's Recommendations

Earlier, in Colombia, Currie had discussed with President Ospina the desirability of establishing a small committee of eminent persons to study the report upon its publication and make recommendations for policy. He was also enthusiastic about setting up a separate mission to study and recommend reforms of public administration that would enhance the implementation of the economic program. In March 1950, therefore, Currie was invited back to Colombia to discuss these proposals in more detail. Robert Garner also supported these ideas and suggested that Currie urge that the mission report study committee be bipartisan. This would increase the probability that its recommendations would be accepted.

As a result of these discussions a contract was drawn up for Currie, acting in a private capacity, to perform a threefold follow-up to the report. First, he was to head a full-scale public administration mission composed of technicians from the U.S. Public Administration Service. Second, he was to head the secretariat of the Economic Development Committee which was to be set up to study the recommendations of the IBRD report and advise on policy. And third, he was to act as adviser on technicians to be sent to Colombia under Truman's Point Four Program and the UN Technical Assistance Program, with a view to enlisting their support in the work of the public administration mission and the Economic Development Committee.

Currie addressed himself to the respective roles of a government planning agency and foreign lending and technical assistance agencies in a paper entitled "Some Prerequisites for Success of the Point Four Program," delivered before the American Academy of Political and Social Sciences in Philadelphia in April 1950:

> If a government is prepared to make considerable effort to develop and follow an integrated development program, it should expect to be able to supplement its own relatively meagre savings with capital from abroad. . . . In the absence of an overall plan, the elimination of waste and the proper determination of priorities, it is highly questionable whether foreign loans or private capital investment by themselves can make a significant impact on the standard of living of the masses of the people. . . . Under conditions of complete political stability and demonstrated willingness to embark on

> a broad program . . . I am confident that foreign capital, both institutional and private, will be attracted to the country in substantial volume. In short, Colombia may very well prove to be an admirable test case of what can be accomplished through the cooperation of many agencies both foreign and domestic in an integrated and coordinated program of development.[7]

Currie spent much of the summer of 1950 recruiting and organizing the personnel for the public administration mission for which he obtained the services of experts through the U.S. Public Administration Service and the Bureau of the Budget. The work of the mission began in September. The first of the technicians appointed under the Point Four Program was Walter Rubichek of the IMF but it was several months before most of the Point Four and UN technical assistants arrived and so were unable to have as big an influence on the work of the public administration mission or the Committee of Economic Development as had been hoped. However, Jacques Torfs, Carl Flescher, and Frederick Gill, members of the survey mission, were provided by the IBRD to help the committee on a few specific topics.

The composition of the six-man Committee of Economic Development was a crucial concern. An essential qualification was that they possess a sense of the national rather than sectional interest. Currie sought to model the committee on the British Royal Commission, taking advantage of the latent desire of prominent citizens to serve their country voluntarily in an influential and prestigious capacity. Six outstanding persons were eventually nominated, largely on the advice of Mauricio Obregón and Mario Laserna. This was done in advance of the publication of the IBRD survey report in August to prevent representatives of special interests getting on the committee to block or oppose various recommendations. Despite a difficult interview that Currie held in July with Carlos Lleras Restrepo, president of the Liberal party (who was reluctant to approve of any collaboration with Conservatives at that controversial time when Laureano Gómez was about to assume office as President of Colombia) nevertheless, three Liberals were appointed to the committee, together with three Conservatives. Also, three were from the east and three from the west of the country.

In Currie's last interview with Laureano Gómez, who was already a sick man and would be unable to carry on his full duties as President, Gómez again stated his agreement as to the importance of the bipartisan approach in giving greater weight to the committee's recommendations and helping overcome opposition to reform within his own Conservative administration.

Mauricio Obregón was appointed general coordinator, with responsibilities relating to the committee, the public administration mission, Point Four, and the UN technical assistance programs. The Banco de la República, then in the charge of Luis Angel Arango, also made available the services of their technicians, with Jorge Franco Holguín the head of technical studies.

The six members of the committee were Rafael Obregón, Alfredo García Cadena, and Pedro Nel Ospina Vasquez, for the Conservatives; and Martín del Corral, Emilio Toro, and Juan Pablo Ortega, for the Liberals. Currie was adviser and Jaime Córdoba the secretary. Among the Colombian consultants and advisers, either of the committee or of the public administration mission or both, were Jorge Franco, Hector Becerra, Rafael Bernal, Miguel Fadul, Fernando Gaviria, Rafael Gonzalez, Hernan Hernandez, Rodrigo Llorente, Jaime Malagón, Miguel Nuñez, and Jorge Videla.

The Committee of Economic Development, 1950–51

The first meeting was held on September 28, 1950, and for nine months thereafter the committee met regularly two or three afternoons a week to work through the survey report by subject, looking at each to derive specific recommendations for policy, and always on the basis of a supporting technical paper that updated or elaborated on the material in the survey report. In this way the IBRD program for Colombia was, to a remarkable extent, converted into a Colombian program for Colombia instead of collecting dust on a shelf in Washington, the fate of most IBRD reports that failed to be followed up by the committee device which Currie had hoped would serve as a model for all future IBRD country surveys.

At the time it was hoped and expected by Currie and by the Colombian government that substantial loans would be forthcoming from the World Bank if the government adopted most of the committee's recommendations as an integrated policy package or program. In the event the World Bank did offer loans, but did not make these conditional on the adoption of the overall economic program. Furthermore, the Bank refused to finance social projects. "Social" was defined to include even waterworks. As a result, they lost the opportunity to exert more leverage in favor of a program, as opposed to a specific-project approach to development. This remains true today and may account for the disappointing results that have been achieved generally from the extensive aid programs of the international agencies.

Nevertheless, as a result of the follow-up work of the Colombian Economic Development Committee in 1950–51 much was achieved. The committee's first priority was to tackle the chronic problem of inflation which was running at an annual rate of around 30 percent during the first nine months of 1950. The committee, whose meetings on the subject were attended by the minister of finance and the head of the Banco de la República, had endorsed Currie's recommendations for a reorientation of monetary policy toward control of the means of payment rather than support for credit programs as such, and for strengthening the power of the central bank.[8] Monetary expansion thereafter subsided sharply and a relatively long period of quite stable prices followed, despite a relaxation of direct price controls as recommended in the mission report and endorsed by the committee.

Next the committee turned its attention, with the collaboration of Jorge Leyva, the minister of public works, to the integration of the national transportation system as recommended in the IBRD report with modifications made in the light of fuller information then available. The minister quickly agreed to suspend work on various scattered railway construction projects that had been going on for many years and to concentrate instead upon a survey of the feasibility of the extension of the railway down the Magdalena Valley. This project was later completed successfully. Instead of the Cartagena-Calamar railroad, a contract was awarded to dredge the Canal del Dique to permit free passage for barges pushed or towed from Cartagena to the railhead on the Magdalena. However, neither railroad nor water transport has been very well used or managed in Colombia. The more flexible road transport system has always been more fully utilized, and increasingly so as the network developed. Rather absurdly, in 1983 the railroad unions brought a lawsuit (denuncia) against Currie and the past manager of the railroad for "abandoning" the railroad system thirty-three years earlier. Though the denuncia was thrown out Currie, nevertheless, was obliged to appear in court to present a defense.

When the committee made its recommendations on roads, again based on the IBRD report, the minister also agreed readily to the proposals. These were to suspend work on a variety of scattered and small new road projects throughout Colombia and instead concentrate on the rehabilitation and reconstruction of the main trunk lines of the country. This played a key role in integrating national markets, permitting economies of scale, and comparative advantage to be exploited more fully.

Also in the transportation field the committee endorsed the missions's recommendations on air transport. This field was then completely monopolized by the private airline Avianca, one of whose directors, Juan Pablo Ortega, was a member of the committee. He clashed bitterly with mission member Frederick Gill who had proposed the breaking of Avianca's monopoly in domestic air transport, their control of airports and landing rights for international airlines, and monopoly of postal services. Despite Ortega's opposition the committee supported Gill and an independent civil air transport authority was established, Avianca's monopoly was broken except in the field of postal services, and new airports were built.

Currie had hoped that the World Bank would delay new loans until the committee had published its final report so that greater leverage could be exerted on the government to adopt as much of the integrated program as possible. However, early in 1951 Jorge Leyva insisted on flying to Washington to expedite financing for the transport program recommended by the committee. He succeeded in securing a $16.5 million loan.

In one sense this was a setback for the committee's overall aims. But at the same time Leyva's triumph increased the committee's prestige, which it badly needed at that time for it had recently suffered a major reverse when it failed to stop the grossly uneconomic Paz del Río integrated steel mill project.

When the IBRD mission arrived in 1949 a promoting company for the steelworks had already been formed, with the backing of a public agency created to promote industrialization but relying almost exclusively on taxes and forced savings for financing. The cost of the project was put at $41 million which was, as the IBRD mission and a majority of the Economic Development Committee suspected, much less than its final cost. By 1955 these costs had already escalated to $160 million, rising to almost $200 million by 1959—a sum that almost equaled the net amount borrowed for all purposes in the 1950s by Colombia from public agencies abroad—the earnings were nil, and other Colombian industry was handicapped by high-cost steel of inferior quality.[9]

The IBRD mission had recommended the far cheaper solution of fabricating facilities for the processing of local and imported scrap in Barranquilla on the Atlantic coast and in Medellín, despite the fact that President Ospina had warned Currie that political and social considerations favored a new steel mill in the relatively remote, impoverished region of Boyacá. The mission concluded, however, that these local benefits were small relative to the enormous costs (mostly spent on imported capital equipment) of an integrated steel mill, which, to be economical, had to produce at a capacity far greater than the potential market demand for its products in Colombia. Exports were ruled out by the inferior quality of the local ores, and by high transportation costs.

In order to minimize the damage to the national economy and yet meet the tremendous pressure of regional and social arguments in favor of a steel industry in Boyacá, the Economic Development Committee seized on a compromise suggested by Carl Fleshcer in November 1950 for a small, simple, beehive coke oven plant at Paz del Río to make a limited tonnage of a few products from native ore, requiring an investment of $15 million. The promoting company rejected this proposal, even though it was addressed not to the company but to the government. The government remained silent and the original project proceeded by default with taxpayers' money and expensive short-term suppliers' credits from France. Paz del Río demonstrated that steel could be produced in Colombia entirely from local materials. But nobody had doubted this. The only question at issue was whether such steel could be produced economically. Here was an excellent example of the need to view projects not in isolation but as part of an overall program that established priorities in the allocation of scarce resources for competing uses. But the World Bank, unhappy at the resistances and antagonisms Currie was encountering, failed to use its leverage to stop it.

However, undaunted, Currie next turned the attention of the committee to the sensitive question of the exchange rate which had become heavily overvalued by internal inflation. They persuaded the President to announce a surprise major devaluation from 195 pesos to 250 pesos to the dollar in March 1951, with a progressive movement to a unified rate, which implied some benefit for coffee growers, though the coffee rate was to remain lower than the main exchange rate.

Despite the President's fears, this program was carried through smoothly with no accompanying rise in prices. At the same time it helped permit a considerable liberalization of imports and improved reserve position. Currie also persuaded the committee to recommend complete freedom for foreign capital but they did not agree to make his distinction between "productive" (direct) capital investment and "acquisitive" (portfolio or financial) investments.

One of the few suggestions made in the IBRD report that the committee did not accept was the proposed tax on the nonuse of the land in the Sabana de Bogotá and the Valle del Cauca. This proposal had aroused fierce opposition and was not thought feasible until more work had been done on cadastral surveying. However, most of the tax proposals made by Richard Musgrave for the mission were endorsed by the committee. Some of these were subsequently adopted, including improvements in the capital gains tax, though the committee insisted that proper care be made to distinguish between real and purely monetary gains that reflect inflation.[10]

Throughout this period Currie was also directing the work of the public administration mission and its final report was presented to the President in August 1951,[11] shortly before that of the committee. The President agreed with the suggestion that a small and distinguished committee be set up to study the public administration mission report and make recommendations, just as the Economic Development Committee had done. However, nothing came of this second committee, partly because the World Bank lost whatever interest it had in this work. Jacques Torfs, the Belgian economist on the Bank's staff, had frequently clashed with Currie, for example over foreign exchange proposals, the land tax, Paz del Río, and the degree to which the Bank should delay loan agreements pending publication of the overall program recommended by the Economic Development Committee. Torfs was lukewarm toward problems of administration, though he did support the creation of a planning office.

A very weak three-man committee (with no adviser or support staff) was eventually set up to study the public administration mission report and it soon fizzled out. Thus, far fewer of its recommendations were adopted than was the case with the mission report. However, the Economic Development Committee itself made some recommendations on administrative reforms, and so some things were achieved. The Ministry of Agriculture was reorganized and the budget office was strengthened but placed in the Treasury rather than in the President's office as recommended in the mission report, following U.S. practice. However, an independent national planning board was established that, as Currie suggested, was directly responsible to the President (and not located in the Ministry of Finance, as suggested by Garner and Torfs at the World Bank).

The National Planning Council, 1952–53

Currie recommended a three-man committee form for this National Planning Council as being more suitable than a single individual for the formulation of policy advice and the reconciliation of differences before proposals were presented to the President.[12] The main qualification laid down was that the council members enjoy the complete confidence of the President. As with the Council of Economic Advisers in the United States, Currie envisaged that the Consejo Nacional de Planificación would concern itself with the overall macroeconomic picture, concentrating on budgetary policy, monetary and exchange policy, and pointing out conflicts and inconsistencies in overall programs in agriculture and transport, for example, while leaving specific program planning to existing ministries. It would be an advisory not an executive body, whose role, drawing on its own technical support staff, was to establish guidelines and priorities and to coordinate overall economic policy of the government.

In line with these recommendations the consejo was established with Emilio Toro as chairman and Jesús María Marulanda and Rafael Delgado Barreneche as the other members, all of whom carried a good deal of weight with the acting President, Roberto Urdaneta Arbelaez. It held its first meeting in April 1952, at which time Currie was engaged in "a strange mission to Caldas where I set myself the truly heroic task of trying to separate the Departmental Government from the bottle—I mean the Licorera—with, naturally, a complete lack of success."[13] (The departmental governments were, and remain, jealous of their local liquor monopolies whose revenues were an important source of local financing. Tariffs are still imposed on liquor imported from other departments.)

During this time Currie remained in close touch with Emilio Toro and the work of the consejo and gave advice informally. After the Caldas report[14] had been completed, Toro persuaded Currie to be associated formally with the consejo as an adviser, despite the misgivings of Robert Garner at the World Bank who had secured the services of Albert Hirschman as adviser for two years and feared, rightly as it turned out, that there would be difficulties between Currie and Hirschman since Currie seemed to "create resistance." That Currie's unusual combination of tact and firmness had proven a winning formula seemed secondary compared with IBRD's preoccupation with harmony. It is ironic and puzzling, however, that Hirschman is famous for his theories that the *deliberate* creation of tensions, bottlenecks, and disequilibria enhance development by "economizing on the scarce factor of decision-making."[15] (As if there were not enough of these in less-developed countries already!)

In any event Currie joined the consejo as adviser in August 1952 and immediately set about preparing a more systematic work program for the consejo and identifying the required support staff. Emilio Toro requested seven technicians from the World Bank, including a specialist in housing, for example, but this the Bank then regarded as outside its interests and all it offered were the services again of the ubiquitous Jacques Torfs. Currie also endeavored to increase the consejo's interest in the public administration reforms that were needed to accompany the consejo's economic policy proposals but Hirschman and Torfs had little interest in those matters, which was perhaps understandable since the consejo, in the absence of greater support from the World Bank, had only a small staff. Instead they turned the consejo's attention mainly to specific project appraisals. In Currie's judgment these appraisals were viewed too often in isolation and divorced from an overall action program.

However, the consejo did fill a serious gap in monetary policy (despite a tendency for Currie and Hirschman to disagree here too), since there was at that time no monetary board and the board of directors of the Banco de la República, which acted as such, was composed mainly of private bankers and other borrowers from the Banco. Consequently, the consejo devoted a lot of attention to this area. In fact the consejo played a more prominent role here in 1952–53 than it was ever to do subsequently.

During this time Currie worked closely with Enrique Peñalosa—the beginning of a long association[16]—analyzing in functional terms the budget for 1950–53. This was the first time such an analysis had been made of the national budget, and called attention to the need for many reforms in budgetary presentation and procedures. He was soon to discover that departmental and municipal budget statements were in equally bad shape when he and Peñalosa undertook to prepare for the consejo an urban study of the city of Barranquilla in October 1952. Currie's plan for Barranquilla involved an infrastructure program for which a prerequisite was an expansion of the waterworks.[17] After a bitter exchange in April 1953 between Currie and the World Bank's representative, Albert Waterston (once a junior of Currie's at the Foreign Economic Administration in Washington ten years earlier), the waterworks project was rejected as too social to qualify for a World Bank loan. So Currie secured on behalf of the consejo and the city of Barranquilla a loan from the Banco de la República's stabilization fund (whose abolition, Luis Angel Arango reminded him, he had earlier recommended!) with a provision suggested by Currie that a "Watchdog Committee" (Comité de Vigilancia) should report monthly to the Banco on the progress of the plan until the loan was repaid. This committee proved to be a most productive "Royal Commission," replicating the success of the earlier Economic Development Committee that studied the 1950 IBRD mission report. Although it had no real authority, the prestige of the three prominent citizens who served the committee, the fact that it was reporting to the powerful Banco de la República, and the rapid turnover of administrations of the city of Barranquilla and the Department of Atlántico, which made the committee the only organization with stability and continuity in the city and state, ensured its life throughout the period of the loan, and 90 percent of the plan was fulfilled.

In early 1953 Currie and Peñalosa worked on an urban plan for Bogotá that centered around water and electricity projects and the creation of a "Special District" (Distrito Especial). However, on June 13 General Rojas Pinilla effected a coup; personal relations on the consejo and among its advisers became increasingly strained; Emilio Toro resigned the day after the coup (and also because of disputes with Jacques Torfs); and Currie became increasingly frustrated at the lack of interest in the Bogotá study by the consejo, the IBRD, the mayor, and the new President. For the first time in his life he felt he was working for money rather than because he enjoyed the work. So around this time he bought a farm in Albán on the edge of the Sabana, about thirty miles west of Bogotá. His contract with the consejo was to expire in February 1954 and he did not seek its renewal. It was time to fulfil a lifelong desire to be a farmer.

Nevertheless, these three and a half years had been highly fruitful. It was one of the very few times that the recommendations of a country study by foreign economists were accepted and implemented by a developing country, and the newly created institutions survived. Although the economic report and recommendations of the subsequent planning committees were not couched in modern macroeconomic terms (using IS and LM terminology) they were consistent with them and resulted in new and highly productive investment (especially in transport), while checking inflation and ushering in a period of relative stability with an outward-looking trade orientation. One of the chief benefits was an intangible. The report was widely read in Colombia and for the first time thousands of educated Colombians could see the interconnection of what had appeared hitherto as isolated and unrelated phenomena. This must have helped to raise the prestige of economics as a discipline and attract more able students. But the procedures that Currie devised to accomplish all this were not generalized by the Bank for application in other countries or for Colombia on subsequent occasions; and the Bank did not use its great influence to have the same prodecures applied to the reforms recommended by the public administration mission. The latter recommendations were still valid and urgent at the time of writing, and, in tacit acknowledgment of this, in 1988 and 1989 the National Planning Department arranged to have Currie's early reports reprinted.

CHAPTER 7

A Farming Interlude, the Return to Economic Advising, and the Magdalena Valley Mission, 1954–60

A New Career as a Full-Time Dairy Farmer, 1953–59

Driving west from Bogotá one eventually leaves the flat, fertile lands of the Sabana. The road then twists treacherously into the mountains. It first rises above the 2,600 meters highland plateau and then descends the western slopes of the eastern cordillera of the Andes into warm coffee-growing country and then into the tropical Magdalena Valley. Just as the road begins to descend one arrives at the small, rather depressing town of Albán. It was just outside Albán that Currie purchased a decaying farmhouse with about sixty-five hectares of land, of which about a third was cultivable, the rest being steep and spectacular mountain slopes. He named it Los Robles (The Oaks) after the live oak trees that grow there.

In late 1953 the farm was very run-down and required a considerable amount of work and investment to bring it up to the very high standard of operation that Currie was determined it should attain. He had a great deal to learn about dairy farming but was assisted at the beginning by one of his son's friends from the United States, a student of agriculture at the University of Nebraska. For the next five years he devoted himself full-time to the farm, a slave to the cattle seven days a week. In those early days a typical month's program of work was very similar to the following list for March 1954:

1. Prepare stable for milking.
2. Build corral for vacas (cows).
3. Build stable for terneros (calves).
4. Build stable for toro (bull).
5. Build corral for toros.
6. Build gallinero (henhouse) and corral.
7. Prepare potrero (field) 3 and 4 for vacas.
   Repair fences and extend to camino (road).

Cover up old zanja (trench) in 3. Mow pastures in 4. Cover up old zanjas in 2.

8. Mow old part of No. 5.
9. Plant sides of represa (dam).
10. Spread cal (lime) and abono (manure) in chicken corral.
11. Cement zanja along house by guest room.
12. Plant potatoes.
13. Make gates to enter 3 and 4.
14. Make alberca (drinking trough) in corral.
15. Make depression in camino below alcantarillado (sewer).

During this period frequent journeys had to be made into Bogotá for spare parts and supplies and he kept his downtown apartment. The interior designer who was recommended to furnish and decorate this apartment was Elvira Wiesner, daughter of a well-known Colombian artist. In May 1954, Currie's first marriage having ended in divorce, she became the wife of an apprentice dairy farmer. In 1956 their son Ronald was born and in 1958 a daughter, Elizabeth.[1] Lauchlin Currie became a Colombian citizen in 1958. He had become a naturalized American citizen in 1934, but in those days U.S. citizenship had to be forfeited for naturalized Americans if they resided abroad for more than five years, and Currie had no desire to live in the United States at that time. He made his permanent home in Colombia, except for the time he was later to spend abroad as a visiting professor in the United States, Canada, and Great Britain—for one semester in 1965 and for four years between 1967 and 1971.

At his farm in Albán he gradually built up a herd of one hundred head of cattle, but with a milking herd of only about thirty—he had been let down by the laws of probability, with many more male calves born than heifers. However, his farm was converted into one of the technically most efficient farms in Colombia, albeit mostly using secondhand equipment; he eventually won the prize, for three consecutive years, for the highest-yielding herd of Holsteins per cow per lactation in the country. As an economist, Currie placed productivity ahead of type and so embarrassed the Holstein Association by having lower-graded cows produce the most milk! One day his mayordomo was sent on a visit to the nearby Rockefeller Foundation agricultural station. He returned saying he had learned nothing but had invited the Rockefeller people to visit Los Robles.

A lesson from his farming experience that was impressed on Currie more profoundly than ever before was the difference between techni-

Currie at his farm in Albán, 1962.

cal and economic efficiency. He developed the highest-yielding dairy herd in Colombia but this required a tremendous amount of work and careful observation and experimentation. Climate and soil conditions vary enormously in Colombia, even for neighboring farms, so there was no substitute for individual experimentation, and there was little that the government's experimental stations and technical assistance programs had to offer him. As for the farm workers, their productivity was influenced little by the formal part of their schooling, though the informal part—inculcating habits of discipline and punctuality—was more important. Whether literate or illiterate made little difference to their ability to learn farm work on the job, though they were required to make accurate records of inputs and milk yields. However, the ambition of most of the boys on the farm was to move on to the big city, away from the dreariness and boredom of the small town of Albán.

The higher yielding the cows the more susceptible they were to illness. A very strict watch had to be kept on their feeding habits, on the quality of their pastures, on the use and maintenance of the milking machines, on clean hands, and the general standards of hygiene.

Also on the sobriety of the workers! Quite high expenditures on drugs and veterinary bills were incurred. Many years later he was to read James Herriot's delightful veterinary reminiscences with great interest and entertainment, recalling the constant emergencies that arise in dealing with animals. Some of those crises occurred when he was alone on the farm on a Sunday or holiday. Immediately after calving, a very high-yielding cow could collapse with milk-fever. The remedy was an injection of a drug in the jugular artery in the neck but it had to be done immediately or the cow would die. Currie recalls ruefully jabbing away with a hypodermic needle at the animal's neck until he encountered the artery and made the injection.

About a week after calving, milk yields begin to decline inexorably until the next calving, and the best one can do is to reduce the rate of decline as much as possible through high quality feeding and by providing as calm and unexciting a life as possible for the cows. Thus physical yields were high but so too were costs. His farm was not large enough to use his machinery economically, and he hired more workers than he really needed. On the revenue side, the price of milk was set by the government, though the higher grades produced at Los Robles (nearly 4 percent fat) would have commanded a premium price. The farm provided Currie with a living but not a fortune and his *hourly* rate of pay was even more modest, at least up to 1959, by which time the farm's operations had been routinized and he was able to spend much less time at the farm himself.

Nevertheless, these were satisfying years and it gave him an insight into the inner life of the country that few visiting economists could possess. Currie subsequently lamented that it is a pity that one of the few occupations left that give a person such a sense of personal achievement should yield such a low return and is consequently available for less and less people. It is the unavoidable price paid for growth. Currie's own psychic income was very high and he did feel he had demonstrated to his dead older brother that he could do things with his hands and not just his head! But having demonstrated this and getting bored with the routine and busy with economics again, he eventually disposed of the farm in 1966.

The Return to Economic Advising

Having established a relatively smooth routine at his farm, in late 1958 and early 1959 Currie partially came out of retirement from economics to undertake two small consultancy jobs. In 1957 General Rojas Pinilla had been overthrown by a military junta and, after reaching an accord on a National Front coalition, in 1958 Conservative and Liberal leaders returned from exile in Europe to reestablish a system of civilian government by which the two main parties would share power. It was agreed that a common presidential candidate should be nominated by the National Front, alternating between a Liberal and a Conservative for each of the next four presidential four-year terms. In this way it was hoped not only to return to civilian government but also to dampen the widespread "violencia" that had been sweeping the country for the past decade and that had cost many thousands of lives, mostly in remoter rural areas that were divided along traditional party lines. The first of these National Front presidents was a Liberal, Alberto Lleras Camargo. He assumed office in August 1958.

Around this time Currie was retained as a consultant to a private group that had earlier contracted Arthur Altmeyer to make recommendations on a national social security system. As was noted in chapter 3, Currie and Altmeyer had clashed before in 1937 on this issue. Altmeyer's approach then for the United States, and again now for Colombia, was to build up a large reserve fund that would eventually yield sufficient interest to finance expected payments for insurance and retirement claims, based on actuarial calculations and following the practice appropriate for and commonly adopted by individual private insurance companies. Currie, however, distinguished between private and national systems and explained that a national system could operate on a pay-as-you-go basis. Current revenues paid into the national social security fund could be used to finance current insurance claims and pensions. It was not necessary to build up a large fund (which in the condition of depression in the United States in 1937 constituted a significant deflationary force). With state support and with the assurance that current contributions would grow steadily with a growing national membership and growing national income, a national scheme did not face the same risk of insolvency that a private company faced. However, it was Altmeyer's advice that the sponsor accepted.

In early 1959 a second small consultancy study was undertaken for the Economic Growth Ministry (Ministerio de Fomento). The brief was to make recommendations on the organization and duties of this ministry which then had few responsibilities of its own. Currie suggested it merge with the Ministry of Mines.[2] This merger did take place, but later it separated again into the two ministries, but with a change of name for the growth ministry which became the Ministry of Development (desarrollo). This ministry was again left with relatively few powers other than control over the low-cost housing institute, the Instituto de Crédito Territorial. It would seem appropriate for a ministry of development also to have responsibility for encouraging exports, and it has been proposed that the ministry take over the export promotion institute, Proexpo. This move, however, has been blocked by the Banco de la República which has traditionally controlled Proexpo.

The Magdalena Valley Mission, 1959

In March 1959 Currie was appointed director of a major study of the Magdalena Valley region and so became a full-time economist again and part-time farmer. Over the next seven years, to the end of 1966, despite the many studies and missions he was to direct, he spent almost every weekend and holiday at his farm, which was now running to an efficient routine (in technical if not in economic terms). It was during this period that on three occasions he won the annual prize for the highest yielding herd of Holsteins, per cow per lactation, in the country and was made an honorary member of the Colombian Academy of Veterinary Sciences.

In 1958 President Lleras appointed Dr. Virgilio Barco as his minister of public works. (Barco became President of Colombia in 1986). Barco was a friend of Enrique Peñalosa who had worked closely with Currie a few years earlier. When Currie retired into farming he put Peñalosa in touch with Robert Nathan, his old friend from the New Deal, who had established an important economic and engineering consultancy firm in Washington. Nathan retained Peñalosa and his associate Miguel Fadul as his representatives in Colombia. Peñalosa and Fadul promoted the idea of a study of the Magdalena Valley and north Colombia which was soon to be opened up by a major, very costly extension of the Magdalena railroad. This extension had been initiated under the military junta in 1957. On Peñalosa's recommendation Barco invited Nathan's firm to undertake the study (Peñalosa and Fadul were probably considered too close to Barco to take it on themselves) but asked Currie to be the director and the coordinator. The National Railroad Board provided most of the financing of the mission. Work began in March 1959. Apart from Currie, the mission comprised five foreign technicians provided by Nathan's firm and nine from Colombia, including Rodrigo Botero, a future minister of finance. The technicians whom Currie found to be the most valuable members of the mission were the American hydraulics engineer, Charles Senour, formerly chief engineer of the Mississippi River Commission, Glen Parker, an industrial economist, George Dahl, an ichthyologist from the National University of Colombia, and Henry Eder, a prominent Colombian businessman, trained as an electrical engineer, but who undertook an excellent survey of forest resources for the mission. Eder later was head of the Cauca Valley Corporation and mayor of Cali. Currie subsequently undertook further specific studies relating to the Magdalena Valley with Senour and Eder.

The main purpose of the mission was to identify the opportunities and problems that the extension of the Magdalena railroad would present.[3] A survey of the economic feasibility of the section of the Magdalena railroad that stretched from Puerto Salgar to Puerto Wilches, where it would connect with the navigable part of the Magdalena River, was recommended by Currie's 1950 IBRD mission. An IBRD survey team subsequently recommended that the project be undertaken and the rail-river link with the Atlantic coast at the important city of Barranquilla was made in the mid 1950s at a relatively low cost.

The far more costly extension, over very swampy terrain, was then initiated, with little prior study, to join the Magdalena railroad with a short section of railroad in the banana zone between Fundación and the relatively unimportant city of Santa Marta and its small port. However, by 1959 a great deal of the capital expenditures had already been committed so that the *marginal* cost of completing the railroad was by then relatively small compared with the potential benefits of opening up the virgin northern plains, rich in natural resources of all kinds. Thus Currie pressed for its earliest completion. (It opened in August 1961, and Currie was among the passengers on the first historic journey to Santa Marta.) Nevertheless, without a rail connection between Santa Marta and the port of Barranquilla the Atlantic railroad would lose much of its attractiveness. Thus in a subsequent report prepared in 1960 with the help of Charles Senour, Henry Eder, and a soils expert, Pedro Ramirez, Currie examined the technical and economic feasibility of a line to Barranquilla branching from the main Atlantic railroad at Ciénaga.[4]

Preliminary studies indicated that this line could be built at low cost by simply widening the existing road to accommodate rail tracks and modifying the proposed bridge across the Boca de la Barra, the narrow mouth of the Ciénaga Grande de Santa Marta. For a few minutes twice a day the bridge would be closed to road traffic to allow the trains to pass over. However, this interruption of the traffic flow did not appeal to the secretary of the Ministry of Public Works, Alfredo Bateman. When Virgilio Barco left Colombia in 1961 to take up the post of ambassador to the Court of St. James in London, Bateman seized the opportunity to press ahead with the original bridge structure, which ruled out the railway plan.

This was a major blow for the national railway system whose enormous infrastructure has always been grossly underutilized because of the small capacity of the port of Santa Marta and the inconvenience of moving freight by road between Barranquilla and Ciénaga and tranferring it there to or from the railway cars. Pilferage during such loading and unloading operations, poor management, and labor problems have combined to discourage use of the railway system which has declined progressively in the years since the opening of the Atlantic railroad in 1960.

Returning to the work of the original mission in 1959, about 100 separate recommendations emerged, one of the most important being the creation of an autonomous regional development agency of coordinate transportation plans and other infrastructure projects. In particular, it was to follow the example of the Tennessee Valley Authority in supervising major land reclamation projects, flood control, and promoting the conservation of the region's rich natural resources of rivers, forests, flora, and fauna. It would also manage national parks located in that region, including the famous Parque Tairona that was created a few years later by Enrique Peñalosa, using his powers as head of Incora (the agrarian reform institute) to acquire most of the land for the nation. This recommendation was adopted soon afterward, in July 1960, with the creation of the Corporación Autónoma de Los Valles del Magdalena y del Sinú (CVM). The corporation was given only a small budget and staff, completely inadequate to deal with the destruction that followed on the opening of the region. Currie was retained as adviser.

Writing years later in the newspaper *El País*, April 17, 1985, he recalled:

> On two occasions, one on the west bank of the Magdalena and one on a stream leading into the Ciénaga of Ayapel between the San Jorge and Cauca Rivers, I had the opportunity of navigating by canoe in waters crowded with tropical fish and the air equally full of aquatic birds, with iguanas crawling on the banks, only to return later to these streams to find them practically devoid of fish, birds and wild life generally.
>
> We tried to protect the eggs of the large sea turtles that were laid on the beaches of the Guajira but it was a hopeless struggle. We tried to ensure that dynamiting and the use of small mesh nets would not destroy the fish of the ciénagas and lead to the destruction of the smaller fish in the annual subienda (rise) of the bocachico (fish). The sound of exploding dynamite was one of the most characteristic sounds of the Coast and the lower Magdalena. We tried to limit the slashing and burning of the virgin forests and engage in reforestation of the regions near Barrancabermeja. But while the Corporación was planting some 200–300 hectares of eucalyptus, the campesinos were destroying some 2 million hectares of virgin forests. The C.V.M. contracted with a United Nations mission to make an inventory of the trees on the edges of the vast forest that once extended from the Magdalena deep into northern Antioquia. To do this they made trails but these were promply utilized by colonos to enter, slash and burn, plant corn and then move on to repeat the process. As an inventory of the forest was being made the forest itself was being destroyed.
>
> It is difficult to believe that as late as the 1950s there was still a large population of caimans in the Magdalena. I visited by small boat a large finca of friends below Barrancabermeja (Emilio Toro and Fernando Londoño Londoño) but on the west bank of the river we saw a caiman on the bank, and the boatman took a shot at it and made a hit. While it was thrashing about in the shallow water near the bank, the boatman jumped into the water with a knife and stabbed it to death so as not to lose its skin if it succeeded in getting into deeper water. . . .
>
> The harrowing experience of these years reinforced my conviction that regardless of how good the conservation laws may be, if the majority of the people do not believe in them they cannot be enforced. There were just too

many very poor people who made a bare living by destruction for us to be able to stop them. The remedy, I felt, must be the creation of better paying jobs and better living conditions in the cities, if we were to save what was left of the natural wilderness, wild life and flora of the countryside.

The first manager of the CVM was Rodrigo Botero, advised by Currie and a board of volunteer directors. Although the CVM had a very limited impact, one of its successes worth mentioning was its promotion of a significant African palm oil export industry. Shortly after Currie left Colombia in 1967 for a period of teaching in Canada and Britain, Botero, who was then the economic secretary to President Carlos Lleras Restrepo, who wished to give Incora precedence over the CVM, abolished the corporation without even informing the board. His view was that most of the corporation's potential activities lay in the jurisdiction of some other public body such as the Caja Agraria or Incora, without need for a coordinating body. Thus the CVM was converted into a national conservation body, Inderena. Inderena possessed fewer powers and responsibilities for regional development but has had some success in increasing public awareness of the importance of conservation.

Currie's 1959 mission itself did focus attention on both the potential exploitation of the region's abundant natural resources and on the urgent need for greater conservation controls. One of the most important mineral resources in the region was the vast coal field at Cerrejón in the remote Guajira desert. The mission concluded that at that time it was premature to put government money into its exploitation, though relatively small sums could be spent on continuing exploratory studies and no obstacles (but also no subsidies) were to be placed in the way of any foreign company that wished to assume the high risks and high costs of operating there.

The main problems with El Cerrejón coal were that there was no local market in the Guarjira; on the coast it had to compete with cheap natural gas; and transportation costs also would not make it competitive in Colombian markets in the interior. Thus the operation could not rely on a stable home market as a base from which to develop exports competitively, especially since there were very poor or nonexistent transportation and other facilities in the area, and the nearest port of Santa Marta had very limited capacity. Years later, however, the enormous investment sums (over $2,000 million) required to exploit the field were spent and the mines came into production in the mid-1980s, unfortunately at a time when world coal prices were becoming very depressed, falling below even the current costs of production.

One interesting and potentially very important land reclamation project that Currie tentatively identified while flying over the region, and which he later explored in greater detail with Henry Eder, Charles Senour, and Pedro Ramirez, concerned the 135,000 hectares between the Magdalena River and the Ciénaga Grande de Santa Marta.[5] From the air the old bed of the Magdalena River is clearly visible, running from near Piñon, on the present course of the river, to the south of the Ciénaga Grande. It would be relatively easy to reopen the old channel and thus let the fresh waters of the mighty Magdalena River into the Ciénaga. If a weir could be build at the narrow mouth of the Ciénaga (Boca de la Barra) then the Ciénaga's salt water, along with the flow of fresh water from the Magdalena, could escape into the sea, with the weir preventing any return flow of seawater. Thus the Ciénaga could be converted into a vast freshwater lake. At relatively small cost a freshwater canal system could then be constructed to run off the western side of the Ciénaga to irrigate a vast area of rich, accessible land. To date, however, nothing has come of this proposal. One major difficulty (apart from possible technical problems with the weir) is that a large number of fishermen derive their livelihood from fishing in the Ciénaga. The project would kill off their supply of saltwater fish, and it would be some time before the Ciénaga could be restocked with edible freshwater fish that could survive in tropical waters.

One of the most important problems of the Magdalena Valley identified by the mission was the invasion of the area by colonizers. Flying over the area Currie was concerned at the large number of forest fires that reduced visibility to a few hundred yards. These were caused by the slash-and-burn mentality of the colonos who were destroying, without replacement, the forest resources built up over millions of years for the sake of short-term gains.[6] The permanent loss of topsoil, washed away by the rains in the absence of adequate vegetation to protect it, was a common consequence. This led to the silting of rivers and, hence, to widespread flooding. Another common practice, mentioned above, was the use of dynamite, often stolen from roadworks, thrown into rivers and lakes, killing far more fish than were edible and upsetting the ecological balance. In short, the increased agricultural production achieved by the colonos was often negligible relative to the destruction caused.

Under Colombian land laws—passed, Currie insisted, under the influence of ideas from a bygone and primitive era—if a person occupies or uses land belonging to the state or to other private individuals and is not evicted within a few weeks he gains legal title. In practice it has been very difficult to enforce evictions, and in any case local officials often sympathized with squatters' rights. Under these circumstances Currie was convinced of the need to educate public officials and strengthen their authority. However, strongly influenced by his own experiences as a farmer and disabused of the type of romantic notions about an idyllic rural way of life commonly held by urban-based intellectuals, Currie was by this time coming increasingly to emphasize that the only fundamental solution to rural poverty and ecological destruction was the creation of jobs outside of agriculture for the great mass of low-productivity marginal farmers and farm workers.

Currie was convinced that the main problem of Colombian agriculture was not excessively large landholdings, or latifundismo, but rather, excessive parcelization or minifundismo, primitive technology, and soil erosion arising from a short-term, unscientific approach to land use. The future lay with modern, technically efficient agriculture on plots of sufficient size to make mechanization and soil conservation practices more economical. To the extent that this reduced the unit costs of production it would make it more and more difficult for small-scale subsistence agriculturalists to compete in the major markets, especially those located in more remote regions of the country. There were simply too many farmers and Currie deplored what he called the pseudo-economics and sentimentality stemming, for example, from the influential Lebret report of 1958, which in turn deplored migration from rural areas to the towns and cities and sought to arrest this trend.[7] By contrast, Currie explained that the depopulation of rural areas was not an undesirable phenomenon but rather an essential corrollary of economic and social development, which incidentally would have the important effect of conserving natural resources.

Currie emphasized once again that the basic objective was a rise in the general standard of living. This ultimately depended most of all on increased productivity. But increased productivity in agriculture would, speaking realistically rather than romantically, depend primarily on larger, commercially oriented, technically advanced farms located favorably relative to markets. As productivity advanced so fewer and fewer people, at first in relative and later in absolute terms, would be needed to work in agriculture if average agricultural incomes were to rise. Thus Currie insisted that the fundamental right of the Colombian people was not the direct ownership of the land they occupied or worked but a decent standard of living. Farmers required secure title to the land they had bought if they were to make long-term plans for its use and improvement. On the other hand, ownership rights were not absolute and Currie strongly recommended that more resources be devoted to updating cadastral values, made by the Instituto Geográfico Agustín Codazzi to ensure adequate revenues from the rural property tax.[8] This was another area in which inflation wreaks its havoc upon public finances and equity.

Lastly, however, we should also mention Currie's emphasis on the encouragement of export agriculture, again based on the development of modern, larger-scale farming in products such as beef cattle, cotton, sugar, and palm oil. He deplored the common practice of export controls designed to divert production to the home market at a lower price. This yielded at best only short-term effects on the cost of living, invariably followed by a reduction in production to a level that supplied only the home market, and by a subsequent increase in price to a level equal to the long-run unit costs of production. An increase in export agriculture would provide more useful work in agriculture than would exist in its absence. Nonetheless, the surplus agricultural population was so large and the potential so great for further displacement by machinery and improved techniques and management that Currie remained convinced of the need to place greatest emphasis on the conditions that would facilitate rather than impede the historic process of mass movement from countryside to town and city.

These were themes that Currie was thereafter to refine and extend with increasing vigor. The theme was crystallized at the end of 1960 with the publication of the first edition of the famous *Operation Colombia.* This small book was to pitch Currie into the center of an extensive, long-running, and often bitter debate on national development policy. The debate was always being decided in Currie's favor by the natural forces of the market but also, more satisfyingly, by the adoption, in 1971, by the administration of President Misael Pastrana of a refined *Operation Colombia* under the name of the *Plan of the Four Strategies* based on *Guidelines for a New Strategy,* written by Currie shortly after he had been invited to join the National Planning Department as chief economic adviser.

CHAPTER 8

The Origins and Development of Operation Colombia, 1960–67

Operation Colombia: Toward a Theory and a Program of Development

In November 1960 President Alberto Lleras invited Currie to be his representative on the National Planning Council. At that time, however, Currie was directing a study of the Department of Meta under a private contract with the National Planning Office. Because of this conflict of interests Currie had to decline the invitation. However, the invitation set him thinking more deeply about the appropriate lines that a national, as opposed to a regional or sectoral, development program should take.

When he first came to Colombia in 1949 he had no special theory of development and his diagnosis and action program was not particularly novel except insofar as his was the first comprehensive national survey of a developing country sponsored by a development agency. As we have seen, it emphasized the integration of the national market through integrated national road, rail, and air transport programs. It also advocated greater reliance on the price system and fewer controls, land taxes to stimulate agricultural production, a realistic exchange rate, and greatly improved public administration, especially in the fields of central banking and the fiscal system. Individual projects, such as road and rail links, waterworks, or steel mills were evaluated in terms of their contribution to more integrated national and international markets in order to promote economies of scale and efficient resource allocation according to comparative advantage. He also persuaded the World Bank to include the study of social sectors, particularly public health, in the mission survey.

By 1960 Currie had already undertaken a wide range of more detailed economic and administrative studies in various regions: Caldas, the Magdalena Valley, the Sinú Valley, the Atlantic coast, Barranquilla, Bogotá, and now Meta and the Llanos Orientales (eastern plains). He was an active dairy farmer, and he had carried out studies on the problems of the beef cattle industry in the Magdalena Valley and Meta.[1] We have seen already how, in his travels around Colombia, particularly in Nariño, Boyacá, and later in the Magdalena Valley, he had been struck by the intense poverty and ignorance of the minifundistas and colonos. These people were either eking out a bare subsistence with primitive traditional techniques on tiny plots in remote and difficult terrain or were causing untold damage to the environment with their short-sighted slash-and-burn mentality. In addition, the birthrate was extremely high.

Meanwhile, from his own experience as a farmer and from his observations of the dramatic technical revolution that was silently taking place on the best and most accessible lands in crop after crop, he was becoming more and more convinced that there was absolutely no economic future for the great majority of Colombian agriculturalists. The agricultural future lay with just a small fraction of the present rural population, working much larger plots on the best and most accessible lands with modern methods, new seed varieties, and much machinery. Nowadays the truth of this perspective has, albeit often reluctantly, gained widespread acceptance. In 1960, however, it was heresy both in Colombia and even among North American and European intellectuals in their great urban universities or in the development agencies in Washington, New York, Rome, and Geneva.

When, therefore, in late 1960 and early 1961 Currie uncompromisingly pushed the implications of his observations to their logical conclusion in *Operation Colombia*, he aroused bitter opposition at home and abroad. But by now he was accustomed to controversy and his resilience was fortified by an absolute conviction in the soundness of the basic ideas, by the support of a few people whose judgment he respected, and by the inadequacies of the opposing plans and criticisms that he encountered. "Any economist worth his salt," he wrote in a memorandum in February 1961, "is accustomed to espousing views that run counter to public opinion (otherwise there would be no justification for economists)."

Operation Colombia was originally written not for publication but rather as a study document for President Lleras and his advisers at the National Planning Agency. The original version, which ran to 153 pages of typescript in English, was written in a great hurry following a moment of inspiration in December 1960 when Currie suddenly recognized that, despite inflation and the fact that there appeared to be relatively little *open* unemployment, in essence the nature of the problem in Colombia was very similar to that of the Great Depression in the United States. What Colombia had in common with the Great Depression was in fact mass unemployment, albeit disguised, and gross underutilization of its capital and natural resources.

During the Second World War real output in the United States increased by around 15 percent a year for three consecutive years and thus it was possible to meet massive war expenditures and at the same time increase production of consumer goods. In Colombia Currie believed that the potential could be equally great if a concerted effort, strategically directed, was launched to mobilize the country's grossly underutilized resources for productive employment. Devising a strategy to accomplish this, however, first required a correct diagnosis of the nature of the problem. The problem was pervasive poverty arising from extremely low productivity for the mass of the population. However, not only was productivity extremely low, most people were producing things for which actual and potential demand was extremely limited relative to the labor required. This was especially true of agriculture. Half the agricultural labor force was producing only a small fraction of total agricultural output. If these workers were to leave agriculture and work elsewhere, Currie was convinced that the commercial farms could easily make up their small output. The output potential of larger-scale modern farms using the latest techniques and practices on the better, more accessible lands was enormous and was limited primarily by lack of effective market demand.

Currie noted that all of the recent increase in market demand had been met by modern commercial farmers. In fact, the increasing misery of subsistence farmers and their migration to the cities indicated that modern farms were increasing their output faster than the growth of markets, with the result that they were capturing a larger share of that market. Overall agricultural output was growing at about the same pace as effective demand, or a little faster than population growth, so that farm prices evidenced no secular tendency to rise in real terms (that is, relative to other prices), despite the violence that had torn Colombia's rural areas in the 1950s.

No one was against measures to increase agricultural productivity, least of all Currie. But where Currie's diagnosis and proposed solution differed radically from the conventional wisdom of the vast majority of economists and politicians in Colombia and elsewhere was in his acute sensitivity to the possibility of the fallacy of composition and the need to view the workings of the economy as an interrelated system. No part of the machine should be viewed in isolation. The most appropriate cure for a breakdown may lie not in a direct attack on an isolated part, but on some other related part of the machine. The reason a wheel is not turning may be that the motor has no gas.

For Currie, the motor of development was not agriculture as such but technology and the most economically efficient use of resources directed to satisfying the most urgent needs of the mass of the people. Needs, however, had to be converted into effective demands. But in an inflationary economy this could not be accomplished simply through increased government spending and monetary expansion. Furthermore, balance-of-payments considerations had to be examined very carefully.

When comparing the mass consumption needs of the Colombian people with the existing allocation of resources some most striking mismatches were to be observed. On the one hand, nearly half the labor force was engaged in some kind of agricultural activity, most of them producing very little of economic value that could not easily be produced on a relatively small number of modern farms employing relatively few people. On the other hand, there was a gross deficiency of nonagricultural products, including low-cost housing, related construction materials such as cement, bricks, glass, and timber, and social infrastructure such as urban roads, waterworks, sewage, schools, clinics, and related services. Almost all these products could be produced more cheaply and efficiently not in the existing scattered rural villages and towns but in larger cities that offered greater economies of scale and interdependence, together with larger and more concentrated markets.

Natural forces were already bringing about the appropriate reallocation of resources toward a more industrialized and urbanized economy. However, the technical revolution that had occurred over a 150-year period in North America and Europe was available for developing countries such as Colombia to use immediately. But Currie was convinced that this technology was being applied in a most wasteful fashion and its potential benefits largely unexploited. Technology makes possible a larger output with fewer resources. But if the resources displaced by technology are not mobilized for use elsewhere then the benefits will be unequally shared and unemployed or underemployed labor will be worse off, despite growing national output. Despite and because of this widespread misery population growth was accelerating, which in turn contributed to the further spread of poverty and underemployment.

Poverty, unemployment, and high birthrates were concentrated in the rural areas. Why? Because technology was being introduced at an historically unprecedented rate, albeit on a relatively small number of farms, and at a rate significantly greater than the growth of effective demand. Paradoxically the agricultural revolution was accompanied by widespread malnutrition but, again paradoxically, most of this was to be found among the rural population or among those who had recently migrated from the countryside to the towns without finding remunerative work.[2] The orthodox response to this unhappy situation was to decry rural-urban migration and to concentrate efforts on raising the productivity of subsistence farmers.

Typically, government policy, supported by the international agencies, emphasized: agricultural credit policies directed preferentially toward small traditional farmers at interest rates often subsidized by the central bank in its ambiguous role as a development bank; technical assistance programs that also emphasized small farmers; extremely costly colonization programs on land often far distant from the main markets but where land was more abundant and cheap (and cheap precisely because it was more or less economically worthless); policies to prohibit or make more costly the importation of agricultural machinery which "displaced labor," but to encourage new seeds and fertilizers because these "created jobs"; and "land reform" programs to break up large estates and redistribute land to minifundistas and landless laborers. All this Currie regarded as either irrelevant or, more often, misguided and positively harmful. This did not win him many friends but it would not deflect him from persistent, uncompromising advocacy of what he was convinced was right. In the Washington development agencies he consolidated his reputation for being conflictive, unrealistic, and uncooperative; perhaps insubordinate too.[3]

The fallacy of composition underlying the conventional view of agriculture and the possibility of maintaining agricultural employment lay in the belief that since an increase in productivity for one farmer is good for that farmer then an increase in the productivity of all farmers must be good for all farmers. Surprisingly few economists, and still fewer politicians and laymen, grasped the distinction between physical and value productivity. Additional machinery, harder work, better organization, improved seed varieties, fertilizers, pesticides, reclaimed land—all these may increase yields per hectare and output per man. They increase physical productivity. They all add to costs, though not necessarily unit costs. If, however, they increase overall output faster than market demand, prices will fall. In the short run prices may even fall below the unit costs of production. This is an ever-present threat to most agricultural products because the price and income elasticities of demand are so low. Home demand grows little faster than population growth because, as incomes grow, most of the additional income is spent on nonagricultural products and services. If a country can produce agricultural goods cheaply enough, and if the exchange rate is competitive, foreign demand may help. But price and income elasticities of demand are also low on international markets and competition is fierce. And the most successful agricultural exporting nations are countries such as the United States, Canada, and New Zealand where even in 1960 only around 5 to 10 percent of the labor force was engaged in agriculture. (Today the proportion is even lower.)

Currie emphasized the "excess competition" in Colombian agriculture, a concept that sounds strange and contradictory to most neoclassical economists, trained to applaud and encourage competition and free enterprise. Currie also applauded these but insisted that their benefits are lost if not accompanied by the equally important phenomenon of mobility, especially labor mobility. If increasing agricultural productivity is not accompanied by mobility then, because of the low elasticity of demand for the product, prices would fall and the great mass of noninnovators would suffer a fall in income. Indeed, even the innovators could suffer some reduction in income since in the short run increased output could cause prices to fall even below the lower costs of production of the more efficient farmers. In the long run prices would tend to equal unit costs of production of these efficient farmers. However, competition from minifundistas willing, or forced, to accept very low incomes would tend to discourage investment in more mechanized agriculture. Such investment would also be discouraged by policies to restrict agricultural credit to smaller farmers, by land redistribution policies, and by the massive diversion of resources into remote "penetration roads" and colonization projects.

Given the interrelated nature of the problem a new type of national plan was called for that attacked poverty, not by throwing money at the problem wherever it was presently encountered, but strategically concentrating the attack or mobilizing idle resources for use where they would create the greatest addition to the wealth of the country and the well-being of the poor. This meant bringing workers to the work, not work to the workers. And it meant bringing people to where services could most cheaply be provided. not expensive services to remote and scattered people in places with no economic future.

In reading *Operation Colombia* one is reminded of Keynes's biography of Winston Churchill. In reviewing Churchill's devastating appraisal of the blunders of the British and German generals in the First World War, Keynes remarked: "The strategic surrender, the deliberate withdrawal, the attempt to lure the enemy into a pocket where he could be taken in flank, all such expedients of the higher imagination of warfare, were scarcely attempted. The ideas of the staffs were from beginning to end elementary in the extreme—in attack, to find out the enemy in his strongest place and hurl yourself on him; in defence, to die heroically in the first ditch."[4]

By contrast, the campaign strategy of *Operation Colombia* was to mobilize all available idle resources and put them to work in the places they were most needed, in the places where they could produce the greatest economic value and so contribute most to the standard of living of the masses. This would best be accomplished by working with, not against, natural forces. Natural forces were displacing labor from agriculture and small-scale, technically backward handicrafts and services, and putting them into the bigger industrial cities for work in modern factories, construction work of all kinds, and more efficiently organized services. But these natural forces were operating too slowly and were being restrained by the wasteful diversion of resources, limitations on mechanization, and resort to inflationary finance that were the hallmark of the official national plan, the Plan Cuatrienal, 1960–63, worked out with the aid of technicians loaned by the UN Economic Commission for Latin America (ECLA), that was being launched at the same time that Currie was preparing his radical alternative.

Having presented the broad thrust of his program it was Currie's hope that the four-man National Planning Council, at that time chaired by Jorge Mendes, would be asked by President Lleras to submit the program to serious study by its technical staff (whose director was Edgar Gutiérrez) both to appraise its theoretical validity and to make more detailed estimates of the quantitative magnitudes that a program of this type implied in terms of overall and sectoral goals for output, employment, and noninflationary financing.

Currie's own tentative target was a two-year crash program that would mobilize an additional 500,000 workers into new urban jobs, mainly in the larger cities and primarily in construction and related industries, but also in other industries of mass consumption such as textiles, and in urban education and public health programs (the latter to focus on the eradication of debilitating diseases such as intestinal parasites that affected almost everyone). This implied about a 20 percent increase in the growth of national income over the two-year period, in contrast to the goal of 2.5 percent annual growth of per capita income envisaged in the official Plan Cuatrienal. Later, at the Punta del Este Conference in Montevideo in July 1961, ECLA technicians (under the direction of Raul Prébisch) persuaded the Colombian planners to convert their four-year plan into a ten-year plan, the Plan Decenal, but with the same focus and the same unambitious targets of an overall annual growth of 2.5 percent in per capita income.

Currie worked out, in broad terms, the financial requirements of his program. The main source of finance was to come from private savings, mostly to finance a target of 300,000 new housing units over the two years. This contrasted with perhaps 30,000 units a year being built under existing programs.[5] These savings, consistent with a 20 percent savings rate out of the greatly increased national income envisaged in the plan, would be encouraged by a new index-linked housing finance system that Currie proposed and explained in some detail in his original draft of *Operation Colombia*. It would be administered by a new national institution.[6] Hitherto, Currie noted, inflation discouraged saving and the limited funds available were distributed to potential house buyers in the form almost of a lottery. Those fortunate enough to buy a house with a fixed-interest mortgage made substantial capital gains while others were homeless, income distribution worsened, and the ethical basis and reputation of the free enterprise system were undermined. *Operation Colombia*, Currie believed, represented the only salvation of democratic economic institutions at a time when Castroist ideology was sweeping Latin America.

A second source of finance was to come from the diversion of a host of nonpriority public expenditures, especially in remote rural areas. There would also be restrictions of private sumptuary expenditures, including luxury housing. The restrictions on luxury and middle-class housing could be relaxed at the end of the initial crash program, to maintain the momentum of private expenditures following the initial pump-priming operations. Currie's ideas on housing priorities were to change somewhat in later years, with greater emphasis on middle-class housing and the "filtration" or "escalation" principle which will be described in more detail in chapter 10 below. In 1960 Currie focused more on low-cost housing, though he was opposed to the *very* low-cost housing programs undertaken by the Colombian Territorial (popular housing) Institute (ICT) and deplored "auto-construction," or self-built housing. He viewed these programs as a desperate resort by persons unable to obtain better quality housing through more conventional professional housing programs and a negation of the principles of specialization and exchange. If people had full-time remunerative work they could afford to buy new or, more often, existing housing of a much better standard in more accessible locations than they could if they had to build their own homes. Better-off workers would occupy new housing in Currie's plan, and the poorer families would occupy the houses the former group would vacate.

A third source of finance would be the peso counterpart of the additional foreign exchange inflows arising, in the first instance, mainly from a large *program* loan that Currie hoped to persuade a consortium of international agencies to make in support of his national plan. The idea of a program loan, unrelated to specific projects vetted by IBRD and other international agency technicians, was at that time very novel, as was the idea of several agencies cooperating for this purpose as a consortium. Currie failed to gain this support for his plan but his proposal was discussed seriously with Barend de Vries and Orvis Schmidt of the World Bank. This resulted in the creation of the Grupo de Consulta shortly afterward. However, this body, which meets regularly in Paris, has not acted in the way Currie had hoped. Instead, the Grupo de Consulta, with representatives of the main international lending agencies, merely sits down to share out the "shopping list" of individual projects requiring finance presented to it by the Colombian government.[7]

In addition to foreign loans, and later to replace these, Currie also placed considerable faith in Colombia's ability to greatly increase foreign exchange earnings from the export of meat. Currie was outraged at the inefficient organization of this industry, at the poor quality of meat brought to market, and at the unnecessarily high marketing costs. After conducting various studies with a British meat-marketing expert he was convinced there was considerable scope for reducing costs and improving quality. With a more competitive, differential exchange rate regime, a major break into world markets similar to that achieved by the Argentinians should then be feasible. Currie agitated vigorously for reforms in the cattlemen's federation, Fedegan, later succeeded in establishing a new organization, and himself became a director for a while of the cattlemen's bank, the Banco Ganadero. However, though Colombia has been very successful in diversifying into other exports, twenty-five years later there has been almost no success in improving the quality of its meat to the standards demanded in foreign markets.

A substantial increase in foreign exchange would be necessary to support Operation Colombia to finance the import of machinery for the technification of agriculture and to break bottlenecks in various sectors of industry. Exchange licenses were to be allocated strictly according to the priorities of the plan. However, it was envisaged that import requirements per unit of output would be greatly reduced through a change in the pattern of demand toward articles of mass consumption, especially housing and construction with its relatively intensive use of domestic raw materials, and through a much more intensive use of the existing capital stock. In Colombia in 1960 very few industries operated more than one shift and, because of frequent patriotic and religious holidays, even for the urban fully employed the work year usually did not exceed 220 days. Operation Colombia would change that too.

The last financial aspect of Operation Colombia concerned the related monetary policy. Currie worked out the appropriate, noninflationary expansion of the money supply equal to the increased demand for money that would be expected to accompany the real increase in output and expenditures envisaged in his program. To the extent that the government would finance part of its spending program by borrowing from the central bank, 100 percent marginal reserve requirements were to be imposed to ensure that the overall expansion in the money supply did not exceed the growth of real production.

That, in bare outline, is the essence of the objectives, diagnosis, and strategy of Operation Colombia. In the next few years Currie was to refine the theoretical framework in greater detail. Eventually, under a different name and in more refined form, it was to be adopted as the official national plan of President Misael Pastrana's administration in 1971. In May 1961, however, when the first confidential draft of *Operation Colombia* was complete, the first task was to get the document studied seriously by President Alberto Lleras and his key officials and to have the quantitative aspects worked out in greater detail. Once the support of the Colombian government had been secured the next step would be to convince the international agencies to support it. And then it could be presented to the Colombian people for public debate, approval, and implementation. It would be a New Deal and a War on Poverty waged jointly by the Colombian people and the international development agencies.

The Campaign for Support and the Refinement of the Theory

Operation Colombia was dashed off in a few weeks of inspired writing as a confidential draft document for President Lleras. Currie was bursting with enthusiasm for his new insights, thinking big, minimizing the difficulties, confident they could be overcome if the objectives were clear and consistent and the basic diagnosis correct. He did not know how much of what he was writing was really novel since he had not worked seriously on economic theory, or kept up with the professional journals, for many years. Years later, looking back on his "youthful" (at the age of fifty-eight!) enthusiasm for Operation Colombia with some sense of embarrassment, he would remark, in excusing its weaknesses and lack of refinement, "ignorance was bliss and twas folly to be wise." Had he been more cautious and circumspect he would never have dared forward his plan in such bold and stark form, would not have aroused such controversy, would not have been led to refine and develop the program or rewrite it, first as the award-winning book, *Accelerating Development*,[8] and then again later (after four years of academic teaching, reading, and thinking in Canada and Britain) as the famous *Plan of the Four Strategies*, that was adopted as the highly successful official development program of the Pastrana administration in the early 1970s.

Nevertheless, Currie has never doubted the broad correctness of his basic diagnosis of the pervasive phenomenon of underdevelopment—at least as found in most contemporary Latin American economies—

nor the main thrust of his proposed development strategy. Nor has he doubted that his ideas in general represent a far superior alternative to the orthodoxy of the ECLA-Prébisch-Hirschman programs for inward-looking, import-substituting industrialization behind protective tariff walls; or to the crude land-redistributing agrarian reform programs of the Alliance for Progress; or to the labor-intensive "make-work" programs of the International Labor Office (ILO) and the Sussex School; or to Schumacher's "small-is-beautiful" approach; or to the Harris-Todaro thesis that rural-urban migration is, for migrants as a group, irrational, increases unemployment, and reduces national income; or to the Marxist "dependency thesis" that metropolitan development exploits and is at the expense of rural "satellites"; or to the IBRD-McNamara direct attacks on the "poorest of the poor" in the remotest, most backward regions—the crude First World War attrition approach. This catalog of some of the more popular and well-publicized approaches to underdevelopment brings out, for those readers less familiar with the favored theories and strategies of development in the past thirty years, just how novel and controversial have been Currie's theories and policy proposals.

Thus the skepticism that greeted the first drafts of *Operation Colombia* early in 1961 is understandable. Nevertheless, President Alberto Lleras read the proposals with interest and urged his Consejo de Planificación to study them. He also encouraged Currie to take his program to Washington to discuss with President Kennedy's closest economic advisers and with the economists at the international development agencies, particularly the World Bank. Copies were sent to his old friend John Kenneth Galbraith—but Galbraith was appointed U.S. ambassador to India so was unable to study it—and later to Paul Samuelson at the urging of Virgilio Barco, who had discussed the plan with Samuelson in London in November 1961. Samuelson was in London to deliver the Stamp Memorial Lecture. Ambassador Barco wrote to Currie:

> I was able to get him to come yesterday to my home where I corralled him for more than an hour to explain "Operación Colombia". I had even the chance of informing him of the stage of the game we are in at present with the organization of the foundation and all that. Also, he was briefed on the outcome of the Washington presentation and I let him read your report in which the reaction of the many economists were consigned. I believe he was quite interested because I pressed on him the urgency of the situation in Latin America and the insufficiency . . . of the "programmes" now be-

ing offered. . . . [Samuelson] stressed that the fact that he was a presidential adviser would make it difficult for him to second a scheme which could have such vast implications on policy. He agreed to read the report and if he felt that he could comment in spite of his commitments to Washington, he would do so.[9]

Though Currie did send Samuelson a copy of *Operation Colombia*, unfortunately it elicited only a polite acknowledgment.

In June 1961 Currie traveled to Washington with Virgilio Barco, the latter en route to London to take up his post as ambassador. Together they sounded out a number of prominent economists. Ironically, in view of the adverse publicity Currie had received during the McCarthy "witch-hunts" and the fact that due to his residence in Colombia the U.S. government had withdrawn his citizenship,[10] on the very first day of his arrival in Washington since losing that citizenship Currie was lunching in the White House!

This arose because the first person whom Virgilio Barco wanted him to meet was Barco's old MIT teacher of economics, Walt Rostow, who was now installed in the White House as the President's (later much discredited) national security adviser. The John Birch Society would have been appalled had it known; and the conservative Rostow was at first somewhat abashed too. But he gave *Operation Colombia* a respectful hearing and promised to follow it up. According to Currie's report on this meeting Rostow saw in the plan opportunities to increase PL 480 loans to Colombia, thus tending to reduce the whole problem to one of the availability of food and fibers.[11] In other words, along with a large number of other critics of accelerated urbanization policies, Rostow's main emphasis was placed on the need to promote agriculture first, because of a supposed highly inelastic supply or to make up for local food deficiencies by foreign food aid programs.[12]

Currie discussed his plan in Washington with many other economists inside and outside of the government and in the international agencies. The plan had a good reception from his old friends from the New Deal, including: Gerhard Colm,[13] chief economist of the National Planning Association, who suggested further study on the value of the Keynesian multiplier during the transition period (the multiplier might be lower in the transition period so that the cutback in other investment could be less; however, they also discussed the inflationary dangers); Walter Salant of the Brookings Institution and E. M. Bernstein, formerly chief economist of the IMF, both of whom expressed interest in doing further work on the balance-of-payments aspects of the program; Emile Despres, chairman of the Council of Development Studies, Stanford University; Robert Nathan, who discussed the problem of expanding exports when GNP was expanding rapidly; and Ben Cohen.

Salant introduced him to Isaiah Frank, director of the office of international financial and development affairs at the State Department, who was very enthusiastic. He in turn introduced Currie to Milton Barroll, a State Department official for Latin American affairs, but he was critical of the consortium idea. At the World Bank, however, Currie's friend Orvis Schmidt was much more positive on this, as was Barend de Vries. However, other Bank economists, Jerry Alter and John de Wilde, were not helpful. Alter apparently believed that once the initial housing program had been completed there would be no further work for the construction workers so that Operation Colombia would shortly cause a big increase in urban unemployment. A few months later Alter headed an IBRD team to Colombia to discuss consortium financing of projects for the Plan Decenal instead!

Back in Bogotá, Currie wrote to Virgilio Barco, June 22, "The Operation survived its baptism of fire very well." However, he continued:

> For my own inner peace of mind, it would have been better if I had not gone to Washington. Now I have a low opinion of the White House gang. The morale in the State Department is bad. I have little faith in "task forces," "teams," committees and commissions as substitutes for personal responsibility. I encountered no great sense of urgency. In short, our "saviours" do not appear too impressive close at hand. And Colombia is so small and unimportant. I'm afraid they'll only get interested in us when we are "lost" to them. Almost all the best economists are outside the Government which is very different from the New Deal days. Clearly, we will have to work out our own salvation.

During Currie's absence in Washington Jorge Méndez, chairman of the Consejo de Planificación, had brought up Operation Colombia at a full meeting of the consejo with President Lleras and four ministers. It was described as "utopian" and more or less rejected. Carlos Lleras Restrepo, who had urged Currie to delay the release of *Operation Colombia* to the public until he had pushed his new agrarian reform bill through parliament, nevertheless himself referred critically to the document in the Senate. He questioned whether the Operation could be accompanied by an adequate increase in agricultural output, and whether the new urban jobs could be sustained after the initial phase of the Operation had passed.[14] By July public criticisms of the Operation by Edgar Gutiérrez provoked further interest in the press, and the Laureanistas (a wing of the Conservative party) accused the government of suppressing the document. In another letter to Virgilio Barco, July 15, Currie wrote: "Méndez has sent an S.O.S. for Pope Prébisch[15] himself to blast me—so I couldn't ask for a bigger build-up. I am told that the Laureanistas and Alfonsistas[16] are going to support it. Opposition of the Ospinistas (Patiño, Pastrana, et al) and *El Tiempo* has stiffened."

In view of the distorted accounts of *Operation Colombia* that were being leaked to the press, Currie secured President Lleras's permission to publish the full text. The press began carrying installments on July 16. On July 20, in opening Congress, President Alberto Lleras formally rejected Operation Colombia in favor of the ECLA-inspired official plan. Ten years later, to the day and the hour, on July 20, 1971, President Misael Pastrana, who in 1961 had wobbled between support and attack on Operation Colombia, and whose relations with Currie were then rather strained due to disagreements over the 1961 transport mission, presented to Congress a revised version of Operation Colombia, now called "The Plan of the Four Strategies." Despite fierce opposition Pastrana stuck to this program even more fiercely and with acknowledged success.

The Foundation for the Progress of Colombia

Around this time Anibal López, who was later to play an important role as a member of Currie's "Wednesday Night Group" that prepared the way for the adoption of the Plan of the Four Strategies in 1971, suggested to Currie that, since the planning office would not undertake a serious study of Operation Colombia, an independent research institute should be established to study and promote it instead.

Thus was born the Fundación para el Progreso de Colombia, which, under Currie's guidance, was to undertake a large number of studies directly or indirectly related to Operation Colombia over the following two years. Other members of the board of directors included Samuel Hoyos (another member of the 1971 Wednesday Night Group), Fabio Lozano (who ran a column in *El Espectador* that often carried satirical articles prepared for him by Currie), and Emilio Toro, who was a prominent member of the 1950–51 Committee of Economic Development (see chapter 6). Klaus Vollert was, for a while, executive director.

The studies undertaken by the foundation under Currie's direction covered agriculture, industry, construction, population problems, and more detailed quantitative estimates of the physical and financial implications of Operation Colombia. Perhaps the most important of the agricultural studies undertaken at this time was the study of the coffee sector, financed by the coffee bank, the Banco Cafetero.[17] The study found that about three-quarters of coffee-growing family farms were cultivating such small minifundios in poor or remote locations—often suffering from soil erosion—that they were not even earning the minimum wage. Many thousands of them had barely enough land to justify more than about one month's work a year. They were marginal in the sense that they earned much less than was customarily earned in unskilled or semiskilled urban work.

Given the very low elasticity of demand for coffee, and Colombia's adherence to quotas fixed by the international coffee agreements, the solution to the extreme poverty of around 140,000 coffee farm families (over 60 percent of the total) could only be found in other occupations. A rise in the coffee rate of exchange in terms of pesos would only encourage increased production that would either have to be destroyed or that would push down the world price. It would also give a windfall gain to the larger, more efficient coffee farmers and reduce government revenues. (Government gains from the differential between the coffee exchange rate and the import rate of exchange: the government pays coffee growers fewer pesos per dollar than the pesos it obtains from sale of dollars to importers.)

However, Currie's study then examined the entire agricultural situation and found that almost any attempt to find alternative work for marginal coffee growers in other crops would only make the situation worse for existing cultivators of those alternative crops. If there was to be a diversification into other crops, this would be most easily and efficiently accomplished by the larger commercial coffee growers, not by minifundistas. But if the larger coffee growers did diversify into other crops, this would further increase the "excess competition" that prevailed generally throughout Colombian agriculture and so could represent at best improved incomes for a few richer farmers, not a general solution to widespread rural poverty and unemployment.[18]

The study examined the *average* yields of the larger, more mechanized, commercial farmers who were earning around the average urban income and, using this figure, calculated for all the main crops in Colombia the amount of land and number of workers that would in these circumstances be required to produce the entire 1960 agricultural production. For coffee only 682,000 hectares would be needed, instead of 2,177,000 hectares; agriculture as a whole would need 1,444,000 hectares instead of 3,066,000 hectares.[19] The number of workers required in coffee was estimated at 154,000 instead of 394,000; and in agriculture as a whole (excluding cattle) 297,000 instead of 1,236,000.[20] A further 280,000 (instead of the current 440,000) would be required for the cattle industry. Under these conditions, supposing that the 1960 *average* commercial practices were spread throughout Colombian agriculture, only 14 percent, instead of 52 percent, of the labor force would be needed in agriculture, working on less than half the presently cultivated land.

Estimates of the income elasticity of demand for agricultural products, calculated by Jorge Ruiz Lara as part of his study for the foundation of the "Quantitative Aspects of Operation Colombia," indicated that a 20 percent increase in national income would yield an 11 percent increase in domestic demand for agricultural products overall which, spread over two or three years would, Currie believed, be easy to meet so long as there were no price controls so that it paid commercial farmers to meet the additional real demand.

This study of the coffee sector and agriculture generally revealed that once moderate technical improvements were introduced—as they would be if demand and prospective profits justified it and if agrarian reform focused on the consolidation of minifundios rather than the further fragmentation of economic-sized farms—then two million of the farm workers of 1960 would be surplus to requirements. Mobilizing these people for more remunerative nonfarm employment was thus the medium- or long-term goal. It suggested that the short-term goal of 500,000 new urban jobs under Operation Colombia was not unreasonable. It was no less than the magnitude and urgency of the problem demanded.

Other agricultural and regional studies that Currie directed for the foundation at this time included several for the Corporación del Valle del Magdalena: on land reclamation in the Municipio de Plato that investigated the possibility of reclaiming some 25,000 hectares of currently valueless land at very low cost;[21] a cattle study aimed at reorganizing the cattlemen's association to promote exports through the changes recommended in the earlier Currie-Anderson study; and a study of the Sinú Valley that changed the emphasis on land reclamation there from flood control and irrigation to the problems of drainage of rainwater.[22] Another regional study was undertaken for the Ministerio de Fomento on the Department of North Santander. This was a more general survey of the development prospects of this region and stressed the importance of developing commercial relations with neighboring Venezuela.[23] In the same department of North Santander a related but narrower study of land reclamation possibilities had been undertaken a year or two earlier.[24] For these various agricultural and land reclamation studies Currie relied, among others, on the help of Charles Senour, Santiago Rueda, Pedro Ramírez, and Julio Bejarano.

A little later Currie conducted a study on the cotton industry which again highlighted the technical revolution that was taking place, the implications of this for rural employment, the elasticity of supply, and the importance of demand-side considerations.[25] And in 1967 he returned to Barranquilla and the Atlantic coast to direct another general survey and make recommendations on agricultural and urban development.[26]

Of equal importance were the studies Currie directed on the possibilities for accelerated industrial and urban development. A study sponsored by the Colombian Construction Association (CAMACOL) in 1962 examined the importance of income growth and the availability of finance for the growth of housing for different income groups. Currie again emphasized the importance of a new housing finance system that, through index-linking, would take care of the serious damage done to the system by inflation.[27]

Meanwhile, for the foundation, Oscar Gómez issued a questionnaire to industrial firms on excess capacity. The results affirmed that a great majority of firms operated on a single shift. The main exceptions were in textiles and in certain plants where it was too expensive to suspend the operation of furnaces. It confirmed the tremendous potential for expanded production if double or triple shift operations were introduced and public holidays reduced. This was also the kind of study that would be useful in indicating where bottlenecks were most likely, and would be a guide to policymakers in the priority allocation of licenses for scarce foreign exchange. Jorge Ruiz Lara's quantitative studies also focused on foreign exchange requirements for capital imports, though Currie felt that his methodology was based too rigidly on the projection of historic coefficients for capital and imports relative to output. Thus Ruiz Lara's estimated import requirements were rather on the high side. Currie insisted that Operation Colombia would involve a much fuller use of capital, hence of foreign exchange requirements, than in the past.[28] Furthermore, the emphasis on housing involved a sector with relatively small import requirements, as confirmed in the earlier CAMACOL study.

In February 1962 Currie was contracted by the mayor of Bogotá to undertake a new study of Bogotá's urban development. Characteristically, this study soon widened its scope to consider Bogotá's growth in the context of the overall rate and pattern of growth of the Colombian economy and to evolve an overall national urban policy—at that time totally absent—that Currie hoped would enable Colombia to avoid the worst mistakes of the North American pattern of costly urban sprawl.[29] These ideas were to be much more fully worked out in a subsequent study of growth alternatives for Bogotá that Currie undertook in 1966–67 for Virgilio Barco when he was mayor of Bogotá and Currie was director of the Center for Development Studies (Centro de Investigaciones para el Desarrollo, CID) at the National University.[30] This latter study became the basis for a "cities-within-cities" design for metropolitan expansion that in turn was to be the basis of major urban development projects carried out in later years.[31]

Currie's 1962 study of Bogotá differed from his later ideas in that at that time he believed that through a system of incentives and deterrents an effort should be made to avoid excessive concentration on a few cities. Later he was to be more impressed by the relative economic efficiency of the larger cities, because of economies of scale and agglommeration economies. Nevertheless, he was always acutely aware of offsetting costs, especially transportation costs, involved in unrestrained and unplanned metropolitan sprawl. In 1962 he hoped to limit this sprawl by restraining the growth of the largest cities. He hoped that cities could be prevented from becoming metropolises by strict prohibitions on the extension of suburbia. Later he became aware of the possibilities for a new urban design for the largest cities that would permit them to avoid some of the worst costs of metropolitan growth. This was the point of his novel "cities-within-cities" design that aimed to create more or less self-contained nuclei within the metropolitan area that could promote a much better matching of jobs, residences, and community facilities, thus minimizing transportation costs. At the same time this design would preserve and maximize the advantages of proximity of industrial plants and services of all kinds within the wider metropolitan area. More will be said about this important aspect of Currie's work in later chapters.

The Political Background and "Economic Illiteracy"

In August 1962 Guillermo Valencia became President of Colombia. Under the National Front agreement it was the turn of a Conservative to assume office, and Valencia was, with the support of the Liberal leader Carlos Lleras Restrepo, the compromise candidate. Valencia was a well-known poet from Popayán, a heavy drinker, and totally unsuited to the post he was to hold for the next four years. The country was drifting into revolutionary violence, with Castro's star in the ascendant and President Kennedy's reputation tarnished by the Bay of Pigs fiasco. U.S. policy in Latin America was to send Peace Corps workers (provocatively described by Currie as boy scouts), to support ECLA's protectionist approach, and to launch the Alliance for Progress with AID money concentrated on support for colonization and land reform programs of the crude land redistribution variety.

Currie's friend Enrique Peñalosa was appointed head of Colombia's Agrarian Reform Institute, Incora, and for a while was cool toward Operation Colombia. Somewhat later he accepted the need to campaign vigorously for "complementary" urbanization programs.

Virgilio Barco, who at first, in an excess of caution, refused to join Valencia's cabinet as finance minister, thinking it would be political suicide to do so, did join in January 1963 as minister of agriculture and so also went down the land reform road with Peñalosa despite Currie's best efforts to keep him behind a massive urbanization program instead. But at that time there were more votes in land reform. Carlos Lleras Restrepo also favored this focus.

Currie's view was that this government was demonstrating Parkinson's "Law of Inverse Infallibility" and "stumbling and fumbling along," avoiding real choices. It was the government's luck that the Communist guerrilla groups were equally badly organized; but rural violence continued. This, together with the technical revolution in agriculture, was pushing more and more campesinos into the towns and cities. President Valencia, his advisers, and the international agencies all agreed that there were already too many people in the cities, so naturally no special efforts were being made to provide urban employment for them. Overt unemployment increased and these critics felt this vindicated their opposition to Operation Colombia.[32] The governing classes stepped up their efforts to build heavily guarded islands of security for their families, or left the country.

The U.S. ambassador did his best to block Currie's influence. By 1964 Currie shared a commonly held belief that the military would soon take over because the President was so incompetent and there was general disintegration of the economy, society, and morals. In December 1964 Virgilio Barco asked Currie to prepare a speech for him on the desirable qualities of a president, which Barco wanted to use for a speech in support of Carlos Lleras's presidential campaign. Barco did not use the speech because he said the qualities Currie had listed made Valencia appear ridiculous.[33] By April 1965 Currie was beginning to fear going to his farm outside Bogotá because of a wave of kidnapping. Partly for this reason, but mainly because he wanted to devote more time to academic work, he decided, very sadly, he would have to try to sell the farm. When he heard of this, his friend Alvaro Gómez (son of the late President Laureano Gómez who died around this time) commented, "all of Colombia is up for sale."[34]

Naturally this was all very disheartening, but Currie retained enough of his old resiliency to carry on his lonely crusade against the tide. The studies carried out at the Fundación para el Progreso de Colombia "turned his faith into a conviction." He tried out his ideas on a variety of audiences: architects and engineers, industrialists and farmers, economists and sociologists. In 1963 many of his speeches and essays were published by Ediciones Tercer Mundo as *Ensayos sobre Planeación* (Essays on Planning), with an expanded second edition published in 1965. Gratifyingly, these essays, together with *Operación Colombia* (reissued in 1965), sold very well. Currie saw these as an important part of his personal campaign to reduce the ghastly incidence of economic illiteracy that prevailed in Colombia. Though thousands called themselves economists (including anyone who graduated in accountancy or business administration) almost none thought like economists, by Currie's standards. Later he was to carry his educational campaign much further; but first he was anxious to work up a completely revised and more academic version of *Operation Colombia*. He felt that, in his early sixties, he had little time left.

Accelerating Development

This, however, was a spur. When late in 1963, the McGraw-Hill Book Company, in collaboration with the Society for International Development, announced a major prize competition for a book on international development, Currie devoted himself single-mindedly over several months to his manuscript. He submitted it in April 1964. During this time he immersed himself in the academic economics literature for the first time in nearly thirty years. He had been unable to enjoy this luxury since his Harvard days. The experience was so satisfying that he resolved to try to create the opportunity to devote more of his time to this kind of serious academic work in the future. With the country "going to the dogs" he also resolved to try to reduce his energy-sapping work on regional, sectoral, and city studies and devote himself primarily to national issues.

It was a great boost to morale, and a politically useful enhancement of his prestige, when in October 1964 McGraw-Hill announced that Currie had won the first prize of $2,500 for his "fresh and pragmatic" contribution. The book appeared early in 1966 under the title *Accelerating Development: The Necessity and the Means*. At a luncheon given in Currie's honor in July 1965 to mark the occasion of the McGraw-Hill prize, two ex-presidents (Darío Echandía and Mariano Ospina) and one future president (Carlos Lleras) were in attendance. Messages from two other ex-presidents (Alberto Lleras and Alfonso López Michelsen) were read out. However, the organizer omitted to read out a speech by Father Camilo Torres, who had helped Currie with studies on education and health at the Fundación para el Progreso de Colombia. In his message he said he hoped Currie would not let the common people down. Father Torres later joined a guerrilla movement and was killed by the army.

In *Accelerating Development* Currie placed even more stress than in his earlier writing on the "inter-locking vicious circles" of underdevelopment pervading every aspect of life. The shotgun approach to development, with hundreds of unrelated projects sprinkled thinly across the country was not equal to the task of breaking these vicious circles. In particular, the impact was feeble relative to the dead weight of rapid population growth, then running at nearly 3 percent a year, or doubling every twenty-four years.

Currie insisted on the urgent need for a more focused strategy, based on a correct diagnosis of the nature of the problem, that would be massive enough to make a real impact, a breakthrough.[35] Only by mobilizing the rural poor into productive, remunerative urban jobs would there be a significant effect on motivation to reduce the birthrate. Citing the important work of Richard and Nancy Ruggles on the factors that affect the birthrate Currie noted the importance of higher incomes, urbanization, opportunities for women to work, and educational level (cheaper to provide in urban areas). Religion was a relatively unimportant variable, though Currie had often urged the church in Colombia to relax its attitude on birth control. As late as the early 1980s, the Colombian church authorities were even unwilling to distribute a Vatican pamphlet on the rhythm method.

In the absence of a breakthrough plan the conventional, thinly spread, capital formation approach, financed largely through foreign loans or inflation, would serve mainly to support more and more people at subsistence level, worsen income distribution, and increase the debt burden. In later visits to the Population Council in New York, Currie despaired of their almost exclusive emphasis on family planning campaigns: "We *know* that family planning can take place among the very poorest," asserted Frank Notestein in an interview with Currie in October 1966. He had never seen the Ruggles study. For Currie, the "population bomb" posed a threat greater than nuclear war.[36] By destroying natural resources it made more and more remote the possible attainment of a civilized standard of living for all. By helping perpetuate poverty and ignorance it widened the gap between rich and poor within and between nations. By widening this gap it engendered the envy and hatred that brought nuclear war closer.

These were the stakes and they both drove Currie to pursue his crusade for his breakthrough plan and at the same time increased his sense of frustration and hopelessness in the face of bureaucratic inertia, political opportunism, intellectual laziness, and lamentable teaching of economics and social studies in the universities of Colombia.

He was convinced that if there was to be any hope of a pilot test of his ideas, he would have to carry them to the international agencies—with the leverage their loans could exert if coordinated in support of a strategic program rather than a collection of unrelated projects—and to the prestigious universities of North America and Europe whose economists the international agencies listened to.

The book received a mixed reception from its many reviewers. P. D. Henderson, in *The Economic Journal*, December 1967, wrote: "Professor Currie has written what must surely be one of the liveliest and most absorbing books that economics has produced in recent years." Milton Taylor, in the *Journal of Political Economy*, May–June 1968, commented: "Professor Currie applies the same talent and dedication to the resolution of social problems that made him one of the stars of a brilliant team of New Deal economists. As a result, *Accelerating Development* is more than a good study. . . . In the literature on growth, it may rank with the contribution of scholars like Domar, Harrod, Myrdal and Nurkse." Peter Wiles, in *Economica*, May 1967, was surprised that "in view of the author's reputation it is entirely unsocialistic." He thought, probably fairly, that the book was not formally a good book since the order of presentation was peculiar and the style too flat to make the new or the important stand out from the roughage. Nevertheless, the book "is very important, since it says a number of new and correct things on development policy" that "deserve the most serious consideration." Unfortunately, Wiles failed to understand Currie's argument in some crucial respects. For example, he thought Currie's strategy was mainly one of industrialization through shift work. He thought shift work impractical, because Stalin could not organize it. Yet in Colombia shift work in the textile industry was widespread. He failed to understand the more crucial role of housing in Currie's plan; nor why Currie rejected building directly for the very poor and auto-construction schemes, which Currie dismisses as Robinson Crusoe economics but which Wiles thought must be positively encouraged.

Less sympathetic reviewers included John Powelson who, in the *International Development Review*, June 1967, claimed it was too simplistic: "the anomaly of Currie's plan lies in its keen comprehension of the direction of history and its simultaneous failure to grasp how vast a change it would require. To create a new industrial complex capable of productively employing the millions of illiterate, surplus peasants is no mean task." (Currie, of course, never claimed it was.) And the influential *American Economic Review* assigned its review to Albert Hirschman, an economist well known for ideas diametrically opposed to Currie, and with whom he had been feuding for years. Hirschman was a strong advocate of the land redistribution solution for agriculture and an industrialization strategy based on protectionism and the "principle of the hiding hand"—deliberately exaggerate the benefits and minimize the costs, in order to persuade people to invest their money (not Hirschman's) in industry. Hirschman dismissed Currie's ideas on the political and cultural factors bearing on economic progress as "remarkably uninteresting and dubious," citing Currie's remark that "Colombians are prone to compromise, to avoid conflicts on principles and to improvise on economic matters."[37] Hirschman continued:

> What seems hardest to accept is the insistence that not only land reform, but almost any allocation of resources for agricultural growth is to be avoided and the correlative assurance that the supply of agricultural output is highly elastic. While the orthodox, alarm-ringing FAO line on this subject may be subject to doubt, Currie merely asserts the opposite point of view and does not pay any attention to the evidence of inadequate growth in agricultural production implicit in recurring relative rises of food prices. He dismisses the need for agrarian reform in Colombia with the simple assertion that "the progressive farmers are generally large, and the small farmers are stagnating or retrogressing" (p. 163) in that country. It does not seem to have occurred to him that the first part of this sentence is perfectly compatible with the statement "the large farmers are not generally progressive"—and therefore with the need for land reform. Currie's apparent belief that in agriculture size is closely correlated with productivity is strangely uninformed.

Actually, Currie did stress the slow growth of agricultural output, but attributed this to low income elasticity of demand and correctly noted that there was no *secular* tendency for the relative price of agricultural products to rise. As for productivity and farm size, he stressed that it was not output per acre but output per person that should be the object of economic policy. Small farms may be cultivated very intensively but, with very labor-intensive techniques, output per worker and income per head were very low. This situation could only be remedied by massive transfers of labor from low-paying rural to higher-paying urban activities.

To explain the message of *Accelerating Development*, Currie made exhausting lecture tours all over the country—in Barranquilla, Medellín, Cali, Ibagué, Manizales, Cartagena, Santa Marta and, of course, Bogotá—at first talking mainly to businessmen whose relatively small numbers were out of proportion to their potential influence, but later increasingly to the more receptive and idealistic young in the universities. Though emotionally exhausting, this was usually rewarding work in helping him clarify and refine his ideas.

In 1964 the Colombian Association of Universities retained Currie as an adviser on the accreditation of new degree courses. In investigating the nature of contemporary economics training in Colombia's top universities he was quite appalled. At great cost the American foundations were sponsoring professors from the top U.S. universities, such as Minnesota and Harvard, to support economics programs in Colombia. Currie sat in on some of these courses and criticized the emphasis on rote learning of (and lecturing from) textbooks and on abstract mathematical theory divorced from current policy problems. This was driving students away from economics, or attracting only a handful of mathematically inclined engineers with little background or interest in basic concepts and traditional economic theory. Because of the poor data available in developing countries Currie doubted whether there was scope for advanced mathematical and statistical techniques in the meaningful handling of any of the urgent problems confronting these countries and certainly not to the extent that would justify the emphasis given to the mastery of such techniques in the curriculum. There was undoubted need for rigorous mental discipline, but this did not come only from the study of mathematics, to which many able minds are tone deaf.

Judging from its backwardness in the face of the most urgent problems awaiting solution, it is fair to maintain, said Currie, that economics is a tremendously difficult field and, indeed, far more difficult than mathematics or any of the natural sciences in which tremendous advances had been made.

> A really good economist who is working on real and not hypothetical problems must try to come up with realistic and appropriate solutions, cannot indulge in the luxury of long sustained thinking in terms of symbols. He is dealing with people, with emotions, beliefs and vested interests. His quantitative data are often poor or misleading. His ability to experiment is almost nil. He must observe, interpret and use his best judgement—sometimes almost intuitive judgement. In dealing with a real problem he must be endowed with imaginary antennae, quick to catch the nuances and changing elements in the problem, underlying conditions and relations to a continually emerging and fluid overall situation.[38]

In 1964 he had his first meetings with a small group of alumni from the University of the Andes, known as the Grupo de Integración, which met with Currie at irregular intervals over the next three years to discuss contemporary problems and benefit from his highly stimulating Socratic method of teaching through questioning and provoking thought and discussion. One of the members of this group was Roberto Arenas, who, as head of the National Planning Office in 1971, was to be responsible for bringing Currie back to Colombia from Canada to advise on the "Plan of the Four Strategies."

After Currie had presented a paper at the seventh Latin American Congress of Sociologists at the National University in May 1964, Professor Orlando Fals-Borda tried to persuade Currie to join the National University, and later Currie did give various lectures to the students there. He also published two short books on the teaching of economics and social studies,[39] stressing the importance of teaching students to think rather than to acquire knowledge for its own sake. "To make a subject interesting," he wrote, "professors must be of a lively turn of mind, use analogies, figurative language, irony and satire and have, it is hoped, a sense of fun and a ready wit, and be themselves keenly interested in what they are teaching." Later he was to be invited to head the department of economics at the National University and to set up a new development research institute there.

First, however, he took his message to the United States and Canada, in a series of lectures that more or less coincided with the publication of *Accelerating Development*. He spent the 1965 fall semester at Michigan State University. During this period he also lectured at Harvard, MIT, and Cornell. Michigan State University Press later published *Obstacles to Development* (1967), based on his Michigan lectures, together with a few other essays, including those on population, cost-push inflation, technology, the need to define and measure "disguised unemployment" in a dynamic context, and the crucial role of factor mobility in boosting incomes and promoting more equal income distribution. After a brief visit to Colombia, he returned to the United States in March 1966 to lecture at Illinois and Cornell and to deliver two Royer lectures at the University of California, Berkeley, on the role of planning in a free enterprise economy, one referring to the case of the United States, drawing on his New Deal experience, the other referring to developing countries.[40] He explained how in both developed and developing economies the basic patterns of the free enterprise system—self-interest, competition, freely moving prices, private ownership, and mobility of factors—had weakened in the course of time, but were especially weak in developing countries. He emphasized how poor was the understanding, in any profound sense, of the functioning of the free enterprise system in developing countries. Thus, as in the Great Depression in the United States, the system was not being allowed to function properly and a mass of rich resources lay idle unnecessarily. The economic system was a delicate machine, requiring fuel for its motor. Instead, governments randomly poked around it with screwdrivers or hit it with hammers, hoping for the best.

In August 1966 Carlos Lleras Restrepo assumed office as President of Colombia. But Currie saw little improvement in official policy. Lleras was "able, but not able enough" and was "charging off in all directions" in an increasingly dictatorial fashion. In March 1967 he imposed martial law giving him all the powers of a dictator and Currie became increasingly pessimistic about the future.

He was appointed dean of the faculty of economics at the National University in June 1966 and he spent a great deal of time trying to persuade organizations such as the Inter-American Development Bank, the Agency for International Development, the Ford Foundation, the Harvard Business School, the MIT School of Industrial Management, the Yale Economic Growth Center, and the New York Population Council to support his idea for the establishment at the National University of a new liberal arts college, a postgraduate school of business administration, and a development research center. Neither the liberal arts courses nor the business school gained enough support from the university authorities, but the Center for Development Research (CID) was established early in 1967. Its first project was the major study of alternative patterns of urban development for Bogotá that Mayor Virgilio Barco had commissioned.

At that time the National University was wracked by intrigue and in-fighting between faculty and among the students. Currie had particular trouble implementing his ideas in the face of opposition from the dean of the social sciences faculty. But he was distressed at the manner of the dean's departure, fired by President Lleras on the suspicion he was a Communist. This helped inflame a volatile student body. Instead of leaving the university to resolve its own problems, in June 1967 President Lleras sent in the army and the university remained closed for an extended period.

Currie felt he had overstayed his welcome. His influence on national policy he felt was minimal. President Lleras retained Currie as an adviser to the ministry of agriculture[41] and on Colombian-

Venezuelan relations. But Currie felt that this was mainly to buy his silence on the central issues of national development programs. In April 1967 he even learned, through Roberto Arenas, that Lleras, without consulting him, was about to adopt his idea on constant-value (indexed) bonds for the Social Security Fund. However, the proceeds were to be invested in risky low-cost housing and with no increase in the principle of the mortgage with the rise in prices, as "mortgagees would object." It was also to be used for other low-yielding projects. Thus Currie feared his ideas were being distorted and that he would later be told they had been tried but shown not to work. He would rather his ideas not be applied at all than that they should be applied as pallid half-measures to be discredited later. He resolved to leave Colombia, maybe for good.

Colombian-Venezuelan Integration Studies

Before concluding this chapter, however, one last aspect of Currie's varied work in Colombia during the 1960s deserves mention. This concerns his important role in promoting integration between Colombia and Venezuela. Currie first mooted the idea of a joint study with the Venezuelans on integration possibilities in letters to Virgilio Barco in July 1962 following Currie's work on the mission to North Santander which borders Venezuela. In June 1963 Barco, then minister of agriculture, led an official team, including Currie, to Caracas to discuss with the Venezuelans the ideas Currie had been working on earlier that year. These were designed to foster greater economic integration with a minimum of damage to the existing industries in each country. These opportunities, Currie believed, would be even greater if the programs of integration were accompanied by an Operation Colombia and a similar Operation Venezuela. It was remarkable that commercial exchange between the two countries was at that time minimal. At the 1963 meeting there was agreement in principle to the idea of closer integration.

In June 1964 a second, larger meeting assembled at San Cristobal, on the Colombia-Venezuela border, to explore these ideas further. At these meetings Barco and Currie were decorated by the Venezuelans with the Order of Francisco Miranda for their earlier work. The San Cristobal Accord called for more intensive studies of the type of exchange that could be most beneficial to both countries and, as a preliminary step a "Frontier Study Commission," concerned with limited trade between border regions, was established. Not much happened over the next two years but in August 1966 Currie was asked to prepare draft terms of reference for a major study of the opportunities for increased trade, and in September President Lleras asked him to head the Colombian delegation to the Caracas Conference at which it was agreed to sponsor a study that followed Currie's guidelines.

Currie's basic idea was to protect the existing production of major industries in the two countries but to allow the principle of comparative advantage to determine future investment to expand capacity and production in these sectors. Thus, for example, the inefficient Colombian steel industry and Venezuelan textile industry would have their existing markets protected, but in future all new steel investment would occur in Venezuela and all new textile investment would occur in Colombia.

Tenders for the integration study were invited from David Lilienthal's Resources and Development Corporations (which, in association with the Inter-American Bank, had been involved in the Frontier Study Commission) and Robert Nathan Associates. In January 1967 Nathan's firm won the contract and the study, which Currie advised, was completed the following August. By this time, however, President Lleras had become more interested in the possibilities of playing a leading role in the more grandiose plans for a common market, the Andean Group, which initially included only Colombia, Ecuador, Peru, and Chile, and excluded Venezuela which did not join until 1973. This grouping involved a far more complex set of vested interests and has never been very successful. The simpler, more realistic bilateral links with Venezuela fell victim to the bureaucratic nightmare of the wider union which probably would have been achieved more easily through a step-by-step approach, beginning with bilateral union.

Departure

And so another of Currie's projects fell by the wayside, another casualty of the politics of compromise. Currie sold his farm in December 1966 and early in 1967, through the help of Murray Bryce, one of the judges for the Society for International Development in the McGraw-Hill prize competition, Currie was invited to Simon Fraser University in Vancouver, Canada, where Bryce was living at that time. At the end of July 1967, after a brief lecturing assignment at the FAO in Rome,[42] Currie returned to the land of his birth—though on the extreme west coast, 3,000 miles from West Dublin, Nova Scotia—to assume the post of professor of economics, a position he was to retain, with a year's interlude in Glasgow and Oxford, until 1971, when the next President of Colombia would recall him to his adoptive home.

CHAPTER 9

An Academic Interlude in Canada and Britain, 1967–71

Visiting Professor in Canada, 1967–68

During the 1960s Currie had worked tirelessly to promote sectoral and regional, but especially national, macroeconomic policies for the acceleration of Colombia's economic and social development. He was too articulate and ubiquitous to be ignored by the three successive civilian governments he sought to influence, but generally he was kept on the fringes of government and, while his advice was usually listened to with respect, it was seldom acted upon. Most of Currie's studies were conducted on a shoestring budget. The National Planning Department never took Operation Colombia seriously and devoted no resources to studying its implications in quantitative terms as the basis for action. His greatest achievement during this period was probably his educational work: through his many books and articles, through teaching students and staff at the National University, and through informal seminars with business leaders and, in particular, with the group of alumni of the University of the Andes that called itself the "Grupo de Integración," a group which included Roberto Arenas, who was later to play a leading role in bringing Currie into the center of national policymaking.

By 1967, however, the frustration he felt at his lack of progress and influence in Colombia, together with personal considerations, including concern for his young children's education and well-being in an insecure environment and the lure of his native Canada which culturally he had never left, induced him to accept with gratitude an offer from Simon Fraser University in Vancouver to spend a year as visiting professor of economics. He left Colombia in July 1967 and remained abroad for nearly four years.

During this period his friends in Colombia, especially Roberto Arenas, sent regular appeals for him to return. Through these professional and family connections Currie remained in close touch with political and economic developments there, though naturally his interests shifted, or at any rate broadened, to more global concerns of developed as well as underdeveloped nations.

At Simon Fraser University in the 1967–68 academic year his formal obligations were to teach courses in development economics to small undergraduate and graduate seminars in which he was able to practice the provocative style of Socratic teaching he had perfected many years earlier at Harvard. This approach rests on the assumption that students learn by being confronted with apparently inconsistent statements and must attempt either to reconcile the inconsistency or reject one of the statements. He has said that his most successful classes are those in which the students argue with each other and the teacher confines himself to guiding the discussion so that students appear to arrive themselves at the conclusion he wishes them to arrive at. This method is strenuous as the teacher must actively adjust questions to the course of the discussion, and the basic premise that students are bothered by inconsistencies may be questioned. But if they are not, taking notes on lectures may not serve either.

He believes that the cardinal sin of a teacher is to ridicule a student or get a laugh from the class at the student's expense. He recalls how in his classes at Harvard Allyn Young would go to elaborate lengths to make sense of the most absurd question of a student, saying, "I see that what you have in mind is, . . ." something the student had not really had in mind, but was pleased the teacher thought he had. Currie has certainly excelled as a teacher and regrets that in his long active life only a few years, at the beginning, middle, and toward the end, have been spent in teaching.

In his classes at Simon Fraser he was forced to read up on even more of the literature on development economics, including abstruse theoretical models rather alien to his own policy-oriented approach, and to debate these and his own writings with his students. Many of his graduate students were well trained in the current orthodoxy of the best North American and British universities but were eager to have their theoretical knowledge confronted and challenged by Currie's wide experience.

In these seminars students were encouraged to approach their subject, first by a searching examination and definition of the nature of the problem and frame of reference, second by diagnosis or explanation of the problem so defined, and third by considering the appropriate strategy for resolving that problem. Thus the aim was to guide students to thinking about ideas that were not just to be played with but used. Or, failing that, at least Currie hoped that through the Socratic method students would be forced to think problems through for themselves to their logical conclusion and so both develop their critical faculties and absorb the ideas into their bones; to regard them as their own ideas, not handed-down ones. This, he felt, was of more lasting value than listening passively to lectures, a style of teaching with which he has never been comfortable.

Currie's Ideas on Underutilized Resources, "Dualism," and the "Big Push"

These seminars enabled Currie to probe more deeply into the analysis and, more importantly for him, the assumptions of the then most influential development theories of economists such as Arthur Lewis, John Fei and Gustav Ranis, Dale Jorgenson, Albert Hirschman, and Irma Adelman and Cynthia Morris, none of whom Currie thought at all helpful or relevant to the conditions facing most underdeveloped countries. Among other reasons, Currie criticized these models for their excessive attention to low agricultural productivity and their tendency to identify increasing agricultural productivity with increasing agricultural incomes without adequate awareness of the implications of low price and income elasticity of demand. Currie insisted that in reality farmers will not, as a group, increase the "agricultural surplus" in advance of demand. If they tried or were helped to do this by technical assistance, subsidized credit, land "reform," or greater rural infrastructure this would only increase dualism within agriculture.

Furthermore, the literature took a narrowly static view of disguised unemployment and defined it to include only that labor whose "marginal product" was zero or close to zero. For Currie any labor was disguisedly unemployed or underemployed if it was earning less than other similarly qualified labor was earning in other occupations. The typical development model assumed that wages were equal in all sectors or, if a premium did exist in the urban sector, that this was due only to a higher cost of living or customary standard in the cities. For these economists it was not the result of faulty or inadequate labor mobility. After all, they would say, there is already *too much* mobility. For look at the growth of city slums and urban unemployment. Surely the need is for less rapid, not more rapid, rural-urban migration? Surely we need to try to create more *rural* jobs, by emphasizing labor-intensive agricultural methods and further fragmentation and more intensively worked land?

Currie, however, insisted that this analysis confuses movement in the geographical sense with mobility in the economic sense. There had been much movement but little mobility. Dualism was not a two-sector phenomenon, but all-pervasive. So long as workers fail to move from low-paying to high-paying jobs so pay discrepancies, inequality, and real unemployment persist, and are symptoms of the faulty functioning of the mobility mechanism. Rapid rural-urban migration was more the result of push factors (labor displacement through some farmers innovating while demand for the product grows relatively slowly) rather than pull factors (better paying jobs opening up outside of agriculture).

The key to development was to create the conditions that would greatly expand the number of better-paying nonagricultural jobs. In the Lewis-Fei-Ranis-Jorgenson models the economy has only two sectors, agriculture and industry. This quasi-Marxist approach leads them to ignore the enormous opportunities potentially available in the construction and services sectors, so often written off in the economics literature as "unproductive," despite the fact that in North America and Europe as much as 75 percent of the labor force derive their livelihood from these occupations by producing something that commands value in the marketplace.

As we have seen, Currie was likewise skeptical of the usefulness of a Keynesian diagnosis of underdevelopment. Keynes, diagnosing the conditions in developed countries, concentrated attention on open unemployment, excessive savings, and deficient monetary demand. In developing countries there is a continuum of unemployment, most of which is disguised in the sense that a very large proportion of the labor force and capital stock is grossly underutilized. The way to mobilize these grossly underutilized resources of manpower and machinery is not through Keynesian demand management but by institutional changes that attack cost-push pressures, overvalued exchange rates, obstacles to shift working, wasteful public spending on economically worthless projects, urban sprawl (because of lack of urban planning for higher densities), and the chronic discouragement to personal savings for housing finance resulting from fixed-interest mortgages in an inflationary environment. Merely to state some of the elements of Currie's diagnosis and strategy is enough to indicate how, though seemingly sensible, they differ sharply from conventional approaches.

So far, however, we have made no mention of population growth. This, for Currie, was perhaps the key issue in underdevelopment. The development economists with whom he felt most affinity were those who likewise recognized the crucial nature of this variable. These included Harvey Leibenstein, Richard Nelson, and, for different but related reasons, Paul Rosenstein-Rodan. Leibenstein and Nelson explained how an initial increase in income tended to reduce the mortality rate while having a relatively weaker effect, in the short run, on the birthrate. This was the "fertility lag" that accelerated population growth and dragged down the growth of income per capita. A "critical minimum effort" was called for. Without this, developing countries (which Leibenstein[1] preferred to call backward countries) would be caught in a "low-level equilibrium trap." Even if there was some rise in per capita income, said Currie, it would in these circumstances be more appropriate to speak of growth without development.[2] For the growth in numbers would tend to keep the real wages of the masses at a subsistence level with the fruits of progress captured mainly by the few. Even if the *proportion* of the population living at subsistence were falling the *absolute* numbers in the "pain" economy would still be increasing alarmingly.

Thus an attack on the birthrate was imperative, not only because this would help make labor scarcer, therefore more highly paid, but also to reduce the worldwide destruction of irreplaceable natural resources. Birthrates are almost universally highest in rural areas where ignorance and low incomes are most prevalent and where fewest opportunities exist for women to work outside of the home. Urbanization is almost universally accompanied by higher average incomes, greater career opportunities for women, and lower costs of providing basic education and birth control propaganda. Policies were urgently needed, therefore, that would maximize remunerative urban jobs to break into the vicious circles of underdevelopment and reduce the rural population.

This requires not marginal change suitable for highly developed economies where the free enterprise system is functioning relatively well and small defects call for small reforms. Rather, it calls for a "critical minimum effort" (or maximum effort) in Leibenstein's terms, or a breakthrough program in the terms Currie used in *Accelerating Development.* Paul Rosenstein-Rodan had earlier called for a "Big Push" to mobilize the underemployed resources of eastern and south-eastern Europe after the Second World War.[3] He was not concerned with a population explosion but only with pervasive underemployment of a labor force that had lost a large portion of its capital stock in the devastation of war. He was bothered by the inelastic demand that would confront a single sector if a significant investment was made in it before similar investments were made elsewhere in the economy. A big push operating on many fronts simultaneously was thought necessary to resolve this problem.

Currie explained, in his classes and in the manuscript of a new book he prepared during his years in Canada and Britain, how writers such as Hirschman had interpreted Rosenstein-Rodan's article as a theory of "balanced growth" which was rejected in favor of their own theories of "unbalanced growth." In Hirschman's case, sectors favored for relatively rapid growth would be ones with greatest technical "linkages," such as the steel industry. If this meant advancing faster than demand, threatening bankruptcy, Hirschman's solution was the "Principle of the Hiding Hand": exaggerate the benefits and conceal the true costs.[4] The fruitless debate over balanced versus unbalanced growth tended to obscure the original point of Rosenstein-Rodan's article. This was to emphasize the enormous extent of disguised unemployment, and the need for a big push.

Currie's diagnosis too was of widespread underemployed manpower, but coupled also with gross underutilization of the capital stock and a rapid population growth with population threatening to double every twenty-five years. For this Currie, like Leibenstein and Nelson called for a critical minimum effort, breakthrough, or big push. Unlike other writers, however, Currie actually had thought through ways and means of achieving this breakthrough that differed from the relatively simplistic and general calls for more capital formation or an increase in the savings ratio and foreign loans, along the lines indicated by aggregative growth models of writers such as Roy Harrod, Evsey Domar and Ragnar Nurkse, or the two-gap models of Hollis Chenery and others, or the two-sector models of Lewis and Fei and Ranis.[5] Currie's strategy also took account of the limited administrative capacity of governments in underdeveloped countries and hence of the need for a selective or strategic attack on the interlocking vicious circles at their most vulnerable points, and operating through, rather than in competition with, the private sector that responds to profit signals. In this way government effort could be concentrated rather than spread thinly across too many battle-fronts at once.

The Doomsday Group

This was one set of themes that Currie discussed with his students at Simon Fraser. Increasingly, however, Currie became absorbed in even broader issues. He sympathized with the handful of economists such as E. J. Mishan and Kenneth Boulding who were beginning to question some of the basic assumptions of modern economics regarding growth and efficiency. Currie, however, made a sharp distinction between the developed and the underdeveloped economies in their concern with growth. There was little dispute about the need to increase material abundance in the "pain" economy, though even there it was essential that the goals of economic policy be specified in less aggregative terms than overall GDP per head. The goals should be spelled out in terms of what and for whom, with growth of GDP the consequence of success in meeting the more specific goals.

In the affluent developed economies material growth had a much more tenuous link with what Currie called well-being to distinguish it sharply from the concept of "economic welfare" that preoccupied modern economic theorists. Currie questioned whether more meant better, and in terms that went much deeper than the theoretical quibbles that dominated the literature on welfare economics over "compensation criteria," income distribution, and "external" costs and benefits. Currie was more concerned with the question of whether and how the satisfaction of consumer demand increased human well-being in a deeper sense. He was thus concerned with the role that economics should play as one of several disciplines within an overarching interdisciplinary study of well-being or the ultimate aims of man in society.

He presented a paper on this theme at the Canadian Economics Association in December 1967 and at a public address at the University of British Columbia in March 1968. In the spring of 1968 he also persuaded some of his ablest graduate students to attend a series of informal evening meetings at his house to examine the values, beliefs, and goals of economists and the role of the economist in defining and working toward the good life. Rather gloomily they called themselves the Doomsday Group, for their discussions were centered on the problems of unprecedented population growth, ecological disruption, the impact of science and technology on modern weapons of war, the genetic balance, the pace of social change, and on what Currie called the "deprivation effect" arising from the creation of new gadgetry and unequal incomes. When asked whether these discussions were unnecessarily somber and unsettling, Currie offered the group a quotation by Eugene Meyer sent to him by his friend Milton Taylor: "As to the age-old question whether it is better to be a pig satisfied or a Socrates dissatisfied I would choose Socrates. If the pig should disagree I have an unanswerable reply: that I have known what it is to be both Socrates *and* a pig."

Visiting Professor in Glasgow and Oxford, 1968–69

Currie's initial contract at Simon Fraser University was for one year. Although as a result of his popularity with students and his publications he was invited to remain there to teach he decided first to seize the opportunity offered by the universities of Glasgow and Oxford to spend a year in Britain with a very light teaching load that would enable him to devote most of his time to reading and writing. He was anxious to write a book on "Development and Well-being" that developed his ideas on both of these great themes in a global context. The Canada Council also provided him with a grant to hire a research student, Peter Gudgeon, one of the SFU Doomsday Group, to help him cover the voluminous literature for part of the time in Glasgow and Oxford.

In August 1968, therefore, he left for the Institute of Latin American Studies at the University of Glasgow. In this decision he heeded more the advice of his friend Jacob Viner—who wrote that he had a high opinion of the economists there— than that of Marriner Eccles who wrote (April 24, 1968) that, though he enjoyed his two years in Glasgow in 1911–13 as a Mormon missionary, when he returned in 1966 for a brief visit he found it had lost all its attraction—"Glasgow is a terrible city." In fact it was not so terrible. Currie enjoyed an excellent library and good working conditions, and his children made excellent progress in their somewhat austere Scottish schools. He stayed in Glasgow for two terms and in the third term of the academic year was a fellow of St. Antony's College, Oxford, where he was able to discuss his ideas with economists such as Paul Streeten, Keith Griffin, and Thomas Balogh (the latter was very critical), with a well-known historian of Colombia, Malcolm Deas, and with a wide range of scholars from all over the world.

During this year his reading ranged widely over the conventional literature on development economics and also over the much broader issues concerning fundamental social needs, as opposed to material wants; of man the social animal, covering the work of, for example, Thorstein Veblen, Frank Knight, Kenneth Boulding, E. J. Mishan, Erich Fromm, Lewis Mumford, Arnold Toynbee, Bertrand Russell, Kenneth Galbraith, Joan Robinson, Nicholas Georgescu-Roegen, Robert Heilbroner, David Riesman, Desmond Morris, Adolf Lowe, and Jacques Ellul.

He began writing his new book that covered the theme of economic development within the global context of the relationships between developed and underdeveloped countries and the ability of material progress to satisfy the deeper social needs of man: man's craving for esteem and a sense of personal worth, his conformism, his emotional equipment inherited from a technically much more primitive time that provided the drives that underlay the growth process and which, in a world of material abundance, remain as strong as ever.

The Deprivation Effect

The "deprivation effect" was the illfare that arises when other people possess what one cannot afford, when new products are launched on the market, or the envy, frustration, and hatred that are created by the existence of inequality within and between nations. In our modern society the link between work and reward is tenuous because workers get not what they produce but only the value of what they produce, thus apparently undermining the ethical basis of income distribution, which instead depends on the caprices of supply and demand. Monetary incomes, and what money can buy, become the badge of status, not work and skills. Where the ideal income is 20 percent more than one already has, the deprivation effect will remain so long as inequality exists. It will be decided ultimately by the consumption patterns of the Texan oil millionaires and aggravated whenever their consumption increases. Modern communications prevent any country from effectively isolating itself from this effect. Other development economists tend to refer approvingly to the "demonstration effect" of modern goods in motivating modern attitudes among the poor.[6] Currie insisted that the pain economy, or privation, sufficiently motivates most poor people to want the opportunity to remove that pain (hunger, cold, illness). The deprivation arising from the cornucopia of luxury commodities (including heart transplants) is unfortunate but unavoidable so long as there is no control over science and technology, nor over the destruction of finite natural resources. And, so long as there is no control over population growth, neither privation nor deprivation are likely to be lessened.

Currie believed that these considerations helped explain the paradox that while for any given product there is a downward-sloping demand curve that induces welfare economists to conclude that we enjoy much "consumers' surplus," measured by the difference between price and the intramarginal demand curve, there is no downward-sloping demand curve for all products taken together, hence no overall consumers' surplus. Incomes increase with output, and all output is sold. The satisfaction or "utility" that consumers expect, ex ante, to get from consumption soon evaporates as other people also obtain the extra goods. So ex ante expectations differ from ex post satisfactions, largely because we are trying to satisfy our social *needs* for recognition and status by gratifying our material *wants*. Our ultimate goal should be to develop the potential of the individual personality rather than to develop the economy. The economy and society need to be adapted to the needs of the individual, not vice versa.

Simon Fraser University, 1969–71

This gives just some flavor of the discussions that Currie carried to the classroom upon his return in September 1969 to Simon Fraser University where he had gained approval to teach a new course in "Concepts and Goals in Economics" for graduates and final-year undergraduates, as well as his course in (relatively) more orthodox development economics. He remained at SFU until May 1971.

His four years in Canadian and British universities were of great intellectual value to him. He had worked for many years in relative isolation from the economics mainstream, but this period now enabled him to catch up on what other economists were thinking and writing and gave him assurance.

However, the book that Currie worked on during these years was never published. The draft manuscript, completed at the end of 1970, ran to several hundred pages and required considerable editing. An English publisher, Allen and Unwin, accepted the manuscript for publication but required that its length first be reduced by one-third and that a companion American publisher be found. By this time Currie had agreed to return to Colombia to be the chief adviser to the National Planning Office and so was caught up in other concerns that prevented him from returning to his book. And as time passed his interests shifted and developed.

Nevertheless, the work on this book was by no means wasted. First it helped him clarify his ideas on the nature and goals of development and underdevelopment and the working of the free enterprise and mixed economic systems. This would enable him to write the basis for an entirely new development plan for Colombia within weeks of his return there in May 1971. Secondly he gave several conference papers and published various articles arising directly from the work of this period. The most important of these were, first, one dealing with the narrower issue of development policy, "The Exchange Constraint on Development: A Partial Solution to the Problem," in *The Economic Journal* of December 1971;[7] and second, an article published later on broader economic goals, "Wants, Needs, Well-being and Economic Growth," in the *Journal of Economic Studies,* May 1975. Currie also contributed a theme paper, "Social Development and Economic Progress" for the 1971 Congress of the International Union of Local Authorities.[8]

The Economic Journal article provoked a critical "Note" from Gustav Ranis and Currie's "Reply," which were published in December 1972. This exchange will be discussed in the next chapter. Here it may just be mentioned that in his 1971 paper Currie expounded his theory that it was not the lack of capital or foreign exchange that was the main constraint on development so much as their underutilization or poor utilization. Factor proportions could be varied considerably not by deliberately opting to encourage labor-intensive (that is, low physical productivity) techniques in any particular sector (Currie was in any case skeptical how far this could be achieved without raising unit costs), but by varying the structure or pattern of demand by reorientating it toward industries of mass consumption. This in turn could be achieved by mobilizing the mass of underutilized capital and manpower to produce these goods of mass consumption, including food, textiles, building materials, and housing. Agriculture, however, faced very inelastic demand, and so improved productivity there necessitated less rural employment. Already there was far too much labor idle in agriculture that could be put to more remunerative use in other sectors if the obstacles to mobility were removed.

These obstacles included premature social legislation that raised labor costs in industry and inhibited shift work and overtime; an inadequate flow of personal savings into housing; wasteful expenditures on unplanned city sprawl and unnecessary rural infrastructure and colonization; and overvalued exchange rates and an inadequate exchange licensing system. By removing these obstacles through institutional reform and by adopting a bottleneck-breaking criterion in the allocation of scarce foreign exchange, Currie pointed to the great increase in output and employment that could be achieved with the existing capital and foreign exchange available in underdeveloped economies. He denied the common belief that in order to accelerate growth it was essential that consumption first be cut (to increase savings) or that agriculture be given top priority.

Contacts with Colombia

Meanwhile, back in Colombia quite different ideas continued to be promulgated and quite different policies were being pursued. In 1968 Richard Musgrave was invited by President Lleras to head a tax commission and advise on tax reform. The commission arbitrarily postulated a 6 percent rate of growth of GDP which would, it was assumed, be achieved via substantial increases in government spending on agriculture, transport, and electrification. This in turn would require higher tax rates. There was not time for the recommendations of the commission to be adopted by the Lleras administration, which left office in August 1970, but they were largely implemented by the administration of President Alfonso López Michelsen after he came to power in August 1974.

In 1969 President Lleras invited another mission sponsored by the

International Labor Office to advise on employment policy. The idea of having this mission was supported by the head of the Harvard advisory service, Richard Mallon, who took a gloomy view of urban employment possibilities and anticipated the view of the ILO mission that additional employment would have to be found in agriculture. The mission chief was Dudley Seers, well known, ironically, for an article he had written on "Why Visiting Economists Fail."[9] His report, *Towards Full Employment*,[10] was rushed into print so it would appear before President Lleras left office in August 1970. Nevertheless, his successor, President Misael Pastrana Borrero immediately appointed an evaluation commission to make recommendations. Pastrana, the Conservative candidate for the National Front, had won an extremely narrow victory in the presidential elections over the ex-dictator General Gustavo Rojas Pinilla who was running on a populist platform as head of a new party, the Alianza Nacional Popular, ANAPO. Rojas's party had capitalized on the rising tide of frustration and resentment of people who felt no benefit from President Lleras's program despite some abatement of inflation and growth in exports toward the end of his administration.

As President-elect, Pastrana wrote to Currie (August 3, 1970) requesting that he sit on this evaluation commission. Currie's teaching commitments in Canada prevented this, but he did send some written comments. In a letter (September 18, 1970) to Roberto Arenas who was very close to the President and who was appointed shortly afterward as director of the National Planning Office, Currie remarked:

> It is much better than the Plan de Desarrollo of 1961 both in its economics and in its orientation and objectives. On the other hand, it is a very confusing document and shows signs of its hasty preparation by many different people. There is little obvious relation between the numerous measures proposed and the precise sectorial rates of growth projected in output and employment. The individual recommendations are too many, too diverse, lack ranking in importance and in some cases are inconsistent. . . .
>
> On the other hand, by using discrimination in selection and emphasis, a practicable program could be put together which could claim support from different parts of the report. (I suppose you noted that the plan attributed to me was not mine at all, and the criticisms were consequently misdirected. As you know, I never relied exclusively nor even primarily on manufacturing for the increase in non-agricultural jobs. I naturally regret that they didn't read *O.C.*, or *Accelerating Development* or *Las Alternativas para Bogotá*.) The treatment of agriculture is not very satisfactory

and I fear they drew the wrong lessons from the Mexican agricultural experience.

The ILO report argued that because industry required much more capital per worker than did peasant agriculture, "industrializaton" was not feasible, so more rural jobs had to be created and migration restrained. Currie argued that capital does not have to be spread evenly and thinly over all workers, and in no country, whether capital rich or capital poor, is this done. All that is needed is greater mobility so that the benefits of capital-intensive projects, employing relatively few workers, can be diffused among all workers, including the many who would be engaged in the services sector. These latter workers, though working with relatively little capital, should earn a competitive wage similar to that of workers in the most highly capital-intensive sectors if the mobility mechanism was allowed to operate properly. Currie's proposed strategy was not an industrialization program but an urbanization program in which manufacturing industry would play its role but, in terms of new employment, a role very secondary to that played by the construction and services sectors. Unlike the ILO strategy it was decidedly not a make-work program. Employment would result from policies to create the effective demand to induce maximum output with the most efficient techniques available.

Dudley Seers's mission also believed that employment would be greater as a result of measures to redistribute income through progressive taxation and land redistribution. The argument was that poorer people spend more of their incomes on labor-intensive goods.[11] Again, however, Currie argued that this was a form of make-work for its own sake. His strategy involved not so much a redistribution of existing incomes, which by itself he doubted would have much effect on overall employment or real wages, but rather a mobilization of unemployed resources of all kinds to create higher real incomes that would constitute the source of *increased* effective demand in a real sense and not simply a *redistribution* of the existing levels of income and, hence, real demand. A redistribution of income would thereby result from a leveling-up process (as unemployed or poorly employed labor finds more remunerative work) rather than by leveling down.

Currie continued to place great store in the role the international agencies would have to play in supporting a different type of national development strategy if this was to have any chance of success. In 1969 Virgilio Barco was appointed as one of the executive directors of the World Bank in Washington and Harold Dunkerley (the ex-head of the Harvard advisory service in Colombia) was working in the Bank's urban division. This helped Currie's efforts to put pressure on the Bank to give more prominence to the role of urbanization as a motor of development, rather than as a necessary evil whose problems had to be alleviated as well as possible with as many specific project loans as could be managed within the resources available after providing for the priority accorded agriculture.

In January 1970, on the occasion of the eventual publication of the 1967 study of Bogotá that he directed, Currie was called in by the Bank for consultations on the implications of the Bogotá study. In January 1971 he was again called to advise a World Bank evaluation team, directed by Christopher Willoughby, whose object was to evaluate the work of the World Bank in Colombia from the time of the original Currie mission in 1949. (Willoughby's report was highly critical on some aspects of the Bank's projects approach and was suppressed.) Roberto Arenas, who by this time had been appointed director of the National Planning Department was in Washington for loan negotiations and continued to put strong pressure on Currie to return to Colombia as his senior adviser.

Arenas had succeeded Jorge Ruiz Lara at the Planning Department. Ruiz Lara had been working for the adoption of a national plan that had been initiated by President Carlos Lleras Restrepo and which Lleras was expecting President Pastrana to follow. Pastrana was not entirely happy with this plan and after a few months of frustration Ruiz Lara resigned, along with a large group of his technicians, leaving Roberto Arenas to take over and appoint his own team. Pastrana continued his appeals for Currie to return to help Arenas develop a fresh plan. Meanwhile, the ILO report continued to exert a strong influence on national thinking and the minister of development, Jorge Valencia, was attempting to promulgate a new "reforma urbana" that differed sharply from the emphasis of Currie's *Alternativas* for Bogotá and for national urban planning. Improvization, discontent, and sporadic outbursts of violent protests continued to characterize the national scene.

Actually Roberto Arenas had himself been supporting Valencia's reforma urbana on the grounds that it did call for more urban renovation, greater densities, and more powers over land acquisition and use. On the other hand, as Currie warned in a letter to Arenas November 4, 1970, the emphasis was still mainly on the construction of houses directly for the very poor and not enough on housing as an engine of development. Currie wrote:

> I would like to see the bill so drafted as to make it possible to attract billions of private and international capital to this field, to permit the financing of the purchase of existing houses when the owners wished to buy new ones, to dampen down on nonresidential and luxury residential as and when physical and financial bottlenecks appeared, and to have an administrative organization that combined the advantages of centralization (broad national powers on overall policy and financing) with decentralization (urban planning and renovation for specific cities). I would like to be able to tie interest rates for lenders and borrowers to the cost of living if it appeared necessary. . . . This matter of financing is vitally important. Most public housing has floundered on decapitalization. . . . The idea that you must try to provide new housing for all the very poor is fine demagoguery but poor economics. Few North Americans, for example, live in new houses constructed for them, or drive cars that they bought new. . . . If one could interest the World Bank, for instance, one might have powerful support to resist demagogic demands that might wreck a policy.

Against the confused and unsettled background described above, Roberto Arenas was more than ever anxious to enlist Currie's advice and support, though other Colombian friends of Currie whom he met in Washington in January, such as Virgilio Barco, Enrique Peñalosa and Eduardo Gaitán were skeptical of what Currie could accomplish and hoped he would not be sacrificing his more tranquil life in Canada for the same professional frustrations of old in Colombia. Currie shared this skepticism and he also hesitated because of various attractive job offers that would enable him to continue his teaching and research in Canada for the next two years. However, he was eventually persuaded that in Colombia at the very least he would be assured of a significant group of technicians in the National Planning Department to help him finally do a proper quantification of the various implications of his "breakthrough" plan. As for its implementation, that remained to be seen. He decided the risk was worth taking, especially since his wife was very keen to return to her relations and friends in Colombia. In February he agreed to a two-year contract with the National Planning Department, with work to begin in May, once he had finished teaching that semester's classes at Simon Fraser University. In fact he was to remain at the planning office as senior economic adviser for the next ten years.

First, however, he continued to stress the importance of seeking the support of the international lending agencies. In March he visited the Canadian International Development Agency (CIDA) in Ottawa, taking advantage of his presence there as a member of the interviewing panel of the Canada Council that awarded studentships and research grants for Latin American studies. CIDA later increased its involvement in Colombia (and even paid Currie's salary at the Planning Department for a while), though their focus was mainly on scattered, small-scale rural projects.

In May, on his way back to Bogotá from Vancouver he stopped off for ten days of consultations with staff at the World Bank and AID in Washington. He was particularly interested in what seemed to be growing interest in urbanization at the World Bank following Robert McNamara's visit to Colombia with Virgilio Barco in 1970. The mayor of Bogotá at the time, Carlos Albán, was angling for World Bank loans to finance various projects arising from an earlier report by the consultants Freeman-Fox, Wilbur Smith, and Restrepo-Uribe on transportation and urban development. This costly study was known as the Phase I Bogotá Study and Carlos Alban wanted to follow this up with an even costlier Phase II Study, for which he had already drawn up the terms of reference and was seeking a World Bank loan to finance it.

The Phase I Study rejected the recommendations of Currie's 1967 Bogotá study for a number of more or less self-contained centers, to reduce movements greatly, on the grounds that this plan "would be difficult to implement and it would involve very high total costs. Although the public sector infrastructure costs are low, the pattern would probably require a heavy commitment to expensive public sector housing" (p. xii). Instead, they were recommending an extensive program of road construction to extend the city to the west, and low-cost self-help housing schemes on the peripheries.

Currie was depressed by the way the Phase I report characterized his plans as relying on expensive public housing, ignored his new private housing finance proposals, and failed to recognize that the acquisition costs of peripheral land is cheap only because it is poorly serviced (thus huge infrastructure costs would be required to make it as desirable and well-serviced as central locations). He also noted wryly the huge difference in the costs incurred by the Centro de Investigaciones para el Desarrollo (CID) to do their 1967 study compared with the costs involved in hiring the international consultants for the Phase I Study, and the even greater costs in prospect for the Phase II Study ($1 million).

In Washington in May 1971 Currie spoke with the World Bank officials negotiating the big new Bogotá study and with his old student, the distinguished urban economist at the Brookings Institution, Wilfred Owen. He determined that one of the first things he would do on his return to Bogotá would be to try to have the terms of reference changed to focus the study on identifying and developing new centers within existing city limits, instead of looking only at the extension of public services and transport to meet existing patterns of urban sprawl.

On May 29, 1971, Currie flew into Bogotá with Roberto Arenas (who was returning via Washington from Rome where he had been for more loan negotiations) to the enthusiastic welcome of his old friends and much fanfare from the news media.

CHAPTER 10

The Plan of the Four Strategies, 1971–74

The Background

In the confused and unsettled country to which he returned on May 27, 1971, Currie had no great illusions about how much he would be able to accomplish. But, despite or perhaps more because of his age, he felt he had a great duty to try. For four years he had been teaching and writing on how to accelerate development. He was now in a key position to exert his influence to that end as chief economic policy adviser to the head of the National Planning Department (DNP), Roberto Arenas, and through him and directly as adviser to the President.

President Misael Pastrana was already nine months into the short four-year presidential term and the constitution did not allow his reelection for a second successive term. He had inherited a relatively conventional development plan from his predecessor, President Carlos Lleras, and Dudley Seer's ILO mission had just delivered its report amidst a blaze of publicity.[1] The Evaluation Commission that Pastrana appointed endorsed the ILO theory on the need for labor-intensive make-work schemes, expanded rural employment, enormously expensive colonization programs, and other restraints on rural-urban migration. The mayor of Bogotá, Carlos Albán, was about to sign a big contract with the World Bank and the United Nations for a study of Bogotá's transport and public service requirements that would be dictated by the existing pattern of urban sprawl. A "reforma urbana" was being sponsored by the minister of development, Jorge Valencia. This focused on rent controls, low-cost (but still heavily subsidized) public housing programs, and land taxes that would discriminate against a scattered multitude of vacant or "underused" urban lots to force them into uses declared "social" by government officials. The bill made no provision for additional financing, contained no vision of the urbanization process as a motor of development and would do little to avoid the high-cost North American pattern of urban sprawl.

Roberto Arenas greatly admired Currie's ideas and abilities but had himself become closely identified with the rather muddled and inadequate ideas contained in the reforma urbana. So Currie's first task was to convince him and the President of the need for the more radical and sweeping measures required for a strategic breakthrough plan. It was also necessary to convince the divisional chiefs and their technicians at the DNP many of whom were initially skeptical or even hostile toward the ideas of a massive urbanization program.

Drafting the Guidelines

During June and July Currie wrote the first drafts of the guidelines for a new national plan and also persuaded Arenas to force a delay in the signing of the important Phase II Bogotá Study contract with the World Bank and United Nations until the terms of reference had been modified. This immediately aroused hostility from the mayor, the Bogotá district Planning Department and officials of the World Bank. But eventually new terms of reference were grudgingly agreed, a steering committee established with Currie as a member, and an international firm of urban planning consultants selected for the study. The progress of this Bogotá study will be described later. At this stage it may simply be noted that Currie was determined that major urban programs of the type under consideration should be subordinated and integrated into overall national planning.

During this time the minister of finance, Rodrigo Llorente, and the minister of development, Jorge Valencia, were proclaiming their own ideas on national planning, the former emphasizing more public spending on agriculture and negotiating external loans for unrelated projects, the latter pushing his reforma urbana. Arenas, meanwhile, was quietly urging Currie's memoranda on the President.

On July 20 the President, in his speech opening Congress, endorsed the main lines of Currie's reorientation of policy, ten years to the day after similar proposals had been rejected by President Alberto Lleras. Whether we like it or not, he said, urbanization is inescapably linked with development: it must be planned, finance must be found, millions of new urban jobs created, to be accompanied by the necessary housing and social services to ensure increased well-being for all. There was much more in the speech, not all of which was consistent with Currie's draft guidelines, but the President made no mention of Valencia's reforma urbana and so Currie was encouraged to press ahead with the final drafts of his plan.

Over the next few months Currie wrote the final draft guidelines of what he called the *Plan of the Four Strategies*. These *Guidelines for a New Strategy* eventually appeared almost as Currie had written them, apart from some minor amendments and rearranging. However, he first had to engage in fierce debate with DNP officials, some of whom were especially hostile to the emphasis on private housing finance for middle income and upper working-class groups rather than public housing for the very poor and sites-and-services or autoconstruction (self-build) programs.

For Currie, these programs would be inadequate for various reasons. Firstly, they depend heavily on public subsidy. Secondly, even with heavy subsidies this kind of housing can be little better than slum buildings. Thirdly, in order to reduce costs these programs usually are located on the periphery of towns and cities where land costs are low. But land costs are low because access and public services are poor. These must later be provided at great cost and the economies of a denser pattern of urban design are lost. Fourthly, the value of what is produced in such programs is low; and, since the potential size of such operations is small, both the quantity and the quality of employment will be relatively low. It is the economics of Robinson Crusoe.

By contrast, Currie's aim was to make urbanization the main motor of development. Palliatives were not enough. The aim was to provide hundreds of thousands of new jobs each year in work that produced high value and was much more remunerative than incomes in subsistence agriculture or in urban disguised unemployment. It was to be a self-financing program relying on an institutional change that would attract a substantial increase in personal savings. It relied also on the rapid increase in personal savings that would be the consequence of the big future increase in real incomes expected from the new strategy. The aim was to increase personal savings flowing into the construction sector from the traditionally very small 1.5 percent of national income (in terms of value added) to 5 or 6 percent of a rapidly increasing national income, similar to the figures attained in Israel, Japan, and Singapore, for example.

The Theory of Leading Sectors and the Role of the Construction Sector

Through the institutional changes proposed it was hoped to redirect demand toward a sector where virtually inexhaustible latent demand existed. The institutional changes were designed to convert that latent demand into effective demand by capturing real savings—the real loanable funds the lack of which had been the main constraint on demand in the construction sector. Currie emphasized that it was not sufficient simply to increase savings. It was essential that the savings be canalized into key strategic or leading sectors where massive latent real demand existed. The constraint on faster growth was not inadequate capital or foreign exchange overall. Most of the capital stock was grossly underutilized. The main constraint was not, Currie insisted, on the side of the supply of inputs but on the side of demand for output, or with the *incentive* to expand output and, subsequently, capacity. However—and this is a point Currie has had great difficulty conveying because it is so alien to the modern Keynesian generation of economists—the deficiency of demand that he speaks of is not a deficiency in the Keynesian or purely monetary sense.[2] Indeed, the existence of chronic inflation in Colombia and most other developing countries indicates that Keynesian effective demand is excessive rather than deficient.

Instead, Currie has emphasized the deficiency of demand in the sense of J. B. Say: a deficiency of supply of output (not the supply of capital or foreign exchange) which is the demand for the output of other sectors. In this sense the constraint on development is the small output or small market size that limits demand. As Adam Smith explained, the division of labor is limited by the size of the market. But the division of labor determines the productivity of labor and the national product, incomes, and expenditures. This circular sequence is, for Currie, the key problem for underdeveloped, slow-growing economies. It is the vicious circle of underdevelopment.

This vicious circle cannot easily be attacked on all fronts simultaneously. That would diffuse and dissipate effort. In this, Currie's leading sector strategy differs significantly from Rosenstein-Rodan's "Big Push" approach. If all available savings and tax revenues were spread thinly over all sectors of the economy there would be little incentive to expand capacity (already excessive), and productivity would grow only slowly. Increased savings would in these conditions either depress income (a Keynesian result) or be used mainly to finance consumer credit.

Currie's solution was to concentrate effort and attack the vicious circle at strategic points. He identified housing and construction as a potential leading sector because, more than any other sector—with the possible exception of automobiles (which would be objectionable on other grounds)—it was heavily dependent on borrowing. Unlike most consumer goods and services, almost every house purchaser relies on substantial loans which are amortized over a long period. Without these loans effective demand is severely restricted and cumulatively repressed for all income groups. It is not so much the incomes of the buyers nor the price of the house that determine demand, but the availability of mortgage credit and the terms on which it is available. This important point was little understood by technicians in the DNP and elsewhere, including the international agencies. The conventional way to estimate potential demand for housing was to project past trends and calculate income elasticities of demand on that basis. Currie was forever being told that demand would soon be exhausted and that the housing program would grind to a halt after an initial spurt.

Furthermore, it was believed that because the middle-class and richer working-class groups were a small proportion of the total population demand would be particularly small for middle-class and upper working-class housing. Since the poor were the largest group new building had to be of a kind they could afford. But the poor could not afford much either. Thus it would be better to invest mainly in agriculture instead and so reduce migration. This was, and perhaps still is, the conventional wisdom among development economists, to say nothing of sociologists, architects, engineers, and politicians, especially those who themselves live in middle-class city housing. Not surprising, Currie was often exasperated, depressed, and "peppery" (a term Lloyd Rodwin, a consultant on city planning for Bogotá, used to describe him when reviewing Currie's 1976 book on urbanization.[3])

Nevertheless, Currie persevered with his characteristic stream of memoranda, speeches, and meetings to explain and win acceptance for his ideas. He believed that a massive housing program, financed through private savings protected from the ravages of inflation by the indexed housing finance system he had first advocated ten years earlier in *Operation Colombia*, was easily the most efficient and effective way to improve the housing conditions of all, not least the poor. This would operate through the "filtering" or, as Currie preferred to call it, the "escalation" principle in housing. As the middle classes vacated their old houses to occupy new ones, those slightly poorer would buy the former units. They in turn would vacate their old houses in favor of other lower income groups; and so on. This process would reach down to the very poorest if each year there were constructed a number of new housing units slightly in excess of the number of new households being formed over the same period.

This would require a massive effort and a massive increase in real personal savings directed toward the building sector. There existed, however, massively underutilized resources and Currie was convinced that with a new savings system and measures to channel the bulk of all personal savings into it, these could be mobilized, first to expand building and then to expand all sectors of the economy. Personal savings out of current and future real incomes would provide a noninflationary stimulus to demand, to which the building industry would respond by employing more labor, utilizing existing capacity more fully, and then investing in increased capacity. Because of the existence of greatly increased real final demand the building materials industries would then also be motivated to expand output, employment, and capacity, mainly utilizing internal corporate savings for the purpose. Profits are the chief source of funds for business expansion and for this reason it is the existence of final demand and, hence, profitability that is the main motivating force here. The same is true of agriculture.

For these reasons industry and especially agriculture (with its very low price and income elasticity of demand) are "following" or "dependent" sectors.[4] They tend to move closely in line with the movement of the overall economy, with some differences, depending mainly on the various sectoral income elasticities of demand. Housing and construction, however, can and often do move independently of the overall growth rate, as Currie already noted for the United States in his TNEC testimony in 1939 (see chapter 3). These movements depended on exogenous factors, including those amenable to policy, especially the availability of funds and the terms of financing in relation to rentals on the existing housing stock. Rent controls, or their absence, therefore, were another exogenous policy variable that could be manipulated by discretionary government action.

This, therefore, was the first of Currie's four suggested strategies: action on the housing finance front on a massive scale to mobilize underutilized resources of labor and capital to expand building by as much as 50 percent a year without running into demand constraints; and anticipating and tackling specific supply bottlenecks as they arose by applying the bottleneck-breaking investment criterion and priority foreign exchange rationing as explained in Currie's 1971 article in *The Economic Journal*—in other words, the economics of warfare, in which Currie was experienced. Housing and urbanization costs were to be reduced not only through the economies of scale to be expected from large-scale operations but also by applying the cities-within-cities type of urban design described elsewhere.

The Other Elements of the Plan

Currie's second strategy concerned exports. This too was a strategic and a leading sector. It too depended crucially on effective real demand, this time external demand and, hence, less subject to domestic control. However, there were key policy decisions, notably on the exchange rate, that had a major bearing on the ability of a nation to penetrate foreign markets. If the authorities ensure the exchange rate remains competitive despite domestic inflation then an individual nation faces an almost limitless world demand for many products. (For Colombia this would exclude the special case of coffee.) Growth rates of 30, 40, or even 50 percent a year (as in the case of countries like Korea and Taiwan) are possible for individual countries without fear of encountering inelastic demand or saturating the vast market. The astonishing success of several newly industrialized developing countries (NICs) in recent years has attracted increased interest and enthusiasm for export-led growth models. Currie explains this phenomenon in terms of the massive latent real world demand capable of being tapped by exogenous policy action, but generalizes the lesson to the potential for similar action on the more controllable domestic front.

The third and the fourth strategies followed naturally from the first two. Measures to raise agricultural productivity were to be emphasized and were expected to be stimulated by the increase in real demand arising from the urbanization and export programs. These programs were also expected to improve income distribution by lessening dualism and providing more and better paying jobs for unskilled and semiskilled workers. The plan was also highly critical of the issue of tax-exempt bearer bonds as a principal means of finance for the government's excessive borrowing requirements and also for the monopolistic Central Mortgage Bank (BCH). These bonds were most attractive to the very rich who could use them to avoid tax. This method of financing concealed the true cost of government borrowing and of BCH financing and greatly reduced the effective progressivity of the tax system. The new housing finance system that was to be introduced would avoid those features. It was also hoped to introduce a more effective valorization tax, to capture the rise in the social value of urban land as cities grew.

Despite fierce oppostion from various ministers and the Monetary Board (Junta Monetaria) the President bravely endorsed the new plan and presented it to Congressional leaders as the official Plan of Development of the government on December 2, 1971. Getting the plan adopted had been an uphill struggle. Currie now had to work even harder against the opposition that was determined to prevent its implementation. This was especially difficult because the President did not have a majority in Congress and so could not rely on its support for enabling legislation.

The Opposition

Fortunately Currie took a keen interest in the legal and administrative as well as the economic aspects of national planning. This was essential if his bright ideas were not to remain just bright ideas. In discussions with lawyers on implementation he was told (by Fernando Cepeda) of the possibility that the President could invoke authority conferred on him by the constitution relating to personal savings and their handling and disposition. Currie met with the President and persuaded him that the use of his own powers had the advantage that he could identify himself personally with the new system and take more personal credit for its success.

The Banco de la República (the central bank) and the BCH were both particularly hostile to the proposed changes. The BCH, which was owned mainly by the Banco de la República, had enjoyed a monopoly over private housing finance based on a very limited supply of fixed-interest, tax-exempt bonds and it did not relish competition. As for the Banco de la República itself, Currie argued, as he had done in the 1930s, that a clear distinction be drawn between monetary policy and credit (or savings) policy, and that, therefore, a new Savings and Housing Board (JAVI) be established to advise the President on the new system. The Monetary Board (Junta Monetaria) and the head of the Central Bank, German Botero de los Ríos, resented losing their control over savings (though the Monetary Board was still to be represented on the Savings Board).

In a January 1972 memorandum from the central bank prepared by Miguel Urrutia, Leonel Torres, and Francisco Ortega ("Consideraciones sobre el Proyecto de Fomento de Ahorro"), it was argued that it would be wrong to divert savings from other parts of the capital market; that it would weaken the Stock Exchange and starve industry of funds; that it would harm the BCH; that it would make it difficult to finance the government's borrowing requirements; that it was somehow improper to allow the real value of capital to remain intact during inflation; and that monetary correction would perpetuate inflation. The minister of finance agreed completely: constant-value bonds would institutionalize inflation and all financial assets should be given equal treatment.[5] Currie explained to the President that these criticisms missed the whole point of the new system which was to create new savings and not simply to effect transfers; and that a stimulus to savings would be counterinflationary. It was excessive monetary expansion (the prime responsibility of the Monetary Board), not excessive saving, that caused inflation.

To rally further opposition to the new plan Miguel Urrutia organized a big conference in March 1972 at the University of the Andes in Bogotá. He invited Professor Gustav Ranis of Yale University to come to Colombia specifically for the purpose of blasting the plan. Ranis argued that the plan would be inflationary because he could not see where the savings were going to come from. His own model of development (reviewed in chapter 7 above) insisted that the main source of savings was an increase in the agricultural surplus and he saw no prospect of this in the plan. He thought rural rather than urban housing should be emphasized and that if more urban jobs were created this would only increase migration, increase urban unemployment, and reduce the agricultural surplus. This was the so-called Harris-Todaro thesis that was then and still is fashionable among development theorists, despite being totally at variance with the historical experience of every country that is now developed. In addition Ranis repeated his preference for labor-intensive technology and for spreading capital as thinly as possibly in order to employ more people in industry.

Currie was furious with Ranis for calling into question the sincerity of the plan's stated goals to increase exports and agricultural productivity and to improve income distribution; for his peculiar and inconsistent definition of terms such as "mobility" and "demand"; for urging uneconomic make-work schemes; and for the absurd logic (shared by many of the other critics of the plan who had been brought to the conference) that an increase in urban employment increases unemployment. Currie's critique of Ranis's paper was strongly worded. He also made full comments on several of the other papers presented at the conference, which caused their authors to make substantial changes before they appeared in print.[6] This occasioned Currie to protest to the conference organizer about the appropriateness of this practice since each change made by the original author necessitated a change in the commentator's comments and he had better things to do with his time. However, the revised conference proceedings were eventually published.[7] In addition, to Currie's delight, because a reply was not difficult, Ranis submitted a "Comment" to *The Economic Journal* on Currie's 1971 article.[8]

Implementation

The conference had the effect—not the one intended by the organizers—of fortifying the morale and commitment to the plan of key officials in the DNP such as Luis Eduardo Rosas, Eduardo Sarmiento, and Alejandro Figueroa. Even more important at this time were the meetings every Wednesday evening of a group of distinguished citizens from varied backgrounds, mainly law and business, who were friendly toward Currie and who met with him to discuss in depth the theory and the legal and institutional practicalities of the plan. This was known as the Wednesday Night Group and each week it worked over the memoranda Currie had prepared in the previous days and offered criticisms and suggestions. Currie found it both stimulating and prudent to try out his ideas first on friendly critics before exposing them to hostile ones. His view was that if he could not secure a consensus in such a group on some aspects of the plan, it would be extremely difficult to secure approval of it later from a more general and undoubtedly more hostile audience. The group was informal and attendance varied, but at different times included Samuel Hoyos Arango, Anibal López Trujillo, Andrés Uribe Crane, Rodrigo Gutiérrez, César Garcés, Gonzalo Córdoba, and Eduardo Gaitán. It included none of the country's best-known economists, since most of those were hostile or lukewarm. Nevertheless, the group was very distinguished and constructive and gave the head of DNP and later the President assurance that the plan had been subjected to careful study.

Though the Wednesday Night Group studied closely the Brazilian and Chilean systems of indexed housing finance, the new Colombian system would differ in many details from those and avoid some of their weaknesses. In particular, the Colombian system allowed for daily (rather than quarterly or half-yearly) monetary correction and provided a high degree of liquidity for savers and adequate central bank support against temporary losses of deposits. These features made the system very attractive for short-term savings.

A second precautionary move Currie made early on was to request AID to send a few experts and to contribute to the original financing. This was not so successful as all the experts were opposed to the idea of monetary correction and all were strongly in favor of mutual savings associations which were the least dynamic of the Brazilian and Chilean savings and loans systems.[9] AID also insisted that lending be mainly on very low-cost housing and wanted significant matching peso contribution from the Colombian government. Currie finally advised dropping the negotiations for the initial financing by AID. However, a subsidiary of the World Bank later made a small investment in one of the new corporations as its gesture of goodwill.

On May 2, 1972, President Pastrana signed Decrees 677 and 678 authorizing the setting up of private, joint-stock savings and housing corporations (Corporaciones de Ahorro y Vivienda, CAVS) under the supervision of the Savings and Housing Board (JAVI). Currie was appointed as the President's representative on JAVI. On May 3, 1972, the Junta Monetaria introduced a resolution permitting the commercial banks to raise interest rates on their savings sections and to increase the margin between rates paid depositors and those charged borrowers. This would increase the banks' profits and competitiveness vis-à-vis the proposed new savings corporations and so sabotage the new system.

This resolution was declared unconstitutional because it usurped presidential powers and so had to be abandoned. Nevertheless, the Junta Monetaria resurrected the proposals in September just before the first private corporation was due to open for business. President Pastrana signed the decree prepared by the Junta Monetaria, but Currie persuaded him to rescind it in November because of the damage it was doing. This hostility was typical. In a letter to Robert Nathan (July 17, 1972) on the occasion of Nathan's honorary Doctorate of Law from Georgetown University, Currie remarked that instead of honors he was receiving only brickbats: "I'm under considerable attack as the sinister force manipulating things behind the scenes. I suppose it is a compliment in an inverse sort of way—if I weren't getting somewhere, there would be no point in attacking me. Actually, not only has my plan become the official Plan of Development of the Government but, after a tremendous battle that is still going on, it is being implemented, which is a different and much more difficult matter."

The New Housing Finance System in Operation

The first charter was given to the BCH to set up a "constant value" savings corporation but the BCH had no real interest in developing the new system, gave almost no publicity to it, and received almost no deposits for several months. Currie has noted:[10] "Time was pressing, and the system, to survive a change of governments, had to be established quickly and had to create its own vested interest." For this he advised that the big commercial banks be permitted to participate with up to 30 percent of the capital and even provide space and personnel for the first year but with separate boards of directors. "These banks had their own savings departments, and we appeared to be putting our little sheep into the lion's den, but we gambled on competition, and fortunately the gamble paid off." When one financial group, the Banco de Colombia under Jaime Michelsen, formed a corporation (Corporación Granahorrar), others, such as the Banco de Bogotá (Corporación Davivienda), felt compelled to form their own or be left out.

The system got off to a relatively slow start in the first few weeks because of the increased attractiveness of savings deposits in the banks, and because Currie failed to persuade the President to scrap BCH cedula (tax-exempt bearer bond) financing and force the BCH to move completely to the constant-value system. In a letter (October 16, 1972) to Zane Spindler, a consultant who had been helping him on problems of the budget, Currie spoke of the series of crises:

> The margin of interest provided the savings deposits in commercial banks between rates on deposits and rates on loans was so generous (8 percentage points) as contrasted with the valor constante savings (2½–3 points) that they are all pushing fixed-sum savings and sabotaging valor constante. So I've been fighting to save the basic implementation of the Plan.
>
> Sometimes I get so weary and frustrated that I'd be almost relieved if, as and when the opposition kills the Plan. But as long as Arenas and the President support it, I must fight.

During this period Currie's main relaxation was tennis which he had relearned in 1971 after many years away from the game. He was later to say that one of his main regrets in life was that he had not played more tennis earlier. It was a game he greatly enjoyed and, apart from brief periods of injury, in subsequent years he continued to play four or five times a week, for at least an hour each time. He has maintained this exacting physical program into his 87th year (1989). In 1971 and 1972 he was so busy that these hours of tennis were almost his sole relaxation, but essential if he was to maintain his physical and, hence, mental fitness. His formula was to take time off work to play tennis to enable him to work even harder to save the plan.

In a highly confidential memorandum dated November 21, 1972, which he handed personally to the President, Currie expressed some of his anxieties:

> The declared opposition to the valor constante system of the possible next president of the country poses an extremely urgent question of time. We have only 1½ years to implant the system so firmly that it cannot be scrapped and even less if it is to be so firmly established and supported that the opposition dare not make it a campaign issue. What was done over a period of years in other countries must be done quickly here.
>
> This means that hundreds of thousands of individuals must become accustomed to and use the system within the next few months. That virtually all of the mortgages be written in valor constante terms, that the volume of valor constante savings and mortgages increase rapidly and that a large segment of industry becomes dependent on such savings and mortgages, that the system is used to ease the impact of wage advances, that life insurance and annuities are written in valor constante terms and finally that true interest rates to borrowers can be brought down to 7 or 7½ per cent.

The President acted swiftly on Currie's recommendations relating to competition from the banks' savings accounts (mainly used to finance consumer credit, euphemistically known as "working capital") and thereafter the new system was almost overwhelmed by a massive influx of savings deposits. Despite this, demand for mortgage loans increased even more rapidly. Loan applications were soon running at more than double the rate of savings, amply vindicating Currie's theories so fiercely attacked earlier, about the true nature and potential of housing demand. The experience also vindicated his faith that, given the right conditions, Colombia could be converted into a nation of savers. As Currie recorded later: "Starting from scratch with 200 million pesos at the beginning of 1973 . . . deposits in the new system rose to 7,300 million by March 1974, when legal and political uncertainties arose. This was a net gain. Total personal savings rose from 788 million in 1971 to 7,496 million in 1973 in current pesos (or from 220 million to 1,539 million in 1958 pesos)."[11]

As a result, over this period there was a tremendous upsurge in the construction industry in general and housing in particular. Also exports expanded rapidly thanks to the maintenance of a competitive exchange rate. These results again vindicated Currie's theory that the constraint on growth was not inadequate supply of resources and that the tremendous slack and underutilized resources would respond to incentives and real demand. Under the stimulus of these leading sectors industrial output also rose rapidly, by nearly 10 percent in 1973, the highest on record. Agriculture also grew at a very respectable rate of over 5 percent. Total employment increased by approximately 1 million in the four-year period since 1970, increasing in each successive year and well in excess of the assumed growth in the work force.[12]

Dudley Seers and his associate Richard Jolly returned to Colombia in February 1973 to review with local members of the 1969 ILO mission the progress that had been made in adopting the mission's recommendations (minimal, he complained). The President was angered by the criticisms of his government. Seers and Jolly had written in a report for the ILO entitled "The Pilot Missions under the World Employment Programme": "But suppose the government rejects the proposals, the report could still have a positive effect in the hands of those inside the administration, and outside it, who are trying to mobilize support for the necessary changes in the direction. Indeed, in such a case, it should not be held against a mission if its report may be one of the factors which leads to a change in government." Currie drew this and other highly critical passages to the President's attention. The President told Seers that the new plan was the official plan of the government and that he wanted only constructive criticisms. So Seers did not stay long. He found it hard to swallow that what his ILO report insisted could not happen on the employment front was in fact happening, thus refuting his analyses and prediction that if his recommendations were not followed more than one-third of the labor force would be openly unemployed by 1985.

Inflation and Monetary Policy

The record of the Pastrana administration was less impressive on the fiscal and monetary fronts, and accelerating inflation was the result. The annual rate of inflation was around 13 percent from June 1971 to June 1972, rising to around 23 percent in each of the two succeeding years. Currie prepared many memoranda on the subject during this period and was highly critical of the absence of any good monetary theorists on the Junta Monetaria. The Banco de la República acted as both a central bank with responsibility to control the money supply and as a development bank. The Junta Monetaria and its advisers emphasized its role as a development bank and urged "selective credit controls" and "productive credit" for "working capital." Membership of the junta was (and remains) dominated by spokesmen of different borrowing groups. The commercial loan theory of central banking, therefore, was as alive in Colombia at this time as it had been forty years earlier in the United States when Currie first wrote of its fallacies and dangers.

Belief in productive credit as the criterion of monetary policy increased the likelihood that the central bank would accede to the many pressures placed on it to open new lines of credit. The advisers to the Monetary Board, Francisco Ortega and Leonel Torres, and other key officials in the central bank, including the manager, German Botero de los Ríos, and Miguel Urrutia, resisted Currie's calls to introduce open market operations to offset exogenous expansionary pressures on the money supply arising from increasing international reserves (from increased exports and external borrowing) and heavy government borrowing requirements. Over the next fifteen years Currie would have to repeat his criticism of central bank policy over and over again since several of the key officials remained in positions of influence for much of this period. German Botero de los Ríos, for example, was manager for the long period from 1968 to 1978, and Francisco Ortega remained an influential adviser throughout, becoming the manager in 1986. Neither had much formal training in monetary theory.

These officials had little understanding of or sympathy for the theory of leading sectors and instead believed that the leading sectors diverted credit from other sectors. Thus it was their reluctant but solemn duty to open central bank lines of credit to these other sectors when pressed to do so. The money supply was then expanded by a multiple of the initial allocation of credit, and monetary spending then expanded by an even greater multiple (depending on the velocity of circulation of around six or seven per year). They did too little to offset the monetary consequences of the excessively high government deficit or the increase in international reserves. They rejected Currie's repeated calls for measures such as a widening of the spread between the buying and selling rates of exchange as a means to increase government revenues and reduce borrowing requirements. Currie arranged (directly or indirectly) for a number of distinguished international economic consultants to visit Colombia to advise on various aspects of monetary, fiscal, and exchange policy. They included persons such as Wilfred Lewis, Zane Spindler, Ronald McKinnon, Michael Posner, James Hanson, Robert Barro, and Dick Netzer. They had little influence on ingrained central bank thinking and practice.

When inflation accelerated many central bank officials tended to pass the blame on to the new housing finance system and monetary correction. Yet monetary correction was paid only *after* inflation had already occurred. Furthermore, the system did not really get started until December 1972 and the money supply and inflation had been accelerating long before then. Throughout 1973 and early 1974 the capture of new savings greatly outstripped disbursements. Thus a substantial volume of savings was concealed in a special fund (FAVI) in the central bank.[13] This acted as a fortuitous but helpful contractionary, hence anti-inflationary, influence on the money supply. However, the strange theory of the system's critics in Colombia and abroad was that an increase in savings was inflationary.[14] They rationalized their position by adding savings to the money supply, to obtain a series for "quasi-money," so that the faster the growth of savings the greater the "inflationary" increase in "money." Currie once remarked that whoever invented the concept of quasi-money should be awarded a Nobel prize-in-reverse. In any case the Monetary Board continued to resent the existence of a separate body to deal with savings and successfully pressed the next government to abolish it. Thus the confusion between monetary and credit policy persisted.

As inflation accelerated Currie wrote more and more memoranda and articles explaining the difference between the effects of an increase in Keynesian or purely monetary demand on the one hand, and real or "Sayian" demand (after J. B. Say) on the other. Though the theory of leading sectors emphasized a demand constraint this certainly did not involve inadequate monetary demand. The chronic persistence of inflation testified to that. Rather, institutional constraints reduced factor mobility and so kept output and, hence, real demand low. Real demand was particularly repressed by these institutional obstacles in the fields of housing and exports. Accelerated development with overall growth rates in excess of 5 percent was invariably accompanied by extraordinarily high growth rates in one or two key sectors, as shown by the increasingly familiar export-led growth experience of countries such as South Korea, Taiwan, Singapore, and Hong Kong.

By March 1973 Currie visited Singapore, mainly to observe the nature of urban planning there. But he was equally impressed by how Singapore had achieved one of the highest growth rates in the world over the previous decade, with extraordinary expansion of exports and housing, yet had experienced an annual average inflation rate of only 1 percent. Currie tried to impress on the President that this showed that it was possible to combine a rapid growth in real (Sayian) demand with austere monetary policies (though the more rapid the real growth rate the greater the permissible expansion of Keynesian or monetary demand without incurring inflation).[15]

In November 1972 Roberto Arenas was appointed to the important post of minister of government and his position as head of the DNP was taken over by his deputy, Luis Eduardo Rosas, who had a Ph.D. from Brown University in the United States where he had specialized in monetary theory. Rosas, therefore, was also predisposed to emphasize the important distinctions between monetary and credit policy and as a member of the Junta Monetaria he pressed for greater monetary control. He also argued that a policy that gives equal priority to all sectors gives priority to none and would fail to accelerate real growth. He encouraged Currie to organize a major two-week seminar in September and October 1973 on "the Plan in Action" at which Rosas and Currie, together with various chiefs at the DNP and others, explained these and other important aspects of the theory and practical implications of the plan.[16]

A little later Rosas also decided to devote an entire issue of the DNP's academic *Revista de Planeación y Desarrollo* to the subject of monetary theory and policy; he, Currie, Antonio Hernández, and Robert Barro contributed technical articles. This appeared in February 1974 a few days after Currie had had a long private meeting with the President at which he finally made him understand the relevant theory and persuaded him of the seriousness of the lack of adequate monetary control. On February 18 the President gave a long speech on television in which he frankly admitted the mistakes that had led to serious inflation, that there was a need to distinguish between the different roles of a central bank and a development bank and that hard decisions on monetary control were now called for. Thereafter the President took much more decisive action, overruling the Junta Monetaria, to control the money supply and fiscal deficit. As a result inflation fell to a very low level in the final months of his administration.

When at the end of February the *Revista* appeared with the few articles on money which, though very technical in nature, were implicitly very critical of the theory and practice of the Junta Monetaria, the minister of finance, Luis Fernando Echavarría, who chaired the junta, was furious. He made the serious accusation that Rosas was "disloyal" to the government. Unfortunately for Echavarría the President had a few days earlier endorsed Rosas's viewpoint. The President had also known for some months (letter to the President, August 27, 1973) that Currie was going to publish his paper showing the very close relationship between inflation and the excess expansion of the money supply.[17] Rosas shrugged off the challenge and Echavarría was admonished by President Pastrana.[18]

By the end of 1973 the government's whole program and record was being placed in jeopardy by the inflation caused by the monetary and fiscal mismanagement. But because indexation was being made the scapegoat, several unfortunate modifications were introduced to the system. The index base was extended from a three-month to a twelve-month and then a twenty-four-month moving average which, with rising inflation, had the effect of reducing the amount of monetary correction paid. Thus savers began to receive a lower real return.

Secondly, on January 28, 1974, a decree was signed that permitted borrowers to deduct from their income tax liabilities not only interest payments but also monetary correction.[19] This was an exorbitant privilege (in Brazil and Chile borrowers were allowed to deduct neither monetary correction nor interest) and shortly before President Pastrana's term of office ended, Currie, Luis Eduardo Rosas, and Samuel Hoyos signed a "constancia" (dissent) against this ruling which they presented to Finance Minister Echavarría. He rejected it, as did his successor, Rodrigo Botero. These ministers accepted the spurious, purely political argument that the "poor" borrower was being exploited by "rich" savers. But most borrowers in the private housing finance system were relatively wealthy. And the wealthier they were the greater the tax concessions. No doubt most government ministers who were proclaiming the virtues of distributive justice were among those who would enjoy the greatest benefits from their "reforms."

A System Too Strong to Dismantle

In March 1974 Alfonso López won the presidential election and was due to assume office in August. He and his closest economic advisers let their hostility to the new savings system be known and a "demanda" (suit) was lodged with the Consejo de Estado (Council of State) against its constitutionality. The effect was that the rate of growth of savings slackened off after March. In terms of constant 1972 pesos savings grew from 200 million pesos at the end of 1972 to 3,556 million at the end of 1973. By March 1974 they had leapt to 5,143 million but then grew more slowly to 5,892 million in June and 6,088 million in September (around $300 million).

President López and his economic team dearly wished they could dismantle the system. But to Currie's delight the system had been so enormously successful in attracting savings and financing new building that too many vested interests had, as he had hoped and planned, by now been created.[20] By mid-1974 there were ten corporations, offices throughout the country, 8,000 million of current pesos on deposit ($320 million), 1,000 employees, and 125,000 individual accounts. It would be extremely dangerous to attempt to dismantle such an organization. When President López assumed office there was panic among savers and the system began to lose deposits rapidly. The new

President and his team got cold feet and promised they would after all maintain the system. However, a number of measures were taken all of which benefited the powerful lobby of rich borrowers at the expense of savers. These included a ceiling on monetary correction at 20 points (while at the same time the monetary and fiscal policies of the new government immediately had the effect of increasing inflation to an annual rate in the final quarter of 1974 of over 30 percent), a reduction in the interest rate to savers from 5 percent to 4 percent, and confirmation of tax deductions for borrowers while imposing new tax liabilities on the purely monetary gains of savers. Following their peculiar theories on how to control inflation they succeeded in reducing savings while accelerating the growth of the money supply.

Nevertheless, the new system survived and, indeed, eventually expanded enormously. However, it was never again to play the role that Currie had planned for it: to create a dynamic leading sector out of construction and, through it, to achieve the critical minimum effort needed to break the vicious circles of underdevelopment and put the economy on the self-sustaining, noninflationary high growth path that he was convinced was possible for a nation with the abundance of underutilized resources that Colombia possessed. But the system has survived and is available to any future government that may wish to exploit more fully its potential as an instrument to accelerate development. To have done so much personally to conceive, establish, and nurture this important yet initially so unpopular system, must stand as one of Currie's most notable achievements.

CHAPTER 11

The "Cities-within-Cities" Design for Urban Growth

The Phase II Bogotá Urban Development Study

As was noted in chapter 10, one of the first things Currie determined to do on his return to Bogotá in May 1971 was to change the terms of reference that the World Bank and the mayor of Bogotá, Carlos Albán, had agreed for the Bogotá Phase II Study. The expensive Phase I Study had been carried out by a firm of transport planners and engineers and basically made recommendations to meet the transport requirements implied by existing urban trends. It assumed a monocentered city with dispersion following existing lines to the north and west. It ignored the alternative of a multicentered city that Currie had proposed in his 1967 study for the then mayor of Bogotá, Virgilio Barco.

The terms of reference for the $1 million Phase II Study now being proposed were again heavily transport oriented and made no reference to the need to study the idea of creating new, largely self-contained centers within existing city boundaries to prevent further costly sprawl on to the valuable agricultural lands of the Sabana. Currie feared that if another engineering consulting firm was given a single lump-sum contract following inflexible terms of reference laid down in advance, it would place too great an emphasis on accommodating traffic rather than on planning to prevent traffic generation, and would commit Bogotá to the horribly expensive North American style or urban sprawl based on the private automobile.

Currie, therefore, persuaded Roberto Arenas to ask the World Bank to send Wilfred Owen to Bogotá at the end of June to discuss the relationship between national urban planning and plans for Bogotá. Specifically, he was to consider how the terms of reference of the Phase II Bogotá Study could be reconciled with views held in the National Planning Department (by Currie and Arenas) with respect to the effective use of the urbanization process as an instrument for accelerating economic growth and raising levels of living for the mass of the population.

Owen was an old student and friend of Currie's. They had discussed urbanization problems many times in the past and had a common outlook. Currie later gave Owen's well-known book *The Accessible City* (Washington, D.C.: Brookings Institution, 1972) to President Pastrana to read, and had some of his papers translated for publication in Spanish in the DNP journal.[1] Owen's report to the World Bank endorsed Currie's misgivings:

> What the national planners would like to guard against is a prior commitment in the terms of reference to already designated routes for the construction of a subway. They believe that much of the million dollar study will be devoted to the feasibility of rapid transit before sufficient enquiry has been made of the ways in which development patterns could be altered to change commuting patterns.
>
> A specific complaint is that there is insufficient attention in Phase I of the survey to a pattern of high-density centers throughout the Bogotá region, in which a mixture of residential and work places and associated community facilities would reduce the average length of work trip and make many transport trips unnecessary. The existing pattern of development, based on outmoded zoning principles, separates housing in the suburbs from work places at the center, and misses the opportunities for providing good residential community development in the vicinity of industrial plants, and vice versa.[2]

Bogotá at that time was a city of around 2.6 million, a population that was expected to double in a decade and reach 9 million by 1990. The city was expected to grow by some 200,000–300,000 persons each year, around half due to immigration from the countryside and smaller urban centers. This phenomenal growth presented both great challenges and great opportunities. Whereas it was extremely difficult to change the form of a city of a given population that had already established itself, it was not too late to plan a more efficient design for the additions to a city's population in which the central concern is housing and jobs and not highways and automobiles. On the other hand, to permit a laissez-faire policy of urban land use (essentially the U.S. model) would mean a repetition of the U.S. automobile-dominated cities with high-cost suburban sprawl, a decaying center, pollution and congestion, decline of public transit, and the neglect of housing and amenities.

Owen told the World Bank that building a city was not like building a bridge. Many alternative designs were possible and a flexible approach, dominated by social scientists to whom engineers would be subordinate, was called for. A strong steering committee was needed, with representatives from the national government, to control the study and ensure flexibility in the terms of reference.

Eventually the terms of reference were rewritten, but only after several month's delay occasioned by disagreements between the National Planning Department, the Bogotá District Planning Department and the World Bank. Bogotá officials were not enthusiastic about having representatives of the National Planning Office on the steering committee. In the end, however, Currie was appointed to fulfil this role and was the only member to attend all of its meetings over the next two or three years.

The World Bank refused to be moved from its practice of awarding a large, lump-sum contract rather than a flexible cost-plus, open-ended series of smaller contracts for specific action-oriented studies whose need would be identified as work progressed. Thus Currie was all the more insistent on a strong steering committee and modifications to the terms of reference to reflect the new guidelines for national planning that he had been writing and which, by December 1971, had been adopted by the government. These guidelines insisted on the inextricable link between national development and urbanization. If urbanization was to be the motor of national development and well-being then the future of Bogotá was a national issue, a pilot test for national urban planning.

Urban congestion, pollution, violence, and alienation had given big cities a bad reputation. Currie insisted, however, that these costs could be avoided or greatly reduced if the pattern of urban growth was better planned and guided. This planning would be even more urgent in the future as the growth of cities was to be accelerated through the creation of the new housing finance corporations to capture a massively increased flow of personal savings for building. Measures to increase agricultural productivity would also release even more rural workers for employment in urban industry, construction, and services.

Currie had to fight off at least three types of opposition to his ideas on urbanization and development. The most basic was typified by the criticism of the British ambassador and his wife at a luncheon for the former British minister of overseas development, Judith Hart, in September 1971. They told Currie that people were happier in the countryside and should be encouraged to stay there. Judith Hart thought this would be possible were it not for the selfishness of the ruling classes who were blocking land redistribution. These critics, themselves invariably the product of urban civilization, seemed incapable of understanding the logical contradiction between their romantic idyll and the inescapable negative consequences for rural employment of increased agricultural productivity and inelastic demand for agricultural output. They also ignored the implications of high rural birth rates, the horrendous destruction of the natural environment arising from the growing rural population, and the enormous per capita costs of bringing to their scattered communities the amenities of civilization that they craved but were unable or unwilling to pay for.

The second type of opposition came from those who believed that the best kind of urbanization and development would arise naturally from the unhindered operation of the price system. Changing land values would guide resources into the optimal locations. It was the function of government to bring services to the places where people chose spontaneously to live and to work, perhaps with some modification of choice through zoning norms that segregated land use according to type of activity, especially where this protected property values in the better neighborhoods.

A third line of attack came from those who rejected Currie's approach to metropolitan development on the grounds that it was "too costly" and/or too oriented to building new housing that the very poor could not afford. These critics favored the growth of smaller cities where land was cheaper. Geographers and politicians, in particular, liked decentralization and regional balance, to bring work nearer to where the workers (and their votes) were currently located. To these people it was axiomatic that if land values were higher in large cities then development there would be more expensive and so, at best, would favor only the rich.

Nevertheless, if more people came to the big cities (where, inconveniently for the opposition case, average real incomes were highest), then emphasis should be placed on the "sites-and-services" approach to housing those in most desperate need. This was seen as the cheapest possible solution and, therefore, the most appropriate if the maximum number of poor people were to be helped. Since many poor people are unemployed or underemployed, it was argued, they could build their own homes at little opportunity cost. To keep costs down it was also obvious that cheap land on the periphery of the big cities was the best location for "sites-and-services" projects.

Currie's "Cities-within-the-City" Approach

Currie addressed himself to all these issues in a stream of memoranda, articles, and books over the next few years. He persuaded President Pastrana to incorporate some of his basic ideas on urbanization and urban design in important speeches: opening Congress on July 20, 1971, to congressional leaders on December 2, 1971, when it was adopted as official government policy, and, most comprehensively, to the Congress of Planners in September 1972. The basic principles were early set forth in a seventy-seven-page statement for the National Planning Office, dated August 13, 1971, "An Urban Policy for Developing Countries," and in "The Multiple Objectives of Urban Development," March 10, 1972 (thirty-one pages).

After attending the meetings of the American Economic Association in New Orleans in December, where he presented a paper in the special session on the New Deal, Currie went to Washington for talks with World Bank officials, including S. S. Kirmani, Jerry Alter, Harold Dunkerley, and Hollis Chenery, on the new national plan and the Bogotá Phase II Study. Also, at the Brookings Institution he discussed with Wilfred Owen potential urban development firms that had experience in planning whole new communities.

Early in 1972 the terms of reference for the Phase II Bogotá Study were revised to incorporate the study of the multiple-center or "cities-within-cities" concept of urban design as set out in Currie's writings, with a view of identifying appropriate sites for implementation as soon as possible. Several firms submitted proposals for the study. Eventually the British firm of Llewellyn-Davies, Weeks, Forrestier-Walker, and Bor was selected by the World Bank and the steering committee to undertake the work. Llewellyn-Davies was the firm that had designed the new town of Milton Keynes near London. A contract was signed in July 1972 and work began the following month in association with Kates, Peat Marwick and Co., Cooper and Lybrand, and a local consultancy firm, Consultécnicos. All of the firms presenting proposals had emphasized transportation and relatively conventional urban design concepts. These points still loomed large in the terms of reference which, despite the modifications Currie had introduced, retained most of the original draft terms drawn up by the World Bank and the Bogotá Distrito.

As Currie later commented:

> The first progress report (October 9, 1972) confirmed all my previous misgivings. The consultants saw no difference between a socioeconomic study of a city facing a tremendous period of growth and the building of, say, a dam or a bridge. After two introductory chapters in which soothing words were inserted on the change in emphasis to an "action-oriented" approach and a perfunctory discussion of the "cities-within-cities" alternative, mostly negative, the report laid out the work of 48 staff members and consultants in 78 different "tasks" requiring 305 man-months, with flow diagrams indicating precisely the dates on which the various tasks would be started and finished. Any real possibility that the study could be significantly modified in its course was an illusion. Staff and consultants were already hired, and work was subcontracted. (A total of 114 man-months were assigned to a firm of transport specialists to start immediately.)[3]

From the beginning Currie had to battle relentlessly to orient the study toward the cities-within-cities concept and to make the consultants understand the full implications of the new national plan for housing demand and urban employment. The study team director, Jonathan Smulian, and several key consultants including Christopher Foster, a London School of Economics transport economist, Alan Gilbert, a London University geographer, Douglas McCallum, an urban planner at Glasgow University, William Doebbel of Harvard, and Lisa Peattie and Lloyd Rodwin, urbanists at MIT, were in varying degrees enamored with the sites-and-services approach and "progressive" building (auto-construcción) or what Currie called the do-it-yourself approach to economic development.

It was not until January 1973 that the cities-within-cities concept was accepted by the consultants, in their second progress report. But, as Douglas McCallum remarked in a lengthy report to the ILO on the experience of the Bogotá study:

> None of the conclusions reached by the Study were arrived at easily or without controversy: within the Team, or between the Team and the Steering Committee, or within the Steering Committee, or with outside parties. In actual practice, the Steering Committee was ultimately dominated by Lauchlin Currie and the DNP point of view; other points of view gen-

> erally lacked the continuity, coherence and political weight needed to match Currie. . . .
>
> The dominance of Currie was a function both of his position (representing the mainstreams of current national policy through his close relationships with decision-makers in DNP and with the President himself) and of his greater intellectual force, aggressiveness and tenacity. It is also significant that District Planning was represented by a succession of three Directors, none with any real personal or professional commitment to the post, whereas DNP was continuously represented by one man (Currie) with a very strong commitment. This domination was evident to most observers, including among others the various World Bank visiting boards.[p.48][4]

Thus the study team and other participants remained lukewarm or hostile toward Currie's ideas. Even after the consultants formally accepted the new design concept little was done to advance its study because by that time most of the work had been subcontracted in accordance with what the consultants believed to be the original terms of reference. McCallum's report itself is a good reflection of the skepticism prevailing among the study team.

He complained that in the early stages of the new housing finance system most of the savings were financing offices, houses, and apartments for the rich in Bogotá. He claimed that because of the very unequal distribution of income there could be little prospective demand for indexed (UPAC) housing finance and that these funds were creating a "false" boom that could not last. Forty to sixty percent of people were excluded from the normal housing market by their low incomes. UPAC funds were used to build for only a small class and therefore, he claimed, would have no effect on lower income groups. In fact it harmed the poor by causing the price to rise of the building materials they used to build their own "progressive" housing. "There is a real danger that the cities-within-cities programme as set out by DNP will turn out (especially if they are largely financed with UPAC funds) to be mainly high- and middle-income residential developments, with little employment of any kind, and very little employment or housing for the low-income populace." (p. 59). The welfare of the poor majority was being "studiously ignored." (p. 53).

McCallum's account is revealing for what it ignores. It ignores the enormous excess of demand for housing finance even over the tremendous increase of funds made available by the new system. Applications were running at over twice the funds available. As the system developed branches opened up throughout the country and more funds were lent to middle- and lower-middle-income groups. Effective demand for housing fell only when the next government deliberately reduced the attractiveness of the new system to savers, so that there was less available to translate the manifest latent demand into actual demand. This caused a slump in building and a big increase in unemployment which must have aggravated inequality. When Currie made this claim in his 1981 book on the role of economic advisers in developing countries, Miguel Urrutia, who was one of those responsible for the hostile approach to housing finance, angrily dismissed this claim as "irresponsible." Urrutia was reviewing the book for the influential *Journal of Economic Literature* (volume 21, March 1983). It is interesting to compare his harsh review of the book with that of the more disinterested Sir Alexander Cairncross, who wrote that Currie's book "not only talks more consistent sense about the theory of economic development than any other book I have read but is full of useful guidance on problems of policy based on personal experience."[5]

McCallum's claim that the building of a major city within the city for around 400,000 to 500,000 people would "provide little employment of any kind" can hardly be taken seriously, expecially when he himself acknowledges the big increase in unemployment in 1975 when building was allowed to slump. However, following the fashionable Todaro thesis, he repeats the theory that the more urban employment that is created the more migrants will arrive, so the more unemployment there will be. Presumably the answer is to destroy urban jobs in order to reduce unemployment.

Direct versus Indirect Attacks on Poverty

McCallum dismissed Currie's explanation of the way that the poor could benefit indirectly from a major construction program—through the "filtering" process—without, however, giving any arguments against it. Currie's argument was that the root cause of the housing problem was not inadequate housing but inadequate incomes. The poor benefit most from well-paying jobs that give them more income to purchase better accommodation. If many more of them also find good employment, and the total stock of housing is increased faster than the growth of new family units by building decent (nonslum) housing, then *all* families can improve their housing conditions, with the vast majority moving from their existing home to another existing home of a somewhat better standard in a somewhat better location. Only a few, as in all North American and European countries, would move into homes newly built for them.[6] Building directly for the poor results, he argued, in extremely poor housing on cheap land is only cheap because it is poorly serviced and poorly located. Even then it usually involves a heavy subsidy element. Subsidies have their place but are an extremely precarious basis on which to plan the main thrust of development policy.

Instead of wasting resources by bringing relatively expensive services to poor barrios in distant locations, Currie urged that the poor be brought to those places where services can be provided most cheaply. Although the land element is more expensive in the more central city locations, he explained that this is a pure transfer payment that does not absorb real resources. Furthermore, if a public urban development corporation could acquire large blocks of land in advance of the building of new cities within the city it would be possible to buy at pre-development land values. The building of the new city would itself create enhanced land values that could be captured by the development corporation in higher rents charged to the wealthier residential, commercial, and industrial tenants. This would not only obviate one of the most important sources of inequality by preventing private owners from capturing the increase in socially created land values, but it would also enable the corporation to finance more community facilities and subsidize the rents of poorer tenants with jobs nearby (who thus impose fewer transportation costs on the community). This strategy would also help reduce the social segregation that is a feature of traditional urbanization patterns in developing countries. These emphasize zoning to protect property values in wealthier neighborhoods and encourage sites-and-services auto-construction schemes on peripheral locations, with housing usually divorced from nearby job opportunities and social amenities.

Partial Precedents

A partial precedent for the model of metropolitan development that Currie had in mind was to be found in Singapore. Currie made a brief visit to Singapore in March 1973, accompanied by Rafael Villate, director of planning for Bogotá, and reported his findings at the UN interregional seminar on new towns in London in June 1973.[7] Over the previous decade Singapore had rehoused one-third of its entire population in a series of large, relatively compact new towns. Currie revisited Singapore in 1984, following an official visit to China and Hong Kong. By that time three-quarters of the population had been rehoused and Singapore's new towns were increasingly self-contained cities-within-cities.

Singapore's new housing developments were almost exclusively high-rise apartment blocks of ten to twenty stories. An unusually high proportion of national income was diverted to building, yet Singapore had one of the fastest growth rates in the world. Savings for building were increased dramatically by substantial employee and employer contributions to a national pension scheme. These contributions could be used for the downpayments on the purchase of apartments and for servicing mortgage debts. The Singapore experience may be contrasted with Douglas McCallum's criticism of Currie's proposals for Bogotá: "The idea of housing the poor in high-rise apartment buildings in high-density new cities-within-the-city is too unrealistic to deserve much serious treatment" (McCallum, 1975, p. 60; 1978, p. 117).

McCallum insisted such an approach was too expensive because high-rise, well-serviced, centrally located apartments cost more than traditional low-density building. He also noted, on the basis of opinion surveys carried out by the Llewellyn-Davies study team, that the poor *preferred* their own single-family house and garden. This finding echoed the views of Bogotá's planning director, Patricio Samper, in an article for the newspaper *La República* in July 1971, that high-rise living was an imperialist foreign idea and that the Colombian tradition was a house and a garden in which to raise chickens and grow vegetables.

Despite these sentiments, all these commentators endorsed the study team's projections that Bogotá's population would grow to over 8 million by 1990.[8] Bogotá as a garden city of 8–10 million is impossible to imagine unless the whole of the agricultural Sabana was to be lost. Currie's solution did not offer everyone a private garden and it implied much higher densities per hectare.[9] But it offered much lower densities per room. It also offered ample communal space. And, by economizing on infrastructure costs it released more resources for education and health. No doubt if the opinion survey had asked, respondents would have said they preferred all these things too. Of course it would be ideal if people could have private gardens also, but economics is about choices and the poorer the economy the harder the choices that are called for, except in the language of the populists.

However, despite Currie's enthusiasm for Singapore's achievements he did not fully endorse their urban model. He noted that the private automobile played a too dominant role, so that an excessive amount of land was given over to streets and parking lots. Private cars also caused heavy congestion in the traditional center (though later severe restrictions were placed on the entry of cars into that center during peak periods). Furthermore, little was being done to capture the rapid increases in socially created land values and inequality, therefore, was excessive. (Later, however, draconian land acquisition powers were acquired by the state.) Also, at that time the new towns in Singapore tended to be dormitory suburbs rather than true cities. Again, however, much more was done later to provide all the basic community facilities and recreation areas for each center and to create a much better mix of housing and jobs which has considerably reduced the need for movement. Currie was particularly impressed by Singapore's clean, efficient, seven-story "flatted factories" that greatly economized space and that were being located in the middle of the new centers.

He believed that one of the defects of planning in Singapore was that each new center did not have its own urban development corporation. In this they differed from the British new towns that he toured in June 1973 after the London seminar. Instead, Singapore had one very large Housing Development Board responsible for all public housing on the island, and a separate industrial development agency, the Jurong Town Corporation. Initially, therefore, housing and industry were excessively divorced from each other.

Currie was impressed by the efficient integrated management of the British new towns. Also by the fact that their general policies were supervised by central government to ensure coordination with overall national priorities—a judicious mixture of centralization and decentralization. Furthermore, they had been able to purchase large blocks of land at predevelopment prices and so capture much of the rise in land values created subsequently. A few months later Currie addressed another UN seminar on urbanization in New York and there learned more of the similar principles in the planned communities created by private development corporations in, for example, Columbia (Maryland), Reston (Virginia), and Staten Island (New York). However, both the British new towns and the American privately planned new communities suffered from the great disadvantage—from the point of view of Colombia and other developing countries—that they were dominated by the private automobile which greatly increased infrastructure costs and long-distance commuting.

In view of his dissatisfaction with the orientation of the Phase II Bogotá Study team, and in order to benefit from different approaches to the general problem of an efficient design for rapid urbanization in Colombia, Currie arranged in 1972 and 1973 for two U.S. urban planning firms with experience of planning new communities to undertake studies and prepare designs for new cities-within-the-city in Cali, Medellín, Barranquilla, and Bucaramanga. These firms were the American Cities Corporation and Planners Incorporated. In 1973 Currie arranged for the latter firm, with AID financing, to conduct intensive seminar programs for Colombian urban planners from these provincial cities and to take them on an international tour of cities where the multiple-center, cluster, or cities-within-cities design had been applied: in Paris, Stockholm, Singapore, England, and the United States.

El Salitre

Toward the end of the Bogotá Phase II Study, which had not identified any specific site for a new self-contained center, Currie initiated discussions on new contracts with new firms to undertake this action-oriented work. The World Bank wanted Llewellyn-Davies to do this follow-up but Currie argued the need for three separate firms, preferably new ones, to initiate three pre-feasibility studies of the possible physical layouts and land use patterns of three different sites to satisfy certain specified parameters on density and total population. In August 1973 the director of the National Planning Office, Luis Eduardo Rosas, persuaded the United Nations to transfer to the World Bank $100,000 of a sum they had earmarked for urban studies to be sponsored by DNP so that these various pre-feasibility studies could be undertaken at a total cost of around $250,000 (the balance to be made up with money the World Bank had itself earmarked for the Bogotá study).

Shortly afterwards, however, there were major changes of personnel in the World Bank's urban division and the new officials supported Llewellyn-Davies's claim to be the only firm contracted by the Bank—using the whole $250,000—to do another rather general study of one large block of more than 7,000 hectares to the west and north of Bogotá, capable of accommodating 1.75 million people; far too many for a single self-contained center. Angry exchanges ensued, in Bogotá and Washington, between the director of DNP and World Bank officials over this decision and the terms of reference for the new study, but to no avail. Therefore, Luis Eduardo Rosas persuaded AID to finance another of the many smaller, quicker, much cheaper action-oriented studies that they had so successfully sponsored earlier.

Currie and Rosas, with the support of the President, were particularly interested in the unique opportunity afforded by a 450-hectare site known as El Salitre adjacent to a major complex of government offices (Centro Administrativo Nacional) and other institutions that already employed around 40,000 persons. El Salitre was an almost vacant site only five to seven kilometers from the traditional city center (close, but also far enough distant to form potentially a separate center). In its immediate area of influence there were 1,500 hectares of already urbanized land occupied by nearly 200,000 people who would presumably wish to use a new commercial center at El Salitre. The lands of Salitre were owned entirely by a single public charitable agency, La Beneficencia. The District Planning Office and the Llewellyn-Davies people, however, were unenthusiastic about this site, arguing that it was too close to the existing center and that it was too expensive for the low-cost, low-density type of housing they favored.[10] They were more interested in more distant, green field sites.

Therefore, Planeación Nacional contracted the American City Corporation to undertake the survey of El Salitre. Within a few months, with the help of the econometrician John Delaplaine and Currie himself, they had prepared a detailed three-dimensional maquette showing their proposed physical layout of the new city, with accompanying financial calculations, cash-flow details, and recommendations on administration.[11] The new city would accommodate 450,000–500,000 residents (with about 300,000 on the lands of El Salitre itself) with a minimum base of 125,000 jobs in manufacturing, business and government offices, institutional positions, and a wide range of services. It provided for a full range of social services and institutions; commercial facilities to meet all the basic shopping requirements of residents; open spaces and recreational facilities that exceeded the current standards in Bogotá; a public transit system that was nowhere more than 300 meters distant from any apartment block; and a land-use design that practically eliminated the need for private auto trips between home and work, recreation, or social services, thus requiring less land for vehicular movement. The proposal offered a full range of housing sizes available at various rentals and prices to accommodate a broad range of family incomes and family sizes. Buildings would occupy only 20 percent of the total land area. Half would be four to five stories in height, the rest a mixture between ten to twenty stories.

The American City Corporation and the Llewellyn-Davies team both initiated their respective studies on April 15, 1974. In a letter to Wilfred Owen on July 23 Currie noted wryly: "American City did an excellent quick job of the sort I was talking about at our meeting last September. Physical and economic feasibility study on a specific site, 3½ months, $80,000. Llewellyn-Davies is doing another year's general study for $250,000." Meanwhile, on the privately owned lands that Llewellyn-Davies was studying and on which they preferred that the first new city be built, private speculators and developers were grabbing all they could.

The windfall gains from rapidly appreciating land values as urbanization accelerated was a subject that had preoccupied Currie for some time. In 1972 he had arranged for Robert Huck, a land valuation expert at the Institute of Public Administration in New York, to undertake for the National Planning Department an important feasibility study on ways of capturing the land value increment with annual assessments.[12] His report was encouraging. In 1974 Currie discussed the issues extensively with the World Bank expert on the subject, Orville Grimes, and worked up a draft bill with the legal experts Hugh Mields and David Blum. Currie hoped to incorporate this in the broader urban legislation he was helping to prepare. This included the setting up of urban development corporations to manage the new cities-within-the-city, in particular El Salitre.

The López Administration

The spectacular success of the new indexed savings and loan system in 1973 and early 1974 appeared to have settled the question of how to raise an adequate volume of finance for building as a motor of economic development. The main preoccupation then had become where, how, and what to build. Thus the importance Currie attached to the planning of new city centers, renovation of existing centers, and legal powers to control urban sprawl. For the latter purpose the regional corporations of CAR (Corporación Autónoma Regional), responsible for the rural areas surrounding Bogotá, and the CVC (Corporación del Valle del Cauca) were transferred from the jurisdiction of the ministerio de agricultura to the Deparamento Nacional de Planeación in July 1974. The next step was to set up public urban development corporations to manage the new cities, starting with one for the proposed Ciudad El Salitre.

In August 1974, however, the new government of President Alfonso López Michelsen was due to assume office. As discussed in chapter 8 the new savings system was the subject of fierce political attacks and savers feared the López government would dismantle the system. The Junta Monetaria also succeeded, even before August, in passing resolutions that made the new system less attractive to savers. One of the advisers to the Junta Monetaria was Miguel Urrutia who had little sympathy with Currie's leading sector strategy. Currie's position, therefore, looked very precarious when President López appointed Urrutia to head the National Planning Department. However, Currie had had fairly cordial personal relations with López over the previous years. In the 1960s when López was seeking support for his new dissident wing of the Liberal party, the Movimiento Revolucionario Liberal, they had lunched together fairly regularly. Although López was to rely on a team of economics ministers that was very hostile to Currie, nevertheless he probably respected, or feared, Currie's opinion and perhaps felt he was less inconvenient inside than outside of his administration. In any event, despite the personal animosity between Currie and Urrutia that the former at least tried his best to conceal, "in order to live to fight another day," Currie remained at the Planning Department throughout the López administration (Urrutia left in 1977).

Currie met with President-elect López in July 1974 and discussed the role of personal savings and planned urban development. In subsequent letters Currie warned of the gravity of the panic withdrawals from the savings corporations. López responded by offering some reassurance to savers in a public pronouncement on August 2, 1974. Savers remained nervous, however, and various measures taken by the new minister of finance, Rodrigo Botero, further reduced the attractiveness of savings. In real terms savings and hence new building and employment slumped significantly over the next few months.

With the change of government Currie duly resigned his position as the President's representative on the Junta de Ahorro y Vivienda (Savings and Housing Board, JAVI). President López failed to appoint new members to replace those who were due to resign. Thus, control of JAVI passed to the members of the Junta Monetaria who were then in a majority. The savings and loan system thereafter lacked any effective defense against the hostility of the Junta Monetaria and the Banco de la República. Actually JAVI never met after August 1974, and was formally abolished in 1976. JAVI ceased to publish statistics on the new system and for many years the Bank of the Republic also refused to make any statistical reference to it in its monthly review, despite publishing figures on all other financial intermediaries, many of much lesser significance than the private savings corporations. One of the main complaints of the head of the Bank of the Republic, German Botero de los Ríos, about these corporations was that he had to pay monetary correction on their reserves deposited in the FAVI (Fondo de Ahorro y Vivienda) account at the bank. This conflicted with his implicit view of the central bank as having as one of its prime objectives that of maximizing its profits. Thus he disliked paying interest on FAVI deposits and for similar reasons disliked open market sales of bank liabilities to control the money supply. On the other hand, lending money to, say, the Caja Agraria that yielded a nominal return to the bank of 2 percent was good business. Currie's criticism of this theory of central banking was a constant source of irritation.

Generally, however, Currie attempted to maximize his influence on affairs by mainly confining his attention and memoranda to the creation of the urban development corporations needed to implement the cities-within-cities program. Urrutia was impressed by the American Cities' physical plans and renewed their contract. However, he himself took little interest in urban planning though he headed the Colombian delegation to the UN Habitat Conference in Vancouver in 1976. His main interests were in industrial decentralization and nutrition programs. Nevertheless, President López endorsed the El Salitre proposal when the National Planning Department published it in October and he asked Currie to stay on at DNP to work on urban problems. Currie continued to work for the requisite legislation, aided in particular by Luis Ricardo Paredes and Rafael Obregón.

Also in October Currie traveled to Ottawa, financed by the Canadian International Development Agency, for discussions with government officials and academics on the Canadian urban planning experience. He also discussed Canada's experience with index-linked tax systems that he hoped could be introduced in Colombia along with indexed social security schemes. He believed these would help prevent the arbitrary and undesirable effects that inflation normally has on income distribution. However, President López's economic team, which claimed to be emphasizing income distribution before development in the new national plan ("Para Cerrar la Brecha"—"To Close the Gap"), disagreed. The following February Currie quietly continued his work to promote indexing schemes by presenting a paper at a major conference on the subject in São Paulo.[13]

Eventually, in 1976, a development corporation for El Salitre was created along the lines Currie had proposed, though he was not too happy that major control was in the hands of the ICT (Instituto de Crédito Territorial), a low-cost popular housing agency whose administrative record was poor. Currie had hoped that the DNP would have the decisive influence but in practice this opportunity was not seized. Furthermore, by 1975 saving had been discouraged by the various economic reforms introduced by the government, and it had been intended that the comprehensive development of El Salitre would be financed through the saving and loan corporations (corporaciones de ahorro y vivienda, CAVS). These now had fewer funds than expected. Also the ICT, partly under the influence of Rafael Villate, whose career Currie had earlier fostered and who was now assistant to the director of the ICT, chose to push several much smaller urban development projects (mainly purely low-cost housing) in smaller cities. Villate called these cities-within-the-city, thus greatly devaluing the concept.

The intention was for the Salitre Development Corporation to buy the lands from La Beneficencia but initially deposit the money in the CAVS. Later the Beneficencia would receive cash payments with monetary correction and interest. The CAVS in turn would finance residential and commercial building with index-linked mortgages. Tenants would also pay rents that were adjusted for inflation and for any rise in the real value of land as the city developed, though poorer tenants with nearby jobs would be given rebates.

A price of $750 million and the terms of payment were agreed between the El Salitre Corporation and the Beneficencia after an independent appraisal of the entire 450-hectare site by the Instituto Agustín Codazzi. However, the deal was stalled by the difficult financial position of the CAVS and by the finance minister who, on learning that the principle of monetary correction was to be used in the financing, opposed the scheme on grounds of moral principle. Thus for many years almost nothing was done on this prime urban site.

In the early 1980s the minister of finance, Eduardo Wiesner, acquired 200 of the 450 hectares for a Japanese-type park. The Beneficencia received no payment for this. In 1984 Currie directed a new study of the possible development of the remaining lands as a smaller but still largely self-contained city-within-the-city.[14] This study was, however, largely ignored and eventually in 1987 President Virgilio Barco decided that the area should be developed by the Banco Central Hipotecario (BCH), acting as trustee for the Beneficencia. The BCH has thus naturally felt obligated to raise maximum profits for the Beneficencia by planning a conventional, large, middle-class housing estate, selling lands piecemeal to the highest bidders. In this way much of the community-created increment to the value of land will accrue mainly to the early private purchasers and partly to the Beneficencia. None will go to any public urban development corporation (none now exists). Thus the opportunity was lost to develop the area as an integrated and large-scale project, using the resources not just of the BCH but of the whole UPAC system. That would have enabled the development corporation to capture most of the valorization through higher rents and sale prices for apartments, shops, and offices from the beginning. Instead, however, the piecemeal development actually implemented has involved selling small apartments relatively cheaply, in advance of community facilities and jobs. This makes it much more difficult to subsidize poorer tenants with nearby jobs, reduce traffic movements, and finance community facilities and new government offices to provide employment that will be needed to make El Salitre a true, low-cost but efficient, self-contained city-within-the-city.[15]

The UN Habitat Conference, Vancouver, 1976

At the big 1972 UN Conference on the Human Environment, held in Stockholm, it was resolved that the United Nations should sponsor an even bigger conference in 1976 on human settlements. It was to be held in Vancouver, Canada, and Enrique Peñalosa of Colombia was appointed its secretary-general.

In 1974 Peñalosa asked Currie to prepare a series of background papers for the conference which Currie eventually worked up into his book, *Taming of the Megalopolis: A Design for Urban Growth* (1976). Currie was also hoping at this time that the Salitre project would serve as a showpiece to take to the Vancouver conference. During 1975 and 1976 he served as Colombian delegate or adviser to various UN habitat regional and international preparatory meetings. In February 1975 he was sponsored by the UN Center for Housing, Building, and Planning to visit large cities in Argentina, Brazil, Chile, and Venezuela to advise the United Nations on criteria for multilateral financial assistance in urban development. It had always been Currie's view that what mattered for development was not how much the international agencies lent (the emphasis arising from "two-gap" theories of development) but on the *kind* of lending they promoted. So too in the general field of urban development.

He was critical of the extremely broad frame of reference suggested by the title of the forthcoming UN conference—"human settlements." He tried, without success, to get Peñalosa to narrow the focus to "urbanization." Human settlements covered everything from rural hamlets in Africa and Asia to the great cities of New York, Leningrad, and Mexico City. In a paper he prepared for the ad hoc intergovernmental working groups meeting in Geneva in September 1975 he urged a more selective approach, with delegation of more of the specialized topics and problems to some of the UN agencies already working in them, such as the FAO for rural development and WHO for health. The main theme of human settlements should be broken into a number of subheadings that allow common treatment of common problems: villages and small towns, cities in developing countries, cities in developed countries, socialist and nonsocialist. He urged his characteristic problem-solving approach: identify a problem in terms of a failure to obtain an objective, list and discuss the advantages and disadvantages of proposed courses of action, assess the resources available and the feasibility of proposed policies, drawing on precedents, and follow this with institutional and other problems of implementation.

At an earlier regional preparatory meeting in Caracas, Currie's background paper[16] explained how "the" urban problem changes both in degree and magnitude as the size of cities grows. He insisted that the number of very large cities in the world would multiply, regardless of whatever efforts may be made to restrain migration or encourage the growth of small cities under 100,000 inhabitants. He noted the commonly cited disadvantages of larger cities, created by the threefold forces of the pricing system, inequality of income, and the private car. These forces have led to sprawling suburbs, highly congested centers, enormous sums spent on movement, high and rising land values in certain areas and blight in others, segregation, fragmentation of living, and intensification of the sense of deprivation and of the loss of significance of the individual.

He set forth his cities-within-cities alternative and the nature of decentralized public urban development corporations. Their planning of land use would not be guided by present land values or values expected in the immediate future (the private accounting approach). "The type of building appropriate to these values, say in a new, sparsely built suburb may be totally inappropriate to the type of building if a city of 400,000 is shortly to occupy the area. If an area develops, pressure is brought on the planning authority to modify the norms to permit greater density and then to modify zoning requirements to permit commercial use. The result is premature obsolescence and demolition of buildings with useful life, and a ragged, unplanned area of higher density that in a relatively short period of time either strangles itself by traffic congestion or must be served by a new system of throughways put in at great expense in an urbanized area" (*Taming of the Megalopolis*, p. 140). Instead, the public urban development corporations would plan according to the land values expected to be created by a new city. Ownership of land and buildings would be retained in order to recapture the socially created land value increments.

More generally, he continued,

> it is a striking example of our economic illiteracy that we have more or less quietly acquiesced in the private appropriation of socially created gains, letting fortunate owners and their heirs levy tribute or claim a share of the national income to which they have contributed nothing. . . . Generally, the case for capture of all or a large portion of the pure monopoly gain of rising urban land has been impaired by failure to distinguish between land and capital in general, between land and building, and between the rise reflecting inflation and that traceable to pure scarcity. (pp. 142–43)

Among other proposals he put forward (several of which were later adopted at the Vancouver conference) were that the social or unearned income from urban land values should be obtained through a levy to be called a recapture (that is, by the community that created the rise) and not a tax; that liability should be initially restricted to the largest cities or urban areas which are rising in value most rapidly; within such areas that liability should be restricted to land only and to "family" holdings above certain size and value, to exempt the great bulk of poorer owner-occupied homes and avoid fragmentation of lots among a family; that the recapture provision could apply only to rises in the future and not be retroactive; that it should be based only on the rise in land values after allowing for general inflation; and that this "true" rise should be assessed and payable every two years, whether or not the property has been transferred. Provision could be made for the extension of the recapture levy to other areas, suburban or urban, as experience is gained and large rises occur. These proposals, which had arisen partly out of Currie's discussions with Robert Huck and Orville Grimes referred to above, would remove one of the main sources of growing inequality and would provide a source of funds for investment in the purchase of land for new cities and in the provision of community facilities.

Apart from these preparatory meetings in Caracas and Geneva Currie also attended meetings in New York, Dubrovnik, and Arc-et-Senans, France. Virgilio Barco was the head of the Colombian delegation at most of these. Currie was also invited to present a paper, "The Application of the Concept of Cities-within-Cities to Developing Countries," at the International New Towns Congress in Paris in November 1975 where he was able to see for himself the French version of multiple-center planning in operation.

The Vancouver conference itself was a gigantic affair. Currie was well aware of the difficulty in managing such an event to achieve some consensus on meaningful and reasonably noncontradictory resolutions. During the preparatory stages he had, in a very confidential memorandum, urged his protégé Enrique Peñalosa to "use extreme care in deciding the few basic issues you want Vancouver to endorse, ensure that the other stuff that must be included is not obviously contradictory, and ensure that these recommendations are included in an increasing number of reports of preparatory meetings."

He continued:

> If we can get Vancouver to call for a re-examination of the basic design of large and growing cities to correct or avoid the ills of urbanization; to ac-

> cept the inevitability, at least in developing countries, of the growth of large cities, so designed; to endorse measures to ensure that the *inevitable* rise in the rentability of urban lands does not all fall into private hands but is captured and used for socially beneficial purposes; that if the private automobile is permitted to become a necessity in urban transport, countries will have to devote a smaller proportion of their resources to housing and other services,—to do all these things would mean that Habitat had contributed something of great value to the world.

Finally, in another characteristic passage that reveals Currie's policy-oriented approach to political economy and his several decades as adviser to decision makers, he concluded: "but to do this requires careful manipulation or leadership on your part. Speeches are necessary. But the more important thing is still the manipulation of people to achieve desired ends (always assuming that the desired ends are really worthwhile!)—the art of getting things to happen."

In the event the Vancouver conference, though well organized as a "show," turned out rather a fiasco in other respects. The two-week conference took place in May–June 1976 with around 4,000 delegates and observers. Virgilio Barco led the Colombian delegation for the final preparatory meeting in the days before the conference itself began. For the actual conference the delegation was headed by the director of the National Planning Department, Miguel Urrutia, attending his first urban planning conference. The official Colombian position, endorsed by the President, favored the cities-within-cities approach to urbanization. Urrutia followed this general line also and spoke in favor of it in a speech to a plenary session. Barco also supported it. Others in the delegations, however, were hostile.[17] In particular, Mariano Ospina Hernandez, the son of ex-President Ospina, was vehemently antagonistic to any increase in city densities, multifamiliar housing, and the whole concept of cities-within-cities. However, he was put on the drafting committee for the commission that discussed the nature of urban design. He used his position to delete all reference to cities-within-cities from the final documents and resolutions submitted to the plenary session.

Currie wrote in his notes that at a subsequent "strategy" meeting Miguel Urrutia staged a debate on the cities-within-cities and Ospina "was vicious on the subject. I finally got up to leave but our Ambassador to Canada[18] (also on the mission) whispered to me to stay and listen to what he had to say. He thereupon hit into Ospina—but hard. Practically accused him of being disloyal and sabotaging the head of the mission—who had defended cities within cities in his speech to the Plenary—and the Government of Colombia's position." The ambassador ridiculed Ospina's assertion that no expert could find anything good in the idea and was angry that on the drafting committee he had deleted references made to it by the Mexican delegation.

On another occasion there was also some bitter disagreement with Miguel Urrutia over a speech Currie had drafted for Virgilio Barco on the capture of the increment to land value. Urrutia objected to the exclusion of buildings so that the provision, passed in one of the conference committees, applied only to land. He also objected to confining the recapture levy to the rise in the real value of land only (exclusive of the rise due to general inflation). Currie offered to withdraw the whole amendment but Urrutia insisted he try to include the taxation of buildings and at least make only a partial allowance for inflation. Currie asked sarcastically if Urrutia's favored figure might be 8 points, the same arbitrary concession that in 1974 the government had given savers when tax was imposed on the "income" arising from monetary correction on their UPAC savings deposits.

The conference did eventually accept the principle of capturing "unearned increment" to land values but did not accept the key provision that the recapture be levied even when there is no transfer of title. This made the recommendation similar to the legislation on land in Britain during the 1960s and 1970s. Britain's "betterment levy" and "development gains tax" legislation applied only on transfer of land title or use. This greatly restricted the transfer or development of real estate while owners waited for a new government to repeal the legislation.

There were plenty of other frustrations for Currie at the conference. Galley proofs for his book, *Taming the Megalopolis*, were lost in the mail so publication was delayed and only a few copies of the rather poorly produced book were available at the conference. Instead, great publicity was given to documents of Barbara Ward and John Turner, for example, who propagated very different ideas on development and urban design. Barbara Ward's televised speech was generally well received but Currie thought this was because she hit out emotionally in all directions. Currie's style was selective and analytical. He disliked emotion that came at the expense of reason. In a letter to Currie, August 31, 1975, Barbara Ward (Lady Jackson) asked:

> Do you see any conflict between the scale of self help that clearly will be needed in many of the developing world conurbations and the more struc-

tured concept of "cities within the cities", corporations and the building up of a valid construction industry? . . . Is there a risk that self help creates permanent cities of the poor with no admixture of classes and incomes? There are times when I feel that advocates of different approaches are attacking each other with almost theological zeal. My own feeling is that in settlements there is no one answer but at least three thousand. . . .

Currie replied, September 9, 1975:

> The dilemma of self help vs conventional building surfaces very clearly in the recent Position Paper of the World Bank (and even more in the unpublished Background Paper). I finally worked out to my own satisfaction why, despite all the acknowledged disadvantages of self help in poor urban design, expensive services, segregation and so forth, the Bank plumped again for it. It came back to the statement that from 40 to 60 percent or more of the residents cannot afford a conventionally built house; so there seems no alternative other than heavy subsidies or self help in building on cheap land, which can be found only in the peripheries of cities, badly located.
>
> But all these people are living in some quarters already and the Bank is also opposed to demolition. Hence the immediate problem is not to build new housing for this 50 percent but to establish whether or not there is effective demand for conventional housing and accompanying building for a yearly growth of families, let us say, of 5 percent. If we can establish this and raise it to 6 percent, we ease the pressure on the active housing stock. In other words, the process of filtration can function (I prefer the word escalation!).
>
> . . . As you see, I am still a bit of a zealot and hope that your forthcoming book does not come up with the three thousand answers you threaten.

As for John Turner's approach, Currie had long taken issue with him for his emphasis on do-it-yourself housing. At one of the committees Currie tried to stop a blanket endorsement of auto-construction by inserting "in many countries." But this amendment was rejected. At the same session he supported a French amendment that favored incentives to mobility. A Ghanaian said he thought it had been agreed that mobility was bad. Currie tried to make a distinction between movement and mobility. The group decided that the concept of mobility was unclear so rejected the French amendment.

Toward the end of the long conference the whole affair disintegrated into a platform for a venemous political row over the Palestine question. The Arabs and their African and Cuban supporters presented resolution after resolution denouncing the Israelis. The Panamanians also seized the opportunity to condemn the U.S. presence in Panama. Others attacked South Africa. Perhaps this was inevitable with a theme so broad and vague as "human settlements." One of the final, protracted debates then centered on whether the UN Center of Housing should be moved from its New York headquarters. Various countries pushed their claims. It was finally moved to Nairobi and renamed the UN Center for Human Settlements (Habitat).

Currie returned to Bogotá intensely disappointed that two years' work had produced so little.

CHAPTER 12

Perspectives on the Future and the Past in the Light of Allyn Young, 1975–82

Introduction

Unable to exert much influence on current macroeconomic policy, in 1975 Currie turned his attention to long-range issues. He remained at the National Planning Department where he prepared some memoranda for the director, mainly on urban policy, and also, as a favor, wrote occasional speeches for his old friend Virgilio Barco who was now ambassador in Washington with his sights on the presidency. But between 1975 and 1978 Currie devoted most of his time to two major research projects, the first looking mainly to the future, to the year 2000, the second looking back over the record of economic advisers during the past two or three decades.

Resources for the Future

In 1975 Resources for the Future Inc., of Washington, and the UN Latin American Institute for Economic and Social Planning (UN-ILPES), based in Santiago de Chile, sponsored Currie to direct a multifaceted study of the availability and adequacy of resources to permit accelerated growth in Colombia over the next three decades, and to review Colombia's use of resources since 1950.[1] Historical reviews and projections were undertaken for all the major sectors of the economy and the variables that had the most important effect on the nation's well-being: population growth, growth of GDP and GDP per capita, energy resources, agricultural potential, exports and the balance of payments, pollution and ecological trends, the housing deficit, the requirements of accelerated urban development, and the provision of social services and infrastructure. The study was not confined to mere projections, and certainly not to a mere projection of past trends. Rather, the focus was on appropriate policy and the potential for accelerated growth based on recommended policy changes. Currie's study team included eleven Colombians. James Hanson, the chief adviser, provided invaluable assistance in checking the consistency of the various quantitative projections. Other consultants included Ronald Ridker of Resources for the Future, Alan Strout (who had recently conducted a similar study for Indonesia), and Luis Eduardo Rosas (who was at that time the director of UN-ILPES).

One of Currie's major conclusions was that, in general, resources had not been, nor were likely to be for some time, the main limitation on economic growth. His study appeared to confirm that resources of all kinds had been grossly underutilized and that policy was more important than resource availability. Naturally he emphasized the relevance of his leading sector strategy for a selective stimulus to building and exports, together with his cities-within-cities design for rapid urbanization. He also dwelt on the distinction between growth, development, and well-being, and the importance of addressing policy to the deprivation effect in its domestic and international manifestations. For Currie these were crucial considerations affecting the nature of the problem and, hence, the indicated solutions and future trends and possibilities. For some of the directors of Resources for the Future, however, much of this discussion seemed extraneous. Their main preoccupation was with hard facts and the goodness of the econometric methodology and technique rather than with the assumptions and implications. This caused some straining of the personal as well as the technical relations of the study, and some publication delay.

Nevertheless, interesting conclusions emerged from this work. The demographic studies undertaken with the help of José Olinto Rueda showed that the larger the urban center, the lower the birthrate. Currie believed this offered a further very important argument in favor of big cities (appropriately designed). Bigger cities were economically more efficient as measured by higher average incomes and employment opportunities, especially for women of childbearing age. They also offered greater opportunities to provide education at lower per capita cost. Higher income, better employment, and better education were key correlates of the birthrate, because they acted on motivation. They were far more important than the mere availability of contraceptive techniques and knowledge.[2]

This finding was of relevance to the conclusion that policy that acted on real market demand was of much greater significance for development than the mere availability of factor inputs, including, in particular, labor inputs. It was Currie's contention, which he later elaborated, that a growing labor force hindered rather than helped the growth of per capita incomes. Thus a high birthrate was a drag on development. A low birthrate, induced by rapid urbanization and larger cities, was a help.

Currie went so far as to suggest that the size and rate of growth of overall GDP would be little different if population growth had halted years ago. Thus a larger population and labor force was a dilutant that simply reduced GDP per head. Further, he showed that very small differences in the growth rate of per capita income would over time give rise to very large differences in the projected *absolute* size of income per head. This was due partly to the power of compound interest and partly to the fact that the faster the growth rate of income the faster the decline in birthrates. A 10 percent growth of overall GDP would be accompanied by faster urbanization and a sharper decline in the birthrate. Thus per capita incomes would be significantly increased. A more modest 5 percent growth of overall GDP would be accompanied by higher population growth and thus there would be an even greater gap between the per capita growth rates implied by the two scenarios. The percentage difference in the per capita rates of growth would, after a few years, imply enormous differences in the absolute level of per capita income. It was calculated, for example, that a 10 percent growth of overall GDP would double per capita GDP within only 9.5 years. Growth based on existing trends would double per capita income after 48 years. This justified supreme efforts today to make a success of growth-promoting urbanization and export strategies.

Finally, as to the *type* of urbanization strategy that is indicated, the study arrived at novel conclusions (chapter 9) on likely trends in the size of the housing deficit in the light of different policy options. Currie and his collaborator on this part of the study, Homero Cuevas, defined the housing deficit not in crudely narrow terms of families sleeping on the streets but in terms of location and minimum standards of space, services, durable materials, separate entrances, and separate cooking facilities and toilet. Estimates were made of the proportion of national product required to reduce the absolute deficit on these criteria, under different assumptions on growth rate of national product and growth of new family formations. The study indicated how small a proportion of annual product had historically been devoted to building in general and housing in particular; it also showed that the constraints were not physical but manmade and institutional. With a higher but feasible growth rate the deficit could be wiped out in a few years if around 7 percent of all resources were allocated to housing and associated infrastructure. The solution, however, did not lie with the typical housing programs sponsored by the Instituto de Crédito Territorial (ICT), which specialized in building tiny, poorly serviced housing shells on the distant peripheries of cities or in small towns remote from services and remunerative employment. Paradoxically, such programs could actually increase the housing deficit as defined above.

In a concluding chapter on policy implications (chapter 14) he noted: "Perhaps the most irritating characteristic of the direct actionists is their bland assumption that poverty can be abolished only by direct action and that people who favour other and in some cases more indirect approaches are reactionaries, indifferent to the evils of poverty and inequality. It has to be insisted most strongly that the issue is not the objectives, on which there is general agreement, but the longer term effectiveness of the means to achieve the objectives" (p. 322). In support of this approach he cited admiringly the works of Arthur Okun, who once noted that the cure for a sore throat is not an injection of penicillin directly into the throat.

The Evaluation of Economic Advisers and Their Advice

After more than forty years as economic adviser, administrator, and negotiator it was natural that Currie should want to draw some generalizations from his own experience and observations on the advice of other individuals and institutions. The Twentieth Century Fund in New York made this possible with a grant that enabled him to devote most of his time between June 1977 and the end of 1978 to a research project to appraise the recommendations of economic advisers in developing countries.[3] More time was spent in 1979 toning down and pruning the manuscript to appease various referees who were not happy with Currie's attacks on the conventional wisdom and who may have been offended personally. It was a rather watered-down version that was eventually published but which nevertheless won praise from most reviewers.[4]

John Naranjo and Eduardo Wiesner, successive heads of the National Planning Department during this period, encouraged him to pursue this work. At the same time they solicited his advice on current issues, especially monetary and exchange policy on which their predecessor Miguel Urrutia requested he remain silent.

Currie's study focused partly on the degree of influence an economic adviser has and the conditions that enhance that influence. It depends as much on the attitudes and motivations of the sponsoring institution or individual minister as on the goodness of the advice itself; and it requires not just the submission of the report but active concern over the political, legal, and administrative aspects of implementation so that reports do not merely gather dust on a shelf. Regardless of the quality of the advice, Currie noted that advice in the form of conditions attaching to loans made by the international aid agencies is relatively influential. He also noted the influence of fashionable theory on the advice proffered by these agencies. He discussed too the importance of personal values, personalities, and timing.

Of greater interest to Currie, however, was the evaluation of the advice tendered. This could only be judged in the light of an appropriate theory of development. Advice can only be as good as the general theory on which it rests. Often the underlying theory is not made explicit, though generally it can be inferred. But an appropriate theory of how the economic system works is not enough. Advice must also be appraised in terms of an appropriate definition or criterion of development and related objectives. In the 1970s the "basic needs" approach to development became fashionable. Paul Streeten, editor of *World Development*, believed that Currie's 1950 World Bank mission report on Colombia and his 1966 *Accelerating Development*, with their emphasis on elevating the standard of living of the poorest half of the population, made him "the father of the basic needs approach." He invited him to write an article, "The Objectives of Development,"[5] explaining his approach.

Actually, despite superficial parallels, Currie's approach was very different from the typical "basic needs" literature associated, for example, with the analysis and policies of the World Bank under Robert McNamara, or the ILO-Sussex approach, or the prescriptions called for by UNCTAD and the New International Economic Order (NIEO). Mostly these involved what Currie called the "direct" approach to poverty: sites-and-services housing programs; "small is beautiful"; protectionism; extremes of decentralization (what Currie would characterize as the "fill-in-the-spaces-on-the-map" approach); labor-intensive make-work approaches to employment with scant regard for productivity because of a supposed incompatibility between maximum productivity and better distribution; and targeting project aid to "the poorest of the poor" wherever they happen to live now (mainly in rural areas).

Currie explained, in his 1978 *World Development* paper and in his book on economic advisers, that the direct ("Harpo Marx")[6] approach to poverty and inequality was often less effective than an indirect ("Sherlock Holmes") approach based on an efficiency criterion. If modern technology, no matter how capital-intensive, reduces unit costs of production then this expands the size of the market by reducing prices relative to money incomes. Full employment, and better employment, can best be ensured not by promoting inefficient, labor-intensive techniques, but by promoting labor (and capital) mobility. Theories that rejected this conclusion and decried mobility usually suffered from a too narrow sectoral frame of reference. For Currie it was important to evaluate advice from a macroeconomic perspective.

He was given access to the minutes of all meetings of the President's Economic and Social Policy Council (CONPES) from 1964 to 1977 and he was struck by the amount of time and attention this high-level committee gave to the isolated evaluation of individual projects presented for its approval by the National Planning Department. This emphasis was very much in line with the approach recommended in the 1960s by Albert Waterston of the World Bank whose slogans were "learn to think small" and "plan from the bottom up."[7] It was what Currie called the engineer's approach to development planning. Engineers had dominated the World Bank and national planning agencies, not least the one in Colombia that has often been headed by engineers rather than economists.

While the President's time was taken up in CONPES approving small projects, sometimes less than $10,000 in value, the really important macroeconomic decisions were being made elsewhere, in committees not attended by the President. CONPES seldom discussed monetary, fiscal, and exchange rate policy. These were decided mainly in the Finance Ministry and by the Junta Monetaria (also presided over by the powerful finance minister). For years Currie has vainly urged that the Budget Bureau be moved to the office of the President to enable the President to exercise closer control over macroeconomic policy.[8]

Allyn Young and the Theory of Economic Progress

Around this time Currie was engaged in correspondence relevant to these themes with Nicholas Kaldor, the influential British economic adviser and Cambridge professor. Kaldor and Currie had both been students of Allyn Young in the 1920s, Kaldor for a year at the London School of Economics, Currie for two years at Harvard, and both had been profoundly influenced by him.[9] Currie was greatly interested in two well-known articles that Kaldor had published a few years earlier, "The Irrelevance of Equilibrium Economics" (*The Economic Journal*, 1972) and "What is Wrong with Economic Theory" (*Quarterly Journal of Economics*, 1975), in which Kaldor follows Allyn Young in placing stress on increasing returns and economic progress, the title of Young's famous presidential address to section F of the British Association in Glasgow in September 1928. Disequilibrium rather than equilibrium, therefore, characterized the economic system and made much of economic theory irrelevant to our understanding of the real world.

Professor Young had explored and developed new implications from Adam Smith's dictum that the division of labor depended on the size of the market. Young insisted that the growth of the market was the main explanation of fuller exploitation of the division of labor through more roundabout, capital-intensive methods and, hence, economies of scale. Thus real demand was at least as important as supply-side considerations in explaining economic progress. But demand involved the exchange of real products for other products, a variant on Say's Law that supply creates its own demand: "The capacity to buy depends on the capacity to produce. In an inclusive view, considering the market not as an outlet for the products of a particular industry, and therefore external to that industry, but as the outlet for goods in general, the size of the market is determined and defined by the volume of production."[10] Young was skeptical of the helpfulness of conventional supply and demand apparatus in illuminating these broader aspects of increasing returns, because this apparatus is too partial. However, he suggested that this apparatus could be used if we thought in terms of the operation of *reciprocal* demand. The simplest analysis of reciprocal demand was "when the commodities exchanged are produced competitively under conditions of increasing returns and when the demand for each commodity is elastic, in the special sense that a small increase in its supply will be attended by an increase in the amounts of other commodities which can be had in exchange for it. Under such conditions an increase in the supply of one commodity *is* an increase in the demand for other commodities, and it must be supposed that every increase in demand will evoke an increase in supply" (pp. 533–34).

Young continued, in a passage that could be read as an early, cryptic statement of Currie's "leading sector" theory of development: "The rate at which one industry grows is conditioned by the rate at which other industries grow, but since the elasticities of demand and of supply will differ for different products, some industries will grow faster than others. Even with a stationary population and in the absence of new discoveries in pure or applied science there are no limits to the process of expansion except the limits beyond which demand is not elastic and returns do not increase."

These quotations implicitly reveal that Allyn Young is using the term "increasing returns" in a very different sense from the conventional modern textbook concept of "increasing returns to scale." The distinction, seldom appreciated (even, it will be maintained below, by Kaldor), is fundamental. The concept of "increasing returns to scale" refers to the relationship between equi-proportional increases in all inputs and the resulting increase in output. It assumes that technology is given, so that it can distinguish the separate contribution of increased inputs of the same type. It is thus essentially a microeconomic and "comparative statics" concept. Young nowhere uses the term "returns to scale" and begins his paper by stating: "I do not propose to discuss any of those alluring but highly technical questions relating to the precise way in which some sort of equilibrium of supply and demand is achieved in the market for the products of industries which can increase their output without increasing their costs proportionately" (p. 527).

Instead, his concern is with "increasing returns," a concept that is macroeconomic and dynamic. It refers to the reduction in unit costs that are made possible, in each industry and throughout the economy, by an extension in the overall market size. It does not depend on an increase in inputs nor on new inventions, though the growth process itself may induce and make possible both capital accumulation and funds for the promotion of research and development.

At the macroeconomic level it is impossible for all inputs to grow equi-proportionally, if only because the factor of land is fixed. Furthermore, empirically, capital almost always grows faster than labor. But even if there was no change in inputs, the enlargement of the market makes "increasing returns" possible by expanding the opportunities for using *existing* inputs and existing, *known* technology in more efficient ways. The source of growth is then seen as growth itself. It makes profitable the use of known technology that previously it did not pay to use. This technology may or may not be embodied in new capital. It may be introduced with only small net additional capital expenditures. In this view technical progress is endogenous to the growth process and cannot be "held constant" as the size of the market increases.

As these improvements occur in one industry, as *internal* economies, so they are passed on as *external* economies to other industries in the form of lower-priced inputs or in the form of increased real demand, because consumers' real incomes are enhanced by reduced costs or prices. In this growth process some individual sectors will employ more inputs of all kinds. But an implication which Currie drew out of Young's analysis is that it would be a fallacy of composition to conclude from this that an *overall* growth of inputs is an indispensable precondition for growth. Rather, growth calls for a reallocation and better use of existing inputs. Growth may also induce and pay for a faster rate of capital accumulation and growth of employment. But in this view the increased employment of capital and labor is more the consequence than the cause of growth.

Young's use of the term "demand elasticity" is also a macroeconomic rather than a microeconomic concept. An individual product may face inelastic demand if its output increases, but *overall* demand usually keeps pace with supply unless interrupted by inappropriate monetary policy. If monetary demand for one product falls this money is usually directed elsewhere; it is spent on all other products combined. This ensures that income elasticity of demand is unity in an overall sense.[11] The "law of diminishing marginal utility" lies behind individual, microeconomic demand curves and demand elasticities. It has no place in macroeconomics except as another fallacy of composition.

Here it may be noted that this way of viewing the nature and potential of the economic system—a perspective shared by very few modern economists, brought up as they are to treat demand in terms of indivdual commodities only or in terms of the Keynesian approach to aggregate demand—which is very different from aggregate demand in the sense of J. B. Say or Allyn Young—led Currie to insist on the justification for active policy measures to promote leading sectors by ensuring that demand is *made* elastic in a broad sense of that term, and so to ensure that returns continue to increase. Thus, for example, if the demand for housing or the demand for a country's exports is repressed by institutional and policy factors such as inadequate and inappropriate housing finance, or a chronically overvalued exchange rate, then policy changes are called for accordingly. These changes, by diverting a larger part of current real production, domestic and international, into a real exchange with the output of the housing and export sectors, can ensure that the process of economic expansion does not reach "the limits beyond which demand is not elastic and returns do not increase."

In a developing country the point at which decreasing returns may set in is a long way off, thanks to the vastness of the pool of technology that is known but not yet exploited because it has yet to be "made practicable and economical by an enlarged scale of production" (Young, p. 534n). Furthermore, as explained above, Currie stressed the tremendous degree of slack and underutilization of resources of all kinds in developing countries, an observation that adds force to the conclusions of Allyn Young's analysis and suggests even greater potential for accelerated and sustained development for this class of country than for the countries about which Young was writing.

Currie, therefore, was pleased that Kaldor was calling attention to Young's novel conception of real demand and the size of the market and its importance in explaining economic growth. However, he was less happy with the way that Kaldor sought to remedy a deficiency he thought he had found in Young's treatment. Hence the exchange of letters and papers between the two during 1977 and early 1978. They discussed the issue personally at a conference they both attended in Dubrovnik in November 1977.[12]

An Exchange between Currie and Kaldor on Allyn Young

Before continuing the account of Kaldor's and Currie's discussion of Allyn Young one or two incidental anecdotes from this trip to Dubrovnik may be recorded. Returning via Heathrow airport Currie tripped over Joan Robinson's luggage trolley (she was returning from another conference), was thrown on to the conveyor belt, and badly gashed his leg. In Dubrovnik the Oxford economist Thomas Balogh, noted for his outrageous manners, engaged Currie in conversation about wartime China. Currie mentioned that he was responsible for the creation of the Flying Tigers. "Never heard of them. Who are they?" scoffed Balogh. Currie explained that they were in effect U.S. mercenaries being paid bounties by Chiang Kai-shek for every Japanese plane shot down. "Well!" exclaimed Balogh, "that's one for the book. Lauchlin Currie helping the Fascist Pigs!" Subsequently Balogh expressed surprise that Currie was going to Washington after Dubrovnik to visit the World Bank (in connection with his book on economic advisers). "Do they let you in?" he asked. "Yes, why shouldn't they," asked Currie, knowing perfectly well that Balogh was alluding to the houndings of the McCarthy period. Balogh shifted uneasily and replied, "Oh, nothing."

On the second day of the conference Currie was called on to chair a session at which one of the speakers was François Perroux. He was given strict instructions by the Yugoslav organizers to restrict each speaker to fifteen minutes. After fifteen minutes Perroux had managed to read, very slowly, only a few pages of a long, prepared manuscript so Currie sent a note to say his time was up. This note was brushed aside. Arm-waving and tapping the mike were to no avail and the minutes ticked by. Eventually Currie intervened over the microphone to insist he must stop. Perroux said he had to get through his manuscript. Currie repeated that his time was up and that the audience had copies of his manuscript anyway. Perroux insisted he had to continue reading it because the manuscript contained many errors. Currie would not relent. Thereupon Perroux stormed out and took the next plane back to Paris. Currie claimed he did not know it was the famous "development pole" Perroux until afterward. Had he known he would have been even firmer. Later, in Washington, Paul Streeten told Currie that Perroux was one of the three people in the world whom he thought could not be stopped. Though Currie may have been the first to stop him speaking, he regretted that Perroux's growth poles continued to dominate the policy of influential French-trained Colombian decisionmakers for many years.

In conversations with Kaldor in Dubrovnik, Currie discussed the former's insistence on the need for priority attention to the primary sector, to avoid cost-push inflation. Kaldor insisted that food shortages, not excessive money, were the main cause of inflation. He is well known for his detestation of monetarism of any description. He handed Currie a letter he had written in reply to the one Currie had sent in September. Kaldor's letter and Currie's reply to it reveal clearly their points of agreement and differences in interpreting Allyn Young and their approaches to development theory and policy in general. Currie hoped the exchange would lead to a publication that would clarify the agreement and differences between them. However, Kaldor never replied to Currie's last letter and a publication did not result. Hence, despite their length, these letters merit reproduction here:

24 October 1977

Mr. Lauchlin Currie
Adviser
Departamento Nacional de Planeacion
Republic of Colombia

Dear Mr. Currie,

Thank you very much for your letter of 2 September enclosing Chapter 14 of your forthcoming book, which I read with great interest. I was very glad to see that your "paradigm" of the economy is so similar to mine, and that we both agree that economic development is mainly demand-induced and that the demand which is relevant in this connection is derived from economic activity of other economic sectors at home or abroad, so that taking the world as a whole, growth is the result of an interaction between increases in demand induced by increases in supply, and increases in supply which arise in response to increases in demand.

I feel, however, that you may have misunderstood my comments on Allyn Young concerning the operation of this chain reaction. What I meant to say was that spontaneous increases in supply, for whatever cause (some new invention or innovation, climatic change or possibly a change in expectations—but the latter is only one of many possibilities) are always associated with an increase of *investment*, and not just in the *flow* of production, and this is an integral component of the argument that an increase in the *supply* of commodity *A* comes to the same as an increase in the *demand* for commodities B, C, D etc. A high "elasticity of demand" in the sense used by Young does not do the trick by itself, since it merely means that when more A is produced there is a sufficient substitution in favour of A as a result of the consequential fall in its price (but which also implies a corresponding fall in the demand for B, C, D, which have become relatively dearer) to increase the aggregate income of the A-producers and correspondingly decrease the income of the B, C, D . . . producers. However, it can be shown that increased production due to a *spontaneous* cause, such as the discovery of new oil fields, is *invariably* associated with an increased investment in new plant and machinery (in the form of a larger carry-over of stocks, if nothing else) in the sense required to establish the simple proposition that the increase in the incomes of the A-producers will *not* be cancelled by a corresponding decrease in the incomes of producers B, C, and D because *total expenditure* on goods will increase *pari passu* with the increase in activity in the A industry.

Applying this to your example about house-building being chosen as the "Leading Sector", it is not the fact that people spend a higher proportion of their income on accommodation as they get richer which is the relevant factor that makes it a suitable "leading sector" but the fact that increased building activity increases the incomes earned in the building industry and the building materials industry, without any offsetting decrease in the incomes earned in other industries. The reason for this lies precisely in the fact that increased building activity by its very nature necessarily involves an increase in *investment*. (You create a durable good—a house—only a small fraction of which is currently consumed, or which enters into current expenditure in the form of rent payments.) The Keynesian element which was missing from Young is the fact that for total demand to increase, either exports or home investment must increase and in the Keynesian terminology an increase in exports is a *form* of increased investment.

On a practical plane I am not sure that I agree with you that the housing sector is a *promising* "leading sector". It is true that the import content of building materials etc. is small, but on the other hand housing does nothing to increase export potential, and the increase in incomes earned through greater housing activity, as well as the increase in incomes in other home industries due to its multiplier effects, are bound to lead to an increase in *imports*.

From the point of view of any one country the leading sector must be a sector which *either* immediately *or* after a brief interval can enlarge the country's export potential, since it is inconceivable that a country's import needs should not be increased as a result of higher real incomes and more employment. Whether in the case of countries like Colombia the growth of export potential should be looked for in the agricultural field (including, of course, plantation agriculture) or in the industrial field, I am not competent to judge, but I am quite sure that the main problem why Latin American countries have failed to sustain the rate of economic growth associated with the early stages of their industrialisation was due to their failure to develop their export potential at least in line with the growth of their G.D.P. (The manufactured goods produced as a result of the "import substitution" process were too dear, or too poor in quality, to be exportable.)

I am also a little sceptical of your proposition that the elasticity of supply of foodstuffs in a country like Colombia is high, so that it only needs increased demand to bring about an increase in food production. If this is so, then Colombia contrasts sharply with other countries of Latin America. As regards the countries I do know something about (such as Chile, Brazil, Venezuela and even the Argentine), this is certainly not the case. Indeed, it was the insufficiency of food supplies to meet the needs of growing urban populations which I think was the main factor behind the chronic inflation of some Latin American countries. (In countries like Venezuela and Peru, where large-scale inflation was avoided, this was due to the fact that their foreign exchange earnings permitted the liberal importation of grains to stabilise the internal price of foodstuffs.)

Yours sincerely,
Nicholas Kaldor

January 16, 1978

Professor
Nicholas Kaldor
King's College
Cambridge, England.

Dear Professor Kaldor,

Do forgive my delay in answering your letter of Oct. 24. Actually, I wrote a draft reply while still at Dubrovnik but I put it aside for revision and typing and got swamped with other things on my delayed return. Only in the Christmas vacation was I able to return to it and to a reading of other offprints of yours kindly sent to me by Dr. Sandilands. However, I shall restrict this letter to answering your letter of Oct. 24.

Although, as I'm afraid is customary, I shall concentrate on points of difference, let me first note how pleased I am to find that we appear to be in agreement on a most important point—that economic growth is mainly demand induced and is the resultant of an interplay between supply and demand in real terms.

But to turn to points of difference: You appear to feel that the stimulating effect of a "leading sector", if any, arises entirely from the increased investment it generates and not from an increased flow of production. Otherwise, an increased supply of (or demand for) commodity A merely means a *shift* in demand from products B and C so that the aggregate demand (and supply) is no greater. However, you appear to feel that a spontaneous increase in supply-demand, like the discovery of an oil field, increases "investment" and is therefore not at the expense of existing demand for other products.

On this point several comments may be made

Is there not, in your observation, an implicit assumption that there is no slack in the system—a useful expository assumption but hardly in accordance with reality, especially in LDC's? If the increased supply came from the work of previously underutilized factors, there need be no diminution in the aggregate production of goods and hence, in the Sayian sense, in aggregate demand nor a shift in demand. (We can assume that money incomes can be increased in line with real output so that aggregate money demand increases with aggregate production). You recognize a large degree of slack in the Agricultural Sector in your 1977 (1971) Paper. If there is no slack in the system, even an increase in "investment" in one sector will only result in a substitution of demand and production, as in the case also of an increase in consumption; but if the financing comes from outside the system, through the mechanism of a rise in prices, the only increase in aggregate supply (and demand in a real sense) would come from the presumed greater yield or productivity. So it is not the increase in investment in the Keynesian sense that is the key but the increase in output arising from (a) the economies of scale induced by the actual growth (b) the taking up of slack (unemployed labour) or (c) the possible economies of more roundabout production (a special Harrod Domar case of increased productivity from division of labor and specialization). I shall return to the "investment" point later.

Another point: I did not rest my case on the high income elasticity of demand as the cause of the increase in demand (and even less on the high price elasticity of demand which is a case you cite), and I did not maintain that people must spend a higher proportion of their incomes on housing. I distinguished two types of demand as desirable for the products of a sector which might qualify as a leader to which exogenous stimulus might be given. The first was the existence of a *latent* demand which for some reason is blocked or impeded, say by the absence of mortgage funds. Removing this impediment could give the initial impetus (in this case, to "investment"). To prevent thereafter a quick saturation of the demand, a high income elasticity of demand is highly desirable. In the case of building, the combination of (a) removing the initial impediment (b) exploiting the high income elasticity of demand (c) utilizing previously underutilized capacity and (d) securing more economies of scale and obtaining the stimulus of a high price elasticity of demand, can lead to a large, long sustained stimulus to growth. But the same, though less desirable, results would arise from the stimulus to the demand for a consumer durable good like the private automobile. (In this case the initial "block" might be, for example, the absence of an installment credit system). In the case of private cars the only increase in "investment" would be in the pipe-line and additional productive capacity and the big increase would be in "consumption" and production of consumers' goods. I have not urged automobiles as a leading sector in developing countries because of other socially undesirable side effects, but the possibility of being a leading sector would appear to apply to it. An increase in exports may tap an existing *latent* demand which can be activated (market penetration), and benefit from high income or price elasticity of demand (as in the case of oil or many durable consumers' and producers' goods). To call this "investment" is a bit strained though it would be justified in Keynesian terminology. In your 1977 Cambridge Journal of Economics article you mention the possibility of consumption-led booms.

The Foreign Sector: On the practical side, you object to building as a leading sector largely because of considerations relating to the foreign field. Building, you feel, does not increase the export potential but, mainly because of the secondary expansion or multiplier effect, increases the demand for imports.

Possibly here our differences arise in part from our different environments. The United Kingdom is particularly sensitive to an adverse balance of payments and is adverse to taking restrictive measures on imports. Colombia, and most developing countries, has had a long experience in restricting imports other than by restricting aggregate domestic monetary demand for goods and services. Consequently, a *doubling* of the rate of growth in Colombia sparked, let us say, by building construction, need not be stopped by an exchange constraint. The country is largely self-sufficient in foodstuffs and fibres and the volume of capital equipment (other than plant and part of the infrastructure) necessary to sustain a much higher rate of growth is relatively small (even in the U.S.A. "producers" equipment amounts only to 4–5 percent of the GNP). For the building industry itself, it is very small.

Without a more intensive study of the alternatives I would hesitate to express an opinion on Britain's policy. But, to a foreigner, it appears that Britain has paid a high price in lost production in recent years through unemployment and underutilization to avoid taking measures that might invite retaliation, which price, however, has not prevented a poor record in exports, on a comparative basis.

Low Growth Rates in Latin America: You appear to accept unreservedly "the exchange constraint" explanation of the unsatisfactory rate of growth in per capita income in Latin America. As you gather, I have some reservations on this explanation. If, in the case of Colombia, certain years are selected, it is possible to match a simple geometric growth rate in imports with the gross domestic product or the growth in industrial production. If, however, somewhat more sophisticated measurements are made measuring trends over periods, the growth in manufactured imports is very small in relation to the growth in manufacturing production or the GDP. It may be noted that Diaz Alejandro disagrees rather sharply with Vanek on the matter of an exchange constraint in Colombia.

More recently, while the growth in GDP moved up to a rate of around 8 percent in 1973–74, and exports expanded, imports showed little growth even though previous restrictions were relaxed. During the coffee boom of

1975–76, exports in value spurted whereas the growth in GDP, even with the recovery from the recession of 1974–75, was less than the growth experienced in the period 1950–1973. A growth in exports is desirable but if there is not an exchange constraint, the measures adopted to prevent inflationary repercussions may have an inhibitory effect on induced domestic production, including production of a large volume of "minor" exports, which is what has happened recently in Colombia.

To say that domestic manufactured goods, originally undertaken as substitution for imports, are too poor in quality to compete in the world's markets, is surely too sweeping. The growth in Colombia's minor exports from 1967 to 1974 was highly satisfactory and were mostly of goods that were once imported. The export of Volkswagen motors from Brazil to Germany is a dramatic example of improvement in quality and relative lowering of costs following on economies of scale.

Elasticity of Agricultural Production: You appear to be sceptical of my findings of a high degree of agricultural elasticity of supply in Colombia, and particularly sceptical that it applies to other Latin American countries. The subject is too large and controversial to enter into in any depth here. I can only cite a few facts that I think are pertinent:

(1) There is admittedly an enormous degree of underutilized capacity in agriculture in Colombia and most other Latin American countries—especially labor, but also land and equipment.

(2) Despite constant campaigns and abundant and cheap credit at negative interest rates, agricultural production increased by little more than the increase in population and exports in the period 1950–73.

(3) The expansion of production in commercial farming in some crops has been spectacular (such as sorghum and soybeans) without any decrease in the production of other crops or change (up to 1972) in the terms of trade of agricultural for non-agricultural goods.

(4) The gaps between the physical yields of crops per hectare between experimental, commercial and traditional farming, are very large. Consequently, with the growth in commercial farming, about the same number of agriculturalists have been supplying the food for a *doubled population* and increased exports without any advance in relative prices, again up to 1972. (Starting with 1972 there were a series of bad harvests abroad and in Colombia that has improved the terms of trade, at least for the time being. But the weather is still (1977) abnormal, and there has been a grave decline in security—property and personal—in the countryside. But the elasticity of supply of agricultural output can only be treated over a period of time. Government policies, as in the Argentine, can always discourage agricultural production but can hardly be cited as illustrative of inelasticity of supply except in a very peculiar sense). You stress the surplus manpower in agriculture in Latin America in your *Capitalism and Industrial Development*.

Young and Keynes: Since both you and I find inspiration in Young's Economic Journal article of 1928 as well as in Keynes I hesitate to express some disagreement here. However, the point you raise is important and deserves consideration. It is that Young implied that economies of scale in themselves would generate growth, omitting the necessity of increased investment, which Keynes supplied.

It is, I think, true that Young was concerned to stress the real growth that arises from economies of scale and with the amplifications of Adam Smith's dictum that the division of labour (as in turn amplified by Young) is limited by the size of the (real) market. An implication of Young's treatment is that a rate of growth, whether low or high, tends to be self-perpetuating, but he was not concerned to explain the process by which one passed from a low to a high rate, or contrariwise. *Any* expansion of the market makes it profitable to change factor combinations and makes a higher degree of specialization (including capital equipment) economically feasible and leads to a further growth in real output. The process is not dependent on an increase in investment though it may very well be accompanied by an increase. For instance, better management or technical advances that economize capital may also serve.

Keynes, on the other hand, was, I think, more concerned, at least in the General Theory, with accounting and monetary concepts than with real things. An increase in real production may or may not follow an increase in "investment" or even just spending. An expansion of installment credit, for example, when there is slack in the economy, can result in an increase in monetary (and real) income, with the increase in "investment" being confined to the relatively small but necessary increase in inventory or goods in the pipe-line of production. If there is no slack or there is cost-push inflation, there may still be increased "investment", in a Keynesian sense, the effect of which is dissipated in higher prices with no increase in real output or growth.

In short, I would not agree that Young's treatment, for the task he had set himself, suffered from the lack of Keynes' concept of investment. "Real" investment was included by Young as one of the forms of specialization. Keynes' treatment, it appears to me, runs too exclusively in monetary terms to furnish an adequate theory of growth. The leading sector strategy makes use of the concept of economies of scale but in addition stresses a feasible means (within Young's analytical framework) of making a transition from a lower to a higher rate of growth by identifying sectors to which an exogenous stimulus may be successfully applied. How, in the Keynesian treatment, bring about an increase in investment in general or in real growth rates?

One is forced back to a spontaneous improvement in expectations, increased exports or deficit spending financed by bank expansion or drawing down of balances or buying from abroad. I have always felt it unfortunate that the Keynesian model and terminology forces us to lump together as "investment" such disparate things as capital expenditures, voluntary and involuntary increases in inventories, fiscal deficits and favorable trade balances. "Investment" is too big a category for policy purposes and can be monetary as well as real. Deficit spending is in a sense a leading sector but again may be only monetary or may lead to an undesirable permanent expansion of the public sector or the wrong kind of "expectations". Successful stimulation of output in real terms may be combined with austere monetary and fiscal policies and appears to offer a means of combining high employment, rapid growth and price stability. That it may encourage a growth in imports is not a sufficient objection as *any* successful policy of raising the rate of growth will have this tendency. The problem is to combine high rate of growth with price stability.

I'm afraid what was meant to be a short reply has grown into a memorandum. I hesitate to impose it on you but I hope that you feel that the subject matter is sufficiently important to merit a more extended discussion. Maybe it could lead to a publication of agreement and differences!

My warmest regards to Lady Kaldor and with best wishes for the New Year.

Yours sincerely,
Lauchlin Currie

Kaldor's subsequent writings on Allyn Young basically repeat his earlier interpretations,[13] but Currie continued to explore the subtle reasoning of Young's seminal but little understood article in a number of subsequent publications, notably in his book on economic advisers, completed in 1979, and in a paper published in 1981.[14]

Currie believed that Allyn Young was being excessively (but characteristically) modest when he stated that his celebrated address was merely a variation by a minor composer on a theme of the master, Adam Smith; that the extent of division of labor depends on the size of the market. Kaldor also referred to Young's exceptional modesty and suggested that this is why his paper had not had more of an impact.[15] Currie thinks it was also because Young's theme, the long-run growth process, appeared at a time when such concerns were soon to be overtaken by the worst setback to growth the Western world had known. By the time the Great Depression and the Second World War had passed, interest in growth had shifted in new directions, for example to Keynesian-inspired theories such as Hansen's secular stagnation thesis and Harrod-Domar models. The enormous postwar literature on growth contained few references to Young. Interest in growth theory also gave way to focus on fluctuations around the growth trend rather than the trend itself, and on the difficulties of continuing price stability with full employment.

Even at Kaldor's hands, Young's theory was criticized for supposedly neglecting Keynesian-type considerations of effective demand. According to Kaldor aggregate demand would be unable to support growth if one industry lowered its costs and prices so that demand switched in its favor and away from other sectors (see letter above). A Keynesian-type injection of investment demand was called for to rescue Young's growth process. This may reveal that Kaldor did not fully understand or accept the Sayian type of reciprocal demand to which Young and later Currie were referring. His criticism would seriously restrict the self-perpetuating or cumulative element of growth.

For Young, an increase in the demand for a product was met by an increase in supply, and that supply was an increase in demand in exchange. The greater the demand (and supply) the greater the size of the market and, hence, the greater the opportunities for extending the division of labor by more roundabout, capital-intensive methods and improved organization. Currie insists that Adam Smith's statement that the division of labor is limited by the size of the market was not developed by him into a theory of growth. For Smith the size of the market was a restraint on the division of labor. Once the division of labor is fully adapted to a particular market size, growth ceases. Further growth is then dependent on exogenous improvements or inventions and an increase in thrift through which new capital is accumulated. Foreign markets are useful as a means of disposing of any actual surplus (a "vent for surplus"?), but are not seen as a way to create or develop new "surpluses."[16] The word "surplus" seems to suggest that exports are created by accident rather than design. The classical theory of growth is then a theory of how to increase factor inputs, particularly capital via savings, and of how to exploit exogenous inventions. Claims to the contrary are usually reading into Adam Smith what Allyn Young appeared to be attributing to the master but which in reality he was himself pioneering.[17]

Young developed Smith's insight into a theory of self-sustaining growth based on the endogenous creation of opportunities to adopt new and known technology to increase productivity (increasing returns) as the size of the market expanded. With the extension of the division of labor the market was further extended. That was the same as saying that the extension of the division of labor extended the division of labor; growth created growth; new markets created new markets; expanded demand created expanded supply. Change "becomes progressive and propagates itself in a cumulative way."

Thus, whereas Smith's fundamental insight is the proposition "that the division of labour is limited by the extent of the market" (the title of chapter 3 of *The Wealth of Nations*), Young offers a profound new insight, namely that the size of the market is limited by the extent of the division of labor and, therefore, that the division of labor is limited by the division of labor. In this way growth theory is no longer dependent on the supply of inputs and exogenous technical change. Rather, it is a theory of self-sustaining growth that Smith's approach only hints at and in some respects even denies.[18]

Young was clearly aware that in the real world his real (Sayian) demand would be expressed as a monetary rather than a barter exchange. He was also keenly aware that the flow of monetary demand that is needed to give practical expression to an increase in reciprocal Sayian demand could be interrupted. Although Young does not refer to monetary demand in his 1928 paper he was aware of its complementary importance. In his less well-known *Encyclopaedia Britannica* article on "Supply and Demand" he wrote: "There is a sense in which supply and demand, seen in the aggregate, are merely different aspects of a single situation. It is for this reason that some of the older economists hold that general overproduction is impossible—a theorem which, though not really erroneous, has proved to be misleading. . . . There may be and often are maladjustments of supply and demand. Furthermore production in general may at one time outrun and at another time fail to keep pace with the expansion of money incomes."[19]

Currie insists that Young would have had no difficulty in appreciating the need to maintain a steadily expanding flow of monetary demand in the conditions confronting the United States and the world after 1929. Subsequently, however, the Keynesian concept of monetary expenditure flows have dominated thinking and the definition of demand, while real demand in the sense of Say and Young has been greatly neglected. Keynes is generally thought to have buried Say's Law so the traditional approach to real demand is considered disreputable. For years Currie has been attempting to rescue the old idea from oblivion and to discuss "demand management" not only in the useful Keynesian sense[20] but, equally importantly, in the sense of Say and Young.

The Two Types of Demand and Implications for Demand Management Policy

The policy implications are far-reaching both for long-term growth theory and policy and also for short-term macroeconomic stabilization. Currie extended Young's ideas in various theoretical and policy directions. Firstly, while Young explained why "change becomes progressive and propagates itself in a progressive way," Currie explained why this change tends to perpetuate itself at a constant rate unless accelerated or offset by exogenous events. A slow rate of growth induces further slow growth; a fast rate induces a continuation at that fast rate. Thus, 3 percent growth begets 3 percent growth, and 8 percent begets 8 percent. So although Young's vision was optimistic in that growth was seen to proceed by its own momentum, he offered few explicit prescriptions on how to move from one trend growth rate to another; in particular, he did not explain how growth may be *accelerated* except to point out that this was related to real market size and involved the adoption of more roundabout methods and greater geographical and sectoral reallocation of resources.

However, Young's reformulation of the nature of the growth process was highly suggestive and inspired Currie's development of policy prescriptions to accelerate growth by acting on potential real demand in the sense of Say as well as, or instead of, demand in the sense of Keynes. Another implication brought out by Currie concerned the enormous gains potentially to be had from breaking free of growth trends below the economy's potential. Great present sacrifices in the pursuit of faster growth would be amply rewarded by great "compound interest" benefits from growth. For, if successfully achieved, a higher growth path would tend to be self-perpetuating except insofar as it is affected by exogenous events, including new policy measures and exogenous inventions and improvements.

As Young himself emphasized, however, purely exogenous inventions are much less important than inventions that are stimulated by the more profitable opportunities afforded by increased market opportunities and the extra resources made available by increased incomes for research and development expenditures. And perhaps equally important, especially for less-developed countries (as Currie emphasized), were the greater opportunities for adopting and adapting known methods and machines as the size of market demand expanded. In this view both inventions and innovations are in large part related endogenously to growth and growth is endogenously related to technical change. As the division of labor is limited by the division of labor so, by implication, is growth limited by growth.

In the long run better distribution follows on fast growth and high incomes. High incomes not only make labor scarcer and hence better paid, they also permit a greater volume of income transfers from rich to poor without the bitter social conflict that is generally associated with transfers from given incomes (leveling down) compared with transfers of some of the additions to national income (leveling up).[21] It is also part of the endogenous growth-sustaining process of change that, with growth, real wages rise which, in turn, induce factor proportions to shift toward more productive, capital-intensive techniques that previously were uneconomic.

What policies are called for to escape the inertia of a slow-growth trend? Currie has stressed the leading sector strategy for many years. This is a demand-side approach to growth and development, but with demand clearly defined in the sense of Say rather than Keynes. It will be recalled that in the leading sector strategy Currie has focused on sectors where real demand can be greatly increased so that real supply can expand without prices falling below costs. Sectors that are favored for this role are ones that are quantitatively significant and which face elastic demand in the broad sense of a large *potential demand* (a term Young also italicized) that can be actualized by exogenous policy and institutional changes. Housing and exports are, for the reasons discussed in chapter 10, sectors that Currie would select and that have fulfilled a strategic leading sector role in various fast-growth economies in recent years.

In Currie's theory the economy is seen as an interdependent whole. The growth of individual sectors depends on the overall growth rate of GDP which, in turn, is made up of the individual sectoral growth rates. Each individual sector tends to expand only in line with the historic growth of demand which, in turn, emerges from the overall growth rate and the particular income elasticity of demand for that sector's product. If, however, an exogenous policy can switch demand toward quantitatively significant leading sectors then the growth rate can be accelerated, not only for the leading sectors but for "following" sectors too, though the growth rate of followers would naturally be much slower than that of leaders. We may note that the accelerated increase in demand for and supply of the output of leading sectors is, in fact, the same as the supply of and demand for the products of other sectors in exchange. Constructors build houses in exchange for money which is derived from, and can be spent on, the output of the rest of the economy. The mortgage funds that finance housing arise from savings out of the current earnings of farmers, industrialists, and service sector workers. The earnings and receipts of those engaged in the building industry are spent, in turn, on a variety of other goods and services.

The increased output of leading sectors thus constitutes the effective demand, in real terms (preferably backed by appropriate monetary policy to maintain a steadily expanding flow of monetary expenditures at constant prices), for the output of other sectors. In this way even sectors with very low price and income elasticities of demand, notably agriculture, can expand more rapidly.

"Increasing Returns" as a Macroeconomic Concept

Contrary to interpretations of Allyn Young by Nicholas Kaldor and Charles Blitch[22] (who followed Kaldor), Young did not necessarily expect a sector such as agriculture to be subject to decreasing returns in the broad sense. Kaldor maintained that agriculture has an extremely low elasticity of supply and that only by government policies such as land reform, technical assistance, subsidized credit to finance more inputs of labor and capital, or through food imports can we avoid a halt to the growth process that would otherwise be brought on by food price inflation.[23] In this Kaldor and Blitch follow the "structuralist" interpretation of inflation and advocate "productive credit" programs. The approach is also similar to that of the Fei-Ranis-Lewis models discussed in chapter 9 above.

Blitch correctly noted that Young shunned the partial equilibrium approach that treated individual industries or firms in isolation. But he goes on to claim that "Young proposed that a sectoral view of the economy should be taken as an approach" (Blitch, p. 18). Young did say that "we have to go back to a simpler and more inclusive view, such as some of the older economists took when they contrasted the increasing returns which they thought were characteristic of manufacturing industry taken as a whole with the diminishing returns which they thought were dominant in agriculture" (Young, p. 528). However, he then noted that improvements were being made in agriculture that offset the tendency to diminishing returns in that sector and criticized the older economists for failing to provide any explanation of why agricultural as well as manufacturing improvements were sought and obtained. Instead, according to them, they just happened.

In the rest of Young's article he does not refer to agriculture again, probably because his approach was, in fact, not sectoral but global or because increasing returns cut across industrial and sectoral boundaries and were all-pervasive. He stated that we may miss the nature of increasing returns, or "economies of more roundabout methods," if we "look too much at the individual firm or even . . . at the individual industry" (p. 531). He accepts that there may be limitations imposed by specific factor shortages, including land, but he does not use this to limit his conclusions about the possibilities for technical and organizational improvements of all kinds in all sectors. "Even with a stationary population and in the absence of new discoveries in pure or applied science there are no limits to the process of expansion except the limits beyond which demand is not elastic and returns do not increase" (p. 534).

He goes on to say that, despite various obstacles and costs, it would be "a conclusion repugnant to common sense" to say that no real economic progress could come through the operation of forces engendered *within* the economic system. It is likely that Young would not have been surprised by the tremendous increase in agricultural as well as manufacturing productivity in the United States and would undoubtedly have attributed this to the operation of increasing returns in all sectors, despite the fixity in the supply of land and despite inelastic demand for agricultural output.

In fact, a superb example of the way that the agricultural sector can gain from external economies, which in turn spark further endogenous opportunities to increase productivity, is given in the chapter "Rent of Land," in the famous textbook *Outlines in Economics* (New York: Macmillan, 5th ed., 1930), which Young co-authored with Richard T. Ely and others. There he showed how technological advances in railway and ocean transport (coupled, he might have added, with the repeal of the English Corn Laws in 1846) opened up European markets to U.S. grain farmers. These changes permitted the abandonment of *millions* of acres of U.S. land in favor of the more intensive cultivation of the best lands, using more roundabout and hence more productive methods that also required far less labor than before. All this became economical only because a much larger market had opened up first. This offsetting of the "law" of diminishing returns in agriculture was not a "happy accident" but all part of the endogenous, self-sustaining, sectorally interrelated growth process.[24] It was stated (*Outlines*, p. 417) that the law "operates in an exceedingly elastic manner," and it would be "absurd to make the fundamental tendency toward diminishing returns in agriculture a basis for pessimistic views regarding the possibility of economic progress."

Young mentioned a hypothetical limit "beyond which demand is not elastic." As explained earlier, this refers to elasticity of *overall* demand, though Kaldor and Blitch interpret Young's words in a narrower sense.[25] Currie insisted on the insatiability of overall wants that ensured that over time (though not always in the short run) all income is spent. The income elasticity of demand for goods in general is unity. Young, an intimate of Frank Knight and Thorstein Veblen who were both noted for writings on the powerful psychological and social aspects of consumer demands, would no doubt have agreed with Currie on the insatiability of wants.[26] However, individual products can and do face inelastic demand. Young thought this could present some problems for the growth process but only because the displaced labor would have to learn new trades, a new geographical distribution of the population would be needed, and established communities would have to be broken up (p. 534). Despite inelastic demand, producers "often share in the advantages of the increase of the general scale of production in related industries, and so far as they do productive resources are released for other uses" (p. 535).

If the overall income elasticity of demand is unity an inelastic demand for some products implies an elastic demand for the rest. Over time resources naturally flow from the former to the latter. If the overall flow of money incomes is maintained at an appropriate level there should be no major problem in securing a steady growth of real supply and demand, both overall and even for commodities whose demand is inelastic.[27] Though the demand for labor will fall most drastically in those sectors facing inelastic demand, with adequate mobility there should not be a general unemployment problem. There is no evidence that the fastest-growing economies, experiencing the greatest growth of labor productivity and labor displacement, are ones where unemployment is highest. Generally their unemployment record is better, not worse, than in the economies where labor-displacing productivity growth is slower. The perspectives of Allyn Young and the extensions and policy implications drawn by Lauchlin Currie could not be further from those of the International Labor Office, for example, or the bulk of recent literature on development.

Currie's interpretation of Young places far more emphasis on potential demand conditions facing individual sectors than on the particular production (supply-side) conditions that characterize them. By contrast, Kaldor places most stress on whether a particular industry or sector faces greater increasing returns than others. He subscribed to the controversial "Verdoorn's Law" that the faster the rate of growth of the manufacturing sector, the faster the rate of growth of productivity.[28] In fact, in recent decades agricultural productivity in the United States has grown much faster than productivity in manufacturing.[29] Similarly, the microelectronic revolution is liable to have its greatest impact on service sectors such as banking and finance.

Actually Kaldor himself found that productivity growth in agriculture and commerce was much more closely correlated with changes in their output than was the case in manufacturing, though there were very different trend coefficients for productivity growth.[30] Trends supposedly show the degree to which a sector's productivity growth is independent of that sector's own output growth. This separation of the nature of productivity growth is examined in more detail below but, meanwhile, it may be noted that Currie chooses his leading sectors not according to whether they potentially enjoy greatest scale economies but according to whether they face great potential demand. If, for example, a doubling of the textile industry was to reduce unit costs more rapidly than would, say, a doubling of the construction sector, this would not necessarily make the former a better candidate. For unless textiles can be exported easily demand may fail and prices could then fall more rapidly than costs. This "failure of elasticity of demand" (Young's phrase) would halt further expansion. On the criterion of the sector with the greatest productivity-increasing potential, it would, in fact, have to be agriculture that is chosen. However, because of its very low demand elasticity agriculture is one of the slowest growing sectors of all and could never be made an effective leading sector.

Kaldor's emphasis on the particular production conditions of individual industries suggests that he is thinking more of internal than of external economies. He states that the markets for commodities in which increasing returns are important are ones which, "for that very reason, are only 'imperfectly' competitive—as is the case with manufactures."[31] But this is precisely the view advanced by Piero Sraffa in 1926[32]—that increasing returns lead to monopoly—that Allyn Young vigorously rejected in his 1928 paper. Young's concept of increasing returns applies generally to the whole economy. Particular sectors may face particular expansion problems that give rise to increasing costs, usually only temporary. However, expansion of the *entire* market enables *all* sectors to exploit their own potential productivity at the level justified by the size of their particular market, and this depends on each sector's elasticity of demand with respect to the growth of overall incomes (the overall market).

Internal economies are important but may be of secondary importance relative to external economies (cost reductions passed on by other sectors that supply improved capital, technology, and cheaper services) arising from general expansion in the whole economy. External and internal economies are limited by overall and specific market demands. Thus demand conditions may be more important than particular supply conditions though the latter are not irrelevant. If external economies are more important than internal economies, and if the entire market is growing, then increasing returns as defined by Young need not lead to monopoly. Contrary to Sraffa and Kaldor, increasing returns can be consistent with intense competition as firms struggle with each other in a keen search for new markets and to protect existing market shares.[33] If competitors are gaining a larger *share* of the market, which signifies a *relatively* larger volume of physical sales, they will be in a position to reduce costs more rapidly. This is consistent with Young's stress on the importance of the marketing activities of businessmen.

Young pointed out that growing industries have a tendency to break up into a number of new, more specialized industries. In fact, the division of labor increasingly takes the form of new, specialized firms and industries, often relatively small-scale ones. Furthermore, he thought *large* production (a large overall market) was more important than *large-scale* production (large firms or industries) in securing increasing returns in his sense (p. 531). He warned his readers not to expect too much from rationalization and mass-production methods that arise from the internal reorganization of industry independently of an expansion in demand that is occurring for other reasons. It is not the scale or size of firms, nor even, indeed, the size or scale of individual industries, but rather size or scale of the whole economy or the entire market (including foreign demand) which really counts.

On the same reasoning, agricultural productivity is most likely to increase not because of an increase in the average size of farms but because an expanded overall market size (a) enables individual farms to be more specialized and (b) enables firms that supply agriculture with machinery and other inputs to reduce their real supply price, thus increasing *external* economies to agriculture.

The conclusion arising from Kaldor's way of viewing increasing returns in sectoral terms is that manufacturing in general should be emphasized and resources directed toward it (through selective bank credit and other Keynesian-type policies to supply what he thought was the missing link in Young's analysis). Growth would be boosted in the first instance mainly because of internal economies of scale.

Furthermore, since it is in manufacturing industry that these internal economies of scale supposedly predominate, Kaldor and others have advocated protection for that sector against foreign competition.[34] Kaldor writes:

> "Dynamic" economies of scale do not extend to all forms of economic activity but are largely concentrated on manufacturing industry. They have no equivalent in agriculture, even though technical progress in agriculture is equally the joint result of experience and the progress of scientific knowledge, but their realization does not depend, or only to a minor extent, on the size of the market; and they do not really extend to services. . . . [T]here can be no doubt that manufacturing is the true engine of growth; the greater spread of scientific and technical knowledge, which is both a consequence and a cause of continued progress in manufacturing, reinforces this tendency to "polarization" of economic activity.[35]

In other words, "polarization" and "cumulative causation" are mainly the result of different technological conditions in the various sectors of the economy rather than the different demand conditions that confront them. Kaldor's growth theory is demand-oriented in the sense that output is driven not by growth of inputs but by demand; but demand is seen from a Keynesian perspective, to be stimulated by "elastic credit conditions" and guided by supply-side criteria that direct demand to sectors where increasing returns (to scale) are concentrated, or where output growth has the greatest impact on productivity growth.

Actually, as mentioned above, Kaldor himself found that, abstracting from trends, the growth of output (or demand) by itself increases productivity in agriculture and services by much more than it does in manufacturing. However, in the case of agriculture the "trend" explanator of productivity growth was much more important, and this has been taken to mean that agricultural productivity growth is "exogenous" and independent of demand.

However, in Allyn Young's inclusive view of increasing returns improvements in agricultural productivity would be the result of an increase in the overall market size (that is, growth of GDP) as well as the result of growth in demand for agricultural output. Since GDP generally grows much more rapidly, on average, than the growth of agricultural demand, the former effect is likely to be greater than the latter. We would expect to see a high "trend" coefficient (a) in the Verdoorn equation, $p = \mathrm{a} + \mathrm{b}q$, where p measures sectoral productivity growth and q measures output (or demand) growth. As mentioned above, the trend effect on productivity in agriculture was indeed found to dominate the Verdoorn coefficient (b), even though b is considerably greater for agriculture than for manufacturing.

In the Young view, however, the trend may be largely a measure of the external economies that boost agricultural productivity as overall market size expands, while the Verdoorn coefficient captures the less important internal economies. Both, however, arise from an enlargement of the market, or from demand-side considerations in a broad sense. The great difference in the growth of demand for agriculture compared with overall demand growth—that is, the very low income elasticity of demand for agricultural products—would also explain why agricultural employment is falling sharply while employment elsewhere is rising.[36] These employment differences are endogenous to the growth process, being the result of labor demands that are derived from different rates of growth of product demand in different sectors when overall GDP increases. These different employment patterns both influence and are influenced by the measured trend coefficient (a) and the Verdoorn coefficient (b). Thus Young's theory can be used to explain not only how fluctuations around a growth trend may endogenously affect and be affected by productivity and increasing returns, but, more importantly, also to explain the growth trend itself. This too is endogenously related to the trend growth of labor productivity, with cause and effect running in both directions.

Kaldor described much of the "trend" growth of agricultural productivity as "merely the passive consequence of the absorption of surplus labour in secondary and tertiary occupations, and not necessarily a reflection of true technical progress and of higher capital investment per unit of output."[37] If, however, much of the exodus of rural labor is the consequence of faster growth of output and demand in non-agricultural sectors (especially services) it is endogenous to the overall growth process. Hence agricultural productivity growth arising from this influence would also be endogenous. Furthermore, Currie has emphasized that as labor leaves agriculture for higher paying work elsewhere, real wages rise and this motivates the remaining farmers to increase labor productivity by adopting more capital- and technology-intensive methods.

Currie argues that labor "shortages" encourage productivity growth. Indeed, the greater the shortage of labor the better for growth and real wages, which should be one of the ultimate objectives of development. Young remarked, optimistically: "As every economist knows, the greater the degree to which labour is productive or scarce—the words have the same meaning—the greater is the relative economy of using it in such indirect or roundabout ways as are technically advantageous, even though such procedure calls for larger advances of capital than simpler methods do" (p. 532). Kaldor, by contrast, argues that labor shortages hamper investment; hence his controversial explanation for the slow growth of the United Kingdom—that it can draw on less surplus agricultural labor than can other countries. In his model growth is not self-sustaining in the long run. On the supply side it will be limited by shortages of food and raw materials and growing labor shortages; and on the demand side by a slowdown in the growth of investment demand which, he maintains, will be hampered by labor shortages.

Kaldor, like Currie, also stresses export growth, but here too their approaches differ. Kaldor was worried that a country's success in pushing manufactured exports is constrained mainly by the foreign income elasticity of demand (via the Keynesian or Harrodian foreign-trade multiplier[38]). The higher the foreign income elasticity of demand the better it is for the exporting nation. By the same reasoning, however, the exporting nation's success may be achieved at the expense of the rest of the world (the importing nation or regions).[39] On this view growth is a very mixed blessing. Increasing returns are accompanied not by Allyn Young's vision of economic progress but by sectoral, regional, and international conflicts of interest. So here too

Kaldor's conception of demand-oriented growth bears little resemblance to the kinds of real, Sayian, reciprocal, and mutually beneficial demand stimuli stressed by Young and Currie for whom the growth of exports would represent a greater real demand for the output of the rest of the world.

Luigi Pasinetti has written of Kaldor's approach:

> Kaldor has devoted much effort recently to building a theoretical construction based on the idea that the "Keynesian" features of an economy may apply to its industrial sector, while, side by side to it, the primary sector, providing food and raw materials, may be operating with "non-Keynesian" features. This antithetic sectoral analysis may also be applied to the relations between developed and less developed countries. If the "industrial" sector (or country) operates with "increasing returns to scale" (an idea going back to Allyn Young), and the primary sector (or country) operates at decreasing returns to scale (*à la* Ricardo, only mitigated now and then by "land-saving" innovations), then a whole series of important consequences follow, though it may not be easy to formalize them neatly.[40]

This passage suggests that Pasinetti follows Kaldor in interpreting Young's approach to demand in a conventional monetary or Keynesian sense. And Young's treatment of "increasing returns" again becomes not a macroeconomic engine of growth (which in Currie's treatment develops a self-perpetuating trend rate), but a conventional search for those sectors where internal *returns to scale* are greatest, which leaves technical progress in agriculture to be explained (or, rather, not explained) as a chance (exogenous) offsetting of the law of diminishing returns.

Similarly, Thirlwall writes:

> The difference between industrial and land-based activities has profound implications for the growth and development process in the world economy, where some countries concentrate on activities subject to diminishing returns while others produce goods subject to increasing returns. The existence of increasing returns not only undermines the concept of a competitive equilibrium but makes the whole growth and development process a cumulative one in favoured "regions" relative to others. Trade and factor mobility between "regions" become disequilibriating rather than equilibriating as far as income, employment opportunity, and other indices of welfare are concerned.[41]

Again, this reasoning may be questioned because it fails to analyze increasing returns in Young's inclusive sense in which *all* sectors can benefit from the endogenous spread of cost-reducing methods made worthwhile and feasible as the overall market expands. The relatively much more rapid growth of agricultural productivity cannot be dismissed simply as an autonomous phenomenon, independent of the growth process itself. Technical change may be autonomous or external to agriculture when, for example, farmers use but do not themselves produce improved tractors (just as automobile manufacturers use but do not produce improved computers and robots). This does not necessarily mean, however, that it is autonomous or independent of the overall process of economic growth. Such a conclusion would be, in the words of Allyn Young, repugnant to common sense.

The manufacture of tractors can be made more economical, not only if there is an increased demand for tractors following an increased demand for food but also if the market for automobiles increases. This is because it may then be possible to produce more economically many components (and services) used by both automobile and tractor manufacturers. If tractors then reduce the real cost of producing food and raw materials this in turn cuts the real cost of industrial production, and so the process continues. Thus Young's message was that economic growth throws up at least as many external as internal economies if, indeed, it is possible to separate them conceptually.

For agriculture, however, the elasticity of demand is generally very low. It is this, not diminishing returns, which causes much slower growth in the primary sector and in countries and regions that depend thereon. It is differences in potential demand, not differences in "returns to scale" that justify policies that foster one sector rather than another. In fact, as Currie has emphasized for many years,[42] it is the very rapid productivity growth in agriculture, coupled with very low price and income elasticities of demand, that has depressed per capita agricultural incomes in the face of very poor labor mobility. Greater, not less, mobility is needed to raise per capita incomes both for the migrants and for the remaining agricultural workers.

On this view, Thirlwall's claim that factor mobility between regions is "disequilibriating" is misleading if by this he means that mobility creates undesirable inequalities. It is true that factor mobility causes or, rather, accompanies marked differences in *gross* output growth in different sectors and regions. It does not follow, however, that it causes more unequal output and incomes *per capita* and it is *per capita* measures that are indicators of economic development. Unequal growth of sectoral and regional *gross* product is part of the natural process of resource reallocation in response to shifting patterns of demand and technology, and is the means by which the desired end of higher and more equal per capita incomes is achieved.

Kaldor stated that because increasing returns characterize industry and diminishing returns characterize agriculture (and maybe services too), the principle of cumulative causation implies that "some regions gain at the expense of others, leading to increasing inequalities between relatively prosperous and relatively poor areas."[43] He criticized Allyn Young for failing to emphasize that the process of increasing division of labor "tends to cluster agound geographic centres (which may be thought of as cities, and in a wider sense, countries as political entities)."[44] This is unfair; firstly because Young did in fact note several times in his 1928 paper that increasing specialization in industry and commerce would favor the growth of cities; and secondly because Young nowhere suggested that this process necessarily harmed the slower-growing sectors that faced inelastic demand. On the contrary, to repeat, such sectors "often share in the advantages of the increase of the general scale of production in related industries, and so far as they do productive resources are released for other uses" (p. 535).

The "Marshall-Young-Romer" Model of Growth

Paul Romer has recently produced a model which he has dubbed the Marshall-Young-Romer model of growth in which the main focus is on the presence of increasing returns to scale due to large fixed costs of setting up new firms when, with increased market size, the opportunities increase for new firms to produce new intermediate inputs.[45] Romer claims that "the degree of specialization, or equivalently, the number of different firms that are available at any point in time or location, is limited by the presence of fixed costs." This is somewhat different from Young in that he claimed that the degree of specialization depends on the size of the market. However, it is true that since a larger market promotes more roundabout, capitalistic methods of production, fixed costs would increase. Nonetheless, Young does not claim that this will cause monopoly (in which profit maximization implies that price is above marginal cost) to be a normal outcome, nor even that the average size of firm necessarily increases. It must be remembered that in his 1928 British Association address

(p. 527) he explicitly warned that the presence of external economies that result from changes in the organization of an industry as a whole when the market expands ought to be "a safeguard against the common error of assuming that whenever increasing returns operate there is necessarily an effective tendency toward monopoly."

Young's point was that a larger market size permits more of the infinite potential stages of production to be undertaken by a larger number of specialist firms, big or small. It is conceivable that most will be adapted to the existing market size or, rather, will be *tending* to adapt to a *growing* market, so that in most cases unit costs will be falling to their (moving) short-run minimum or even tending to rise. In these cases average cost and price would be equal to or lie *below* marginal cost, and then the private benefits of savings and investment would apparently *not* exceed social benefits, so the conventional case for investment subsidies is undermined.

However, Romer argues that the opening up of international trade would increase the return to investment in new (intermediate) goods and so boost growth in both countries that exchange their respective sets of new products. However, where trade is not possible because of transport or other barriers, then investment would need to be stimulated in some other way, perhaps by subsidies, though these subsidies would be constrained by society's intertemporal preference function for consumption. This then suggests that if society chose to forego more consumption and instead saved and invested, growth would be more rapid. But in this case there may well be a problem on the side of demand. Why invest more when consumption is being restrained?

Romer's model becomes a model of growth in which the constraint is on the side of the supply of capital inputs, rather than on the side of demand. We are thus rather remote from Young's theory, which depended not on inputs as the cause of growth and not on fixed costs, but rather on the extent of market demand and on how an expansion of market demand increases the *incentive* and *ability* to specialize in new firms, products, and processes, to invest, to accumulate capital, and, if necessary, to employ more labor. Given all this, progress in one industry yields external economies to other industries, which further increases the opportunities for specialization and, hence, further exchange, in a self-sustaining process of growth. This growth would be at a high rate or a low rate depending primarily not on the proportion of GDP that is saved and invested, but on the endogenous properties of the growth process itself that yields macroeconomic "increasing returns" rather than, or as well as, microeconomic returns to scale.

The "Currie-Young Multiplier" and the Sources of Growth

In Currie's interpretation manufacturing in general faces an overall demand constraint determined by the overall trend rate of growth and the associated income and price elasticities of demand for manufactures. The demand for many manufactures such as processed food and clothing is not very elastic and moves closely with the trend rate of growth of GDP. The demand for many consumer durables, especially cars, is more volatile and potentially elastic if credit is made available. For developing countries, however, this is not the most desirable leading sector on other grounds. The demand for manufactured products such as steel, cement, bricks, glass, sanitary ware, and electric cables is an intermediate demand. Thus it cannot easily be manipulated without a corresponding change in the demand for the final products into which these are inputs. That leaves construction as a prime candidate, and/or exports.

Even if the construction sector itself enjoys fewer internal economies of scale than other sectors its main function would be to expand the real market for other products. These in turn can then exploit new opportunities to increase their productivity by employing higher technology. These improvements then become the external economies of other sectors (including construction). Growth becomes self-sustaining.

As Currie himself writes:

> Any increase in the market itself sets in motion forces to create economies, which increase output per capita not only in the original sector but in all other sectors (since, in Sayian terms, an increase in output *is* an increase in demand through barter terms of trade) which in turn creates further economies. As this concept of increasing returns was (and is) so novel it might be thought of as "the Youngian Multiplier"—any increase in real demand in a period creates economies which tend to increase the rate of output correspondingly in the succeeding period. It not only makes technical change an integral element of the growth process, but provides what is now missing—a causal explanation of the growth in technical change itself.[46]

Currie elaborated on this point in a subsequent paper:

> The word "multiplier" is perhaps not the most appropriate to use to describe the growth process. There is a significant difference between the Keynesian and the Young Effects. The impression conveyed by the former is that of a continual starting up and running down. Something (a high efficiency of capital, a deficit, a favorable balance of payment) initiates an increase in investment. A psychological "law" of a propensity to save immediately starts to bring the increase in investment to an end, an interesting link of the "psychological law" of Keynes and the textbook Law of Diminishing Returns. In the case of the Young Effect, the impression is that of a continuing momentum generated by whatever the rate of growth happens to be and a tendency to continue at that rate. While this may seem a minor difference, it is in reality profound. Instead of mixing the theory of growth with the explanation of oscillations around the growth trend, it permits separate treatment. It permits a treatment of historical growth in terms of forces endogenous to the economic system instead of being a chance offsetting of the Law of Diminishing Returns by technological change. It permits a repeal of the latter "Law" and makes it a result of a particular combination of factor proportions of no particular heuristic importance except in the case of an excessive rate of population increase.[47]

Finally, we may emphasize that Currie's theory of growth from increasing returns differs sharply from conventional classical and neoclassical growth theories that stress a causal relationship running from growth of inputs to growth of outputs. This is also the typical way in which textbooks treat the concept of economies of scale: they consider the relative degree to which output expands when an individual firm or industry expands all inputs proportionally. Currie, by contrast, places little stress on the prior increase in inputs, in the economy as a whole, to produce a growth in output. Solow's finding, that 87 percent of the growth of output per man-hour is not accounted for by additional inputs, but rather by a "residual" or "technical progress," is consistent with Currie's theory that capital accumulation is more the result than the cause of growth.[48]

Currie was struck by how small, quantitatively, is the addition to the capital stock in the form of machinery and equipment as a proportion of GDP (around 2 percent). Even the *gross* figure for investment, including plant as well as equipment, amounts to only about 8–9 percent of GDP in the United States. Many new techniques, notably modern computers, greatly reduce both capital and labor requirements per unit of output. Output, then, is raised not so much by inputs as by higher technology, which, however, requires wider and faster-growing markets to make it pay.

As for increased labor inputs, these have little effect on overall GDP growth, and, as noted earlier, instead tend merely to dilute the fruits of growth, reducing per capita income below what it would have been otherwise. Population growth increases the supply of labor relative to its demand, reducing wages. This in turn inhibits the adoption of potentially more efficient, roundabout, capital-intensive techniques of production.[49]

In accounting for the sources of growth, Currie criticized conventional neoclassical approaches for confusing the *contribution* of factors with what is *attributed* to them in the national accounts. Attribution, or distribution of income, results from a complex interplay of supply and demand for factors. It says nothing about the relative contributions, overall or at the margin, of factor inputs to growth. Labor enjoys around 75 percent of national income in advanced economies and this share has increased somewhat over time. This must not be taken to mean that labor has been the main source of growth, a conclusion implied by marginal productivity theory. Even more serious, the identification of marginal product as the contribution of factors to growth also yields mistaken growth and population policies:

> The weight given to "inputs of labour" is particularly misleading. Would it have led to the complete reversal of population policy in China today, or recently in Singapore and Hong Kong? Indeed I very much doubt whether an overall increase in labour leads to any increase in aggregate, to say nothing of per capita, output. At least in Colombia it may be argued that *all* the significant advances in technology that have characterized growth in the past 35 years would have occurred anyway, even with a stationary population. . . . The important consideration is the aggregate effective demand, not the number of individual consumers. (ibid., p. 545)

The trick is to allocate labor to the sectors offering the highest remuneration, so that the distribution of income can improve. But the growth of the gross product and, still less, the growth of output per capita, has relatively little to do either with the growth of the labor force or, even more heretically, with the sectoral allocation of labor. Employment is the consequence rather than the cause of output growth, both overall and by sector. Consequently it is a drag rather than a stimulus to labor productivity and per capita incomes. These heresies are explored further in chapter 13.

CHAPTER 13

Toward a General Theory of Reactivation and Growth, 1978–89

Introduction: Advising and Teaching

The previous chapter was mainly concerned with the evolution of Currie's thinking on the theory of long-run growth and demand management. Throughout this period Currie remained closely involved in current macroeconomic policy issues. Whenever possible he tried to explain the policy implications of his theories to those who were shaping current policy. However, his immediate influence during these years appears to have been very limited. Increasingly he worked for a longer-term influence through teaching and writing.

When President Julio César Turbay assumed office in August 1978 Eduardo Wiesner was appointed director of the National Planning Department where he remained until his appointment as finance minister in January 1981. During this period Currie maintained cordial relations with Wiesner (who was, incidentally, a cousin of Currie's wife) but made relatively little impact. He also met with President Turbay and warned him of the danger of continued inflation. However, generally the main thrust of government policy was little different from that under President López: the individual project-by-project approach to planning, a bias in favor of decentralization away from the four larger cities, inflationary finance, and a proclivity for direct attacks on poverty that included ad hoc rent, price, interest, and exchange-rate controls plus "selective credit" programs ultimately financed by emission from the central bank. Buoyant coffee prices obscured many policy errors. Despite high coffee prices and a huge increase in illegal earnings from the narcotics trade, Colombia's foreign indebtedness continued to increase alarmingly.

Currie prepared dozens of memoranda on current monetary, fiscal, and foreign exchange policy during this period. These memoranda were sent not only to Eduardo Wiesner but also to Luis Eduardo Rosas who in 1978 was appointed to the Junta Monetaria. Currie subsequently decided to do for Colombia what fifty years earlier he had done for the United States: write a book on the supply and control of money in Colombia, relating practice to theory.[1] More will be said later about this book and other work in the monetary and foreign exchange fields.

For Currie teaching was a source of great stimulation, to himself as much as to his students. For most of his years at the National Planning Department he gathered small groups of young economists for informal classes on basic economic concepts. Often it was the original text of Keynes's *General Theory* that was the subject of critical discussions. He also encouraged his students to translate important articles into Spanish for publication in the National Planning Department's *Revista de Planeación y Desarrollo.* These included a translation by Saúl Amézquita of Allyn Young's 1928 article.[2] In August 1979 two separate groups of Currie's students joined together to organize an homenaje (tribute) to mark the thirtieth anniversary of his first arrival in Colombia. These were his Planeación class, led by Saúl Amézquita,[3] and a group of young economists at the economic research foundation, FINES, most of whom were students of his from the National University in 1966. FINES had been formed by Rodrigo Manrique, had Currie as its honorary director, and met regularly to discuss research projects with him. The big dinner at the Tequendama Hotel was attended by ex-President Pastrana, while congratulatory messages were sent by ex-Presidents Lleras Restrepo and López Michelsen. Currie made a lighthearted speech replete with reminiscences.[4] A few days before this banquet the minister of finance, Jaime Garcia Parra announced the creation of the Lauchlin Currie Scholarship, administered by the Banco de la República, to send students to study at Currie's first university, the London School of Economics (of which Garcia Parra was also an alumnus).

In 1980 Currie began teaching part-time at the Universidad Javeriana. The invitation to teach in their new graduate school followed a seminar there in October 1979 at which Currie had been the discussant of a paper presented by Professor William Baumol. Currie was amused and intrigued by the paper Baumol had recently published on the eight versions of Say's Law,[5] and they enjoyed their exchange of notes on J. B. Say and Allyn Young. The course Currie gave at the Universidad Javeriana on economic theory and development was built around the general writings of Arthur Okun, Joan Robinson, and Milton Friedman, plus Kaldor and Currie on Allyn Young, and Keynes's *General Theory,* all with reference to the statistical evidence on broad historic

Currie with ex-President Misael Pastrana, 1979.

trends and economic relationships published in the indispensable annual *Economic Report of the President* (Washington, D.C.: U.S. Government Printing Office), the latest copy of which always lay on Currie's cluttered desk.

One of Currie's brightest students at the Universidad Javeriana was Alvaro Montenegro whom Currie took on as a part-time assistant at the National Planning Office in 1981. They were subsequently to coauthor a small book, *Crecimiento con Estabilidad: Un Modelo* (1984), that showed how the insights of Allyn Young could be used to reactivate the real economy while at the same time pursuing orthodox deflationary policies in terms of monetary demand.

In early 1981 Currie changed his part-time teaching program by moving to a research seminar in monetary economics for final year undergraduates at the Universidad de los Andes. He was to continue teaching there at least until 1988. These classes, as well as being a stimulus to all involved, also enabled Currie to find other bright students whom he could later recruit as his own research assistants.

In early 1981 Currie was also devoting a lot of time to speech writing for Virgilio Barco who was hoping to run as a presidential candidate in 1982 with the support of ex-President López and the Liberal party machine. It was Currie's hope that if Barco was elected he would be able to have more influence on him than he had when Barco was a minister and the mayor of Bogotá, and also more influence than he had been having for the last few years as adviser at the National Planning Department. However, eventually Alfonso López withdrew his support for Barco in order to run again for President himself. In the event he was beaten badly in the polls by the Conservative candidate Belisario Betancur. López was discredited and Barco was nominated by the Liberal party to contest, successfully, the 1986 election. He assumed office as President in August 1986.

As usual Currie was also kept busy with invitations to give talks at home and abroad; Dubrovnik in June 1980 to talk again on Allyn Young and the transfer of technology;[6] to Washington in October 1980 for seminars sponsored by the State Department and Resources for the Future, followed by visits to various urban renovation projects in Baltimore and Florida; to Cali in November to speak at a conference on the development of the cattle industry in Colombia; to Washington again in April 1981 to be interviewed in front of the Federal Reserve building by London Weekend Television for a documentary on the Great Depression; and in June 1981 to revisit Simon Fraser University where he was awarded a much-appreciated Honorary Doctor of Laws. There he gave the convocation address to a graduating class of 1,450 students, a public lecture, and an economics department seminar on the themes of "Development and Culture," "Economics and Survival," and the theory of growth.[7] Also, in June 1981 he was in Mexico City to speak again on urban policy.[8]

In May 1988 he received a second honorary doctor of laws, this time from St. Francis Xavier University in Antigonish, Nova Scotia. Currie had attended this college from 1920–22 but had left without a degree. Sixty-six years to graduation must be an all-time record. It was a nostalgic occasion and he was delighted at the opportunity it gave him to meet for the first time some of the younger members of the families of his Nova Scotian nieces and nephews. Returning to Colombia via Washington he was invited to attend, as one of the few surviving original participants, the fiftieth anniversary of the founding of the famous annual conference on income and wealth, where his early contributions to economic measurement were remembered.

His frequent visits to Washington gave him the opportunity to receive specialist medical checkups there. In 1981 he needed treatment for severe back strain caused by lifting awkwardly a heavy rock while gardening. Also there were dizzy spells. Later, in 1985, he suffered from growing weakness and tiredness which he reluctantly attributed to his advancing years (he was then eighty-three) but which his Washington doctor recognized as one of the worst cases of thyroid deficiency he had encountered. This was treated by daily doses of synthetic thyroid, with dramatically beneficient results: his game of tennis greatly improved and the dizzy spells ceased.

He also sought advice on the nature of the aging process. Some years earlier he had been alarmed to read of the millions of brain cells that disappear every day in older (and younger) people. His doctor in Washington told him in 1981 that he had the cardiac system of a man of 25, but otherwise offered little advice. Currie's own philosophy was that, as with tennis for the body, so constant mental exercise for the brain was the best insurance against senility. In a letter of congratulations (September 24, 1981) on the recent conferment of the honorary degree at Simon Fraser University, J. K. Galbraith wrote: "I notice, with appropriate sorrow, your commitment to tennis. Do bear in mind that Emerson said there was an absolute apposition between physical and mental exercise. However, if you have continued the two this long, there may be hope."

Currie has noted that Supreme Court justices seem to go on forever, and wishes that an important lesson would be learned from this for retirement policy. In any case, he made few concessions in his own tough routine. However, naturally he has been increasingly aware of his bodily machine wearing out and of the need for more frequent visits to doctors and dentists for diagnosis, repair, and maintenance work, with a complicated routine of pills for various ailments at different hours, all designed to keep him functioning in comfort "a little longer," as he has been saying for many years now.

For relaxation at weekends he has hacked terraces out of a dry mountainside at Hato Chico on the edge of the Sabana where later a small house was built for his daughter. On these terraces he planted scores of different varieties of iris that he imported from the United States, despite the many obstacles to be overcome at customs. After years of experimentation with the different varieties in different soil and water conditions, he discovered which were most resilient, most attractive, and most adapted to conditions on the Bogotá Sabana. He has had vague notions about commercialization but has settled for the great psychic income they have given. He hoped that those new varieties he was introducing to the Sabana would give pleasure to some people long after his writings were forgotten. Unlike the United States, irises of every hue bloom on his hillside terraces the whole year round. After these terraces had been completed and his daughter had married and settled in the house there, Currie bought himself, in 1987, another small house on the Sabana with about five acres of fertile land. After installing better irrigation he set about building more terraces and planted another few hundred colorful irises.

After his successful seminars on monetary theory and policy at the University of the Andes, Currie was invited in July 1981 to direct their School of Regional and Urban Studies, with a place on the university's academic council. After ten years at the National Planning Department he finally resigned his position there in August 1981 to take up this new full-time university post. He began a heavy teaching schedule of ten hours a week at the Interdisciplinary Center for Regional Studies (CIDER) within the school, plus two hours each in the economics faculties of both the Universidad de los Andes and the Universidad Javeriana. This was emotionally and physically taxing, but work he enjoyed so long as he dealt with reasonably small discussion groups.

The Institute of Social Studies at the Hague was financing CIDER, though it was staffed mainly by Colombians and Chileans. Currie soon became very dissatisfied with the extensive range of courses and the heavy teaching and examination load the students were expected to bear. They were "being stuffed like sausages," but doing very little economics or independent thinking. Furthermore, hardly any research had been undertaken or published by the center since its foundation six years earlier. Currie's attempts to shake the place up and shift the emphasis from "regional" to urban planning encountered bitter opposition and resentment. An independent evaluation commission was appointed. Their report strongly supported Currie's criticisms but, in order not to lose financing from the Dutch by making a stand on autonomy, the university authorities suggested in February 1982 that Currie quietly move over to the economics faculty with the rank of professor, the same salary, and some new research contracts he had secured. This suited Currie admirably, for the economics faculty was the best in the country and he would be better placed to work with and influence its professors and full-time students of economics.

Growth with Stability

During 1975–79 the frosts in Brazil drove coffee prices to record levels and gave Colombia a massive coffee bonanza, peaking in 1978, that concealed many policy errors. Coffee became Colombia's only major leading sector and when in 1979 coffee prices began to tumble the economy lost its momentum, though this was concealed for a time by heavy foreign borrowing. In the early 1980s the world economy was in recession. In Colombia inflation averaged around 25 percent a year but this was insufficiently reflected in exchange rate devaluation so Colombian products increasingly lost their competitiveness in increasingly competitive world markets.

At the May 1982 presidential elections the Conservative candidate, Belisario Betancur was the victor and was due to assume office in August. Around this time, therefore, Currie and his assistant, Alvaro Montenegro, drew up a new statement of the theory of growth in an inflationary environment and of the potential role of leading sectors in compensating for various recessive influences. Currie hoped this would form the basis for a new government program to escape the evils of stagflation. GDP growth had fallen to 2.3 percent in 1981, barely keeping pace with the 1.8 percent growth of population.[9] By 1982 overall GDP growth was falling to less than 1 percent. GDP per capita was, therefore, now actually declining. Currie and Montenegro's work not only spelled out their diagnosis of these stagflationary conditions but also explained both the nature of and the quantitative magnitudes involved in a program of reactivation for the real economy accompanied by deflation of monetary expenditures and prices. Currie now also resolved to try to publish as soon as possible the manuscript of his new book on the supply and control of money in Colombia which was highly critical of Central Bank policy over the years.

The day after the elections, May 31, 1982, Currie was writing to the present author: "I'm not sure that my services will be called on by the new government but if they are I know what I will advise. Monetary restraint and a full use of the leading sector to pick up the unemployed priced out of the market by cost-push. Simple! There were a lot of glum faces around the University this morning. The head of CEDE was insisting to me that money expansion had to be at least 30 percent a year to keep up with prices and avoid unemployment. These things go deep."

During the transition or handing-over period between governments (empalme) Currie was invited to attend various committees, particularly on housing policy which the outgoing government belatedly decided was important for reducing the now very high levels of unemployment. Currie again urged, again to no avail, that the old Junta de Ahorro y Vivienda (JAVI) be reconstituted, with more full-time members and fewer ministers, to establish the distinction between policies on money and policies on savings and selective lending.

At the end of July the President-elect decided to create a council of economic advisers. It comprised three Conservative members, three Liberals, and Lauchlin Currie. Its secretary was Diego Pizano Salazar who was also to be President Betancur's economic secretary. Pizano convened meetings and set the agenda for the council. It met irregularly on only twenty-four occasions over the next four years and so was not especially influential. In some ways Currie felt it inhibited his own influence because it made it difficult for him to meet privately, and so more effectively, with the President, or to criticize publicly. Also his relatively poor command of the Spanish language made it difficult for him to argue his case persuasively in the council meetings especially since these were attended not only by the President but often also by a number of ministers in addition to the regular members. Usually about twenty people were present, and Currie's soft voice tended to be crowded out.

However, he made his first written submission to the council on August 11, 1982, a few days after the new government assumed office. It was a basic statement of his ideas on combining policies of monetary restraint with measures to stimulate the real economy, to achieve "growth with stability."[10] Over the following months he and Alvaro Montenegro completed the more detailed and quantitative exposition of these ideas and policies for the council's consideration.[11] Naturally, there was considerable emphasis placed on the role of the construction sector in the reactivation program, but in practice the official policy on housing followed the very different advice offered by the President's personal housing adviser, Javier Ramírez. This will be examined below.

In essence, Currie's model of growth with stability stated that actual growth was the result of various expansive and recessive forces that Currie placed into three groups. The first of these was the "Young

Effect" or the underlying tendency for any given rate of growth to perpetuate itself because of the way the expansion of the market affords new opportunities for internal and external economies to be exploited. This tendency should perhaps be called the Young-Currie effect because of Currie's extension of Young's insights that growth begets growth to the related insight that a given *rate* of growth also begets that same rate of growth, as explained in chapter 12 above.

The second group of forces is related to exogenous policies and events that raise or reduce the underlying (endogenous) trend rate of growth. These would include international events beyond domestic control, such as the world price of coffee or world recessions. They also included cost-push forces, especially those relating to the most important element in total production costs, namely money wage rates. Total monetary expenditures (MV) are equal by definition to the money value of national production (PQ). A cut in the rate of growth of MV because of restrictive monetary policies will thus necessarily reduce output (Q) and employment if the rate of growth of money wages, and hence prices, does not fall proportionately. Trade union pressures and the resistance to money wage cuts cause prices to be sticky downwards so that conventional austerity measures usually have negative effects on output, employment, and growth. Downward money wage resistance accompanied by a fall in the rate of growth of the money supply (with the demand for money and, hence, velocity relatively constant) causes output to be priced out of the market (defined by the volume of money expenditures) both at home and, with a relatively inflexible exchange rate, abroad also. Every effort, therefore, should be made to resist cost-push pressures, especially those arising from the unionized labor market since labor costs are the most important element of total costs.

The third group of forces affecting the actual growth rate was related to the behavior of "leading" sectors that for various reasons can move independently of the overall growth rate but which could have a significant impact on movements in the latter rate. In the context of stabilization policy to reduce inflation Currie preferred to call these sectors "compensatory" sectors. When deflationist monetary and fiscal policies confronted downward wage rigidity or cost-push pressures, a new gap was created between the actual and the potential level of national production. Currie and Montenegro calculated the size of the gap so created under the assumption that the rate of growth of the money supply would be reduced progressively over a four-year program period to a level equal to, or only slightly greater than, the desired rate of growth of the real economy (which Currie was persuaded could be pushed to 8–10 percent a year). They then estimated the quantitative magnitude of the effort required in the leading or compensatory sectors to close the gap and achieve the desired real growth targets. Their calculations revealed that tremendous efforts were required if these sectors were to take up the resources released by the sectors that would price themselves out of the market through the inertia of cost-push pressures.

Nevertheless, Currie was convinced these goals could be achieved if the government was sufficiently committed and understanding. In the terminology popularized by Harry G. Johnson[12] the program would combine "expenditure reduction" with massive "expenditure switching" toward not only the tradables sectors (the sectors that interested Harry Johnson in his celebrated paper) but even more importantly toward construction. Johnson and others have stressed the improvement in resource allocation arising from a switch of expenditures toward sectors in which a country possesses greatest underlying comparative advantage, an advantage that monetary inflation combined with exchange rate and other controls so often erodes.

Currie generalizes this insight by noting the tremendous underutilization of resources in general and the need to provide real incentives to improve the mobility mechanism to shift resources toward leading sectors with elastic demand and to increase thereby the real (Sayian) demand for the output of all sectors while simultaneously reducing overall monetary (Keynesian) demand. An additional advantage of the construction sector in this process of reactivation and growth is that it is, in Colombia and many other countries, one of the least unionized of sectors and, therefore, less subject to cost-push pressures. Furthermore, its product (mainly housing) enters the cost-of-living index only indirectly via rents and mortgage debt service payments. A successful leading-sector or compensatory-sector strategy that maintains or accelerates real growth while rates of growth of *monetary* expenditures are being curtailed necessarily reduces the rate of inflation. This in turn reduces debt-service charges under the index-linked housing finance system.

A New Theory of Housing Demand

Currie's prime interest in housing lay in its potential as an instrument of macroeconomic policy. Housing is important, of course, in itself, but so are many other things. Its greater significance lay in its potential for very rapid expansion without saturating demand, for offering better employment both directly and in supplier industries, and also in increasing real demand for the products of the whole economy. These macroeconomic benefits would translate into pervasive social benefits from more and better-paying jobs for the poor, better housing for all, and greater incomes from which to finance social programs of all kinds.

These achievements, however, depended crucially on a thriving, dynamic private housing finance system based on attractive, inflation-proof returns for personal savings, as explained elsewhere. Since 1974, however, successive governments had shown themselves in varying degrees hostile to the private housing system. Since President Pastrana's time none was prepared to foster it as a leading sector. President Betancur's administration was no exception. Nevertheless, this administration did decide to place greater stress on housing as a social policy. Influenced by his housing policy adviser, Javier Ramírez, in 1982 the President decided to channel more resources into very low cost "social" housing for the poor. Unwilling, however, to devote more state revenues to the public low-cost housing agency, the ICT, the government introduced a series of measures to force the private housing finance corporations, the CAVs, to channel more of their resources in these directions. They were obliged to buy ICT bonds (which were seldom properly serviced) and to devote large fractions of all lending to poorer families wishing to purchase low-cost housing. Furthermore, these loans were to be at relatively low rates of interest, longer term, and with zero downpayments.

These measures increased the risks for CAVs, increased delinquency rates, reduced their revenues and, hence, made it more difficult to increase their capitalization and capture of deposits. Other discouraging measures adopted from time to time in subsequent years included a lowering of the ceiling on monetary correction so it fell below the current rate of inflation, reserve requirements against CAV savings, and increased capital requirements.

The CAVs had formed a trade association, the Instituto Colombiano de Ahorro y Vivienda (ICAVI), to publish information and defend their interests.[13] In October 1982 they appointed Luis Eduardo Rosas as the director of ICAVI. Rosas, who played a key role in the early days of the new indexed (UPAC) housing finance system when he was director of the National Planning Department, had recently been serving as adviser to the Junta Monetaria. President Betancur had in August 1982 appointed another ex-director of planning, Edgar Gutiérrez, to be his finance minister. Gutiérrez quickly removed both of the existing advisers to the Junta Monetaria, Luis Eduardo Rosas and Jorge Garcia Garcia, on the grounds they were both "monetarists" (Garcia held a Ph.D. from Chicago, Rosas from Brown). Gutiérrez prided himself on his "structuralist" view of inflation in which money has only a passive role. The result was that after 1982 there was no one on the Monetary Board who thought money had anything to do with inflation, or, if they thought so, had enough influence to modify current establishment opinion.

So Rosas moved from the Monetary Board to ICAVI and from there persuaded Currie to offer his services as part-time adviser. Later in 1983 ICAVI made comfortable offices available to Currie where, over the following years, he would spend more and more of his working time, though he retained his rather spartan office at the University of the Andes for his continuing duties there. Dr. Rosas remained at ICAVI as director throughout this period and so the warm collaboration that Currie had received from him extended, by 1990, to nearly twenty years, having begun in the early 1970s when Rosas was deputy director (then director) of the National Planning Department helping to implement the Plan of the Four Strategies.

Currie's insights into the importance of the housing sector and into the nature of the demand for housing continued to evolve during this period. Of particular significance was his realization in 1983 that much of the confusion regarding the nature of demand lay with the failure to distinguish between the stock and flow demands for housing. The total demand for housing was a demand for both the existing stock and for new housing. The existing stock was of enormous value, nearly one half of all private fixed capital. (The proportion is similar in the United States.) The annual value of this stock, and hence the current value of total housing demand, is equal to the actual or imputed annual rental value of the stock.

The current value of newly built housing, however, is only a very small fraction of the existing stock. Large variations in the supply of new housing, therefore, produce only a small effect on the total stock. Likewise, the current supply would itself exert an insignificant effect on the price, or rentals, of the total stock. The total supply of and demand for housing, therefore, may appear to move only slowly and on this basis calculations of the income elasticity of demand may appear to be only a little higher than unity.

If, however, the demand is decomposed into two elements, one for the existing stock and one for new housing, interesting implications emerge. Percentage variations in the demand for the latter can differ sharply from percentage movements in overall demand. The latter demand may be highly stable while the former is subject to wide swings. These swings are the result of variations in the relative price or rentals of the existing stock compared to the financial costs of new housing. The financial cost of new housing depends mainly on the terms and conditions on which mortgage funds are made available. These are affected by nominal interest rates, monetary correction schemes that alter the repayment schedule, the mortgage period, and downpayment requirements. It also depends on whether the desired funds are actually available or whether queues and rationing are the norm.

Potential purchasers of new houses compare the monthly financial costs of these houses with the rents and prices of comparable existing units. The comparison favors new housing when the monthly mortgage debt-servicing costs are relatively easy and funds readily obtainable. By contrast, rent controls on the existing stock discourage demand for new housing. Small variations in the relative terms on which new and existing housing is available can cause shifts between the two types of demand. A shift in demand from the existing stock to new housing that is very small as a percentage of the stock can represent a massive percentage change in the demand for new housing.

This new way of looking at the nature of housing demand cast new light on the reasons why activity in this sector moves independently of the trend for the whole economy. It also helped to show how construction activity can be manipulated by conscious policy on housing finance. And finally it showed how such policy can rapidly effect very large variations in current production in the building industry. These large variations in current supply can be accompanied by equally large variations in demand by measures that switch housing demand between the existing stock and the new supply. These policy-induced changes in current supply and demand can be sufficiently large to have significant macroeconomic effects. As such, housing policy can be seen not just as a potentially important and socially useful microeconomic or sectoral policy but as an instrument of macroeconomic policy that can have as significant an effect as conventional fiscal, monetary, or exchange rate policies, discussion of which dominates contemporary macroeconomic textbooks and advice.[14]

Currie's work at ICAVI was wide ranging because of the wide ramifications of housing and construction. Currie believed that the supply of and demand for housing and construction could be greatly furthered by the promotion of major cities-within-the-cities urbanization programs such as were discussed in chapter 11. The reader is reminded of the work Currie directed in 1983–84 on a new design for the remaining lands of El Salitre after more than one-third of them had been set aside in 1981 for an ornamental park. Also in 1984 he initiated a study, completed by a group led by Luis Ricardo Paredes, an able lawyer, into the 141 different items of paperwork needed to effect the purchase of a house with a mortgage loan and to make recommendations—few adopted—on how this bureaucratic nightmare could be reduced.[15] The "formal" sector of the economy was plagued by such regulations and was a major reason why a low productivity "informal" sector continued to survive alongside the potentially much more efficient formal sector.

In November 1984 Currie was invited by the Chinese government to join a Colombian group that was to attend the twenty-fifth anniversary celebrations of the founding of the People's Republic of China. This arose from Currie's connections with ex-President Misael Pastrana who had been taking a great interest in Chinese affairs. Currie used the trip to visit major new urban projects in Hong Kong. In addition, the party was given the traditional tour of attractions in Xian, Shanghai, Canton, and Shin Tien. In Beijing he attended the enormous twenty-course celebratory banquet attended by 3,500 guests at the Palace of the People. Although Currie's invitation was unconnected with his earlier visits to China, nevertheless, Chinese leaders made a great fuss of him when they learned of that connection, particularly the fact he had met with Chou En-Lai. On his return from China Currie stopped off to visit the present writer, who was then living in Singapore, and to examine the remarkable progress achieved in urban and social development in the republic since his last visit in 1973, with exports and housing the main leading sectors.

The Exchange Rate Controversy, 1982–86

The performance of the Colombian economy throughout the Betancur years, 1982–86, was one of the poorest on record, with overall growth averaging only about 2 percent a year, only slightly above the population growth rate. Inflation averaged 22 percent a year. In this stagflationary environment Currie was convinced that a big noninflationary stimulus for the leading or compensatory sectors of housing and exports was vital, especially since there was now a general clamor to cut the fiscal deficit.

As a consultant to ICAVI he devoted much of his energy to defending and strengthening the UPAC system against repeated attacks. And as a member of the President's Committee of Economic Advisers he also spent much time arguing for a massive adjustment of the exchange rate which had become greatly overvalued due to domestic inflation.

In his work at ICAVI Currie did not confine himself only to issues that bore directly on the fate of private housing finance. If housing was a key element in macroeconomic stabilization and growth policies so too were monetary, fiscal, and exchange policies all relevant to the fortunes of the housing sector. After 1982 he saw the question of the exchange rate as of particularly vital concern.

By the time President Betancur assumed office the rate of exchange had become severely overvalued. The President himself conceded that it was about 45 percent too high. At the first meeting of the Council of Economic Advisers in August 1982 Currie argued for a faster rate of devaluation to make Colombian tradable goods more competitive. He soon came to believe, however, that a policy of accelerated mini-devaluations would be a great mistake. Announced in advance, it would offer Colombians a wonderful opportunity to make substantial riskless profits by investing in dollars and dollar-denominated assets abroad. This could easily be accomplished by false invoicing of exports and imports and in other ways. Between 1982–84 the exchange rate was moved very little relative to domestic inflation. Official reserves began to fall sharply and continuously from August 1982 onward.

Currie argued that a sudden, unannounced maxi-devaluation was called for to preempt further speculation. In December 1982 he met with then minister of agriculture Roberto Junguito (who later took over from Edgar Gutiérrez as finance minister in June 1984) and urged that he should think of a surprise devaluation during the Christmas holiday period. Junguito suggested a meeting between himself, Currie, and the finance minister. But Gutiérrez rebuffed this idea and forbad any discussion of devaluation. He seemed determined to defend the exchange rate to the last dollar of reserves.

In early March 1983 Currie had the opportunity to press the President on this issue personally. The occasion was a (slightly belated) tenth anniversary celebration of the UPAC system at which Currie and ex-President Pastrana were the guests of honor. President Betancur delivered a fulsome tribute to Currie's contributions to Colombia and conferred upon him the country's highest decoration, the Cruz de Boyaca. Though flattered and gratified by this honor, Currie later complained that too often people praised the advice he offered in the past and ignored what he had to say in the present. He would willingly have foregone the decorations in exchange for a little of his advice being accepted. At the banquet Currie was seated next to the President and expressed his grave concern over the continuing massive loss of reserves and international competitiveness. One hundred million dollars were flowing out each week. The President asked him to prepare another memorandum. This Currie presented at the next meeting of the Council of Economic Advisers in May.[16]

One of the major objections that had been raised with Currie in private conversations with council members and others was that Colombians with substantial foreign debts would suddenly be faced with a large increase in their obligations in peso terms following a maxi-devaluation of, say, 50 percent. Currie's paper sought to alleviate this problem by proposing that a new, "special" or "provisional" rate of exchange be established for most imports and noncoffee exports, while initially leaving other items, in particular debt-service payments, at the existing official exchange rate. This proposal was based on an analogy with the policy adopted by President Carlos Lleras in 1966–67 when he devalued the rate for some items only and then progressively transferred all other items to that higher rate (in pesos against the dollar). This higher rate was then further devalued under a "creeping peg" system and was eventually unified with the even higher capital rate of exchange. This complied with the IMF's general insistence on a unified exchange rate system.

Currie had private meetings with IMF officials before the May 1983 council meeting and was satisfied that, though they would not officially propose it, the IMF would not raise any serious objections to an interim or transitional system of dual exchange rates with different rates for commercial and capital transactions. Currie's proposal was that the commercial (special) rate be devalued massively while the official rate for capital items be left unchanged initially but subsequently progressively devalued until eventually it was unified with the special rate. Once a competitive rate of exchange for exports and imports had been established through a maxi-devaluation it could thereafter be subject to conventional mini-devaluations to maintain the rate in real terms. Actually Currie preferred a floating rate system but thought that opposition to the maxi-devaluation would be less if the apparently sacred creeping-peg principle were preserved thereafter.[17]

At the May meeting of the council, Currie's proposal was rejected strongly by the finance minister who repeated his assurances that recovery was just around the corner and that there was no need for panic action on the exchange rate. The basic strategy of fiscal restraint should be continued instead. The emphasis on the supposed positive effects on business confidence that would result from reduced fiscal deficits at the IMF's behest reminded Currie of the 1930–32 Hoover years. There would be no official policy to stimulate compensatory sectors.

Influential opposition to a maxi-devaluation and support for a policy of "continuity" and gradualism also came from Francisco Ortega at the central bank and from the head of the prestigious research center, CEDE.[18] At first ex-President Pastrana also opposed Currie on this issue but later changed his mind and by the middle of 1984 was strongly urging the maxi-devaluation line on the minister of finance, Roberto Junguito, and the head of the central bank, Hugo Palacios. The story was told to Currie that in March 1984 President Betancur was about to act on Currie's recommendation when the minister of justice was assassinated and he judged the time inopportune. All the time, more and more reserves were being lost.

By December 1984 Currie was at last able to persuade the council to endorse his proposals on a maxi-devaluation and an interim dual exchange rate system. However, the item had been placed last on the agenda and the President had left the meeting before it was discussed. The council was not convened again until several months later and another opportunity was lost. In 1985 Roberto Junguito finally decided on a policy of accelerated mini-devaluations. This encouraged further purchases of dollars, though most of the reserve loss had already occurred by then.

The government's main response to the dramatic loss of international reserves was to impose more and more import restrictions. An ex-colleague of Currie's at the University of the Andes, Norha Rey de Marulanda, was appointed head of the Import Licencing Agency, INCOMEX, and had a wonderful time vetting the thousands of pleas for licenses that flooded into her office every week.

Altogether around $4 billion of official reserves were lost during the Betancur administration, mostly ending up as privately held Colombian dollar balances abroad or foreign balances previously held in Colombia. This was money much of which might otherwise have been placed on deposit in the Colombian housing finance system, or in other ways spent inside Colombia. It represented a major deflationary influence that must go a long way to explain the extremely depressed state of the Colombian economy during these years, with rising unemployment, growing disaffection, and guerrilla activity. President Betancur's attempts to negotiate with guerrilla groups proved a failure, culminating in the dramatic tragedy of November 1985 when the M-19 guerrilla group stormed the Palace of Justice in the center of Bogotá. It was rumored that the army refused to allow the President to negotiate and in the seige that followed the palace was totally destroyed, with the loss of nearly 100 lives, including those of eleven Supreme Court justices.[19]

The relatively wealthy Colombians who seized the opportunity to invest in around $4 billion of high-yielding dollar assets received their payoff with the accelerated mini-devaluation policy in 1985, a result that Currie described as one of the most notable cases of reverse redistribution in recent Colombian history.[20] Just as with the failure of the reforms of the 1974–78 López administration, its actual results belied all the official rhetoric and declared policy goals.

The Supply and Control of Money in Colombia

Almost fifty years after the publication of his first book on the control of the supply of money in the United States Currie published in 1983 a book on the same topic for Colombia.[21] A second edition followed in 1988. In these books Currie set out once again to expose the recurrent fallacy of the theory of productive credit that underlay so much of the theory and practice of central banking in Colombia and elsewhere.

Currie explained that the Banco de la República attempted to perform two basically contradictory functions. First it was a central bank with responsibility for controlling the nation's money supply. It acted as the bankers' bank, and controlled the money supply through its control of bank reserves—occasionally through open market operations but more usually through discretionary changes in marginal reserve requirements. When necessary it acted as lender of last resort to the commercial banks. Currie was highly critical of the timidity with which open market operations were pursued by the Banco de la República, perhaps because of its unwillingness to pay a competitive interest rate on its obligations. He criticized the bank for being more concerned with its own profits than with the control of the money supply. Monetary control was mainly through changing reserve requirements but this was often too little too late. He also criticized the way that savings deposits in banks, but especially in nonbank financial institutions such as the Savings and Loan Corporations (CAVS), were subject to reserve requirements.

Currie objected that this resulted from a basic confusion between money and savings and between money and credit. It was the excessive growth of money that caused inflation and required tight control. In Colombia when savings increased this increased reserve requirements. If total monetary reserves were given, this would reduce banks' reserves against money proper, which of course Currie continued to insist should be defined as means of payment only, or cash plus demand deposits subject to transfer by check.[22] A rise in the ratio of reserves to money may or may not be appropriate at a time when savings are increasing. The point was that the criterion should be the behavior of the money supply and total monetary expenditures. The behavior of savings and lending (credit) was a separate issue, not linked in any precise mechanical way to money and total expenditures. Savings and lending affected the composition of expenditures and the prospects for real economic growth; they had no causal link with aggregate monetary expenditures. The latter were determined by the interplay of the supply of and demand for money. Inflation was often lowest in countries where the rate of growth of savings was fastest. The trick was to combine a rapid growth of savings with a slow growth of the money supply.

The Banco de la República, however, has seen itself as responsible for a second major function besides the control of the money supply. It has seen itself as a major agent of economic development; it operates as a development bank. As such it offers lines of credit (cupos) to a variety of public and private entities. Its balance sheet, therefore, is extremely complex and its operations an intricate mystery understood by very few. Informed criticism is consequently very scarce and in recent years Currie has regarded it as one of his most important responsibilities to unravel these mysteries and explain in simpler terms the nature of central bank theory and practice, why inflation has been so endemic, and how this inflation has inflicted pervasive economic and social costs on Colombia. In trying to operate as both a central bank and a development bank, the Banco de la República's inherent bias is toward financing development through monetary inflation rather than by encouraging real savings.

In treating of monetary theory Currie followed Marshall, Pigou, and Cannan in showing how the apparatus of supply and demand could be extended to money, with velocity of circulation derived from the demand. He became increasingly reluctant to refer to the concept of velocity except through examination of the forces motivating the demand for money to hold. Velocity itself is merely an arithmetic number obtained by dividing income by money. The demand for money, by contrast, can be analyzed in terms of the benefits to be derived from holding money rather than other assets. This approach to the theory of the demand for money can be seen as part of traditional demand theory for any commodity or service. Insofar as the velocity of money can be deduced from the demand for money, the velocity concept can then also be seen not only as a mere arithmetic ratio but also, implicitly, as part of the general theory of value.

The demand for money arises from the lack of synchronization between receipts and payments, the convenience of holding it ready for the moment when it is required to effect payment, and the opportunity cost of foregoing interest and utility on alternative assets in relation to the transactions costs of converting these assets into money when money is needed. Currie defined the demand for money in terms of the proportion of national income households and businesses wished to hold in this form. Thus he distinguished between the absolute demand for money and the demand relative to income or output.

The absolute amount of money held at any moment was by definition equal to the amount in existence, or supplied. If this amount was greater than the desired proportion of current income then there is excess supply that will be spent rather than held. Spending, however, merely transfers money; it does not destroy it. Increased spending will expand money incomes, via an increase in real output or prices or both, until the desired demand for money as a certain proportion of income is restored.

This supply-and-demand analysis shows how the treatment of money can be subsumed under the general theory of value. The price of money becomes its command over real resources: the proportion of national output that the stock of money can purchase. In other words, its price is the price of the goods and services which exchange for money, or the exchange value of money. Thus the price of money is not the interest rate, though the interest rate is one of the variables that affect the demand for money. Currie sees the interest rate not as the price of money but as the price of loanable funds. Money is only one part, sometimes a small part, of the total supply of loanable funds.

It follows from this treatment that the price of money (its purchasing power) cannot be controlled by controlling the rate of interest. If the authorities attempt to hold down interest rates by expanding the money supply the exercise is very likely to fail. Typically the money supply is expanded to provide "productive credit" on cheap terms to favored agencies and projects. The demand for credit (loanable funds in general) may be strong enough to absorb the new funds, but there is no reason to expect that the demand for money will be increasing too. The whole of the absolute increase in the supply of money will be held by someone. No one refuses to accept money in exchange for the sale of goods or services. But if the demand for money to hold has not increased as a proportion of output, the extra money will continually be transferred (spent) until the money value of national income has risen proportionally. Most of this rise will normally be due to a rise in prices that will encourage an increase in the demand for loanable funds at the original interest rate. Nominal interest rates will be forced up. An increased supply of money will eventually increase, not decrease, the interest rate, a conclusion at odds with standard, static monetary theory, and a conclusion with profound policy implications.

It is to be noted that since rising prices and high nominal interest rates increase the opportunity cost of holding money, there may well be a fall in the demand for money at the same time as the demand for loanable funds, or the demand for credit, increases. In practice, these results may be observed because initially an exogenous rise in the money supply may drive down the rate of interest. By itself a lower interest rate increases the desired demand for money, or "k"—

the fraction of real income over which the community wishes to have purchasing power—but this would be trivial relative to the increase in the money supply. Most of the extra money would be unwanted in that form and individuals would try to exchange it for real and financial assets.

As expenditures on real goods and services increase, prices and profits would increase. This increases the demand for loanable funds. The interest rate would rise and the real demand for money would return to its original level. (If nominal interest rates are forced to very high levels the real demand for money could even fall below the original level during the adjustment period.) The process ends when the desired k is restored to its original level, assuming that the markets are not disturbed again by a further expansion in the nominal money supply.

The general conclusion from this analysis was similar to that emphasized by Currie as long ago as 1933:[23] the demand for loans and the demand for money can vary inversely, and monetary policy guided by the former criterion (the banking school theory of productive credit, now associated with Keynesianism) is in opposition to the latter criterion (associated with the Cambridge version of the quantity theory), and policy becomes pro-cyclical.

The main concern of Currie's book was with policy implications. He traced the complex movements of central bank assets and liabilities and the relationships between these changes and changes in the money supply through their effect on commercial bank reserves. In this way he could show how the coffee bonanza of the late 1970s, or the seasonal changes in the demand for cash, especially in December, altered these reserves. However, he was insistent that the reason why reserves changed was not because of these mechanical relations but because of policy. For policy could always alter or offset these relations, through open market operations or new reserve requirements that operate through or on the money multiplier. Thus rules were no substitute for understanding. Rules should not dictate policy; at best they were only the instruments of policy. They should not be used to excuse a loss of control.

Unfortunately monetary policy was usually conducted in Colombia by administrators rather than trained monetary theorists. A loss of monetary control was typically blamed on uncontrollable exogenous forces or on the needs of industry, agriculture, equity, or development. And there were far too few expert commentators to expose muddled thinking, conflicting objectives, and contradictory policies. Consequently, in recent years the government has resorted increasingly to direct borrowing from the central bank to finance its deficit.

Currie's books lack the formal theoretical and mathematical rigor of the typical modern undergraduate and post-graduate university macroeconomics texts with their extensive adumbration of the post-Keynesian and monetarist IS-LM syntheses. In fact his 1983 and 1988 books on money are not very systematically or tightly written and are somewhat repetitious in places. Nevertheless, the books are replete with interesting and novel insights or emphases that expose the limitations of the conventional approaches. To an extent seldom found in the popular textbooks Currie addresses squarely the question of the definition of money and the distinction between the demand for money and the demand for credit. He shows that it is impossible to speak of an increase or decrease in the demand for money without an accompanying shift in the Keynesian savings schedule. The two schedules are not independent in the way they are usually assumed to be. If the Keynesian multiplier exists it exists only through a change in the supply of and demand for money and cannot, for policy purposes, meaningfully be analyzed in isolation.

Currie's analysis also casts doubt on the traditional exphasis given by Keynesians and monetarists to the interest rate as the main motivating force in expenditure decisions. Currie emphasizes that interest rates move pro-cyclically rather than counter-cyclically. In an upswing the demand for loanable funds is strong and investment expands, despite the upward pressure on interest rates. In a downswing falling interest rates do little to halt or reverse the trend in business investment since changes in interest costs represent only a very small fraction of total business costs.

Moreover he stresses the *availability* of funds at any given rate and the changes in standards of credit-worthiness to qualify for loans, citing the hundreds of billions made available by the secondary mortgage market in the United States.

A full understanding of the macroeconomic forces at work during the business cycle and during secular growth requires a less aggregative approach than is normally offered in the popular texts. In particular, Currie would focus on the important role played by independent or leading sectors such as building and exports. The building sector, unlike business investment in general, is very sensitive to the rate of interest the authorities allow the housing finance institutions to offer relative to those offered by banks and other institutions. This affects the flow of funds and the terms on which borrowers can buy new houses rather than renting the existing stock. This in turn has an important bearing on the profitability of new building activity which in turn bears on the real profitability of investments elsewhere in the economy.

Another novel feature of Currie's writings on money is his disaggregated analysis of the demand for money to discover who owns the money stock and whether different holders of money are all similarly motivated. In chapter 3 reference was made to the large deposit study carried out by Currie at the Federal Reserve Board in 1935 and 1936. This was the first and perhaps the only study of who owns the money stock in the United States by size of deposits. In Colombia in 1982 the banks were required to provide periodic information on the size distribution of their demand deposits. As in the United States in the 1930s it was found that a very small number of depositors owned the great bulk of all demand deposits. In 1984 a mere 0.4 percent of depositors held 45 percent of the total value of current accounts; and 15 percent of depositors held 90 percent of the total. Since at least 70 percent of the nation's total money supply (M1) is in the form of these demand deposits it is clear that an understanding of the demand for money (hence velocity and total spending) must focus primarily on a relatively small number of very large account holders. Currie concluded: "Much of the literature on the demand for money runs in terms of the motivations of individuals. But it appears that the motivations most relevant in explaining the demand for money are those affecting the behaviour of a relatively few businesses and financial firms. It would not appear, therefore, that the individual use of credit cards and the ability to secure money outside of banking hours have much effect on the overall demand for money."[24]

Currie's discussion of the motives for holding money helped throw light on the distinction between money and not-money. "Since the demand for money is for various services the possession of cash and checking accounts provide, and the demand for savings deposits is basically a demand for income, the different nature of the demand provides a basis for the distinction."[25] He rejected the basis on which most studies of the demand for money arrive at their definition of money. Friedman and others look for the definition that yields the best statistical correlation with income over a period. This, claimed Currie, is hardly a good reason: "As has often been said, correlation must be 'reasonable' to have significance. To base a definition on what yields the best correlation and then reason that variations in money, so defined, cause variations in prices, is hardly a scientific procedure. It has been claimed, on the other hand, that it is not of importance whether savings deposits are or are not included in money. The conclusion follows that the stability of the demand for money is largely independent of the definition of money, a strange finding."[26]

A New Hypothesis on the Demand for Money

After the second edition of his book on money had gone to press, in late 1987, Currie gave more thought to the implications of the new information on the skewed size distribution of holdings of demand deposits in Colombia. The very large balances owned by a relatively few businesses and financial firms were greatly in excess of the balances that corporate treasurers needed to settle any actual or potential gap between current receipts and payments. Thus the traditional transactions motive for demanding money to hold was an inadequate explanation. And the Keynesian precautionary and speculative motives were really motives for demanding liquidity rather than money in the form of cash or demand deposits. Liquidity with interest could be obtained from a variety of nonmoney liquid assets.

Currie, therefore, proposed a new hypothesis on the demand for money. He suggested that for the bulk of the money supply in the form of large current account deposits the demand arises from cost-benefit analyses on the part of the holders of large deposits and by the banks themselves of their own costs and returns.

> Viewed from the point of view of the depositors the unique service rendered by banks is the provision of an essential element in business accounting. Receipts and payments by check provide a safe, legal and convenient way of doing business. Payments made and received are identified and recorded. The more a company's dealings can be routed through checking accounts, the less danger of robbery and the greater the contribution to efficient bookkeeping.
>
> Viewed from the point of view of the banks the more active is an account, the more costly it becomes. Each of the thousands of checks in the daily flow must be scrutinized, recorded, collected or paid in cash. The bulk of the operating expenses of commercial banks can be attributed to the render-

ing of this service. Naturally, banks expect to be reimbursed. The more active the account, the larger it must be to enable the bank to make a loan the revenue from which will cover all administrative costs and leave a profit.

In short, a highly important element in the determination of the demand for money can be found in the requirements imposed by the banks themselves. Doubtless company treasurers could so average their payments and short-term borrowings as to get along with a very small balance in relation to the activity of their accounts. That they are, in reality, large, accounting for the bulk of current accounts, must be due to the costly nature of the service rendered depositors by banks and the necessity that they be reimbursed for this service. Banks may be prepared to pay a moderate rate of interest on quite inactive accounts, especially if it appears that nominal interest rates are high and rising. But the "market force" restriction on the widespread payment of a rate of interest on checkable accounts comparable to market rates can be found in the cost of handling such deposits. Even in the case of small accounts, banks have steadily raised the initial deposit requirement.

It appears likely that the secular decline in the demand for money in the period up to 1979–80 can be found not so much in the extension of devices enabling small holders to economize in cash (automatic cashiers, credit cards, etc.) as in the growing administrative efficiency of banks in handling the daily flow of checks and the consequent reduced insistence on the maintenance of such large balances. The strong competition among individual banks for loanable funds lead them to pass along these gains in efficiency to their depositors in this form.[27]

In later drafts this novel hypothesis was labeled the "accounting" motive in the demand for money. This motive is so powerful that individuals and corporations are willing to reimburse the banks for the cost of providing this service, either in the form of explicit bank charges in the case of smaller accounts or, more importantly, implicitly by maintaining the minimum balances banks insist on. The interest that banks obtain from the lending of these balances then covers the costs of servicing them. Competition between banks for deposits ensures that the size of these minimum required balances will be related inversely to the rate of interest and directly with banks' costs. With technical progress and increased productivity in the provision of banking services, costs fall. As these are passed on to customers in the form of lower required balances, the demand for money falls and income velocity rises. This is consistent with the evidence of a secular increase in velocity of around 3 percent a year in the United States up to 1981.

The hypothesis is also consistent with a relatively stable demand for money related to slowly changing bank costs and to movements in the rate of interest. It downgrades the importance of the speculative motive for holding money, or liquidity preference, and so removes what is often thought to be a source of instability in the demand for money. Currie's theory provides an explanation for the fall in the demand for money when interest rates rise that also differs significantly from the conventional Tobin-Baumol portfolio approach. That approach suggests that when interest rates rise individuals economize on noninterest-bearing cash balances because of the higher opportunity cost, and are prepared to suffer higher "shoe-leather" transactions costs.[28] Currie thinks this motivation is trivial and that the real explanation is that when interest rates rise banks compete more vigorously for deposits and reduce the minimum size of balances they insist on, especially with respect to the balances of their large corporate customers. Since corporate treasurers are usually holding larger balances than they could get along with, they would have been willing to swap demand deposits for interest-bearing liquid assets even before the rise in interest rates, had the banks allowed this. So the demand for money is determined not so much by the preferences of the holders of demand deposits as by the bankers' need to cover their costs.

It may also be noted that the traditional transactions approach to the demand for money stresses the interval between households' money receipts and expenditures. Typically, however, this interval has been lengthening as more and more workers are paid weekly rather than daily or monthly rather than weekly. This would suggest a tendency for the demand for money as a proportion of annual incomes to rise. In reality, however, there is a secular tendency for the demand for money to fall, or for income velocity to rise. This is therefore another reason why the traditional approach cannot be an adequate explanation of the facts. Clearly, the influence of changes in the typical receipts-payment interval for households is swamped by other influences and motives.

Currie provides a plausible theory of what these alternative influences are. The theory bears little resemblance to any of the currently accepted approaches based on the transactions, or precautionary or speculative demands of individuals. Nor does it resemble the portfolio balance approach of the modern quantity theorists, such as Milton Friedman, who focus on the influence of a wider range of assets, including human capital, and of "permanent income." There is relatively little room for these considerations in a theory that downgrades the importance of individual households and instead focuses on large business balances and banks' costs and earnings.[29]

Currie's approach neatly combines elements of microeconomic theory of consumer demand and business costs with macroeconomic theory and policy that stresses the importance of control over the supply of money rather than the demand for money. The latter is relatively stable and is not amenable to control by the monetary authorities. The authorities' responsibility for managing aggregate monetary expenditures would be enhanced if they better understood and collected information on the variables that affect the cost-benefit calculus of banks and the holders of large demand deposits.

Another interesting implication is that if reserve requirements against demand deposits are increased (in Colombia in 1988 the required ratio was 50 percent) this reduces the earnings that banks can get from lending demand deposits. This consideration, therefore, would induce banks to insist on larger balances, which would tend to increase the measured demand for money and reduce income velocity. It is interesting to note that as far back as 1934 Currie had been concerned, in connection with his original 100 percent bank reserve proposal, with the need to compensate banks for the costs of handling the major portion of the nation's money supply. If the banks are not given a state subsidy to cover these costs their remedy must be to impose on their customers explicit and implicit charges for these services.

Currie concluded his study with a typical focus on the appropriateness of definitions and concepts in monetary theory, and economics generally, in terms of their usefulness for policy purposes:

> The discussion of the nature of the demand for money offers a basis for a definition of money in terms of the service it performs. Money is required and is "paid for" for different reasons. The chief one or at least an important one is because it supplies an essential element in the safe and efficient bookkeeping or accounting of a society. To do this it also has liquidity, is a means of payment, a store of value and a unit of account. But other things possess one or other of these elements. The thing that both possesses these attributes and also serves as an essential element in accounting is composed of means of payment in the form of checking accounts. Checking accounts possess the further essential quality of being quantitatively subject to control, which in turn permits a limitation of the total quantity of demand deposits and hence of money (since unwanted changes in cash in circulation can be offset by induced changes in demand deposits). Finally,

the economic apparatus of supply, demand and price can be "usefully" applied to money so defined. The resulting widening of generalization is in accord with the objectives of scientific enquiry.[30]

A postscript on this work, however, is that, six months after it was submitted to a leading U.S. journal of monetary economics for possible publication, it was rejected (March 1989) out of hand on the basis of a peremptory report by the reviewer whose main reason for rejecting it was that the cost to the banks of handling checks was "microscopic," citing empirical evidence provided by Pesek that in 1977 it was only $0.0007 per $1 of deposits "purchased." He claimed that bank costs could therefore be dismissed as irrelevant in explaining the demand for money, or the proportion that money bears to GDP. What the reviewer failed to appreciate, however, is that in 1977 the average value of each check cleared may have been perhaps $300, giving a cost of $0.21 per check, by no means trivial when many thousands of checks are drawn each year on large business accounts.[31] In 1977 demand deposits in the major New York banks turned over on average 503 times (rising to 2,903 by 1988: *Federal Reserve Bulletin,* 1978, table 1.20, and 1989, table 1.22), so the *annual* processing costs per dollar were much more than $0.0007. For 1986 the Federal Reserve estimated check processing costs to be at least 25 to 50 cents per item (*Bulletin,* March 1987, p. 187).

Money and Savings

Currie's conclusions on the appropriate definition of money as currency plus demand deposits subject to transfer by check, because of the unique services these perform, reinforced his continual insistence on the important distinctions between money and savings. In his 1988 book on money he had shown, theoretically and empirically, how the demand for savings could move in a quite different way from the demand for money. A doubling of savings deposits could occur with no impact on aggregate demand or prices, whereas a doubling of current accounts is unlikely to coincide with a doubling in the proportion of income that it is desired to hold in this form. Normally the result would be a more or less proportionate increase in aggregate monetary expenditures and prices.

After 1983 Currie spent most of his working hours at the Colombian Savings and Loan Institute (ICAVI). During this time the Savings and Loan Corporations (CAVS) were subjected to continuing difficulties that partly arose from the general confusion between money and savings. Currie argued that the distinction between money and savings was basic and could be found in the very different nature of the demand for the two things. As he wrote:

> The nature of the demand for money to hold gives the clue to the explanation of the relative stability of income velocity over a period and hence of the extremely important relation of money to the price level (or the value of money). There is no such relation between variations in savings and the price level. . . .
>
> Nevertheless, there is some overlapping of the concepts of saving and money, especially in the public mind and in Colombia, and in the thinking of monetary authorities. . . . The overlapping is in large part semantic. Savings may take the form of "deposits", may be in commercial banks, and frequently a reserve is required against such savings deposits. Savings accounts in the CAVS are highly liquid and it is understandably difficult for the layman to grasp the theoretical distinction.[32]

Currie analyzed the growth of business investment in plant, machinery, and inventories relative to the growth of corporate savings and found that the great bulk of all business investment was internally financed. The role of banks in financing investment through bank credit was greatly exaggerated. Most bank credit, through fungibility, ended up as consumer credit. The main and distinctive function of banks was in managing the nation's money supply.

Personal savings are generally smaller than corporate savings but are the most important source of funds for the financing of new housing, shops, and offices. Currie believed that this longer-term financing is best left to specialist financial institutions rather than to banks. If personal savings are channeled to the banks rather than to the Savings and Loan Corporations they are likely to be dissipated in consumer credit rather than the finance of new housing. This would then frustrate the leading sector strategy for accelerated growth of GDP, as explained in chapter 11. It would also make it more difficult to achieve growth with stability; for without an expansion of savings for building there would be insufficient new jobs to take up those workers who are priced out of work in sectors characterized by administered prices and wages when deflationary monetary policies are instituted.

In practice the authorities in Colombia continued to impose onerous reserve and capital requirements on the Savings and Loan Corporations. They also increased their forced investments in low-yielding government bonds and obliged them to charge low interest rates to poorer borrowers and increase the proportion of such loans in their total asset portfolio. This seriously jeopardized CAV profitability, making it difficult for them to raise adequate capital for expansion. The real total of their loans declined and this sabotaged the social objectives of policymakers whose professed intention was to increase the total housing stock and employment in the construction industry. Currie found it galling that when he pointed out these contradictions he was accused of being uncaring, while the populists gained plaudits for their apparent greater concern for social justice and equity.

It may have been thought that with the victory of Virgilio Barco in the presidential elections in April 1986 (he assumed office in August) Currie's influence would be greatly enhanced. But as he watched the election campaign on television he was disappointed at the degree to which Barco evidently felt it necessary to make concessions to populism, concessions that Currie believed were unnecessary to ensure electoral victory and that would only make it more difficult for him to pursue sound policies when in office.

However, in the weeks prior to taking office the President-elect did solicit Currie's views on a number of macroeconomic issues and urged Currie to prepare memoranda for him. He spent several hours in Currie's home one Saturday afternoon and the following morning he returned unexpectedly in his car, without a chauffeur or bodyguard, to pick up some papers. To the consternation of his wife, Currie and the President-elect stood calmly talking at the front door on a quiet street for what seemed to her an interminable length of time, during which she feared assassins or kidnappers might appear at any moment.

It was to prove an extremely difficult and dangerous period in which to be head of state in Colombia, with more than one sensational assassination of prominent political figures who had stood up for democratic ideals and against the ruthlessness of certain guerrilla groups and powerful drug barons. In the face of the savage intimidation and killing of judges who attempted to bring the drug barons to justice, it was with considerable personal courage that the President launched a massive crackdown on the traffickers in September 1989; and he successfully appealed to the Supreme Court to endorse his use of constitutional powers to personally sign the orders that were required to extradite alleged criminals to face charges in the United States.

In the period between the presidential elections in April 1986 and the August inauguration date, Currie prepared for Barco a stream of memoranda on objectives, priorities, and institutional reform. It is not clear whether these made an impression sufficient to cut through the large volume of advice that was pressing in on the President-elect at this time, and since they elicited no formal response he stopped sending them once the President had appointed his team of official advisers and ministers in August. Currie, though willing to serve, was actually relieved not to have to take on this responsibility at his age and was content with whatever indirect influence he could achieve through his teaching, writing, and advisory work at ICAVI.

In his search for a broad spectrum of views, shortly before assuming office the President-elect held a two-hour meeting with the celebrated World Bank economist Hollis Chenery, who was heading a commission (composed mostly of Colombian economists) reporting on employment prospects for Colombia. In Currie's opinion this represented a significant advance over the 1969–70 ILO report, but it still gave very little attention to the role of housing and construction in macroeconomic policy. After he took office, President Barco made no important changes at the Banco de la República. Currie could only observe ruefully the continuing loss of monetary control and the continuing assaults on the relative profitability of the housing corporations for their shareholders and depositors, a situation that would soon adversely affect the rate of building.

This was naturally a disappointment, but Currie was well accustomed to that by now. In fact, he had learned not to expect too much and so avoid disappointments. Nevertheless, he continued his efforts to influence events and thinking, although this influence was now more likely to be indirect and long-run, rather than direct and short-run. In 1985 and 1986 he attended most of the eighty-six weekly meetings of the Comisión de Gastos (Public Expenditure Commission), for which he prepared memoranda on the nature and significance of the fiscal deficit, the difference between public and private accounting, and the need to ensure that total debts continue to grow in line with the economy and total savings.

In these meetings he also took a very unpopular stand against a recently enacted law (Law 12 of 1986) for a greater degree of decentralization of public finance and the earmarking of a considerable proportion of value-added tax receipts for the finance of public works in small municipalities, many of which, in Currie's view, had little economic future. This degree of decentralization thus represented a great waste of scarce resources. The future lay, as it had with almost all more developed nations, with the larger towns and cities.[33] As Currie had predicted, by September 1989 the comptroller-general was complaining that the diversion of tax receipts to the smaller municipalities was resulting in unmanageable deficits of the national government.

Currie continued to press instead for the development of self-contained cities-within-cities, and for that concept to be applied to the large El Salitre site in Bogotá. But in February 1988 he was writing that, while the El Salitre project still bore the same name, "it is to be feared that sight is being lost of the original objectives. The land was not acquired; BCH was made the fiduciary agent for the owners, the Beneficencia, which made the cross and internal subsidization for workers' housing improbable or difficult; the original emphasis on creating jobs and minimising urban transport appears to be absent; the BCH is doing the building and the vast latent resources of the Corporaciones de Ahorro y Vivienda are not being used."[34]

During this 1985–89 period Currie was commissioned by the World Bank for a new study of public administration in Colombia; he used the opportunity to restate the need for a stronger Bureau of the Budget located in the President's office, and the need for a reconstituted Savings and Loans Board (JAVI).[35] He also contributed a chapter on the administration of macroeconomic policy to a volume edited by Joseph Pechman of the Brookings Institution.[36] Several studies were prepared in connection with various contracts between the University of the Andes and the National Planning Department, including his lengthy 1986 paper on IMF orthodoxy in which, as mentioned already, he was critical of a prescription for deflation that gave no consideration to the stimulation of compensatory sectors to pick up resources that would be priced out of other markets.

In 1987 he was asked by the UN Secretariat in Nairobi to advise on housing as an instrument of macroeconomic policy.[37] Meanwhile, his day-by-day work of advising and preparing memoranda for the director of ICAVI, Luis Eduardo Rosas, continued. Currie and Rosas prepared a booklet to mark the fifteenth anniversary of the founding of the new savings and loan system, celebrated at the May 1987 conference of the Inter-American Housing Union in Cartagena.[38] At a banquet to pay tribute to the role that Currie and ex-President Pastrana had played in founding the system, the ex-President remarked: "It is with great satisfaction that we celebrate on this anniversary the

Currie with Luis Eduardo Rosas, director of the Colombian Housing and Savings Institute, Bogotá, on Currie's eight-fifth birthday, October 1987.

achievements of the Constant Value System, in large part the fruit of Professor Currie's fertile imagination. I do not exaggerate in saying that it is the only economic revolution that the country has known throughout a history of indecision and the putting off until tomorrow that which could have been done today."

Also in 1987 Luis Eduardo Rosas persuaded the CAV presidents to place more emphasis on macroeconomic advertising of the system's collective role in the economy, as well as stressing, through competitive advertising, the respective qualities of each of the ten separate corporations. Thus a monthly newsletter, the *Carta de Ahorro y Vivienda*, was launched. This provided Rosas, Currie, and others at ICAVI with the opportunity to explain the workings of the system to a wider audience and to monitor its fortunes and contributions in an ever-changing economic environment. It also offered the opportunity to record lighter moments, such as the three-day "Masters Tennis Tournament" held in December 1987 at the Banco de la República sports club in Currie's honor. The participants were all economists and included several ex-ministers, members of the Monetary Board, and, of course, Currie himself, who, according to Luis Eduardo Rosas's account of the event, "demonstrated the solidity of the UPAC system with a display of tennis that was more classical and less Keynesian than that seen in earlier confrontations between Lord Keynes and Fred Perry."[39]

A General Theory of Reactivation and Growth

In 1987 Currie decided to make another "last" effort to set out more systematically, in a book he was still working on in 1990, his views on the nature of the growth process and appropriate macroeconomic policy. This book incorporates the content of his courses at the University of the Andes.[40] In it he reviews the functioning of the mixed economy—how it is driven by continued widespread feelings of deprivation and frustration that in turn drive people to seek higher incomes through competition, mobility, and innovation. Innovation reduces costs and prices but the overall insatiability of wants ensures there is always potential employment for resources that may be displaced from any one activity. This requires mobility. Mobility and the forces of competition yield the greatest value from resources and ensure that the market can expand to make more innovation and specialization profitable and worthwhile. In this sense the main source of growth is growth itself, not the growth of inputs.

This is consistent with Solow's finding that a "residual" accounted for 88 percent of productivity growth. Population growth merely dilutes the gains from growth. And the growth of the capital stock is much less important than innovation. Competition, however, ensures that the benefits of innovation are widely diffused through lower prices, improved quality, and greater variety. The benefits certainly do not mainly accrue to the innovators, yet the innovators' role in growth is very important (though not necessarily more important than the classical market forces of competition and mobility which play a key role even in the absence of technical innovation). Conventional accounting-for-growth exercises that attempt to measure contributions to growth by measuring the growth of factor rewards confuse contribution with attribution. Factors are paid not because they are productive, not because of their contribution to growth, but because they are scarce relative to the demand—insatiable in the overall sense—for the products they help produce.

The essence of Currie's approach finds parallels in the following passage from a little-known article on capital by Allyn Young in the *Encyclopaedia Britannica* of 1929: "Nature furnishes free productive agents which, merely because no economy need be practised in our use of them, they are not productive in an economic sense. Thus in an economic sense the wind is not productive but windmills are. We harness natural forces so as to use them in production, but we *attribute* the product wholly to the harness" (italics added). Currie would add that the same could be said of technology, which, after a while, becomes almost a free good because of the forces of competition, and the benefits are passed on in lower prices or higher wages and better quality and range of products. In his LSE lectures, Young noted that "99 percent of patents are utterly useless" and "the most important improvements in methods of production are not patentable." However, though inventors fail to capture the benefits of their inventions, this does not mean that inventions play only a small role in growth.

In his article on capital, Young continued: "Capital would not be deemed productive if its supply were not limited, nor would it be deemed scarce if it were not productive. Whether the earnings of capital are attributable to its productivity or to its scarcity is therefore a meaningless question. That a larger (physical) product can be got by using capital does not explain why a specific part of the product has to be attributed to capital and assigned to it as its earnings. . . . For an understanding of this relation of dependency between product and capital it is necessary to take account both of the productive uses of capital and of the circumstances of its supply."

The productive uses of capital depend on the size of the market; and the supply of capital depends on the expected demand for the products of capital, which will determine whether all the costs are covered, including the payment of interest—which is bid up when prospective product demand is strong and bid down when product demand is weak.[41] In the long run, wrote Young, "what part of the product is imputed or attributed to capital rather than to labour or to natural resources will be determined by the rate of interest. How much larger the total product is than it would be if no capital were used is mostly a matter of technology. How much of the product is, in the economic sense, attributed to capital as its product, is largely a matter of the price which has to be paid for advances," i.e., the rate of interest. Currie, however, would say that the share of product paid to owners lies in a range determined on the lower side by the lowest acceptable rate of return to savings, and on the upper side by the degree of competition and mobility, which determine how quickly cost reductions are passed on.

Here in brief is a theory of growth and distribution which, in Currie's view, provides an explanation for the substantial unexplained residual in the growth accounting exercises of Solow, Denison, and others. But it also suggests that such exercises should not be based on a Cobb-Douglas production function approach, because that assumes that the contribution of factors to growth can be measured by the value of their marginal products, that constant returns prevail, and that output depends on inputs, rather than inputs being based on output and relative scarcities. It implies or assumes that growth is driven by factor supplies, whereas in Young and Currie growth is demand driven, and employment and even technology are mainly consequences rather than causes of growth.

In Currie's view the Solow approach, by using the assumptions of the Cobb-Douglas production function, assumes what has to be explained. In reality the growth process has an interlocking and interreacting or synergistic nature that cannot be broken into separate elements. Thus Currie does not accept the notion of a separate "residual" element either, because if one cannot determine the "productivity" of labor and capital, one cannot determine what is the residual.[42]

It is true that the individual firm will hire factors according to a comparison of the necessary payment at the margin and the expected incremental revenue product. But that merely says that the wage rate, for example, will *equal* labor's marginal product, not that the marginal product *determines* the wage, nor that it measures the contribution of that factor to growth in the overall or macroeconomic sense. Macroeconomic forces determine wages—in particular the overall market size and flow of real expenditures—with capital receiving a share according to the rate of interest which in the long run is necessary to maintain the capital stock. The rest is then available for wages and rent. Land rents are a payment for pure scarcity; but wages too will depend on how scarce or abundant labor is relative to the amount of GDP left over for it after the payment of interest and rents.

The logic of this analysis, which is basically the same as Young advanced in his 1929 *Encyclopaedia Britannica* articles on capital and wages (which, however, Currie had not seen until they were brought to his attention in late 1989), leads Currie to take a dim view of population growth as a dilutant of wages. He feels that Young may have been too sanguine when he suggested that population growth, by extending the opportunities for the division of labor, at least in a young industrializing country like the United States early in this century (he was more pessimistic about agricultural countries like China and India), may increase productivity and the size of the market. Currie, however, fears that this illegitimately equates the increased needs of a larger population with increased effective demand.

If an expanding population keeps wages down, this discourages the use of more capitalistic, roundabout methods and so reduces the growth of labor productivity. This in turn means that in the long run both the level and the rate of growth of national production will be lower than otherwise, and *per capita* product even more so. The forces of competition and mobility of a *given* labor force will distribute the fruits of growth away from the innovators, managers, and owners of capital and toward labor. But this process is frustrated or diluted if population growth continually adds to the supply of labor. In Currie's theory labor captures—in higher wages with a small labor force or in lower wages with a larger labor force—most of the fruits of growth (along with landowners), and so labor's percentage *share* may be relatively constant regardless of the rate of growth. But labor not only is not necessary to growth, it may actually retard it. This conclusion will not be good for our self-esteem, and so may be unpopular both for that reason and because it conflicts rather starkly with ingrained habits of thought associated with the neoclassical production function approach to growth and distribution.

While most economists may be prepared to accept the conclusion that population growth depresses real wages and dilutes the fruits of growth, they may be bothered, as Currie was, by the observed fact that additional workers are actually working and producing and their "product" is measured by the additional total wages bill. Would not this production be lost if there had been no increase in employment?

Currie found the answer to this objection in the composition and character of production. If population growth were zero or nearly zero while GDP growth continued at the same rate, or even faster, then per capita income and real wages would be higher. This would naturally lead to a change both in the composition of demand and in the production process. More productive technologies would be used, and even in those sectors where no improvement in physical productivity had occurred, such as services (nurses, teachers, porters, bus drivers, for example), there would be a rise in wages due to their greater relative "scarcity." The increase in wages would measure not their contribution to growth but only their greater scarcity.

For the individual employer each additional worker usually makes a contribution to output and sales revenue. But it is a fallacy to infer that for the economy as a whole additional workers make a corresponding contribution to the growth of GDP. As was noted above, the individual firm hires additional workers up to the point where their contribution to revenues equals the real wage. But the firm does not determine the real wage. For the firm that is a datum. The general level of real wages is determined first by those macroeconomic forces that determine the overall level and growth of GDP and second by the size and growth of the labor force. If there is a faster growth of population, wages will be lower and firms will automatically hire more labor. For related reasons employers may be a major pressure group in favor of more liberal immigration policies. However, GDP and growth of GDP are not greater as a result, and may well be lower. In that case, in the macroeconomic sense the marginal product of additional labor may be negative, even though in a microeconomic view it appears positive. Employment, to repeat, is the consequence not the cause of growth, and the individual firm takes the wage rate as given by macroeconomic relationships.

Turning to cyclical aspects, it may be that during the growth process the flow of monetary expenditures may be interrupted by mistaken monetary, fiscal, and exchange rate policies, and such mistakes often do cause divergences between actual and trend rate of growth. Macroeconomic policy determines not only how closely actual growth keeps to trend, but also helps determine the trend itself. But a trend once established tends to perpetuate itself unless reversed by bad policy mistakes or exogenous events. This justifies considerable efforts to ensure that macroconomic policies favor growth. The promotion of competition and the uninterrupted flow of monetary and real expenditures favor growth and disseminate the fruits of growth widely, even in the absence of explicitly redistributive policies.

The so-called residual, or that part of growth that could not be explained by the growth of factor inputs, is usually equated with "technical progress," but Currie thinks this misleading. First, he does not confine technical change to inventions and new products. Equally or more important are the organizational changes stressed by Allyn Young: all of the economies of scale, internal and external, and all the economies of increasing specialization by individuals, firms, and countries. Second, Currie stresses that all this in turn depends crucially on the extent to which the market forces of competition and factor mobility are allowed to operate. These forces are endogenous, tending to vary both with the real size of the market and, by implication, with its rate of growth. They can, however, be affected by discretionary policy actions to promote the greater mobility of labor and savings toward sectors for which potential growth of real demand is greatest.

The implication of Currie's interpretation of the residual and endogenous nature of the Youngian growth process is that market forces alone can perpetuate either a slow or a fast growth rate. This justifies policies designed to *direct* the economy on to the high growth path.

In Currie's view business saving and business plant expansion are consequences of growth and are self-financing, while inputs of work hours, after a point long past, add little or nothing. The main motor of exponential growth is demand working through market forces of competition, mobility, specialization, economies of scale, and the use of every-growing knowledge—all mostly endogenous. The benefits are passed on in lower prices or higher wages or better quality and choice.

The analysis is clearly classical or Youngian in spirit, with considerable faith in spontaneous market forces. The implications for policy are that it should be designed to work with rather than against these forces, but it is not a prescription for laissez-faire, for the system can be guided toward faster progress and better distribution by the operating on real market demand and removing institutional blocks.

Growth and technical progress are seen to be demand driven, not in the sense of aggregate monetary demand stressed by Keynesian theory—though there are times when this is important—but in the real or Sayian sense. Strategically this depends on relative costs and prices in sectors that can perform the leading sector role when adequate latent real demand is directed to them as the result of exogenous policies relating, for example, to the terms of housing finance, the exchange rate, or international agreements on more liberal trade relations.

Efforts by Denison, Solow, and others to explain the residual by attempts to measure variables such as educational inputs, conventional economies of scale, or the effect of labor transfers from agricultural to nonagricultural sectors as measured by earnings differentials are, Currie insists, fundamentally misplaced. Higher earnings of educated manpower or nonagricultural workers do not measure their contribution to growth. They merely reflect the part of the gains from growth that these inputs acquire through their relative scarcity (which in turn depends on mobility: and the greater the mobility, the lower the reward than would be paid otherwise). Scarcity is relative to real demand and relative to other occupations. Thus, just as the general level of wages is a measure not of contribution but of attribution, so too with wage differentials. As for conventional internal economies of scale, these represent only one of the types of increasing return that Young's theory of growth dealt with. Equally, or more important, were external economies and the greater division of labor and specialization.

A further criticism of conventional measures of sources of growth concerns productivity measures. In themselves measures of labor or capital productivity are merely arithmetic ratios of output to inputs. There is a tendency, however, to view growth of GDP as due mainly to technical progress when productivity is increasing, or to growth of inputs if, for the same growth of GDP, productivity growth is slower. Thus in recent years concern has been expressed about the "productivity slow-down" or "productivity crisis" in the United States.[43] The conclusion drawn by some is that the United States is failing to exploit technical advances and instead relies mainly on increased inputs of labor and capital which, therefore, have apparently been the main source of growth.

The Young-Currie theory of growth offers a very different interpretation. Growth of employment (or, rather, growth of wage payments, with or without more employment) and capital accumulation are largely the result, not the cause, of growth. GDP growth is mainly the result not of exogenous technical advances but of policies to enlarge the real market size, or real demand. This both provides the internal sources of funds and makes it pay to innovate and extend specialization, division of labor, and internal and external economies. All this represents increased productivity and endogenous technical change.

As growth proceeds it will pay to employ more labor and capital at existing or higher rates of wages and interest. If the supply of labor is elastic because of a growing labor force or immigration, then the fruits of productivity and income growth will, as we have seen, mainly be captured not by the innovators, managers, and policymakers but by new workers at existing or only slightly higher real wage rates.[44] Measured productivity (output per man-hour) will apparently rise only modestly despite dramatic innovations and changes in work practices and the structure of industry. If, on the other hand, the labor force is fairly fixed, most of the gains in productivity and income will be captured by the existing work force. Real wages will rise more rapidly and measured productivity will also rise impressively.[45]

In both cases, however, the main source of growth was economic policy, innovation, *and growth itself,* self-sustaining growth. Conventional inputs play only a subsidiary role. Employment, in this view, is not so much a means to an end, but more an end in itself, desirable on social grounds to provide people with a sense of purpose, and more acceptable than charitable welfare payments as a way to distribute the fruits of productivity growth. The size of the gross product in the United States or in Colombia would, Currie suggests, be little different today—and conceivably could be larger—if their respective populations were now at the same level as twenty or thirty years ago. The main difference would be in the size of per capita income and in the sectoral composition of the gross product and labor force.

It may be noted that any productivity improvement reduces costs and, if demand is inelastic, releases labor to produce other things. However, the effect of this initial innovation and cost reduction is not confined to the extra output that the released resources can produce. This contribution may be quite minor. Equally or much more important may be the way that the initial cost reduction reduces prices and so increases real effective demand for products as a whole. This in turn enables *all* resources to work more productively.

The gains from an initial increase in productivity in a particular sector may lead to an increase in total production in three ways. First there is the direct reduction in cost and prices in that sector, whose output will then increase depending on that sector's own price elasticity of demand. Second, any resources released from that sector are available for work elsewhere and should be able to find such work because overall real effective demand rises as costs and prices fall in a particular sector.

However, another implication of Currie's downgrading of the importance of conventional inputs in growth is that the contribution of this resource reallocation effect may be quite minor. Instead he would stress a third element, namely that with this overall increase in real effective demand, the productivity both of resources already employed and of those relocated to new sectors is enhanced by the greater opportunities for increasing returns in the Youngian sense as the overall size of the market expands. An increase in productivity in one sector thus expands real, effective, Sayian demand, which in turn leads to increasing returns generally, reducing costs and prices generally, and so expanding the size of the market once again. Thus the process is self-generating and self-perpetuating. Growth is the cause of growth and depends relatively little on a growth of the traditional factors. Growth could proceed unchecked even if unemployment contracted, as would be the case if productivity growth displaced labor which, because of poor mobility, failed to move to new occupations.

Thus, Currie's view of growth is not that it is due to technical progress embodied in new equipment but that growth itself, or policies that expand market size, permit existing resources to be used more productively. This also increases the funds available for research and development, another reason why technical progress is endogenous to the growth of real market demand. Furthermore, the self-financing nature of growth implies that developing countries ought to be able to grow without recourse to heavy foreign borrowing.

These views may be contrasted with the recent writings on growth and increasing returns by, for example, Paul Romer, Robert Lucas, and Maurice Scott.[46] Romer and Lucas emphasize the role of knowledge in increasing returns. The greater the output the greater the stock of knowledge, and this is assumed to yield an increasing marginal product. However, diminishing returns to research expenditures on knowledge creation and to the accumulation of capital are assumed. Investment in new knowledge by a single firm may also be socially suboptimal because the benefits are largely externalized. For similar reasons Scott believes that investment in physical capital is socially suboptimal, and so subsidies are justified.

All these approaches to increasing returns view the growth process largely as input-determined, with growth following on greater investment in research or physical capital that yield external benefits and some kinds of increasing returns. But the process is also associated with some offsetting diminishing returns that eventually yield a balance of forces and a slowing or even a cessation of growth. Thus, while these papers represent a significant advance on standard neoclassical growth models, they still differ significantly from the broader Young-Currie view of the way that growth itself breeds growth by extending the size of the market that in turn motivates and finances the growth of capital, more and/or better paid employment, more roundabout methods of production, new, more specialized firms and industries, pervasive external as well as internal econo-

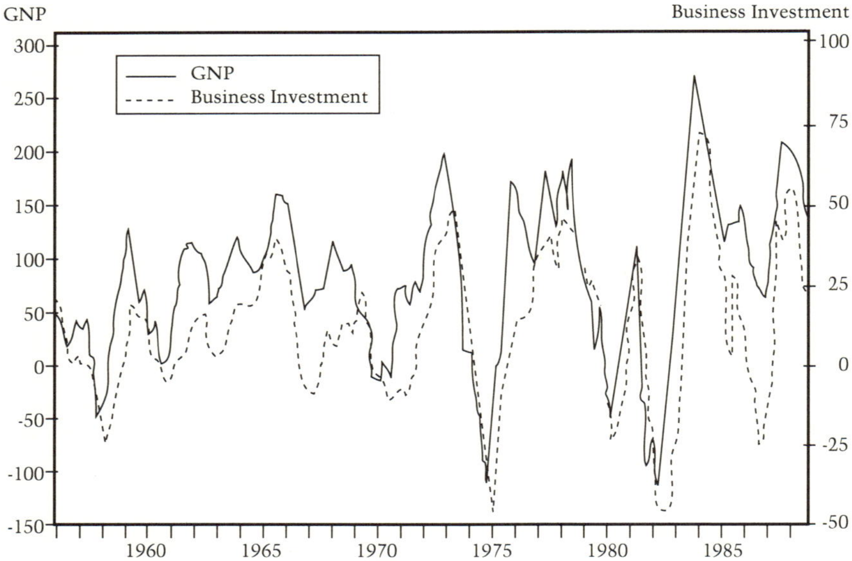

Note: Annual changes by quarters; 1982 prices.
Source: National Income and Product Accounts, U.S. Department of Commerce.

Figure 1. Changes in Business Capital Investment in Relation to Movements in GNP in the United States, 1956–88 (in billions of dollars)

mies, and the greater accumulation of knowledge and learning by doing.

Figure 1, which Currie prepared recently for his forthcoming book, is consistent with the view that in the United States the decision to invest is not the cause but the consequence of movements in GNP. It is a dependent or following sector. Other charts consistent with this show the relationship between movements in GNP and movements in the utilization of industrial capacity, profitability, and orders for capital goods. Normally, all these changes can be seen to precede changes in actual investment.

If the accumulation of capital, the expansion of employment, and changes in the way production is organized are constrained mainly by the growth of the market (GDP), then failure on the side of demand is the main constraint on further growth, and diminishing returns will mainly take the form of a decline in profitability. The role of policymakers is to ensure that real demand can be expanded to the maximum by removing obstructions caused, for example, by an overval-

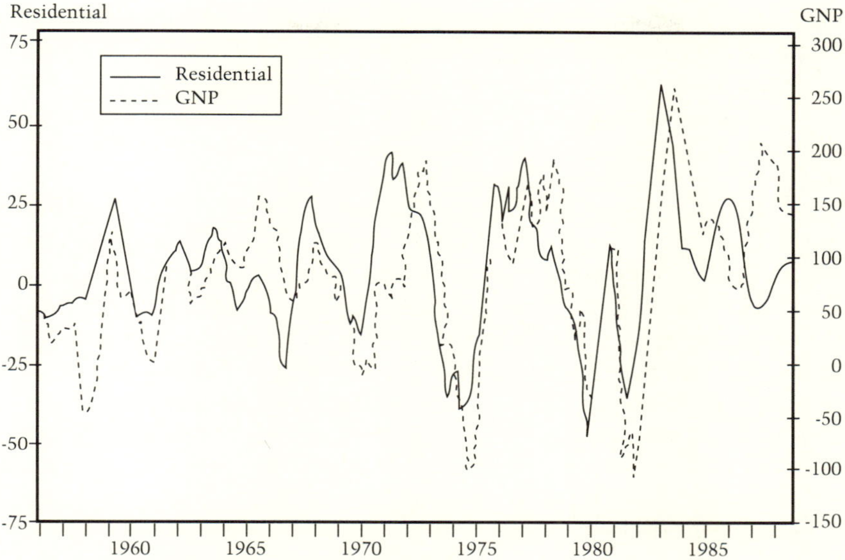

Note: Annual changes by quarters; 1982 prices.
Source: National Income and Product Accounts, U.S. Department of Commerce.

Figure 2. Changes in Residential Expenditure in Relation to Movements in GNP (in billions of dollars)

ued exchange rate that chokes off demand for exports, or by the difficulties inflation poses for increasing the flow of real loanable funds for construction as another potential leading sector. (The sequences indicated by figure 2, which Currie also prepared, are consistent with the theory that housing is a leading or independent sector in the United States and is amenable to significant expansion or contraction by policies that affect the main determinants of housing demand.)

It is the balancing of the growth of demand (size of the market) with the growth of supply that gives us equilibrium growth or, to use Allyn Young's words, a "moving equilibrium" or an "equilibrium rate of progress."[47] It is necessary to ensure that this equilibrium growth is at a high rather than a low level, by operating not only on the supply but perhaps more importantly on the *demand* for inputs and new methods and on the forces of competition and mobility.

Actually, Currie believes there may be no real inconsistency between those, like Nicholas Kaldor, who insist on a constant tendency to disequilibrium and those, like Paul Romer, who insist on a constant tendency to equilibrium. The difference appears to be more a difference arising from the angle from which one views growth. One can either view the growth-begetting-growth process as a continuous historical movement away from equilibrium or regard the constant adjustments to previous changes as an equilibrating process.[48]

If Currie's views on all this are valid insights into the true nature of the economic machine, the implications are, of course, profound, because they undermine the marginal productivity explanation of growth and income distribution and suggest radically different policies to promote faster development and better distribution. It is hoped that this book will help clarify the ways in which Currie's economic thought and method, while by no means eschewing marginalist analytics concerning prices and costs and the signals these give for the allocation of resources through mobility and competition, is, nevertheless, more rooted in a premarginal productivity and premarginal utility classical tradition that emphasizes the togetherness of economic phenomena, the reciprocal nature of overall supply and demand in the real sense, the key role of market forces of competition and mobility in distributing the fruits of growth, and the interpersonal, social nature of individual welfare or well-being.

Ultimately the well-being of individual microeconomic agents as producers or consumers depends on powerful, automatic, self-sustaining macroeconomic market forces. But these forces are not immutable. They can be modified, for good or ill, by the discretionary policies of central bankers, finance ministers, and planners who are guided, consciously or unconsciously, by the economic theories of their teachers and advisers and by their willingness to stick with sound policies even when these conflict with the siren calls of the demagogues for short-term over long-term popularity and success.

CHAPTER 14

Epilogue

A Summary Overview and Assessment

In his late eighties Currie has over sixty years experience as a professional economic thinker and practitioner. His interests and contributions have covered the entire field. They have ranged from the psychological motivations that drive the individual as worker and consumer; to the nature of the interplay between them as individuals, with stress on man as a social animal whose self-esteem derives from the esteem of others; to the nature of the economic and social growth process which in turn is driven by these powerful individual cravings for recognition and acceptance that, in a monetary exchange economy, people believe, rightly or wrongly, are best satisfied by higher money incomes and what money will buy; to a critique of these goals, and the distinctions between needs and wants ("too much is not enough"), between individual and social well-being, between physical privation and social (relative) deprivation at the national and the international levels and in the different contexts of developed and underdeveloped countries.

In terms of macroeconomic relationships he has explored the links between the behavior of the individual on the one hand and group or aggregate behavior on the other, on guard always against the possible fallacy of composition in moving from the former to the latter. Just as it is impossible to understand the nature of economic aggregates without an understanding of individual motivations and behavior, so it is impossible fully to understand the constraints facing the individual unless macroeconomic variables are understood and resolved: the appropriate level and growth of the money supply, aggregate savings relative to their offsets, the external value of the currency relative to its internal value, international monetary flows and indebtedness, and aggregate market demand both in monetary or Keynesian terms and in real or Sayian terms.

To have some idea of what the ecomonic system is capable of producing requires a knowledge of the resources available—natural, manmade, and the potential labor force—but, perhaps more importantly, of the potential technology and form of organization that transforms inputs into outputs for eventual delivery to final consumers.

As far as the resources are concerned, and their distribution geographically and by sector, Currie has kept himself very fully and realistically informed. For him resources are not abstract units of land, labor, and capital—which is one reason why he prefers words to graphs and equations—but instead are described by detailed quantitative and qualitative information on such things as mineral deposits and soil types, and their location relative to actual and potential markets, transport links, and other infrastructure; by demographic details of population and its growth, rural-urban migration, training and retraining needs and opportunities at all levels; and by details of investment in fixed plant, equipment, and inventories, overall and by sector. Though not a mathematician—a grave handicap in modern economics which so greatly values mathematical or symbolic presentation—he has a severely logical mind, an outstanding grasp of quantitative magnitudes, and a remarkable intuitive feel for their reasonableness and relative importance. This enables him to work in fruitful symbiosis with mathematically trained economists.

He is as likely to be found in concentrated study of statistical tables and individual industry reports as of abstract theoretical writing. He by no means downgrades the importance of theory but he values ideas for their utility rather than because they are fun to play with. So he will move back and forth continually from the abstract to the concrete and from the concrete to the abstract, seeking to generalize from the particular and, from the generalizations, to develop policies that will affect in predictable ways both individuals and aggregates. The device of the *reductio ad absurdum* and of imaginative analogies he has often found valuable and illuminating.

Currie's more recent thinking on the nature of the growth process has convinced him of the fundamental importance of technology, the conditions that promote the more rapid adoption of higher, more physically productive techniques, and the respective roles of the market and policy in this process of technological and organizational transformation.

His own detailed study of individual sectors of the economy, such as housing, the cement, iron, and steel industries, transport, and agriculture, and within agriculture, coffee, cotton, beef cattle, dairy cattle, and flowers, and his wartime and postwar work on procurements for and from the aircraft, munitions, and electronics industries, for example, have given him an unusual variety of insights into interdependencies, institutions, actual work practices, and the technological choices available—from the most primitive to the most advanced, from the mule to the jet. This in turn has helped him understand the economic factors that favor or obstruct the introduction of the most productive methods. The obstacles are both natural and man-made.

Over time, and especially as a result of living in an underdeveloped country for forty years, he has been more and more impressed by the silent workings of natural economic forces in allocating resources and promoting more productive technology and organizations. There is a need for intervention but the intervention has to be guided by a profound understanding of and respect for the underlying forces of the economic system itself so that the right levers are pulled, oil is applied to the right parts, and treatment given for the underlying problems rather than to symptoms alone. Administrative capacity is limited and is costly. Therefore, it must be used economically, like any other resource. This means that policy must be strategic, with scarce administrative resources applied only to key parts, as to the key log in a log jam.

Currie's development of the ideas of his Harvard mentor, Allyn Young, has led him to appreciate the fundamentally self-perpetuating nature of the growth process, in which Young's statement that "the division of labor depends on the division of labor" and Currie's that "the rate of growth depends on the rate of growth" are not mere tautologies. Correct or misguided policies can of course boost or retard the underlying growth-promoting market forces. But Currie's stress on the interacting and reciprocal nature of supply and demand, so that every extension of the market sets in motion forces tending to enlarge the market (and production) still more, has caused him to focus not on the scarcity of conventional inputs of labor and capital but on the conditions that have given rise to the poor use of these resources, on the grave impediments to mobility that result in open and disguised unemployment of these resources, and on the conditions that favor the more rapid adoption of new technology.

Increasing output depends only to a relatively small extent on the growth of conventional inputs. Instead, the extent and character of the employment of resources of all kinds, especially labor, depend on the overall size and the sectoral pattern of output, or on market demand in the real sense. However, although employment is more the consequence than the cause of increased output, and although Currie has in general opposed labor-intensive make-work programs as unnecessary and second-best, employment is nevertheless highly desirable for its own sake and as a means of distributing more widely the fruits of economic growth.

As his thinking has evolved along these lines he has, as has been noted already, become more and more impressed by the silent forces of the market and the need to give these freer rein in general. But the market forces can perpetuate a slow as well as a fast growth rate. Government policy, therefore, still has an important role to play, not only in what may be called the passive sense of ensuring that market forces are permitted to operate more freely, with fewer impediments to competition and mobility in response to price signals, but also in the more active sense of ensuring that latent real demand, especially for leading sectors such as housing, other construction, and exports, is fully exploited and promoted by active policy measures.

So Currie is, and has been for most of his professional life, an intriguing, eclectic mixture of economic liberal and economic planner. His approach can perhaps best be summed up in his own introduction to a paper delivered in 1975 at a conference in Panama:

> When I was asked to prepare a paper for this symposium it was suggested that I stress the use of the market mechanism. I conscientiously attempted to do so but I am afraid that although I have a great respect for the power of economic incentives and the efficacy of decentralised decision making, I am still an inveterate planner. Despite my good intentions, the State reappeared, but I hope in acceptable collaboration with the use of economic incentives. The "invisible hand" became two hands, the traditional one working more or less silently through economic incentives, and the more visible one of national policy making. The resulting strategy is a mixed one, difficult to classify. I distrust labels. Personally, I would not call myself a monetarist nor a Keynesian, nor a believer in intervention nor the market, nor a structuralist nor a neo-classicist but a little of all of these, and am prepared to use policies involving elements of all these approaches when the attainment of certain goals appears to make their use appropriate.[1]

This paper elaborated on the respective roles of the public and private sectors in accelerating growth through a strategic leading sector approach. It dealt explicitly with the mixed economy, the predominant form of economy in Latin America and likely to remain so, whatever the preferences of the ideologues of either the left or the right. Based, therefore, on the pragmatic and relevant assumption that progress must be accomplished through the more efficient management of the mixed economy, he concluded that policy should be directed

> both to accelerate the rate of growth through judicious intervention in the market mechanism and to make the basic underlying assumptions of the non-interventionists more realistic. Thus the use of the Leading Sector Strategy implies also action to heighten rather than reduce mobility. It favors not only direct measures to reduce the size of families but fairly drastic changes in socio-economic environmental factors to the same end as well. The quicker unskilled labour can be made scarce, the more effective will be the redistributive action of the Government. The more rapidly, in particular, agricultural labour becomes scarce and worth more, the stronger the incentive to mechanize and to abandon very small and uneconomic sized holdings. Whatever can be done to encourage competition, secure freely moving interest rates in the short run, maintain price stability or, in its absence, protect especially important sectors such as exports, savings, longer-term borrowings, and utility rates from the distortions created by inflation, would be eminently worthwhile.
>
> . . . High and sustained growth appears desirable in developing countries if only to restrain demographic growth and to make possible a raising of standards of housing, diets, health and education of the poorer groups of the economy. Directing more of the flow of new production to this end, in mixed economies, is infinitely less socially and politically disrupting than trying to redistribute an existing stock. But . . . a high and sustained rate in itself facilitates high and sustained rates. . . . This is an implication of the dictum that the profitability of specialization and the division of labour is limited by the size of the market.

In a more recent paper Currie has commented on the importance of the cultural environment in which the economic adviser has to work, with particular reference to the Colombian context. It reveals both the frustrations and the challenges that he has found in his own work:

> In explaining the handicaps under which the Invisible Hand works and indeed the type of economic advice adopted, it is first necessary to say a few words on the culture of the society in question, using the word in the sense of the body of beliefs generally held. In this sense the culture has a profound influence on the type of policies adopted.

In Colombia and . . . most Latin American countries there is little faith in the market. Everything must be controlled and regulated. The rise in prices is generally thought to be due to speculation, hoarding and monopoly. The economic system, by itself, is thought to make the rich, richer and the poor, poorer. This tendency, it is generally believed, must be resisted by direct intervention of the State. The minimum wage scale must be set as otherwise employers would, it is believed, exploit workers. . . .

It is true that many controls and regulations are ineffective in what is euphemistically called the "informal" sector, but that is what enables it to exist. However, they do raise costs in the larger and more modern type of enterprises where the main hope for progress and competitiveness in world markets lies.

Colombia must be one of the most legalistic and, at the same time, lawless countries in the world. Naturally the two characteristics are related as the more pervasive the controls, the more the evasion. All imports require permits in advance and customs duties are very high. Consequently, contraband is general and fairly open. Since there is a chronic "shortage" of exchange, capital export and the possession of assets in foreign currencies are forbidden. As might be expected, all people with means possess unreported foreign assets. The society of constructors recently stated that five hundred legal requirements must be observed to build a house. Naturally many are evaded, particularly in what is called self-construction.

. . . The culture which underlies the resort to controls impedes and places obstacles to the functioning of a mixed market economy and reduces the competitiveness of the "modern" sector in world markets.

. . . There are a considerable number of economists in Colombia, many of whom have received advanced training abroad. But the economics of the people who make economic policy is usually that of the man in the street. Regrettably, in this type of economics in all countries, what is sound is generally unpopular; what is popular is generally unsound.[2]

Concluding Comments

Currie in his late eighties has maintained a work routine which, in its intensity, is not very different from that at earlier periods of his life. One of the few concessions he makes to age is that he has tried to stick more to routine. It economizes on thought. He has tried to reduce, but not eliminate, speaking engagements and consultancy that involve travel or other arrangements that disrupt the routine.

But he is still (early 1990) at home both in the ivory tower and in the hurly-burly of the street and his "real world" office. His time is divided between the offices of the Colombian Housing Finance Institute, which defends the system that Currie founded, the classrooms of the University of the Andes, the tennis courts of the Club de las Americas, his farm on the Sabana de Bogotá, and his home in the attractive Santa Ana suburb of Bogotá whose tranquillity is punctuated only by the staccato of automatic rifle fire on the practice ranges of the nearby cavalry headquarters. This keeps one alive to the turmoil and violence that blight a beautiful country in rapid but erratic and painful transition.

Currie's most satisfying occupation he finds at weekends and public holidays, which are spent in hard physical work (helped by his mayordomo, a Putumayo Indian) digging and planting the land at his small farm in Cota, fifteen miles from Bogotá. Here he conducts experiments to discover which of the hundred or more different varieties of iris he has imported are most suited to the climate and soils of the highland Sabana of Bogotá. He hopes that some of them will be blooming there, long after his writings are forgotten. At his farm he will also be found talking with neighboring farmers about their dairying work or negotiating with contractors over wells and pumps, electricity supplies and repairs to the house.

Invariably his wife Elvira will be there too. She will be keeping a discrete but watchful eye on the small, wiry frame, at once rugged and frail, of her husband. And, as she has done for thirty-five years, she will be doing all in her power to maintain, at some considerable personal sacrifice, as smooth a domestic routine as possible and so facilitate, alleviate, and make more productive the enormous volume of work that he has undertaken in otherwise very difficult circumstances. Her help in this has been invaluable, as it also has been in the raising and education of their two children, Ronald and Elizabeth, to enable them to handle the joys and pains of life and, sadly too soon in the case of their son, death in an enchanting, challenging, and overwhelming country. Also supportive is his American son, Roderick, who makes frequent trips to Colombia from his home in California.

In June 1989 he accepted an invitation to address a forum on "Organizing for Development" in Oslo. This incidentally gave him an opportunity to stop off in Washington to collect new studies on the sources of growth by Edward Denison and others, have luncheon with William Cline of the Washington Institute of International Economics, meet old friends such as Robert Nathan, and, most impor-

Elvira Wiesner de Currie, 1987.

tantly, seek specialist medical advice on a heart condition that had been giving him trouble for some months. He was suffering from an erratic heart that manifested itself in alternations of excessive tiredness interspersed by a few days of his old vigor when he was able to play tennis fairly comfortably.

The Oslo-Washington trip upset his routine and in August he suffered a heart problem that laid him off work for two weeks.[3] Reluctantly he was forced to ask for a postponement of the annual Lauchlin Currie Tennis Tournament organized by the Banco de la República. But he doggedly returned to his work at ICAVI and to his weekly classes at the University of the Andes which he had been persuaded to continue because of their popularity. He was soon feeling fit again and looking forward to delivering conference papers to the American Society of Realtors in Washington and to the Inter-American Housing Union in Lima.

Despite nearly forty years residence in Colombia, Currie remains culturally a Canadian or, as he would prefer to say, a Nova Scotian. Canadians in general and especially those of the Maritime Provinces and of his generation, are hard-working, honest, people of their word, punctual, and suspicious and uncomfortable in the presence of or expression of strong emotion. Currie has shared these characteristics. He once remarked that he could not recall ever having been kissed by his mother, to whom nevertheless he was very close. He has been very critical of demagogues, of people who do not keep their word or who are unpunctual. He made his peace with the generally unpunctual Colombians by always having with him his briefcase full of work.

This obsession with work is perhaps more a personal characteristic than a cultural one. Whatever he does he does with complete absorption. When he was an instructor at Harvard in the depths of the Great Depression, living on $2,500 a year and supporting eight people, he put in twenty-five hours a week teaching, read and graded some 160 honors theses, monitored exams, was chief usher at football games, *and* produced some excellent publications. He has said that in his Washington years he "worked like crazy" and, somewhat later, did the same as a dairy farmer. He is not proud of this characteristic, calling it apologetically an obsession. He rarely takes a holiday. A substantial part of his life has been spent at a desk, intensely absorbed in whatever he happened to be engaged on.

In Washington he also carried on an intense social life, being invited to and accepting a host of meals and receptions, smoking and drinking freely. When nature rebelled, it took the form of attacks of pneumonia. He is now rather more careful. While reserved with strangers he is outgoing and vivacious with intimates, though always a very hard taskmaster. With his critics and opponents, but also with friends, he can be rough and aggressive in debate, exposing fallacious reasoning and not letting his opponents easily off the hook. This approach often wins him respect, and sometimes enemies. Since his early days at Harvard, he has sought out and helped able students. At Simon Fraser University he was renowned for his participation in an informal club of graduate students. In Colombia, his association as a professor at the National University, the Universidad Javeriana, and especially the University of the Andes resulted in continuous contact with the ablest students either as assistants or in recommendations for scholarships abroad.

His attachment to Colombia and Colombians runs deep, rising above the many frustrations and disappointments. His family's native land is now very much his own adopted home. And, while he will never lose sight of how much is still to be achieved, he must surely take much silent satisfaction at his own considerable role in the progress he has seen. Every day and everywhere he goes he sees the results of his thinking—branches of the indexed savings/mortgage system in all parts, the main highways of the country, the airports at which one arrives and departs. Rarely is such satisfaction given to economic advisers.

He would stress that most of Colombia's progress, as in other countries, is the result of the silent workings of market forces. But intelligent policy can help these forces move more quickly along the desired paths. Currie's achievement has been first to help the country attain some of the more discernible benefits of better policy; but a second, less tangible, but possibly more lasting and pervasive contribution is surely his elucidation, for the benefit of future generations of economists and policymakers, of the underlying nature of the economic system in its organic togetherness. Ultimately it is dispassionate understanding, not impassioned demagoguery, that is needed if this organism is to be nourished. Even when cultivating his irises, it is not his passionate affection for these plants that ensures they flourish, but his quiet, painstaking experimentation with different varieties in different soil types, different applications of fertilizers, careful irrigation and drainage, and meticulous recording. A final pleasure from irises is that they do not answer back or resist his policy prescriptions.

Notes

Preface

1. A travel grant was also generously provided by the Colombian Coffee Federation.

1. The Early Years, 1902–25

1. Herbert Stein, *Fiscal Revolution in America* (Chicago: University of Chicago Press, 1969).

2. Currie's own footnote: "Probably a mispelling for Lüneburg, the site of Bach's favorite organ."

3. "LSE in Retrospect," *LSE Magazine* 72, November 1986.

2. "Enter Here and Grow in Wisdom": The Harvard Years, 1925–34

1. A scholarly account of the development and nature of Harvard's economics faculty, and particularly Taussig's role, in the years just prior to Currie's arrival is given by Byrd L. Jones, "Institutionalization of Economics at Harvard University," in William J. Barber (ed.), *Institutionalization of Economics* (Middletown, Conn.: Wesleyan University Press, 1988). Also see Edward S. Mason on the history of Harvard's economics department in the *Quarterly Journal of Economics* 97:3, August 1982, pp. 383–433.

2. "Domestic Stability and the Mechanism of Trade Adjustments to International Capital Movements," in E. H. Phelps-Brown (ed.), *Explorations in Economics: Notes and Essays Contributed in Honor of F. W. Taussig* (New York: McGraw-Hill, 1936), pp. 46–56. Reprinted by Augustus M. Kelly, New York, 1967.

3. "Increasing Returns and Economic Progress," *The Economic Journal* 38, December 1928, pp. 527–42.

4. Nicholas Kaldor, "What is Wrong with Economic Theory," *Quarterly Journal of Economics* 89:3, 1975, pp. 347–57.

5. These lecture notes, edited by the present writer, are to be published in a special issue of the *Journal of Economic Studies,* 1990.

6. See David Rees, *Harry Dexter White: A Study in Paradox* (London: Macmillan, 1973), p. 37.

7. John Kenneth Galbraith, *A Life in Our Times* (New York: Houghton Mifflin, 1981), p. 48.

8. Richard Goodwin, "My Life and Times in the Shadow of Keynes," in Omar F. Hamouda and John N. Smithin (eds.), *Keynes and Public Policy After Fifty Years* (New York: New York University Press, 1988), p. 141–45.

9. The conflicting demands of career and family brought many strains to their marriage, which ended in divorce in 1954. Dorothy died of a heart attack in Washington in 1964. Their son Morgan, who became a journeyman electrician on Nantucket Island, also died of a heart attack in 1980. Rod Currie became one of the early computer experts and settled in California where he still lives.

10. The topic may have been suggested by Allyn Young, since Young had undertaken a similar study on bank deposits and lending policy in *An Analysis of Banking Statistics for the United States* (Cambridge, Mass.: Harvard University Press, 1928).

11. Charles Kindleberger, *The World in Depression, 1929–39* (Los Angeles: University of California Press, 1986), p. 96.

12. According to the "Standard Trade and Statistics Earnings Bulletin" for July 1933, quoted in an undated "Note on Stock Prices and Earnings, 1928–29" in Currie's files, the price-earnings ratio for common stocks reached a not outrageously high peak of 17.1. The average for 1929 before the crash was 15.8 It averaged 14.1 in 1927 and 14.0 in 1928.

13. Senate Hearings on S. R. 71, 1931, p. 134. Testimony of Dr. Miller, quoted disapprovingly by Currie in the revised (1932) chapter 4 of his Ph.D. dissertation, p. 65k.

14. Lionel Robbins, *The Great Depression* (New York: Macmillan, 1934), p. 53. Quoted by J. K. Galbraith, *The Great Crash* (Harmondsworth, England: Penguin, 1961), p. 15.

15. See George D. Green, "Ideological Origins of the Revolution in American Financial Policies," in Karl Brunner (ed.), *The Great Depression Revisited* (Boston: Martinus Nijhoft, 1981), pp. 229–30.

16. See E. A. Goldenweiser, *American Monetary Policy* (New York: McGraw-Hill, 1951), and W. Thomas, "Use of Credit in Security Speculations," *American Economic Review* 25, 1935, pp. 21–30. This view is also endorsed in a recent, much-publicized book by William Greider, *Secrets of the Temple: How the Federal Reserve Runs the Country* (New York: Simon and Schuster, 1987), p. 298.

17. There were two main extensions. The first (chapter 4) was introduced to express more forcibly the distinction between money and other types of credit. He concluded that the ambiguities and inconsistencies in the definition and use of the term "credit" were so great that it would be better if the term was abandoned altogether in favor of more specific terms such as money (means of payment), time deposits, and loans.

The second extension (chapter 8) was a theoretical discussion of the advantages and disadvantages of security loans to explain how Federal Reserve policy in 1928–29 had been disastrously affected by failure to understand the economic effects of such loans.

18. The following papers were based in large part on what was contained in the Ph.D. dissertation: "The Decline of the Commercial Loan," *Quarterly Journal of Economics* 45, August 1931, pp. 698–709; "The Treatment of Credit in Contemporary Monetary Theory," *Journal of Political Economy* 41:1, February 1933, pp. 58–79; and "The Failure of Monetary Policy to Prevent the Depression of 1929–32," *Journal of Political Economy* 42:2, April 1934, pp. 145–77. Also in his dissertation was part of his critical review of H. L. Reed, *Federal Reserve Policy, 1921–1930*, in *American Economic Review* 21, March 1931, pp. 162–64. An "exchange" between Currie and Reed

appeared in the September 1931 issue of *AER*, pp. 501–2. Several other papers dealing with related issues also appeared in these journals between 1932 and 1935, and his 1934 book dealt comprehensively with monetary theory, the nature of the United States banking structure, and implications for policy and institutional reform.

19. *The Paper Pound*, a reprint of the Bullion Report, edited by Edwin Cannan, p. 46; quoted by Currie, *Bank Assets and Banking Theory*, 1931, p. 5.

20. Annual report of the Federal Reserve Board, 1923, p. 33, cited by Currie, *Bank Assets and Banking Theory*, p. 75. Currie was later to hear such arguments advanced even more frequently when he became involved in advising on monetary policy in Colombia.

21. Currie dealt more fully with the defects of the U.S. banking structure in *The Supply and Control of Money in the United States*, 1934.

22. Currie, *Bank Assets and Banking Theory*, p. 262. See also "The Decline of the Commercial Loan," *Quarterly Journal of Economics*, August 1931.

23. Currie's views on the behavior and significance of the performance of stock prices in 1929 find confirmation in G. J. Santoni, "The Great Bull Markets 1924–29 and 1982–87: Speculative Bubbles or Economic Fundamentals?" Federal Reserve Bank of St. Louis, *Review* 69:9, November 1987, pp. 16–29.

24. *Bank Assets and Banking Theory*, pp. 113–16, and *Journal of Political Economy*, April 1934, pp. 150–51.

25. Kindleberger, *The World in Depression*, p. 61, writes: "There is an important school of thought which believes that whatever goes up must come down, and that it cannot come down unless it has gone up." He cites Robbins and Roepke as exponents of such views, though Kindleberger's own chapter on the late 1920s is entitled "The Boom."

26. Donald Winch, *Economics and Policy: A Historical Survey* (London: Hodder and Stoughton, 1969), p. 230.

27. Figures given by Peter Temin, *Did Monetary Forces Cause the Great Depression?* (New York: W. W. Norton, 1976), p. 4, reveal an increase in real GNP of 37.7 percent, 1922–29, equivalent to an average annual growth rate of 4.7 percent. The GNP price deflator was 98 in 1922 and 100 in 1929. Population growth averaged about 1.8 percent per annum over this period.

28. Currie, *The Supply and Control of Money in the United States* (1934), p. 186.

29. Ibid.; and Milton Friedman and Anna Jacobson Schwartz, *A Monetary History of the United States, 1867–1960* (Princeton, N.J.: Princeton University Press, 1963), chart 16, p. 197.

30. *The Economic Journal*, March 1935, pp. 128–31.

31. Friedman and Schwartz, *A Monetary History*, p. 410. Ironically, the year before Friedman and Schwartz published this book, Friedman's Chicago colleagues, Harry Johnson, Albert Rees, and Earl Hamilton, selected Currie's 1934 "Causes of the Depression" paper for the *JPE Landmarks* volume referred to above. These Landmark papers were selected for "the quality and importance of empirical data, originality and validity of analysis, general excellence, impact upon professional economists or combination of these factors."

32. Currie, *American Economic Review* (1931), and *Bank Assets and Banking Theory*, p. 107. Currie also criticized Reed's confused use of the term "credit" to mean alternatively loans and demand deposits. Reed adopted a broad definition of "money"

to measure "credit" conditions and, in Currie' view, was therefore led to exaggerate the degree of monetary expansion that was being permitted in 1928 and 1929. Friedman and Schwartz also focus on a broad definition of money and so they also differ from Currie's assessment of policy in some respects.

33. Thomas Humphrey, "The Role of Non-Chicago Economists in the Evolution of The Quantity Theory in America, 1930–50," *Southern Economic Journal*, 1971, pp. 12–18; and Don Patinkin, *Essays On and In the Chicago Tradition* (Durham, N.C.: Duke University Press, 1981), especially pp. 277–78, and 296–97. But there is a brief discussion of Currie's estimates of the money supply, 1921–33, in Milton Friedman and Anna Jacobson Schwartz, *Monetary Statistics of the United States: Estimates, Sources, Methods* (New York: National Bureau of Economic Research, 1970), pp. 268–69.

34. J. K. Galbraith, *Money: Whence it Came, Where it Went* (Boston: Houghton Mifflin, 1975), pp. 210–11. Galbraith, an old friend whom Currie had helped bring to Washington in 1940, inscribed Currie's copy of this book with the words: "For Lauchlin Currie, a singular and distinguished hero of this history."

35. Humphrey, "The Role of Non-Chicago Economists," p. 14.

36. *American Economic Review* 25, June 1935, p. 339.

37. Review of J. W. Angell, *The Behavior of Money: Exploratory Studies*, in the *American Economic Review*, December 1936.

38. Currie, "Money, Gold and Incomes in the United States, 1921–32," *Quarterly Journal of Economics*, November 1933, pp. 77–95; J. W. Angell, "Money, Prices, and Production: Some Fundamental Concepts," *Quarterly Journal of Economics*, November 1933, pp. 39–76; and Currie, "A Note on Income Velocities," *Quarterly Journal of Economics*, February 1934, pp. 353–54.

39. See Don Patinkin, "Keynes and Econometrics: On the Interaction Between the Macroeconomic Revolutions of the Interwar Period," *Econometrica* 44:6, November 1976, pp. 1107–8.

40. Currie, "Member Bank Reserves and Bank Debits," *Quarterly Journal of Economics* 47, February 1933, pp. 349–56.

41. Ibid.

42. John Maynard Keynes, "Member Bank Reserves in the United States," *The Economic Journal*, March 1932; reprinted in *The Collected Writings of John Maynard Keynes* (London: Macmillan, 1983), vol. 11, pp. 427–33.

43. Joseph Schumpeter, *Business Cycles 1919–29* (New York: McGraw-Hill, 1939), p. 856.

44. See Carol S. Carson, "The History of the United States National Income and Product Accounts: The Development of an Analytical Tool," *Review of Income and Wealth*, 1975, pp. 153–81.

45. See Currie, "The Treatment of Credit in Contemporary Monetary Theory," *Journal of Political Economy* 41:1, February 1933, pp. 58–79. See also the references to Currie in Lester V. Chandler, *American Monetary Policies, 1928–41* (New York: Harper and Row, 1971), pp. 10–11.

46. Karl Brunner, "The General Position of Currie's Work in Monetary Theory," Introduction to 1968 edition of Currie, *The Supply and Control of Money in the United States*, pp. ix–x.

47. Widely divergent movements in the means of payment (M1) and wider measures

of liquid assets caused great confusion in, for example, the United Kingdom in the period after 1979 when Mrs. Thatcher assumed power and attempted the control of quantitative monetary targets. The reasons for the confusion were poorly understood and such targeting was later abandoned, leaving monetary policy in an even more confused state. See, for example, David Smith, *The Rise and Fall of Monetarism* (Harmondsworth, England: Penguin, 1987). As we shall see, similar confusion has existed in recent years in Colombia where it is common to hear commentators blame inflation upon an increase in savings.

48. Currie, "Money, Gold, and Incomes in the United States, 1921–32," p. 92. In the light of adjustments to the income data Currie adjusted these estimates to 2.58 and 3.26, respectively, in his subsequent "Note on Income Velocities," *Quarterly Journal of Economics,* February 1934, pp. 353–54.

49. Angell, "Money, Prices, and Production," p. 75.

50. Friedman and Schwartz, *A Monetary History,* chart 16, p. 197.

51. Patinkin, *Essays On and In the Chicago Tradition,* p. 283.

52. Quoted in Patinkin, *Essays On and In the Chicago Tradition,* p. 296.

53. M. Friedman, "The Monetary Theory and Policy of Henry Simons," *Journal of Law and Economics* 10, October 1967, pp. 1–13.

54. For further discussion of Currie's arguments in favor of discretionary monetary control as against Simon's case for mechanical rules, in the context of Currie's proposals for the changes embodied in the 1935 Banking Act, see Donald F. Kettl, *Leadership at the Fed* (New Haven and London: Yale University Press, 1986), pp. 48–50.

55. Patinkin, *Essays On and In the Chicago Tradition,* p. 254.

56. Currie, "The Failure of Monetary Policy," p. 174.

57. Currie, *The Supply and Control of Money in the United States,* p. 42.

58. Friedman and Schwartz, *A Monetary History,* p. 302.

59. The power to make discretionary changes to reserve requirements was not granted to the Federal Reserve Board until the 1935 Banking Act, most of which was drafted by Currie when he was working de facto as personal assistant to the new Board chariman, Marriner Eccles. This is discussed in chapter 3.

60. Currie, "The Treatment of Credit in Contemporary Monetary Theory," *Journal of Political Economy,* February 1933, p. 77.

61. See Currie, "Member Bank Indebtedness and Net Demand Deposits in the Federal Reserve System," *Quarterly Journal of Economics* 46, May 1932, pp. 509–25; "The Failure of Monetary Policy," April 1934; and *The Supply and Control of Money in the United States,* 1934.

62. Currie, "The Failure of Monetary Policy," p. 175.

63. Peter Temin, *Did Monetary Forces Cause the Great Depression?* and "Notes on the Causes of the Great Depression," in Brunner (ed.), *The Great Depression Revisited,* esp. pp. 112–17.

64. Don Patinkin, *Money, Interest, and Prices,* 2d ed. (New York: Harper and Row, 1965).

65. See G. C. Archibald and R. G. Lipsey, "Monetary and Value Theory: A Critique of Lange and Patinkin," *Review of Economic Studies* 26, October 1958, pp. 1–22; and L. Harris, *Monetary Theory* (New York: McGraw-Hill, 1981), esp. pp. 73–77. Harris also noted (pp. 104–7) that Alfred Marshall had mentioned the role of price expectations in influencing the demand for money.

66. I am indebted to Byrd Jones for this point.

67. Peter Lindert, in Brunner (ed.), *The Great Depression Revisited,* pp. 129–30. It is interesting to note also that Robert Gordon and James Wilcox, "Monetarist Interpretation of the Great Depression," ibid., p. 66, downgraded the importance of money in explaining the depression because the observed link between the broad definition of money (including time deposits) and incomes in the 1920s led them to predict a smaller fall in income than actually occurred after 1929. This result is obtained only because broad "money" increased faster than incomes in the 1920s. But the money supply, exclusive of time deposits, rose much more slowly than income in the 1920s. Had Gordon and Wilcox used Currie's definition of money in their simulations they would have observed a more powerful monetary explanation for the decline in income. Brunner's critique of the papers by Temin and by Gordon and Wilcox is devastating: Brunner, "Epilogue: Understanding the Great Depression," ibid., pp. 316–58.

68. Brunner, Introduction to Currie, *The Supply and Control of Money in the United States* 1968, p. xxiv.

69. Currie, *The Supply and Control of Money in the United States* 1934, p. 147.

70. Ibid., p. 124.

71. Paul Samuelson, "Some Notions on Causality and Teleology in Economics," in Robert C. Merton (ed.), *The Collected Scientific Papers of Paul A. Samuelson,* vol. 3 (Cambridge, Mass.: MIT Press, 1972), p. 429.

72. Joseph Schumpeter, in *The Economics of the Recovery Program,* by D. V. Brown et al. (New York, 1934). For further discussion of the contemporary views on the causes of the depression from economists such as Schumpeter, Wesley Mitchell, Alvin Hansen, and Sumner Slichter, see W. J. Barber, *From New Era to New Deal: Herbert Hoover, the Economists, and American Economic Policy, 1921–1933* (Cambridge and New York: Cambridge University Press, 1985), chapter 5.

73. For a detailed account of these policies see Herbert Stein, *Fiscal Revolution in America,* chapter 2.

74. J. Ronnie Davies, "Chicago Economists, Deficit Budgets, and the Early 1930s," *American Economic Review,* 1968, pp. 476–82. In *The New Economics and the Old Economists* (Ames: Iowa State University Press, 1973), pp. 104–6, Davies also describes the opposition to unbalanced budgets in the early 1930s of Harvard economists L. P. Ayres, C. J. Bullock, and W. L Crum. Davies does not mention Currie's work during this period.

75. Stein, *Fiscal Revolution in America,* p. 36.

76. Currie, "The Failure of Monetary Policy," p. 176. See also J. Pierce in K. Brunner (ed.), *The Great Depression Revisited,* p. 259.

77. See Currie, *The Supply and Control of Money in the United States,* chapter 12.

78. James Angell proposed a 100 percent reserve plan in 1935 which he also saw as a means to eliminate "nearly all discretion" in monetary policy. This, and Currie's criticism of it, is discussed in Joon-koon Lee and Donald C. Wellington, "Angell and the Stable Money Rule," *Journal of Political Economy* 92, 1984, pp. 972–78.

79. Currie, *The Supply and Control of Money in the United States,* p. 178.

80. These points were explored in more detail in Currie's contribution to *Explorations in Economics: Essays Contributed in Honor of F. W. Taussig.*

81. Currie, *The Supply and Control of Money in the United States,* appendix, pp. 187–94.

3. The Treasury and Federal Reserve Board, 1934–39

1. In writing about Currie, "another of the notable Canadians who, in their selfless way, had come south to rescue the republic," John Kenneth Galbraith remarked, in "Maynard Keynes and the Mandarin Revolution," *Harvard Magazine*, May–June 1973, p. 27: "In economics one should never be right too soon. The shrewd scholar always waits until the parade is passing his door and then steps bravely out in front of the band." One such johnny-come-lately, in Currie's view, was his former rival at Harvard, Seymour Harris, whose subsequent reputation as a progressive Currie rather resented.

2. E. H. Phelps-Brown (ed.), *Explorations in Economics: Notes and Essays Contributed in Honor of F. W. Taussig* (New York: McGraw-Hill, 1936), pp. 46–56.

3. See Patinkin, *Essays On and In the Chicago Tradition*, p. 268. Some eighty-five pages of correspondence between Currie and Viner is deposited with the Jacob Viner papers in Princeton University Library.

4. Other members included Harry White, who stayed on at the Treasury for many years as Morgenthau's assistant, eventually becoming under-secretary, and Carl Shoup, the distinguished public finance expert.

5. Edward S. Mason, "The Harvard Department of Economics from the Beginning to World War I," *Quarterly Journal of Economics* 97:3, August 1982, p. 422.

6. Currie, *The Supply and Control of Money in the United States*, pp. 88–89.

7. It was later published with the reprinted edition of *The Supply and Control of Money in the United States* (New York: Russell and Russell, 1968), pp. 195–226.

8. Many years later (see chapter 13 below) Currie was to explore the implications of varying reserve requirements on the costs and benefits to banks of handling the demand deposit portion of a nation's money supply. Higher reserve requirements reduce bank earnings from deposits. This leads them to insist that their customers hold larger balances. This in turn affects the demand for money as a proportion of income, or the income velocity of circulation.

9. In a later memorandum entitled *The 100% Reserve Plan*, submitted to Federal Reserve Board Chairman Marriner Eccles, August 12, 1938, Currie noted (p. 17) that time deposits for a number of banks he had studied turned over on average at a rate of less than once a year. Under the 100 percent reserve plan banks would therefore have much less need to worry about the liquidity of their assets.

10. Currie, *The Supply and Control of Money*, p. 225.

11. Ibid.

12. See Arthur M. Schlesinger, *The Politics of Upheaval* (Boston: Houghton Mifflin, 1960), p. 237.

13. Marriner Eccles, *Beckoning Frontiers* (New York: Alfred A. Knopf, 1951), p. 132. See also Sydney Hyman, *Marriner Eccles: Private Entrepreneur and Public Servant* (Stanford, Calif.: Stanford Graduate School of Business, 1976), p. 128.

14. For a discussion of the influence of the under-consumption thesis on other New Dealers such as Rexford Tugwell and Adolf Berle, see Winch, *Economics and Policy: A Historical Survey*, p. 243.

15. Currie, "Comments and Observations" (on fiscal policy in the 1930s), *History of Political Economy* 10:4, 1978, p. 542.

16. Black later became the second president of the World Bank, a position he held when Currie was appointed to direct the first of the World Bank's country missions, to Colombia, in 1949.

17. Eccles, *Beckoning Frontiers*, p. 166.

18. Dated November 3, 1934, deposited with Eccles's papers in the University of Utah Library. Most of Currie's voluminous letters and memoranda to Eccles are also deposited there.

19. Eccles, *Beckoning Frontiers*, pp. 171–73. The account given by Sydney Hyman, *Marriner Eccles* pp. 157–60, more clearly distinguishes the contents of the memorandum from Eccles's additional comments on the need to make "sound assets" eligible. However, his remark that Eccles welcomed Currie's "refinements on points of detail" does not accurately indicate their respective contributions. For further details of this episode and a lively and comprehensive recent history of the New Deal, see Joseph P. Lash, *Dealers and Dreamers: A New Look at the New Deal* (New York: Doubleday, 1988), pp. 240–43.

20. One issue which Eccles and Currie both thought important for stability and efficiency was an extension of branch banking. Roosevelt, however, opposed this at the November 4 meeting on the grounds that it smacked too much of bigness.

21. Schlesinger, *The Politics of Upheaval*, p. 297.

22. Assisted by Martin Krost, Currie examined the justification for insuring demand and savings deposits in a 52-page *Report on Deposit Insurance*, 1934.

23. See Currie, *The Supply and Control of Money in the United States*, p. 211; and Eccles, *Beckoning Frontiers*, p. 222.

24. See G. D. Green, "The Ideological Origins of the Revolution in American Financial Policies," in Brunner (ed.), *The Great Depression Revisited*, p. 247. It is interesting to note that in Colombia and some other Latin American countries 100 percent reserve requirements have been imposed, from time to time, on additions to bank demand deposits.

25. See Friedman and Schwartz, *A Monetary History of the United States*, p. 448 on this aspect of the 1935 Banking Act, where they draw the distinction between monetary control and credit (lending) control, drawing attention to the fact that Clark Warburton had made this distinction in 1946. They again make no reference here to Currie, who wrote extensively on this distinction several years earlier.

26. See Eccles, *Beckoning Frontiers*, p. 228, and Kettl, *Leadership at the Fed*, p. 49. Currie explained how this new mandate accorded better with the monetary theory of central banking in a memorandum to Eccles, *The Relations of Government to Monetary Control*, March 29, 1935, pp. 17–18. Because it was not given this new mandate the Board was in later years subject to continuous attack over the constitutionality of its actions. Currie renewed his call for a change in *Comments on a Mandate*, memorandum to Chairman Eccles, April 5, 1938.

27. Anderson discussed this episode in chapter 57 of *Economics and the Public Welfare: A Financial and Economic History of the United States, 1914–1946*, first published in 1949 by Van Nostrand, but reprinted by the Liberty Press, Indianapolis, in 1979, with a foreword by Arthur Kemp, who characterized Currie as "a classic figure among the early members of the Chicago School" (p. 11). This is rather misleading since Currie was never at Chicago but it is noteworthy that Currie corresponded with

Professor Viner of Chicago in the preparation of his "A Reply to Dr. B. M. Anderson," *Quarterly Journal of Economics* 49, August 1935, pp. 694–704.

28. See Dean L. May, *From New Deal to New Economics: The Liberal Response to the Recession* (New York and London: Garland Publishing, 1981), p. 46.

29. This memorandum, together with another prepared later in the year with Martin Krost, *Federal Income-Increasing Expenditures, 1932–35,* was published together with an interesting assessment by Byrd L. Jones of Currie's contribution to New Deal fiscal policy in *History of Political Economy* 10:4, 1978, pp. 514–48. Byrd Jones contributed the entry on Lauchlin Currie in *The New Palgrave Dictionary of Economics* (London: Macmillan, 1988).

30. Keynes's *General Theory* developed the theory along rather different lines from Currie's. Currie was critical of various aspects of Keynes's "general" theory when it appeared, including the theory of a stable investment multiplier divorced from explicit discussion of accompanying changes in money and velocity, the declining marginal propensity to consume, and the absence of an adequate definition of money. Currie maintained that these problems in the Keynesian theory partly stemmed from Keynes's relative lack of interest in the empirical checks necessary to make theory useful for policy.

31. As Currie remarked later: "It took too little to keep people alive!" *History of Political Economy,* 1978, p. 545. Harry Hopkins did his best to spend as much as possible through the Works Progress Administration (WPA) but had to battle with Congress for additional appropriations and was also held back by the cautious bureaucratic approach of "Honest" Harold Ickes whose Public Works Administration was charged with major or permanent construction activities.

32. Currie, "Comments and Observations," *History of Political Economy* 10:4, 1978, p. 546.

33. Letter from Currie to Jacob Viner, September 23, 1935, in the Jacob Viner Papers, Princeton University Library.

34. Note that this was *not* a view supporting the chronic under-consumption or secular stagnation theses of Marx, Foster and Catchings, or Hansen.

35. Stein, *The Fiscal Revolution in America,* p. 166, and Alan Sweezy, *American Economic Review,* 1971, p. 120, incorrectly suggest that Currie subscribed to this idea which they rightly criticize as simplistic. But Sweezy also stated (p. 118) that the Currie-Krost "pump-priming" series (though it was never called that, but rather the "net contribution" series or similar term) was "a semantic triumph of the first magnitude."

36. Lash, *Dealers and Dreamers,* p. 318.

37. Published later as William A. Salant, "Taxes, the Multiplier and the Inflationary Gap," in a special issue on the "Origins of the Balanced-Budget-Multiplier Theorem," in *History of Political Economy* 7:1, 1975, pp. 19–27. William Salant, brother of Walter S. Salant, was for a time Currie's assistant in the White House.

38. Currie, "Stabilization of Purchasing Power through the Use of Public Credit," *American Economic Review* 27, 1937, pp. 233–34.

39. *History of Political Economy* 7:1, 1975, p. 11 and p. 45, respectively.

40. A similar point was made by Gottfried Haberler, "Multiplier Effects of a Balanced Budget: Some Monetary Implications of Mr. Haavelmo's Paper," *Econometrica* 14, April 1946, pp. 148–49.

41. See Stein, *The Fiscal Revolution in America,* pp. 123–24 for further discussion of how the economic significance of these transactions was concealed in the reported Treasury deficit: "The concealment of the Social Security Surpluses in the budget accounts contributed to the slowness with which the government and others recognized the extent to which the budget had shifted in a deflationary direction by early 1937."

42. Letter from Walter Salant to Lauchlin Currie, December 26, 1975. Currie comments: "Upon ceasing to receive the monthly series in 1942 Salant enquired the reason and was told that 'the calculated cash income and outlay of the Treasury, regularly published in the Treasury Bulletin, now serves essentially the same purpose.' Yet for 1941 the difference was over $800 millions on a $5,000 millions deficit. Even in 1975 the difference between the cash and national accounts concepts of the deficit was still being annually reconciled. . . . In one form or another the basic *concept* or tool of analysis of the unbalanced budget has never been more alive." *History of Political Economy* 10:4, 1978, p. 544.

43. See, for example, L. Harris, *Monetary Theory* (New York: McGraw-Hill, 1981), pp. 73, 106–7, where mention is made of the views of D. H. Robertson and others on this question. However, much of the modern debate on the distribution of the money supply turns not on the relative size of holding by type of holder, but on the somewhat different question of whether money is of the "inside" or "outside" variety, or whether debtors and creditors have the same spending propensities and, therefore, on whether, and for whom, money and/or bonds are "net wealth."

44. These results were originally presented in the 62-page *Report on the Large Deposit Study,* May 29, 1936, and referred to by Currie in his December 1936 paper to the American Economic Association, excerpts of which were published as "Stabilization of Purchasing Power Through the Use of Public Credit," *American Economic Review* 27, 1937, pp. 233–34. Full details and explanation were presented at the meetings of the American Statistical Association, December 1937, and published as "The Economic Distribution of Demand Deposits," *Journal of the American Statistical Association* 33, June 1938, pp. 319–26.

45. These results were reported in a paper entitled "Behavior of Deposits," presented to the Chicago Forum of the American Institute of Bankers, February 24, 1938.

46. For information on these battles and some of the details of memoranda prepared by Currie for Eccles's meetings with Roosevelt on the subject, see Hyman, *Marriner Eccles,* pp. 208–12.

47. Currie returned to this theme in a short memorandum, *The Causes of the Recession,* which he presented personally to President Roosevelt, November 8, 1937.

48. See Paul A. Samuelson, "The Balanced-Budget Multiplier: A Case Study in the Sociology and Psychology of Scientific Discovery," *History of Political Economy* 7:1, 1975, p. 44. In a 16-page memorandum, *Recommendations Relative to Research in Connection with the Formulation of Monetary Policy,* October 17, 1935, Currie documented many other deficiencies of the Commerce Department statistics which he hoped to remedy by recruiting senior economists for this purpose.

49. Currie also tried to recruit Arthur F. Burns from the NBER in 1936 but was unsuccessful. Many years later the Federal Reserve finally succeeded in securing his services at a rather higher level!

50. Currie, *Recommendations Relative to Research in Connection with the Formulation of Monetary Policy,* Washington, FRB, October 17, 1935, p. 14.

51. Carol S. Carson, "The History of the United States' National Income and Product Accounts: The Development of an Analytical Tool," *Review of Income and Wealth,* June 1975, p. 165. See also Don Patinkin, *Anticipations of the General Theory?* (Chicago: Chicago University Press, 1982), p. 246.

52. Currie, testimony, in U.S. Congress, TNEC, *Investigation of Concentration of Economic Power,* Hearings, pt. 9, 76th Congress, 1st Session, 1939, pp. 3494–3559.

53. See Lash, *Dealers and Dreamers,* pp. 376–80.

54. Stein, *The Fiscal Revolution in America,* p. 168. See also James Tobin, "Hansen and Public Policy," *Quarterly Journal of Economics* 90, 1976, p. 33, where he states that "in the crusade launched at the TNEC, Currie was Mr. Inside, and Hansen, Mr. Outside."

55. See W. J. Barber, *From New Era to New Deal: Herbert Hoover, the Economists, and American Economic Policy, 1921–33* (Cambridge: Cambridge University Press, 1985), chapter 9. See also W. J. Barber, "The Career of Alvin H. Hansen in the 1920s and 1930s: A Study in Intellectual Transformation," *History of Political Economy* 19:2, 1987, pp. 191–205, in which he discusses the Currie-Hansen TNEC testimony and Currie's later efforts to educate President Roosevelt on the theory of New Deal economics.

56. See Stein, *The Fiscal Revolution in America,* p. 164.

57. Leon Keyserling, "Discussion on the New Deal," *American Economic Review* 33, Papers and Proceedings, May 1972, p. 135.

58. "Some Theoretical and Practical Implications of J. M. Keynes' *General Theory,*" in *The Economic Doctrines of J. M. Keynes* (New York: National Industrial Conference Board, 1938), pp. 15–27.

59. See Don Patinkin, "Keynes and Econometrics: On the Interaction between the Macroeconomic Revolutions of the Interwar Period," *Econometrica* 44:6, November 1976, p. 1101. Reprinted in Patinkin, *Anticipations of the General Theory?,* p. 235.

60. Reprinted, with an introduction by Byrd L. Jones, in *History of Political Economy* 12:3, 1980, pp. 303–35. The main arguments of this paper were presented in an address before the Illinois Banking Association in Springfield, Illinois, May 23, 1938, entitled "Some Aspects of Business and Banking Developments in 1936 and 1937," 17-page mimeo in Currie's possession.

61. Jones, introduction, in ibid., p. 309. See also Lash, *Dealers and Dreamers,* pp. 327–28.

62. See Currie's memorandum to Eccles, *Some Monetary Aspects of the Excess Reserve Problem,* Washington, FRB, May 18, 1936.

63. See Green, "The Ideological Origins of the Revolution in American Financial Policies," pp. 247–48.

64. A more detailed analysis of the factors affecting bank assets was made in an earlier 20-page memorandum by Currie, *The Trend of Bank Assets in the Next Few Years,* FRB, November 30, 1936.

65. See Currie, "Causes of the Recession" (April 1938), *History of Political Economy* 12:3, 1980, p. 326, and Eccles, *Beckoning Frontiers,* p. 298.

66. Monthly data on currency plus demand deposits are given in Friedman and Schwartz, *A Monetary History,* p. 715.

67. Ibid., pp. 543–44.

68. Ibid., chart 62, p. 678.

69. See Currie's testimony to TNEC, *Investigation of Concentration of Economic Power,* Hearings, pt. 9, 76th Congress, 1st Session, 1939, chart 1-E.

70. Ibid., table 1e.

71. Walter S. Salant, "The Spread of Keynesian Doctrines and Practices in the United States," in Omar F. Hamouda and John W. Smithin (eds.), *Keynes and Public Policy After 50 Years* (New York: New York University Press, 1988), chapter 5.

72. Two weeks later Eccles met the President to present a memo entitled *Summary of Program to Combat the Recession,* October 31, 1937, containing several of Currie's suggestions. For an interesting discussion of the struggle between Eccles and Morgenthau to win the President's support for their very different programs for recovery at this time, see May, *From New Deal to New Economics,* pp. 117–19.

73. This was a theme dear to Eccles also at this time. See Hyman, *Marriner Eccles,* pp. 238–39. Currie's evidence before the TNEC emphasized the variability of housing expenditures, their much smaller offset to savings compared with the 1920s, and the possibilities for rectifying this.

74. Ibid., pp. 240–41.

75. See Currie's letter to Viner, June 13, 1938, regarding his *Causes of the Recession* memorandum (Jacob Viner Papers, Princeton University Library).

76. Stein, *The Fiscal Revolution in America,* p. 165.

77. May, *From New Deal to New Economics,* p. 155.

78. See Stein, *The Fiscal Revolution in America,* pp. 119–23. Also see Albert Lepawsky, "The Planning Apparatus: A Vignette of the New Deal," *American Institute of Planners Journal,* January 1976, p. 25, for details of Currie's activities at this time as a member of the Industrial Committee of the National Resources Planning Board, under the chairmanship of Tom Blaisdell.

79. See Currie's Memorandum, *United States' Railroad Equipment Authority,* December 2, 1938, Washington, FRB, 9 pages, in which he explains the advantages of renting and leasing compared with RFC emergency loan financing of railroad expansion programs.

4. In the White House: Peace and War, 1939–45

1. Eccles, *Beckoning Frontiers,* p. 333.

2. Schlesinger, *The Politics of Upheaval,* pp. 649–50.

3. Referring to his appointment to the White House, Albert Lepawsky, "The Planning Apparatus: A Vignette of the New Deal," p. 25, writes: "By 1939 Currie had become the fairest-haired economic planner in the New Deal. It was Currie, above all, who possessed that rare combination of intellectual charm and economic persuasiveness which was capable of restraining Roosevelt from relapsing toward the balanced budget."

4. Currie, "The Keynesian Revolution: Discussion," *American Economic Review* 33, Papers and Proceedings, May 1972, p. 141. For further discussion of Currie's intellectual and recruitment role in the New Deal, see J. K. Galbraith, "How Keynes Came to America," in *Economics, Peace and Laughter* (Harmondsworth, England: Penguin, 1975), pp. 36–49. Galbraith writes: "When the *General Theory* arrived they (Eccles and Currie) took it as confirmation of the course they had previously been urging. Currie, a brilliant economist and teacher, was also a skilled and influential interpreter of the ideas in the Washington community. Not often have important new ideas on econom-

ics entered a government by way of its central bank. Nor should anyone be disturbed. There is not the slightest indication that it will ever happen again."

For a description of Currie's role in bringing Galbraith to Washington in 1940—after failing earlier, in 1936, to recruit him as an agricultural economist at the Federal Reserve—see J. K. Galbraith, *A Life in Our Times*, p. 109.

5. David Halberstam, *The Best and the Brightest* (New York: Random House, 1972).

6. Schlesinger, *The Politics of Upheaval*, pp. 651–52.

7. Personal communication.

8. Eccles's memoirs, however, give the impression that Eccles managed to do most of the talking, something which he, like Roosevelt, loved to do. Nevertheless, it seems that Roosevelt developed some novel devices to keep Eccles quiet, such as inviting him to listen to Wagnerian operas, or to watch Roosevelt's dog playing with a ball and doing *its* business on the floor of the Oval Office! See Eccles, *Beckoning Frontiers*, pp. 243, 329.

9. See Currie's memoranda to the President, *RFC and the Budget*, November 15, December 11, 1939. The British government's privatization measures in the 1980s were partly motivated by this same opportunity.

10. In a letter to the President, December 19, Secretary Morgenthau insisted that high cash balances needed to be held by public corporations "for emergencies." Currie responded to this letter by noting that the virtually unlimited lending power of the Federal Reserve banks makes more than a small working balance uneconomical and unnecessary. Memorandum to the President, December 26, 1939.

11. Currie to Roosevelt, Official File 396. Currie noted that the memorandum "represents the progress to date of a line of investigation I initiated at the Reserve Board and which is today being carried on by the brilliant group of young economists in Harry Hopkins' office." This work, by Richard Gilbert, Robert Nathan, V. Lewis Bassie, and George Terborgh is described by Carol Carson, "The History of the U.S. National Income and Product Accounts," pp. 166–67, where she concludes that "Currie's interest in specific components of national expenditure blossomed into a full set of directly estimated gross national product components. These estimates were the statistical framework for appraisals of the economic situation which were circulated to high government policy makers and were being built into forecasting techniques with avowedly Keynesian inspiration." Other staff members, mentioned by Herbert Stein, *The Fiscal Revolution in America*, p. 168, included Walter Salant, Griffith Johnson, Don Humphrey, and Roderick Riley who were all committed to the Keynesian (or Currie-Krost-Keynesian?) approach. Shortly afterward this work was directed by Milton Gilbert who further strengthened his division with new recruits including Daniel Creamer, Charles F. Schwartz, William Shaw, Edward F. Denison, Wendell A. Hance, and George Jaszi.

12. Roosevelt to Currie, Official File 264. See also the paper by Byrd L. Jones, "The Role of Keynesians in Wartime Policy and Postwar Planning, 1940–46," *American Economic Review* 33, Papers and Proceedings, May 1972, pp. 125–33.

13. *Memorandum on Old-Age Pensions*, April 20, 1940.

14. Currie possesses numerous letters and memoranda relating to discussions, on specific army, navy, and air force requirements for equipment, trained manpower, and defense research. He also recommended conscription (July 31, 1940) and embargoes on strategic materials to Japan (July 16, 1940).

15. *Economic Report of the President,* Washington, 1985, p. 234. Real GNP rose by 16 percent in 1941, 15 percent in 1942, 15 percent in 1943, and 7 percent in 1944.

16. For further discussion of the differences of opinion between Keynes and the New Dealers in 1940–41, see Jones, "Role of Keynesians in Wartime Policy and Postwar Planning, 1940–46."

17. The friendly and constructive wartime cooperation between the United States and Canada is discussed in S. D. Pierce and A. F. W. Plumptre, "Canada's Relations with War-time Agencies in Washington," *Canadian Journal of Economics and Political Science* 11, 1945, pp. 402–19.

18. See Henry Morgenthau, *Morgenthau Diary (China),* (New York: Da Capo Press, 1974), vol. 1, p. 349; and Charles F. Romanus and Riley Sunderland, *Stilwell's Mission to China* (Washington, D.C.: U.S. Government Printing Office, 1953), pp. 13–15.

19. Michael Schaller, *The United States and China in the Twentieth Century* (Oxford: Oxford University Press, 1979), p. 61.

20. Ibid., p. 8.

21. Ibid., p. 84.

22. Currie's *Notes on Conference with Chou En-lai at British Ambassador's Home,* February 14, 1941. This, together with hundreds of other memoranda and letters by and to Currie concerning China, is deposited in the Hoover Institution of War, Revolution, and Peace, Stanford University. Some are also to be found in the Franklin D. Roosevelt Library at Hyde Park, New York.

23. Schaller, *The United States and China in the Twentieth Century,* p. 60.

24. In his report to Chiang Kai-shek dated February 24, 1941, entitled, *The Economic Problem.* A 34-page report was also submitted to President Roosevelt, March 15, 1941, together with 44 pages of notes on his 35 hours of interviews with Chiang Kai-shek and Chou En-lai. In these discussions Currie was extremely frank and was especially critical of Dr. Kung, the finance minister whom he urged the Generalissimo to replace by someone more honest and efficient. He recommended K. P. Chen as an alternative.

25. Letter to author, February 22, 1988.

26. Ibid.

27. Michael Schaller, *The U.S. Crusade in China, 1938–1945* (New York: Columbia University Press, 1979), p. 50.

28. For a vivid contemporary account of the immense strategic problems involved in the administration of the lend-lease programs to Britain, China, and later Russia, see Edward R. Stettinius, *Lend-Lease: Weapon for Victory* (New York: Macmillan, 1944). Details of Currie's role in organizing supplies for China are given in Romanus and Sunderland, *Stilwell's Mission to China,* chapter 1; and in Richard M. Leighton and Robert W. Coakley, *Global Logistics and Strategy, 1940–43* (Washington, D.C.: U.S. Government Printing Office, 1955), pp. 82–88. See also Robert E. Sherwood, *The White House Papers of Harry L. Hopkins* (London: Eyre and Spottiswoode, 1948), pp. 408ff.

29. For details of the work of CNAC, see William M. Leary, Jr., *The Dragons' Wings* (Athens: University of Georgia Press, 1976). When the Japanese cut off the Burma Road in early 1942 the CNAC was to play a vital role in its freight service over the "Hump" between India and China.

30. Schaller, *The U.S. Crusade in China, 1938–1945,* pp. 78–85. See also Larry I.

Bland (ed.), *The Papers of George Catlett Marshall, Volume 2* (Baltimore: Johns Hopkins Press, 1986), pp. 570, 657–59.

31. Morgenthau Diaries, vol. 3, pp. 742–43.

32. Schaller, *The U.S. Crusade in China, 1938–1945,* p. 75.

33. Ibid., p. 81.

34. Bland, *The Papers of George Catlett Marshall, Volume 2,* p. 659.

35. Leighton and Coakley, *Global Logistics and Strategy, 1940–43,* p. 105.

36. This episode is discussed in William L. Langer and S. Everett Geason, *The Undeclared War, 1940–41,* (New York: Harper and Brothers for the Council on Foreign Relations, 1953), pp. 710–11, 880–81.

37. Schaller, *The U.S. Crusade in China,* p. 83.

38. Ibid., p. 84.

39. See Barbara W. Tuchman, *Stilwell and the American Experience in China, 1911–45* (New York: Macmillan, 1970), p. 236, for further details on Chiang's offer of troops at this time to General Sir Archibald Wavell, the British commander-in-chief in India.

40. Forrest C. Pogue, *George C. Marshall,* vol. 2: *Ordeal and Hope, 1939–42* (London: MacGibbon and Kee, 1969), p. 356.

41. John Paton Davies, *Dragon by the Tail* (New York: W. W. Norton, 1972), p. 223.

42. In his history of the Second World War, Churchill wrote of these January 1941 meetings: "I told the President how much I felt American opinion over-estimated the contribution which China could make to the general war. He differed strongly. There were five hundred million people in China. What would happen if this enormous population developed in the same way as Japan had done in the last century and got hold of modern weapons? I replied that I was speaking of the present war, which was quite enough to go on with for the time being." Winston S. Churchill, *The Second World War* (London: Cassell, 1951), vol. 4, p. 119.

43. Tuchman, *Stilwell and the American Experience in China,* p. 318.

44. Ibid., p. 340.

45. Ibid., p. 323.

46. *Suggestions for Improving Sino-British Relations,* June 25, 1942, PREM 3/90/5A, Public Records Office, London. See also Christopher Thorne, *Allies of a Kind: The United States, Britain, and the War Against Japan, 1941–1945* (Oxford: Oxford University Press, 1978), pp. 189–91.

47. Acting on Currie's cable, Secretary of State Cordell Hull recorded that on August 12 President Roosevelt issued instructions to U.S. forces in India that they were to exercise scrupulous care to avoid the slightest participation in India's internal political problems. See Cordell Hull, *Memoirs* (New York: Macmillan, 1948), p. 1489.

48. Barbara Tuchman, in *Stilwell and the American Experience in China,* writes admiringly of Stilwell's soldierly qualities and deprecates his critics; but she notes (p. 330) that even Stilwell thought very highly of Wheeler. Schaller, *The U.S. Crusade in China,* p. 113, incorrectly speculated that Currie may have recommended Chennault as Stilwell's replacement.

49. Pogue, *George C. Marshall: Ordeal and Hope, 1939–42,* p. 368.

50. Tang Tsou, *America's Failure in China, 1941–50* (Chicago: University of Chicago Press, 1963), p. 98.

51. Thorne, *Allies of a Kind,* pp. 173–74.

52. Letter, Currie to author, March 17, 1988.

53. Eric Larrabee, *Commander-in-Chief: Franklin Delano Roosevelt, His Lieutenants, and Their War* (New York: Harper and Row, 1987), p. 542.

54. Letter to author, March 17, 1988. Romanus and Sunderland, *Stilwell's Mission to China,* p. 186, state that Marshall first consulted with Stilwell before supporting him so firmly. Stilwell had commented that the Chinese showed a clear disposition to coast and to let others finish the war, but also said that he was not concerned about his relations with the Generalissimo and claimed that he did not understand Currie's references to "strongly antagonistic feelings." However, in his diaries Stilwell made no attempt to conceal his deep contempt for Chiang. See Theodore H. White (ed.), *The Stilwell Papers* (New York: William Sloane Associates, 1948).

55. On August 13, 1948, Currie made a voluntary appearance before the House of Representatives Committee on Un-American Activities (HUAC) to make a Statement on his loyalty to the United States following unsubstantiated accusations by Elizabeth Bentley, a self-confessed former Soviet agent, that he had passed information, albeit unwittingly perhaps, to Communist agents. This is discussed in more detail in chapter 5 below.

56. Currie, memorandum, *Some Reflections on American Chinese Policy,* May 18, 1943.

57. See Gary May, *China Scapegoat: The Diplomatic Ordeal of John Carter Vincent* (Washington, D.C.: New Republic Books, 1979), pp. 96–108, for an account of Wallace's visit. See also chapter 5 below.

58. See Ted Morgan, *FDR: A Biography* (New York: Simon and Schuster, 1985), pp. 725–30, for an intriguing account of the events surrounding the nomination of Roosevelt's running mate in 1944.

59. May, *China Scapegoat: The Diplomatic Ordeal of John Carter Vincent.*

60. Schaller, *The U.S. Crusade in China,* p. 163.

61. Details of this period are drawn from the fourth and final volume of the impressive biography by Forrest C. Pogue, *George C. Marshall: Statesman* (New York: Viking Penguin, 1987), pp. 38ff.

62. Davies, *Dragon by the Tail,* p. 365.

63. Tuchman, *Stilwell and the American Experience in China,* p. 531.

64. Davies, *Dragon by the Tail,* pp. 338–41.

65. John King Fairbank, letter to author, February 22, 1988.

66. Joseph Alsop, letter to author, February 25, 1988. Alsop, a relative of the President, spent most of the first year of the war in a Japanese internment camp in Hong Kong but had known Currie in Washington. Currie helped secure his release from the navy to act as administrative assistant to Claire Chennault and engage in popular reporting.

67. The Harvard historian John Fairbank, who worked closely with Currie in documenting U.S. policy in China, tells of his use of Currie's White House office during this period in *Chinabound* (New York: Harper and Row, 1982), p. 289.

68. These and other details of his work at FEA are summarized in Currie's letter to Roosevelt, January 17, 1945, shortly after his return to full-time work at the White House. See also Dean Acheson, *Present at the Creation* (New York: W. W. Norton, 1969); and J. M. Keynes, *Collected Writings* (London: Macmillan, 1982), vol. 23, pp. 354–57.

69. Keynes, *Collected Writings,* vol. 23, pp. 355–56. Currie had met Keynes on various occasions in Washington in 1941. Roy Harrod, *The Life of J. M. Keynes* (London: Macmillan, 1963), p. 591, records one of Currie's later meetings with Keynes and the latter's alarming reaction when an adverse decision was communicated to him at a dinner in Currie's house. He gasped and clutched his breast on the side of his heart.

70. Currie discussed these issues in lengthy testimony before the Subcommittee on Foreign Trade and Shipping of the House Committee on Post-War Planning, September 28, 1944. This is discussed in Lloyd C. Garner, *Economic Aspects of New Deal Diplomacy* (Madison: University of Wisconsin Press, 1964), p. 267. See also *World Commerce: Free or Controlled?,* University of Chicago-NBC Radio Discussion by Lauchlin Currie, Neil Jacoby, and Nathaniel Pfeffer, September 9, 1945.

71. Keynes, *Collected Writings,* vol. 24, p. 252. See also Alan P. Dobson, *U.S. Wartime Aid to Britain* (London: Croom Helm, 1986), chapters 6–8.

72. Keynes, *Collected Writings,* vol. 25, p. 313.

73. Ibid., vol. 24, pp. 208–9.

74. Reported in James Edward Miller, *The United States and Italy, 1940–1950: The Politics and Diplomacy of Stabilization* (Chapel Hill and London: University of North Carolina Press, 1986), p. 106.

75. Ibid., p. 107.

76. Ibid., p. 115.

77. See Robin Winks, *Cloak and Gown: Scholars in America's Secret War* (London: Collins Harvill, 1987).

78. The *Washington Post,* April 7, 1944, carried a story on a dispute between Currie and the FEA representative in London, Winfield Riefler, over how hard a line to adopt toward Sweden. The United States had lost 60 planes and 600 men in bombing the ballbearing works in Schweinfurt, but SKF were now sending Swedish technicians to help re-build them. This caused indignation in Washington.

79. An excellent account of the issues and of Currie's mission to Bern in February–March 1945 is given by Arthur L. Funk, "American Wartime Relations with Neutral European States: The Case of the United States and Switzerland," in *Les Etats Neutres Européens et la Seconde Guerre Mondiale,* Neuchâtel, Switzerland: Editions de la Baconniere, 1985), pp. 283–302.

80. Letter to Secretary Henry Morgenthau, March 20, 1945. Orvis Schmidt later was director of the western hemisphere division of the World Bank.

81. Co-author with R. Dangerfield of *The Hidden Weapon: The Story of Economic Warfare* (New York, 1947).

82. Dingle Foot gave a graphic account of the negotiations in "Infighting on Neutral Territory," *The Times,* May 21, 1973.

83. A. L. Funk, "American Wartime Relations with Neutral European States," p. 296.

84. Morgenthau's letter to Currie, April 12, 1945. Currie wrote about these negotiations in Switzerland and of other efforts to achieve the restitution of looted property in a lengthy article, "Tumbling the Nazi Financial Redoubt," in the *New York Times,* April 29, 1945.

85. Reports of the Council of Foriegn Relations, EA 39, p. 8, 1943. I am indebted to William Diebold for this information.

5. Postwar America and the McCarthy Period, 1945–54

1. See Miller, *The United States and Italy, 1940–1950: The Politics and Diplomacy of Stabilization,* pp. 185–87.

2. See A. H. Chapman, *Harry Stack Sullivan: The Man and His Work* (New York: Putnam, 1976).

3. Thereafter the allegation that Currie was a Communist was repeated without qualification by sections of the press and by writers such as William F. Buckley, Jr., and L. Brent Bozell, *McCarthy and His Enemies* (Chicago: Henry Regnery Co. 1954).

4. See David Rees, *Harry Dexter White: A Study of Paradox* (London: Macmillan, 1973), chapter 23.

5. Robert K. Carr, *The House Committee on Un-American Activities* (Ithaca, N.Y.: Cornell University Press, 1952), pp. 216–17.

6. Ibid., pp. 153–65, for a full discussion of the Duggan case. See also Earl Latham, *The Communist Controversy in Washington: From the New Deal to McCarthy* (Cambridge, Mass.: Harvard University Press, 1966), pp. 199–201; and Walter Goodman, *The Committee: The Extraordinary Career of the House Committee on Un-American Activities* (New York: Farrar, Straus and Giroux, 1967), p. 267.

7. See Allen Weinstein, *Perjury: The Hiss-Chambers Case* (London: Hutchinson and Co., 1978), pp. 328–29.

8. Carr, *The House Committee on Un-American Activities,* p. 220.

9. See Latham, *The Communist Controversy in Washington,* pp. 169–70.

10. See Owen Lattimore, *Ordeal by Slander* (London: MacGibbon and Kee, 1952), for an account of these proceedings and the tactics employed to discredit him.

11. See the references to the official relations between Vincent and Currie in May, *China Scapegoat: The Diplomatic Ordeal of John Carter Vincent.* Vincent was subjected to particularly vicious treatment by HUAC, the McCarran Committee, and the Civil Service Loyalty Review Board. In 1950 an agent allegedly in the pay of Senator McCarthy even resorted to forgery in an unsuccessful effort to discredit Vincent while he was ambassador to Switzerland. Since it proved impossible to sustain the charge of disloyalty or that he was a security risk, in 1953 the new secretary of state, John Foster Dulles, cynically forced Vincent to retire on the grounds he had shown bad judgment. This ended, at the age of 52, Vincent's extremely promising career that could have had a significant influence in moderating the cold war and altering the course of U.S. policy in Indo-China which was to prove so disastrous.

12. This and other information in this section is based mainly on a lengthy statement sent to Senator Patrick McCarran on May 16, 1952, and also on letters and statements sent to Sumner Welles, January 7, 1953, and to the Department of State, July 5, 1954; the latter in connection with his application to renew his passport.

13. In a letter to the present writer dated July 17, 1989, however, Currie stated that he asked the professor of political science at Harvard for a name when Messersmith declined. He recommended Lattimore.

14. Hornbeck's version of events is reported in Latham, *The Communist Controversy in Washington,* p. 305.

15. Goodman, *The Committee* p. 252.

16. Freda Utley, *The China Story* (Chicago: Henry Regnery, 1951), p. 36.

17. See May, *China Scapegoat: The Diplomatic Ordeal of John Carter Vincent,* p. 190.

18. Ibid., p. 192.

19. Ibid., p. 196.

20. Ibid., pp. 151–52.

21. Ibid., p. 187.

6. The World Bank Mission to Colombia and Its Follow-Up, 1949–53

1. See Edward S. Mason and Robert E. Asher, *The World Bank Since Bretton Woods* (Washington, D.C.: Brookings Institution, 1973), pp. 161–62.

2. See L. Currie, *The Role of Economic Advisers in Developing Countries* (Westport, Conn.: Greenwood Press, 1981), p. 54; and the preface of *The Basis of a Development Program for Colombia,* report of a mission headed by Lauchlin Currie (Washington, D.C.: IBRD, 1950). My account of the 1949 World Bank mission to Colombia and subsequent developments is also based on Currie's personal notes and his voluminous correspondence with World Bank and Colombian officials. See also Mason and Asher, *The World Bank Since Bretton Woods,* pp. 161–63, 299–302, 649–57.

3. Currie (1981), *The Role of Economic Advisers in Developing Countries,* p. 61.

4. For this work additional help was obtained from V. Lewis Bassie who had helped Currie on this kind of pioneering work at the Federal Reserve Board in the 1930s.

5. See Mason and Asher, *The World Bank Since Bretton Woods,* pp. 657–62.

6. *Semana,* October 28, 1950, p. 7. The writer is informed that in Spanish this kind of "program" refers to the wiles of seduction!

7. Currie, "Some Prerequisites for Success of the Point Four Program," *Annals of the American Academy of Political and Social Sciences* 270, July 1950, pp. 102–9.

8. This report, together with the other 17 reports produced by the committee between October 1950 and July 1951, was published in the 370-page *Informe Final del Comité de Desarrollo Económico* (Bogotá: Banco de la República, 1951). This was reprinted in 1988 by the National Planning Department, Bogotá.

9. See Currie, *The Role of Economic Advisers in Developing Countries,* chapter 12, for a fuller examination of this project. Ironically the World Bank itself later ignored the recommendations of its 1949 team and poured some of its money into a profitless expansion of the Paz del Rio plant in 1956.

10. *Informe Final,* p. 87.

11. However, this report was not published until October 1952. Misión de Administración Pública, *Reorganización de la Rama Ejecutiva del Gobierno de Colombia* (Bogotá, 1952,) p. 448.

12. See Currie, *The Role of Economic Advisers in Developing Countries,* chapter 5. Spanish edition, *Evaluación de la Asesoria Económica a los Países en Desarrollo* (Bogotá: Fondo Editorial CEREC, 1984).

13. Currie made these remarks in a speech in Bogotá in August 1979 on the occasion of a dinner in his honor to mark the thirtieth anniversary of his arrival in Colombia. He went on to remark that his 1952 report on Caldas was reviewed ten years later by Mario Calderon who found that nothing had changed except the size of the popula-

tion. Currie's mission report was entitled *Programa Económico y Administrativo para el Departamento de Caldas* (Manizales: Imprenta Departamental, October 1952), p. 427.

14. *Informe Sobre el Departamento de Caldas, 1952.*

15. Albert Hirschman, *Development Projects Observed* (Washington, D.C.: Brookings Institution, 1967), chapter 1. A related idea of Hirschman's was the dubious economics and dubious morality of the "Principle of the Hiding Hand" by which government officials are urged to underestimate the true costs and exaggerate the true benefits of projects, to encourage more of them to be undertaken.

16. Peñalosa was later successively minister of agriculture, secretary-general of the UN Habitat Conference, and ambassador to the United Nations.

17. *Plan para el Departamento del Atlántico,* 1953.

7. A Farming Interlude, the Return to Economic Advising, and the Magdalena Valley Mission, 1954–60

1. Ronald died on October 23, 1988, at the age of 32, in an automobile accident when returning from the small farm near Bogotá that his father had bought the previous year for the cultivation of irises. He had pursued a career in private banking after taking degrees in economics and urban planning at the Universities of Durham and London, England. His sister, Elizabeth, graduated in sociology from Cambridge University and in business from the University of the Andes, Bogotá, before taking up a career with Colombia's central bank.

2. Currie, *Plan para la Reorganización del Ministerio de Fomento* (Bogotá: Ministerio de Fomento, 1959), mimeo, 57 pages.

3. *Programa de Desarrollo Económico del Valle del Magdalena y Norte de Colombia* (Bogotá, 1960), 379 pages.

4. *Estudio sobre la Conexión del Ferrocarril del Atlántico con Barranquilla,* Separatata de la Memoria del Ministro de Obras Públicas Virgilio Barco Vargas, a la Legislatura Ordinaria, Bogotá, 1960, 74 pages. Currie maintained his interest in this scheme through 1961 when he was coordinator of a transport mission to the Atlántico Department sponsored by the new minister of public works, Misael Pastrana. An innovation was to attach an English meat-marketing specialist to this mission because of the potential importance to the railroads of a substantial increase in meat exporting. In March 1961 Currie traveled to England and Holland to study meat marketing and to contract an expert for work in Colombia.

5. *Las Posibilidades de Desecación y Aprovechamiento Económico de 135,000 Hectareas Adyacentes a la Ciénaga Grande de Santa Marta,* in Separata de la Memoria del Ministro de Obras Públicas, Bogotá, 1960.

6. Under the auspices of the CVM Currie later undertook various studies of land use, reclamation, and conservation in the Region of the Magdalena and Sinú valleys. On forestry he emphasized the distinction between reforestation (planting) policies and afforestation, which relied more on natural processes by limiting access by man and grazing cattle through the creation of national parks and other means. See Currie, *El Manejo de Cuencas en Colombia* (The Management of Forestry in Colombia) (Bogotá: Ediciones Tercer Mundo, 1965).

7. Magdalena Valley Report, *Programa de Desarrollo Económico del Valle del Magdalena,* p. 37.

8. However, Currie also resisted populist calls for these revenues to be controlled by local municipalities. He preferred that they be controlled by the national or state government in order to avoid waste. In later years the theme of decentralization was to be increasingly promoted by what Currie continued to describe as populist or demagogic politicians who refused to acknowledge the waste involved, since it would encourage resources to flow to areas where the population is now rather than to where the population will inevitably gravitate (the urban centers) in the process of economic development.

8. The Origins and Development of Operation Colombia, 1960–67

1. For his 1960 study of the prospects for expanding meat exports from the Magdalena Valley region, see Currie, *Algunas Consideraciones sobre la Industria de la Carne en Colombia* (1961). The problems of raising cattle in the Llanos Orientales and the need for improved communications with Bogotá were an important part of his *Informe sobre un Estudio Económico del Departamento del Meta,* 1961.

2. Twenty years later this paradoxical idea was given respectability by Amartya Sen, *Resources, Values, and Development* (Oxford: Basil Blackwell, 1984), especially chapter 13. Whereas few people took notice of Currie's straight-forward diagnosis of *effective* demand for food, commentators applauded Sen's intellectual contribution because he coined the difficult phrase "food entitlements" to refer to the same idea.

3. A few years later, in 1964, he was told on good authority that Washington had instructed the U.S. ambassador, Fulton Freeman, to block Currie's appointment to any government posts. Thus, for example, his proposed appointment to the Monetary Board (Junta Monetaria) did not materialize. Part of Washington's displeasure arose from Currie's advice to the then minister of agriculture, Virgilio Barco, to change the basis of PL 480 wheat import agreements from dollar to peso financing, thus saving Colombia a lot of money.

4. John Maynard Keynes, *Essays in Biography,* p. 55.

5. Estimate derived, on the basis of an average housing unit of 50 m^2, from data on total urban housing construction given by Yezid Soler Barbosa, *El Ciclo de la Edificación en Colombia de 1926 a 1986* (Bogotá: Cámara Colombiana de la Construcción, 1987), table 22.

6. As discussed in chapter 9 below, Currie, on learning more about the bureaucratic nature of the existing state mortgage agency, the Banco Central Hipotecario, and its dependence on tax-exempt bearer bonds and commitment to fixed-interest loans, successfully pushed instead for a totally new competitive private housing finance system with index-linked liabilities and assets.

7. See Mason and Asher, *The World Bank Since Bretton Woods,* pp. 525–26.

8. Currie, *Accelerating Development: The Necessity and the Means* (1966).

9. Letter from Virgilio Barco to Lauchlin Currie, November 13, 1961.

10. President Lleras personally conferred Colombian citizenship on Currie in 1958.

11. Currie, "Report on Trip to Washington, June 12–20, 1961," memorandum to President Lleras, June 23, 1961, 6 pages.

12. At Currie's instigation the present writer undertook a study of the impact of the PL 480 wheat import program on Colombian agriculture and found that, with artificially low domestic wheat prices the elasticity of supply, at least in the downward direction, was extremely high. Within 15 years Colombia changed from being 90 percent self-sufficient in wheat to being 90 percent dependent on wheat imports. Too many of the pessimistic studies of supply elasticity in agriculture focus only on the very short run. See L. Dudley and R. J. Sandilands, "The Side Effects of Foreign Aid: The Case of PL 480 Wheat in Colombia," *Economic Development and Cultural Change,* 23:2, January 1975, pp. 325–36.

13. Gerhard Colm, at the Montevideo meeting in July 1961 that led to the creation of the Latin American Free Trade Association, suggested that a "Committee of Nine Wise Men" (the "Comité de los Nueve") be set up, consisting of the nine best economists in the world, to study Latin America's problems and recommend action. Carlos Sanz de Santamaría, Colombian ambassador to Washington, warned that this idea was naive and correctly predicted that the nine world-famous economists would inevitably be a dumping ground for ex-finance ministers. Jorge Méndez, who sponsored the ECLA-inspired plans at Colombia's National Planning Office, was one of these nine wise men.

14. Carlos Lleras later published the full Spanish text of *Operation Colombia* in the journal he directed, *La Nueva Economía* 1:4, August 1961. In the same issue Alvaro López Toro defended Carlos Lleras's criticisms ("Reflexiones sobre la Operación Colombia"), and Currie replied ("La Operación Colombia y sus Críticas"). Currie's *Operación Colombia: Un Programa Nacional de Desarrollo Económico y Social* had also been published earlier in August.

15. Technicians of Raul Prébisch's ECLA were working as advisers in Colombia's National Planning Agency, drawing up alternative plans.

16. Alfonsistas were followers of Alfonso López Michelsen who became President of Colombia in 1974. Ironically, in view of his apparent support for Operation Colombia in 1961, President López introduced measures in 1974 that severely weakened the new housing finance system that had been established in 1972 to support Currie's later urbanization strategy (see chapter 10).

17. Currie, *La Industria Cafetera en la Agricultura Colombiana* (1962). Study directed by Lauchlin Currie, pp. xvi, 150.

18. Currie returned to these same points in a report dated July 29, 1967, prepared for the Food and Agricultural Organization, Rome, *Notes on Material Prepared by David Wall and Harold Dunkerley on Coffee in Colombia.* Currie again expressed his skepticism of the diversification solution proposed, and emphasized the need for a broader frame of reference in undertaking individual crop studies.

19. Currie, *La Industria Cafetera,* p. 141. These, and related data, were reproduced in Currie, *Accelerating Development,* chapter 12.

20. Ibid., p. 143.

21. Currie, *Estudio Preliminar Agro-Económico de los Playones de Plato y Pinto* (1962), p. 66. In his studies of land reclamation projects Currie repeated his calls for effective valorization taxes as land values appreciated. This, rather than crude land redistribution, was usually Currie's idea of true "land reform."

22. Currie, *Estudio Agro-Económico Preliminar del Valle Aluvial del Río Sinú* (1962), pp. vi, 195.

23. Currie, *Informe sobre un Estudio Económico del Departamento del Norte de Santander* (1962), 86 pages.

24. Currie, *Estudio Agro-Económico de Recuperación de Tierras en la Región del Río Zulia* (1962), 81 pages. During this study Currie had another of his many conflicts with engineering companies who insisted on technical solutions—in this case to an irrigation-flood control problem—regardless of the economics.

25. Currie, *Estudio sobre el Algodón* (1963). See also, Currie, *Accelerating Development,* p. 174.

26. Currie, *Un Plan Socio-Económico para Atlántico* (1965).

27. Lauchlin Currie and Hugo Belalcázar, *Proyecciones de la Demanda de Construcciones y Materiales de Construcción en Colombia para 1962–70* (Bogotá: CAMACOL, 1962), 174 pages.

28. These ideas were later examined by Currie in greater detail in "The Exchange Constraint on Development: A Partial Solution to the Problem," *The Economic Journal* 81, December 1971, pp. 886–903.

29. This study by Currie was published later as *Una Política Urbana para los Países en Desarrollo* (1965).

30. Currie, *Alternativas para el Desarrollo Urbano de Bogotá* (1969).

31. These urban policy proposals, described in more detail in chapters 9 and 10 below, were published in L. Currie, *Ciudades dentro de la Ciudad* (1974), and L. Currie, *Taming the Megalopolis: A Design for Urban Growth* (1977).

32. Jacques Torfs, in a satirical article called "Operación Hormiguero" (Operation Anthill), July 1962, claimed that it was Currie's intention to create a "hostile revolutionary proletariat." A few months later Currie's ex-student Albert G. Hart turned up in town to say he had heard that he had a scheme for the *compulsory* transfer of people from the countryside.

33. Valencia achieved fame of sorts in 1964 when, in proposing a toast to General de Gaulle at an official banquet, he cried out, not "Vive la France," but "Viva España!"

34. In 1988 Alvaro Gómez, who had recently stood as the Conservative presidential candidate, was the victim of a sensational kidnapping by a guerrilla group, but was released unharmed after six weeks.

35. Later Currie learned of the analogous ideas regarding the need for a "critical minimum effort" that Harvey Leibenstein had advanced in his *Economic Backwardness and Economic Growth* (New York: John Wiley and Sons), 1957.

36. See Currie, "Economics and Population," *Population Bulletin* 23:2, April 1967, pp. 25–38.

37. Review by Albert O. Hirschman, *American Economic Review* 57:3, June 1967, pp. 611–13.

38. Currie, *Informe sobre la Escuela para Graduados* (1964), p. 15.

39. Currie, *Enseñanza de la Economía en Colombia* (1965), and *Enseñanza Universitaria en los Estudios Sociales* (1967).

40. Y. Larsson, P. de Wolff, and L. Currie, *Governmental Planning and Political Economy,* The Royer Lectures, Berkeley, University of California, 1967, pp. 53–88.

41. The minister of agriculture, Armando Samper Gnecco, appointed Currie as his representative on the Banco Ganadero.

42. Currie concluded, after his visit, that the UN FAO had no more relevance or purpose than would a UN shoemakers organization.

9. An Academic Interlude in Canada and Britain, 1967–71

1. Leibenstein, *Economic Backwardness and Economic Growth.* See also Richard Nelson, "A Theory of the Low-level Equilibrium Trap in Underdeveloped Countries," *American Economic Review* 46:5, December 1956, pp. 894–908.

2. See Currie's discussion of these ideas a few years later in "The Objectives of Development," *World Development* 6:1, 1978, pp. 1–10.

3. Paul Rosenstein-Rodan, "Problems of Industrialization in Eastern and South-Eastern Europe," *The Economic Journal,* 1943.

4. Hirschman, *Development Projects Observed* (1967), chapter 1.

5. In an otherwise very critical review of Gunnar Myrdal's famous book, *Asian Drama, Journal of Economic Issues* 3:2, June 1969, pp. 166–76, Currie tried to find something favorable to say. He therefore praised the excellent, long appendix on growth models. Its criticisms of the "illegitimate isolation" and "misplaced aggregation" of growth models was "devastating," said Currie. Only later did he discover that this appendix was written not by Myrdal but by Paul Streeten (with whom Currie was later to be associated at Oxford)!

6. Currie included a critique of this view in "Marketing Organization of Underdeveloped Countries," in R. Moyer and S. Hollander (eds.), *Markets and Marketing in Developing Countries* (Homewood, Ill.: Richard D. Irwin, 1968), pp. 117–29.

7. This article was translated and published in Colombia as "La Limitación de las Divisas al Desarrollo: Una Solución Parcial al Problema," *Revista de Planeación y Desarrollo* 3:3, October 1971, pp. 3–24.

8. Currie, "Social Development and Economic Progress," in J. G. Van Putten (ed.), *Local Government as Promoter of Economic and Social Development* (The Hague: IULA, 1971), pp. 19–32.

9. Dudley Seers, "Why Visiting Economists Fail," *Journal of Political Economy,* August 1962.

10. Dudley Seers, *Towards Full Employment* (Geneva: International Labor Organization, 1970).

11. The ILO report, paragraph 256, also projected a 6 percent annual growth in demand for agricultural products, about the same as their projected growth rate of national income. This supposed a far higher income elasticity of demand for agricultural products than ever experienced in Colombia, but it conveniently appeared to justify the emphasis on rural employment.

10. The Plan of the Four Strategies, 1971–74

1. For a discussion of the differences between the approaches of Currie and Seers on employment policy, see Fernando Cepeda Ulloa and Chistopher Mitchell, "The Trend Toward Technology: The World Bank and the International Labor Organization in Colombian Politics," in R. Albert Berry, Ronald G. Hellman, and Mauricio Solaún (eds.), *Politics of Compromise: Coalition Government in Colombia* (New Brunswick, N.J.: Transaction Books, 1980), chapter 8.

2. More detailed discussion of Currie's distinction between Keynesian and "Sayian" demand is to be found in chapter 12 below.

3. Lloyd Rodwin, Review of L. Currie, *Taming of the Megalopolis,* in *Journal of Economic Literature* 16:3, September 1978, pp. 1083–84.

4. Contrast the recent paper by Kevin M. Murphy, Andrei Schleifer, and Robert Vishny, "Income Distribution, Market Size, and Industrialization," *Quarterly Journal of Economics* 104:3, August 1989, pp. 537–64, in which, without fully considering the very low domestic price and income elasticities of demand for food and raw materials, they build a model of growth based on agriculture (and, more plausibly, exports) as a leading sector, whose prior development will "fuel" industrialization. Their paper reflects the continuing influence of the Lewis-Fei-Ranis model. At best, their model is only applicable to the most primitive underdeveloped economy. In it, when the industrial sector expands and the demand for food increases, wages fall because the agricultural production function is assumed to be subject to diminishing marginal productivity, with increased output requiring increased labor inputs. There is no suggestion that agricultural productivity may be endogenously related to the size of the market. (Contrast the discussion on increasing returns in the sense of Allyn Young in chapter 12 below.)

5. Similar views are presented in Jonathan Hartlyn, *The Politics of Coalition Rule in Colombia* (Cambridge: Cambridge University Press, 1988), pp. 131–34.

6. Miguel Urrutia's paper concentrated on supply constraints and insisted that the plan could not succeed because the construction sector was characterized by inelastic supply. He "proved" this by presenting a graph (p. 107 in the published proceedings referred to below) which purported to show that prices of production materials had risen faster than other prices. He obtained this result by using different base years for the price indices being compared. In the year when the overall price index was at the base of 100 the construction price index already stood at 110. Consistent data supplied by Colombian Chamber of Construction, CAMACOL, show a secular tendency for house prices (but not other construction prices) to fall relative to the overall price index, 1950–86. These figures even show a fall in the relative price of housing during the boom of 1973–74. See Yezid Soler Barbosa, *El Ciclo de la Edificación en Colombia de 1926 a 1986* (Bogotá: CAMACOL, 1987), table 22, p. 125.

7. *Controversia sobre el Plan de Desarrollo* Bogotá: Ediciones CORP, 1972.

8. Gustav Ranis, "The Exchange Constraint on Development—A Partial Solution to the Problem: A Comment"; and Currie, "A Reply to Professor Ranis," *The Economic Journal* 83, March 1973, pp. 203–10.

9. See R. J. Sandilands, *Monetary Correction and Housing Finance in Colombia, Brazil and Chile* (Farnborough, England: Gower Press, 1980), for details of the similarities and differences between the three countries' systems and their performance.

10. Currie, *The Role of Economic Advisers in Developing Countries,* pp. 46–47.

11. Currie, "The Colombian Plan 1971–74: A Test of the Leading Sector Strategy," *World Development* 2:10–12, October–December 1974, pp. 69–72.

12. Ibid., p. 71, and *Coyuntura Económica* (Fedesarrollo) 4:3, October 1974.

13. In a memorandum prepared in February 1974 for the Liberal presidential candidate, Alfonso López Michelsen, Jorge Méndez objected to the losses that the central bank incurred in managing these congealed funds. Currie commented that he seemed more preoccupied with making the central bank an individualistic profit-maximizer than a controller of the nation's money supply.

14. See, for example, Albert Goltz and Desmond Lachman, "Monetary Correction and Colombia's Savings and Loan System," *Finance and Development,* September 1974, pp. 24–26; and Miguel Urrutia, "Historia de Planeación en Colombia," *Revista de Planeación y Desarrollo* 18:3, 4, September–December 1986, p. 75. For a critique of these views and a vigorous defense of Currie's position, see Fabio Giraldo Isaza, *El Upac, La Politica Ecónomica y la Construccion,* 1970–87 (Bogotá: CAMACOL, 1987), chapter 4.

15. These distinctions were explained in "El Papel de la Demanda en la Teoría del Desarrollo," *Revista de Planeación y Desarrolo, 4:3, July*–December 1972, pp. 63–70, and more fully in an important article "The Leading Sector Model of Growth in Developing Countries," *Journal of Economic Studies,* N.S., 1:1, May 1974, pp. 1–16. James Hanson amplified Currie's ideas in the May 1976 issue of the above journal ("The Leading Sector Development Strategy and the Importance of Institutional Reform: A Reinterpretation"). In the May 1975 issue of this same journal Robert Barro discussed the beneficial effects of the Colombian monetary correction scheme on the rest of the capital market. ("Monetary Correction, Capital Markets, and Open Market Operations in Colombia.")

16. Currie (ed.), *El Plan de Desarrollo Colombiano en Marcha* [1974]. The other presenters were Roberto Arenas, Eduardo Sarmiento, Alberto Corchuelo, Gabriel Misas, Rodrigo Manrique, Eduardo Gaitán, Samuel Hoyos, Enrique Low, César Garcés, Antonio Hernández, and Alejandro Figueroa.

17. Currie, "La Política Monetaria y el Nivel de Precios," *Revista de Planeación y Desarrollo* 5:2, April–June 1973, pp. 20–45. (The review actually appeared in February 1974).

18. This episode is very reminiscent of the events surrounding the controversial resignation of Britain's Chancellor of the Exchequer, Nigel Lawson, in October 1989. Lawson objected to the Prime Minister, Margaret Thatcher, retaining a personal economic adviser, Sir Alan Walters, who was critical of the Chancellor's policies, which, among other things, involved the abandonment of monetary targets and a reliance on fixed exchange rates to control inflation. This involved a high interest rate policy that attracted a large inflow of foreign funds which, because they were not sterilized by the Bank of England, greatly increased the money base and the overall supply of money. Currie's 1936 paper, "Domestic Stability and the Mechanism of Trade Adjustment to International Capital Mobility," discussed in chapter 3 above, would be instructive here.

19. Currie discussed the full implications of these tax features in a July 1974 memorandum, "Taxation and Monetary Correction." This, together with more than twenty other of his memoranda presented to the President and/or the head of the DNP in 1973 and 1974, were put together as a mimeographed collection entitled, *Savings, Monetary Correction and Building: Essays on Interrelationships in Colombia* (1974), and published in Spanish as *Ahorro, Corrección Monetaria y Construcción* (1974).

20. See Currie, "La Unidad de Poder Adquisitivo Constante: Una Breve Historia de su Nacimiento," *Desarrollo y Sociedad* 6 (1983), pp. 5–12.

11. The "Cities-within-Cities" Design for Urban Growth

1. For example, Wilfred Owen, "Urbanización Planeada: Fin a la Ciudad Accidental," *Revista de Planeación y Desarrollo* 4:1, January–March 1972, pp. 23–36.

2. Wilfred Owen to Special Projects Division, World Bank, on his trip to Bogotá, June 22–26, 1971, Washington, D.C., July 26, 1971.

3. Currie, *The Role of Economic Advisers in Developing Countries,* chapter 11.

4. J. Douglas McCallum, *Bogotá: Urban Development Realities and Plans* (Geneva: International Labor Office, 1975). This report was subsequently published as a co-authored book by Harold Lubell and Douglas McCallum, *Bogotá: Urban Development and Employment* (Geneva: International Labor Office, 1978).

5. Alexander Cairncross, book review, *Journal of Economic Studies* 9:2, 1982, pp. 71–72.

6. Currie has explained these ideas in the writings mentioned earlier and in two books published a little later: *Ciudades dentro de la Ciudad: La Política Urbana y el Plan de Desarrollo en Colombia,* 1974, and *Taming the Megalopolis: A Design for Urban Growth,* 1976, especially chapter 14. See also "The Interrelation of Urban and National Economic Planning," *Urban Studies* 12, 1975, pp. 37–46, and "For Whom Should New Housing Be Built?" *Habitat International* 4:3, 1980, pp. 291–97. His 1976 book was published some years later in Spanish, with a new introduction, as *Urbanización y Desarrollo: Un Diseño para el Crecimiento Metropolitano* (Bogotá: CAMACOL, 1988).

7. "What Colombia (and Other Developing Countries) May Learn from Singapore," ESA/HBP/AC 9/43. He also presented one of the main theme papers of the seminar, "Urbanization Trends and Policies," ESA/HBP/AC 9/1. Currie later found a partial precedent in the new towns of Evry and Cergy-Pontoise, near Paris, which he visited in 1975. Moscow was another example he discussed: "Planeación Metropolitana; Moscú y Bogotá," *Revista de Planeación y Desarrollo* 8:3, September–December 1976, pp. 105–12.

8. In the event a marked slowdown in Colombia's average economic growth rate after 1974, with extremely severe, policy-induced recessions in the 1980s, naturally caused a considerable reduction in rural-urban migration and by 1988 Bogotá's population was still only around 5 million.

9. Thus, contrary to a suggestion by Ralph Gakenheimer, "New Towns-In-Towns for Developing Countries: A Comment," *Urban Studies* 13, 1976, p. 52, Currie's proposal did not involve the "nostalgic bucolic dimension" evoked by the phrase "towns-in-town." Gakenheimer claimed that the reason that the Bogotá plan referred to "ciudades dentro de la ciudad" was because "town" does not translate into Spanish. But Currie's original plan was written in English of course, and referred to "cities-within-cities."

10. See McCallum, *Bogotá: Urban Development Realities and Plans,* pp. 50–51.

11. The American Cities Corporation, *El Salitre: Una Ciudad dentro de la Ciudad* (Bogotá, DNP, 1974).

12. Robert Huck, *The Capture of the Land Value Increment: A Feasibility Study* (Bogotá: DNP, 1973), 149 pages.

13. Subsequently published as "Indexación: Selectiva o General?" in James Hanson (ed.), *La Corrección Monetaria: Cuatro Estudios* Santiago de Chile: Naciones Unidas, Instituto Latinoamericano para los Estudios Económicos y Sociales [UN-ILPES], 1976).

14. *Proyecto Ciudadela Comunitaria del CAN* (Bogotá: FONADE-Instituto Colombiano de Ahorro y Vivienda, November 1984). The study team comprised Lauchlin Currie, Luis Eduardo Rosas, Alvaro Montenegro, Rodrigo Villamizar, Rodrigo Gutiérrez, César Garcés, Rafael Obregón, Juan Manuel Salazar, and Jose Eslava.

15. These contrasting perspectives were brought out clearly in articles published

by Currie and Mario Calderon, head of the BCH, in *El Espectador,* February 23, 26, 1988, respectively.

16. Published as "Controlling Land Use: The Key to Urbanization," *Ekistics* 244, March 1976, pp. 1937–43.

17. The following account of events at the conference are drawn from Currie's extensive personal notes.

18. Santiago Salazar Santos.

12. Perspectives on the Future and the Past in the Light of Allyn Young, 1975–82

1. Eventually published in Spanish as *Recursos para el Futuro: Colombia 1950–2000* (1981).

2. The differences between the "technological" and the socioeconomic approaches to birth control are discussed by William Paul McGreevey, "Population Policy under the National Front," in R. Albert Berry, Ronald G. Hellman and Mauricio Solaún (eds.), *Politics of Compromise: Coalition Government in Colombia* (New Brunswick, N.J.: Transaction Books, 1980). McGreevey states (p. 423) that "no individual was more central to the formulation of population policy in Colombia than was Lauchlin Currie," mainly through his efforts to promote greater employment opportunities in the cities where fertility levels are much lower than in rural areas.

3. Currie, *The Role of Economic Advisers in Developing Countries.* The title, as so often, was chosen by the publishers. Currie objected unsuccessfully that it was a silly title because the role of advisers is to advise. He was interested in the *evaluation* of advice. The Spanish title reflects this better: *Evaluación de la Asesoría Económica a los Países en Desarrollo* (1984).

4. Sir Alexander Cairncross's review in the *Journal of Economic Studies,* 1982, has already been mentioned (chapter 11). Others included John Sheahan, *Wall Street Review of Books,* Winter 1983; Hans Singer, *Journal of Development Studies,* April 1983; Ian Livingstone, *The Economic Journal,* June 1984; J. R. Parkinson, *Third World Planning Review,* 1984; and Guy Pfefferman and Vinod Thomas, *Finance and Development,* March 1983. Miguel Urrutia's hostile review in the *Journal of Economic Literature* was also mentioned in chapter 11 above. Another acerbic review, describing the book as a "diatribe" and particularly critical of Currie's "obtuse" comments on agricultural policy, was written by Gerald O'Mara of the World Bank for the *Southern Economic Journal,* April 1983. In the *Business History Review,* 1982, Louis T. Wells, Jr., of Harvard, objected bitterly to Currie's criticism of the Harvard Development Advisory Service. This selection of reviews is interesting in revealing the depths of feeling that Currie's ideas so often arouse on both sides of a divide.

5. Currie, "The Objectives of Development," *World Development,* 6:1, 1978, pp. 1–10. Reprinted in Spanish in Currie, *La Política Urbana en un Marco Macroeconómico* (1983), chapter 1.

6. He referred to Harpo's headlong dash at any pretty girl he encountered.

7. Albert Waterston, *Development Planning: Lessons of Experience* (Baltimore: Johns Hopkins Press, 1965). The individual project approach to development is also clearly evident in a recent official survey of the World Bank's work by W. C. Baum and

S. M. Tolbert, *Investing in Development: Lessons of World Bank Experience* (Oxford: Oxford University Press for the World Bank, 1985).

8. Most recently in Currie's report, commissioned by the World Bank, *Some Aspects of Public Administration in Colombia,* mimeo, July 16, 1987, p. 170. Published in Spanish by the Comptroller-General's office, Bogotá, 1988.

9. Kaldor preserved extensive notes of Young's lectures at the LSE, 1927–29. (Those for 1927–28 were taken by Maurice Allen and transcribed by Kaldor.) These throw considerable light on Young's ideas on the nature of economic growth and the concept of "increasing returns" discussed below. They have not yet been published but Kaldor's literary executor, Professor A. P. Thirlwall, has kindly given the present writer permission to edit and publish these in a special issue (1990) of the *Journal of Economic Studies,* where they will appear with an introduction by Currie and the present writer, along with a reprint of Young's eleven remarkable but little-known entries in the 1929 edition of the *Encyclopaedia Britannica.*

10. Allyn Young, "Increasing Returns and Economic Progress," *The Economic Journal,* December 1928, p. 533.

11. Walter Salant has pointed out to the present writer that this statement sounds very much like Say's Law. There is indeed a connection, which is why Currie has so often insisted on the distinction between "Sayian" and Keynesian demand. But note that (a) this formulation distinguishes very different sectoral demand potentials and the associated intersectoral relations, thus linking macroeconomics and microeconomics, and (b) recognizes that inappropriate monetary policies can interrupt the real demand flows, which are expressed in terms of monetary exchanges.

12. World Scientific Banking Meeting on International Finance of Economic Development, Dubrovnic, October 31–November 5, 1977. Kaldor and Currie both presented papers at this conference. Currie referred to the contributions of Allyn Young in his paper, "Factors Conditioning the International Financing of Scientific and Technical Research for Developing Countries." He elaborated on this theme at a subsequent meeting of the same group held in Dubrovnic in 1980.

13. See Kaldor's references to Young in his 1985 Arthur M. Okun Memorial Lectures, *Economics Without Equilibrium* (Cardiff, Wales: University College of Cardiff Press, 1985), pp. 63–79. This is discussed below.

14. Currie, "Allyn Young and the Development of Growth Theory," *Journal of Economic Studies* 8:1, 1981, pp. 52–60.

15. N. Kaldor, "The Irrelevance of Equilibrium Economics," *The Economic Journal* 82, 1972, pp. 1237–55.

16. As Young emphasized: "The search for markets is not a matter of disposing of a 'surplus product,' in the Marxian sense, but of finding an outlet for a potential product." (Young, "Increasing Returns and Economic Progress," 1928, p. 537). In other words, new markets *create* production that would otherwise not exist nor be in surplus. Marx, following Smith, tended to miss this subtle but important distinction.

17. This tendency to equate the Smith and Young views on the *endogenous* nature of technical progress is most apparent in one of the few references to Young at the bicentennial celebrations of Smith's *Wealth of Nations* in Glasgow in 1976. See G. B. Richardson, "Adam Smith on Competition and Increasing Returns," in A. Skinner and T. Wilson (eds.), *Essays on Adam Smith* (Oxford: Clarendon Press, 1977), pp. 350–60. See also G. C. Reid, "Disequilibrium and Increasing Returns in Adam Smith's Analysis

of Growth and Accumulation," *History of Political Economy* 19:1, 1987, p. 92, and *Classical Economic Growth* (Oxford: Blackwell, 1989), especially chapter 8.

18. One interpretation of Smith's growth theory suggests that his focus was on the need for capital accumulation in agriculture because this sector provides the greatest potential surplus for investment even though it is manufacturing and, it seems, only manufacturing, that is subject to increasing returns. For related reasons the profit rate tends to fall as economic growth proceeds, thus eventually producing the stationary state rather than self-sustaining growth. See W. A. Eltis, "Adam Smith's Theory of Economic Growth," in Skinner and Wilson (eds.), *Essays on Adam Smith*, pp. 415–54, especially pp. 450–54 where the role of increasing returns is discussed.

19. *Encyclopaedia Britannica* (London, 1929), vol. 21, p. 580. Since 1921 Allyn Young had been an advocate of compensatory public expenditures and banking policies that reduce the extent of cyclical fluctuations. See Charles P. Blitch, "Allyn A. Young: A Curious Case of Professional Neglect," p. 15. In his LSE lectures Young explicitly noted that J. B. Say's view that absolute overproduction was impossible was dependent on the assumption (1) that the supply of money increases correspondingly with production and (2) a view of the world as a whole: "Taking each country by itself it may overproduce relative to the world demand for its products." See R. J. Sandilands (ed.), *Nicholas Kaldor's Notes on Allyn Young's LSE Lectures*, special issue of *Journal of Economic Studies* 17, 1990, lecture 36.

20. However, as was emphasized in chapters 2 and 3, Currie would maintain that an understanding of appropriate demand management in the sense of control over the flow of current monetary expenditures is not dependent on Keynes' *General Theory* and can equally be understood in terms of classical monetary theory, much of which he learned in Harvard classes on money and banking given by Allyn Young and from reading the early Keynes. Currie dedicated *The Supply and Control of Money in the United States* (1934) to Young's memory.

21. Currie, "The Objectives of Development," *World Development*, 1978.

22. Charles P. Blitch, "Allyn A. Young: A Curious Case of Professional Neglect," *History of Political Economy* 15:1, 1983, pp. 1–24.

23. See, for example, Kaldor, "The Role of Industrialization in Latin American Inflation," in D. T. Geithman (ed.), *Fiscal Policy for Industrialization and Development in Latin America* (Gainesville: University Presses of Florida, 1974).

24. A similar modern Colombian example would be the effect on agriculture (and other sectors) of the unification of what were effectively four separate countries into a single country, or national market, through the building of paved interregional, national highways and the Magdalena Railroad, which Currie helped initiate with his 1950 World Bank report and its follow-up, as described in chapters 6 and 7 above. Another example would be the development of refrigerated cargo planes which opened up the North American and European markets for Colombian flower producers, which quickly led to an astonishing boom in the export of flowers grown intensively on relatively little land close to the international airports.

25. See Kaldor's letter above, and Blitch, "Allyn A. Young: A Curious Case of Professional Neglect," p. 20. Blitch claims that Young was arguing here that an elastic demand for a product is a *necessary* condition for the functioning of Say's law. But Young himself does not make any such claim.

26. The reader is again referred to Currie's "Wants, Needs, Wellbeing and Economic Growth," *Journal of Economic Studies,* N.S. 2:1, May 1975, pp. 47–59.

27. Cf. Young: "Although the initial displacement may be considerable and the repercussions upon particular industries unfavourable, the enlarging of the market for any one commodity, produced under condition of increasing returns, generally has the net effect, as I have tried to show, of enlarging the market for other commodities" (p. 537).

28. This proposition, and Kaldor's variants on it, was challenged by R. E. Rowthorn, "What Remains of Kaldor's Law?" *The Economic Journal,* March 1975, pp. 10–19. In 1980 Verdoorn himself conceded that his "law" may have less validity than he believed previously: P. J. Verdoorn, "Verdoorn's Law in Retrospect," *The Economic Journal* 90, June 1980, p. 385. However, in a 1983 symposium on the subject it was defended by A. P. Thirlwall and others. See *Journal of Post-Keynesian Economics* 5, 1983, pp. 333–429.

29. From 1947–84 agricultural output per man-hour rose from an index of 16 to 139 (1977 = 100), increasing more than 8 times, while the index for the nonfarm business sector only doubled, from 52 to 104. *Economic Report of the President* (Washington, D.C.: U.S. Government Printing Office, 1986), pp. 302, 361. Agricultural productivity also rose faster than in the rest of the economy between 1929–47. U.S. agricultural technology is all available for use in developing countries, but only when it pays (i.e., when the size of the market justifies it).

30. N. Kaldor, *Causes of the Slow Rate of Economic Growth of the United Kingdom* (Cambridge: Cambridge University Press, 1966), pp. 36–38, and "Economic Growth and the Verdoorn Law—A Comment on Mr. Rowthorn's Article," *The Economic Journal* 85, December 1975, p. 892.

31. N. Kaldor, "The Irrelevance of Equlibrium Economics," *The Economic Journal* 82, 1972, pp. 1249–50.

32. Piero Sraffa, "The Laws of Returns under Competitive Conditions," *The Economic Journal,* 36, 1926, pp. 535–50. In a recent paper John Hicks agrees that Sraffa's article shows that increasing returns (to scale) are inconsistent with the maintenance of competition. He argues that this shows that the assumption of increasing returns is appropriate only to microeconomic study of the structure of industry while in macroeconomics it is usually necessary and relevant to assume constant returns to scale if neoclassical equilibrium theory is not to be jettisoned, which he himself is clearly reluctant to do. He is therefore critical of, or rather, puzzled by, Allyn Young's assumption of increasing returns to scale (*sic*) in his approach to growth theory, which Hicks seems to identify with the theory of long-run "steady-state equilibrium." John Hicks, "The Assumption of Constant Returns to Scale," in Tony Lawson, J. Gabriel Palma, and John Sender (eds.), *Kaldor's Political Economy* (London: Academic Press, 1989), pp. 9–18.

33. For this reason Young probably (and Currie certainly) would have been skeptical of the assertion, which has little empirical basis, that in the long run the terms of trade between industrial and agricultural products would move strongly in favor of the former—the so-called "Prébisch effect" endorsed, for example, by A. P. Thirlwall, "A General Model of Growth and Development on Kaldorian Lines," *Oxford Economic Papers* 38, 1986, p. 202.

34. See A. P. Thirwall, "A Plain Man's Guide to Kaldor's Growth Laws," *Journal of Post-Keynesian Economics* 5, 1983, pp. 345–58.

35. Kaldor, *Economics Without Equilibrium*, p. 70.

36. Ironically, in a recent major survey of "The Economics of Development" in *The Economic Journal* 99, September 1989, pp. 597–685, Nicholas Stern refers only once to Allyn Young on increasing returns (p. 619) in the context of Rosenstein-Rodan's arguments for a big push and balanced growth, which, he claims, has been developed and made rigorous in important recent papers by Kevin M. Murphy, Andrei Schiefer, and Robert Vishny, referred to in chapter 10 above. In their model, however, agriculture is subject to decreasing returns so that, in the absence of *exogenous* technical progress, its expansion requires more labor working at progressively lower marginal product and wages. Nevertheless, they claim that agriculture can be a "leading sector" that, by increasing the demand for industrial goods, can stimulate the development of industries operating with *increasing* returns to scale. Needless to say, this approach bears no resemblance to the concept of leading sectors developed by Currie, nor to increasing returns in the broad Youngian sense. Stern makes no reference to Currie's work in his long survey article.

37. Kaldor, *Causes of the Slow Rate of Economic Growth of the United Kingdom*, p. 17.

38. This is usually formulated in terms of a fixed exchange rate regime. Variations in the exchange rate can, however, alter import propensities and invoke price as well as income elasticities. The price-elasticity effect may be a far more powerful determinant of export growth, as emphasized recently by James Reidel, "The Demand for LDC Exports of Manufactures: Estimates from Hong Kong," *The Economic Journal* 98, March 1988, pp. 138–48.

39. Many years ago Karl L. Anderson, in a paper that closely followed Allyn Young's ideas, explained why the existence of "increasing returns (to scale)" industries does not undermine the classical vision of mutually beneficial free trade. He concluded: "It must be remembered that the increased production which results from a division of labour constitutes a larger market. When viewed in this perspective increasing returns are seen to be most rapidly encouraged, and diminishing returns most easily defeated, by the spreading of markets through the extension rather than the reduction in international trade." Karl L. Anderson, "Tariff Protection and Increasing Returns," in *Explorations in Economics: Notes and Essays Contributed in Honor of F. W. Taussig* (New York: Augustus M. Kelly, 1967; originally published in 1936), pp. 157–68.

40. Luigi L. Pasinetti, "Nicholas Kaldor: A Few Personal Notes," *Journal of Post-Keynesian Economics* 5, 1983, p. 338.

41. A. P. Thirlwall, "Introduction" to Symposium on Kaldor's Growth Laws, *Journal of Post-Keynesian Economics* 5, 1983, p. 342.

42. Especially in Currie, *Operación Colombia* (1961), and *Accelerating Development* (1966).

43. Kaldor, *Equilibrium Without Growth*, pp. 74–75.

44. Ibid., p. 69.

45. Paul M. Romer, "Capital Accumulation and the Theory of Long-Run Growth," in Robert J. Barro (ed.), *Modern Business Cycle Theory* (Cambridge, Mass.: Harvard University Press, 1989), pp. 51–117. Also see his "Increasing Returns and Long-Run Growth," *Journal of Political Economy* 94:5, 1986, pp. 1002–37, and "Growth Based on

Increasing Returns Due to Specialization," *American Economic Review* 77:2, 1987, pp. 56–67.

46. Currie, "Allyn Young and the Development of Growth Theory," pp. 56–57.

47. Currie, "The 'Multiplier' in Economic Literature," *Journal of Economic Studies* 10:3, 1983, pp. 42–48.

48. R. Solow, "Technical Change and the Aggregate Production Function," *The Review of Economics and Statistics* 39, 1957.

49. See Currie, "Sources of Growth," *World Development* 14:4, 1986, pp. 541–47.

13. Toward a General Theory of Reactivation and Growth, 1978–89

1. Currie, *Moneda en Colombia: Comportamiento y Control* (1983), 171 pages.

2. *Revista de Paneación y Desarrollo* 12:2, 1980. The following year Currie's 1981 article on Allyn Young, "Allyn Young and the Development of Growth Theory," was also translated for this review, 13:1–2, 1981.

3. A few weeks later, in December, Amézquita was killed in an automobile accident. Currie thereby lost a valued colleague, friend, and tennis partner. They had been due to play the day after Amézquita's death.

4. Published on September 1, 1979, in *El Espectador,* whose director Guillermo Cano, sent a congratulatory telegram that was read out at the dinner. Cano was sensationally assassinated by guerrillas on leaving his newspaper offices in December 1986.

5. W. J. Baumol, "Say's (at Least) Eight Laws, or What Say and James Mill May Really Have Meant," *Economica* 44, 1977, pp. 145–61.

6. During this visit to Europe he took the opportunity to visit the writer in Glasgow and from there to fulfil a long-held desire to visit the home of his ancestors in South Uist in the Outer Hebrides. He sailed out into the Atlantic from Oban and arrived at Lochboisdale many hours later. When he saw the barren rocks and scrublands he felt he understood why his ancestors had left. But he could also understand why they decided to settle in Nova Scotia: the barren land there was like home from home!

7. The one on economics and survival was published in a collection of Currie's papers as "La Economia Politica y la Sobrevivencia," in Currie, *Políticas de Crecimiento y Desarrollo* (1982), pp. 223–43. The paper on the theory of growth was published as "La Teoria de Crecimiento," in L. Currie, *La Política Urbana en un Marco Macroeconómico* (1983), pp. 33–46.

8. The paper he presented in Mexico was later published as "Housing as an Instrument of Macroeconomic Policy," *Habitat International* 7:5–6, 1983, pp. 165–71. One of the participants at the Mexico conference, Gerald Dix of Liverpool University, editor of *Third World Planning Review,* also persuaded Currie to write up his criticisms of Hans Schumaker's influential book, *Small is Beautiful.* This was published as "Is Small Beautiful?: A Retrospective Note," *Third World Planning Review* 4:3, 1982, pp. 281–83.

9. In 1989 the National Statistics Department (DANE) revised upward its estimate of population growth during this period, to 2.2 percent, which means that the *per capita* growth record was even worse than previously thought.

10. Currie, "Crecimiento con Estabilidad," in Consejo de Asesores Económicos del Presidente Betancur, *Desarrollo Autosostenido de Colombia* (1986), pp. 37–53.

11. Published later: L. Currie and A. Montenegro, *Crecimiento con Estabilidad: Un Modelo* (1984).

12. "Towards a General Theory of the Balance of Payments," reprinted as chapter 23 of R. E. Caves and H. G. Johnson (eds.), *Readings in International Economics* (Homewood, Illinois: Richard D. Irwin, for the American Economic Association, 1968). Currie refers to this terminology in *The IMF and Growth with Stability*, mimeo, June 1986, published in Spanish as "Los Consejos del Fondo Monetario Internacional: La Teoría en que se Fundamentan," in Currie, *Reactivación, Crecimiento y Estabilidad* (1988), pp. 127–52.

13. Currie had advised them to do this in 1974.

14. Currie explained these ideas in the following articles: "Housing as an Instrument of Macro-economic Policy," *Habitat International* 7:5–6, 1983, pp. 165–71 (with Spanish version in *Desarrollo y Sociedad* 11, May 1983); and "Nuevas Reflexiones sobre Oferta y Demanda de Vivienda," a paper presented at the 26th National Assembly of Affiliates of CAMACOL, Manizales, October 1983, published in Fabio Giraldo Isaza (ed.), *Controversia sobre el Plan de Vivienda sin Cuota Inicial* (1983), pp. 57–69.

15. Eleanora Cuellar, Luis Fernando de Guzman, and Luis Ricardo Paredes, Estudio sobre Agilización de Tramites para la Construcción de Vivienda (Bogota: ICAVI, June 1984).

16. Currie, "La Tasa de Cambio: Una Etapa Intermediaria," in *Desarrollo Autosostenido de Colombia* (1986), pp. 69–74.

17. Actually the famous Decree 444 of 1967 provides for a floating exchange rate but in practice the Central Bank has for many years, without strict legal basis, intervened to peg the rate. Currie further discussed these issues, and the case for a floating rate regime, in *The IMF and Growth With Stability*, mimeo, June 1986, especially pp. 29–37. Published in Spanish in L. Currie, *Reactivación, Crecimiento y Estabilidad* (Collected Papers, 1988), pp. 127–52.

18. José Antonio Ocampo, "En Defensa de la Continuidad del Regimen Cambiario," *Coyuntura Economica* (Bogotá: Fedesarrollo) 13:1, March 1983, pp. 198–214.

19. They included Alfonso Patiño Roselli, recently appointed a member of the Supreme Court, who had served on the President's Council of Economic Advisers.

20. The experience was reviewed by Currie in a contract for FONADE (of the National Planning Department) in "Lo Que se Puede Aprender de la Experiencia Colombiana de 1980–86," in Currie, *Evolución de las Metas de la Política Macroeconomica*, Contrato FNR 282 (November 1986), pp. 10–18.

21. Currie, *Moneda en Colombia: Comportamiento y Control* (1983), 171 pages (2d ed. 1988).

22. In terms of control Currie focused on demand deposits. Demand deposits were the controllable part of the money supply, via discretionary changes to reserves and reserve requirements. Cash was not directly controllable since banks were obliged to provide all that the public demanded when making cash withdrawals against demand deposits. For this reason the monetary base, or high-powered money, consisting of cash and bank reserves, was not directly controllable. Control was effected by operating on reserves and hence on demand deposits, the main element of the nation's money supply.

23. Currie, "The Treatment of Credit in Contemporary Monetary Theory," *Journal of Political Economy* 41:1, February 1933.

24. Currie, *Moneda en Colombia* p. 78 (English edition).

25. Ibid., p. 84.

26. Ibid., p. 79.

27. Currie, *The Nature of the Demand for Money: New Data and an Hypothesis,* mimeo, January 14, 1988, pp. 8–10. Currie presented the basic elements of this theory in "La Naturaleza de la Banca," *Banca y Finanzas,* no. 1, January–February 1988, pp. 23–30.

28. Currie's approach has some affinity in this respect to Case M. Sprenkle, "The Uselessness of Transactions Demand Models," *Journal of Finance* 24, December 1969, pp. 835–47.

29. Friedman himself has acknowledged that "the lack of availability of data has meant that much less empirical work has been done on the business demand for money than on the aggregate demand curve encompassing both ultimate wealth holders and business enterprises. As a result there are as yet only faint indications about the best variable to use" (in the demand-for-money function). M. Friedman, "A Theoretical Framework for Monetary Analysis," in Robert J. Gordon (ed.), *Milton Friedman's Monetary Framework: A Debate with His Critics* (Chicago: University of Chicago Press, 1974), p. 14.

30. Currie, *A New Hypothesis on the Demand for Money: The "Accounting" Motive and Bank Costs,* mimeo, June 2, 1988, p. 20.

31. In the same book as was cited by this referee, we are actually told that in 1977 the total costs of administering $247 billion of demand deposits was $25 billion, or almost 10 percent of the value of the money stock. See Boris Pesek, *Microeconomics of Money and Banking,* New York, New York University Press, 1987, p. 37n.

32. Currie, *Moneda en Colombia* (1988), p. 146.

33. Some of this material was published as "Decentralización: Algunos Interrogantes," in Currie, *Reactivación, Crecimiento y Estabilidad* (1988) pp. 177–94.

34. *El Espectador,* February 23, 1988.

35. Currie, *Report on Some Aspects of Public Administration in Colombia,* mimeo, for the World Bank, July 1987. This was subsequently published by the comptroller-general, Bogotá, 1988.

36. Currie, "Economic Advising in Colombia," in Joseph Pechman (ed.), *The Role of the Economist in Government: An International Perspective* (New York: Harvester Wheatsheaf, 1989), pp. 213–27.

37. Contract UNCHS-87-0097. Currie's four reports were: "Housing as an Instrument of Macro Policy," November 19, 1987, 31 pages; "The Mobilization of Savings for Housing under Conditions of Inflation," November 9, 1987, 29 pages; "Housing Expenditures: Is There a Multiplier Effect?" January 20, 1988, 17 pages; and "The National Accounts of Colombia and Housing," March 12, 1988, 17 pages.

38. Lauchlin Currie and Luis Eduardo Rosas, *Sistema Colombiano de Ahorro y Vivienda: Memorias de los 15 anos, 1972–1987* (Bogotá: ICAVI, 1988). An earlier version was published in English and Spanish: *UPAC: A Theory Converted into Successful Reality* (Bogotá: ICAVI, 1986).

39. *Carta de Ahorro y Vivienda* 1:4, December 1987.

40. The main ideas have been published as "Productividad, Crecimiento Economico y Distribucion: Relaciones Conceptuales," *Desarrollo y Sociedad* (Bogotá: CEDE) 23, March 1989, pp. 13–23.

41. Thus, in contrast to some models of the business cycle, the real interest rate tends to move pro-cyclically, unless counteracted by pro-cyclical monetary policies that expand the money supply when interest rates are tending to rise, and vice versa.

42. In a letter to the author, November 24, 1989, Currie referred to criticisms made of Young—and of himself—by recent writers, that "increasing returns" theory was presented verbally rather than as a formalized model or series of equations: "If sufficient ingenuity were used, this perhaps could be done . . . but the process would be horribly complex and, for policy formulation purposes, more would be lost than gained. To reject an explanation because it is not presented in the form of algebraic equations is surely unreasonable."

43. A notable example, in fact, is a recent book by one of Currie's ablest students at Simon Fraser University some years ago, Martin Baily, now at the Brookings Institution. See Martin Neil Baily and Alok K. Chakrabarti, *Innovation and the Productivity Crisis* (Washington, D.C.: Brookings Institution, 1988).

44. The forces of competition will tend to ensure that cost reductions are passed on to consumers in the form of lower prices, and not retained for long by the innovators and others who are the beneficiaries of growth in the first instance. Lower prices raise real wages unless there is an elastic labor supply which forces a corresponding decline in money wages.

45. Britain recorded its highest increase ever in labor productivity in 1980–81 when its GDP was declining. This was because employment was declining much faster than GDP. However, it would surely be absurd to attribute the cause of the fall of GDP to the decline in labor inputs. Yet that would be the logic of conventional growth accounting exercises.

46. Paul M. Romer, "Increasing Returns and Long-Run Growth," *Journal of Political Economy* 94:5, 1986, pp. 1002–37, and "Growth Based on Increasing Returns Due to Specialization," *American Economic Review* 77:2, 1987, pp. 56–67; Robert E. Lucas, "On the Mechanics of Economic Development," *Journal of Monetary Economics* 22, 1988, pp. 3–42; and M. FG. Scott, *A New View of Economic Growth* (Oxford: Oxford University Press, 1989). Another paper by Romer (1989), in which he develops a so-called Marshall-Young-Romer theory of growth, was discussed in chapter 12 above.

47. Allyn Young, "Increasing Returns and Economic Progress," *Economic Journal*, 1928, p. 535, and LSE Lecture XV: "We need a theory of an equilibrium rate of progress. Probably the optimum rate of progress which will keep the supply curve close up to the demand curve."

48. Currie elaborates on these distinctions in a recent paper, *Growth: Classical and Neo-classical Theories* (Bogotá: ICAVI), mimeo, January 2, 1990, 39 pages.

14. Epilogue

1. "A Leading Sector Strategy as a Complement to Government Fiscal, Monetary and Exchange Policies," Conference on Planning and Short-term Macroeconomic Policy in Latin America; jointly sponsored by the UN Latin American Institute for Economic and Social Planning (UN-ILPES), the Panamanian ministry of planning, and the National Bureau of Economic Research (NBER), Isla Contadora, Panama, November 1975.

2. Currie, "Economic Advising in Colombia," (1989).

3. This coincided with a new phase of violence in Colombia and a massive crackdown by President Barco on the ruthless drug barons after the sensational killing at a big political rally in Bogotá of the popular Liberal leader Luis Carlos Galan on August 18. A few days later Currie was wakened before dawn by the explosion of a bomb in his neighborhood. He was glad that his daughter had left the previous week for a year at the London School of Economics, on study leave from the Banco de la República where she works.

Bibliography of Currie's Writings

1931

Bank Assets and Banking Theory, Ph.D. thesis, Harvard University, 1931.

Review of H. L. Reed, *Federal Reserve Policy, 1921–30,* in *American Economic Review* 21, March 1931, pp. 162–64. An "Exchange" with Reed appeared in *American Economic Review* 21, September 1931, pp. 501–2.

"The Decline of the Commercial Loan," *Quarterly Journal of Economics* 45, August 1931, pp. 698–709.

1932

"Member Bank Indebtedness and Net Demand Deposits in the Federal Reserve System," *Quarterly Journal of Economics* 46, May 1932, pp. 509–25.

1933

"The Treatment of Credit in Contemporary Monetary Theory," *Journal of Political Economy* 41:1, February 1933, pp. 58–79.

"Member Bank Reserves and Bank Debits," *Quarterly Journal of Economics* 47, February 1933, pp. 349–56.

"Money, Gold, and Incomes in the United States, 1921–32," *Quarterly Journal of Economics* 48, November 1933, pp. 77–95.

1934

"A Note on Income Velocities," *Quarterly Journal of Economics* 48, February 1934, pp. 353–54.

"The Failure of Monetary Policy to Prevent the Depression of 1929–32," *Journal of Political Economy* 42:2, April 1934, pp. 145–77. Reprinted in Earl Hamilton, Harry G. Johnson, and Albert Rees (eds.), *Landmarks in Political Economy* (Chicago: Chicago University Press, 1962), pp. 168–98.

The Supply and Control of Money in the United States (Cambridge, Mass.: Harvard University Press, 1934, 1935). Reprinted, with foreword by Karl Brunner (New York: Russell and Russell, 1968), pp. xliv, 231.

Proposed Revision of the Monetary System of the United States, memorandum submitted to the secretary of the U.S. Treasury, Henry J. Morgenthau, Jr., September 1934, reprinted in *The Supply and Control of Money* (1968), pp. 195–226.

Desirable Changes in the Administration of the Federal Reserve System, memorandum to Marriner Eccles, November 3, 1934, 3 pages. Deposited with the Eccles Papers, Marriott Library, University of Utah.

(With Martin Krost) *Report on Deposit Insurance,* memorandum to Chairman Eccles, Federal Reserve Board (FRB) Washington, D.C., December (?) 1934, 52 pages.

"Confidence," memorandum to Chairman Eccles, FRB, Washington, December 1934, 6 pages.

1935

Drafts of the 1935 Banking Act, FRB, Washington

Comments on Pump Priming, memorandum to Chairman Eccles, FRB, Washington, February 1935, 15 pages.

A Suggested Works Program, memorandum to Chairman Eccles, FRB, Washington, March 6, 1935, 11 pages.

The Relations of Government to Monetary Control, memorandum to Chairman Eccles, FRB, Washington, March 29, 1935, 20 pages.

Recovery, memorandum to Chairman Eccles, FRB, Washington, April 13, 1935, 10 pages.

"A Reply to Dr. B. M. Anderson, Jr.," *Quarterly Journal of Economics* 49, August 1935, pp. 694–704.

(With Martin Krost) *Federal Income-Increasing Expenditures, 1932–35,* memorandum to Chairman Eccles, late 1935, published with an introduction by Byrd L. Jones in *History of Political Economy* 10:4, 1978, pp. 514–48.

Recommendations Relative to Research in Connection with the Formulation of Monetary Policy, memorandum to Chairman Eccles, FRB, Washington, October 17, 1935, 16 pages.

1936

"Domestic Stability and the Mechanism of Trade Adjustments to International Capital Mobility," in E. H. Phelps-Brown (ed.), *Explorations in Economics: Notes and Essays Contributed in Honor of F. W. Taussig* (New York: McGraw-Hill, 1936), pp. 46–56. Reprinted by Augustus M. Kelly (New York, 1967), in *Reprints of Economic Classics* series.

Some Monetary Aspects of the Excess Reserves Problem, memorandum to Chairman Eccles, FRB, Washington, May, 18, 1936, 7 pages.

Report on the Large Deposit Study, FRB, Washington, May 29, 1936, 62 pages.

Public Spending as a Means to Recovery, memorandum to Chairman Eccles, FRB, Washington, August 1936, 27 pages.

Keynes' General Theory of Employment, Interest, and Money, memorandum to the FRB, Washington, October 1936, 14 pages.

The Trend of Bank Assets in the Next Few Years, memorandum to Chairman Eccles, FRB, Washington, November 30, 1936, 20 pages.

Review of J. W. Angell, *The Behavior of Money: Exploratory Studies,* in *American Economic Review,* December 1936.

1937

The Practical Importance of the Theoretical Distinction Between Time and Demand Deposits, memorandum to Chairman Eccles, FRB, Washington, January 25, 1937.

Would a Further Expansion of Money Be Injurious? memorandum to Chairman Eccles, FRB, Washington, January 25, 1937, 12 pages.

Analysis of Mr. Altmeyer's Statement on the Old-Age Reserve, memorandum to Chairman Eccles, FRB, Washington, February 25, 1937.

"Stabilization of Purchasing Power Through the Use of Public Credit," *American Economic Review* 27, 1937, pp. 233–34.

An Appraisal of Current Prospects and a Tentative Program, memorandum to Chairman Eccles, FRB, Washington, May 18, 1937.

A Tentative Program to Meet the Business Recession, memorandum to Chairman Eccles, FRB, Washington, October 13, 1937, 8 pages.

The Decline in the Federal Contribution to the Growth in Community Expenditures, memorandum to Chairman Eccles, FRB, Washington, October 19, 1937, 4 pages.

The Causes of the Recession, memorandum to President Roosevelt, Washington, November 8, 1937, 6 pages.

1938

"Some Theoretical and Practical Implications of J. M. Keynes' *General Theory,*" in National Industrial Conference Board, *The Economic Doctrines of J. M. Keynes* (New York, 1938), pp. 15–27.

Report of the Closed Banks Study, FRB, Washington, D.C., February 1938.

Behavior of Deposits, paper presented to the Chicago Forum of the American Institute of Bankers, February 24, 1938, 16 pages.

The Causes of the Recession of 1937, memorandum to Chairman Eccles, FRB, Washington, April 1, 1938. Reprinted, with introduction by Byrd L. Jones, in *History of Political Economy* 12:3, 1980, pp. 303–35.

Comments on a Mandate, memorandum to Chairman Eccles, FRB, Washington, April 5, 1938, 9 pages.

Some Problems in Connection with a Compensatory Fiscal Policy, paper presented to University of Chicago seminar, mimeo, May 1938.

Some Aspects of Business and Banking Developments in 1936 and 1937, paper presented to the Illinois Banking Association, Springfield, Illinois, mimeo, May 23, 1938, 17 pages.

"The Economic Distribution of Demand Deposits," *Journal of the American Statistical Association* 33, June 1938, pp. 319–26.

The 100 Percent Reserve Plan, memorandum to Chairman Eccles, FRB, Washington, August 12, 1938, 24 pages.

United States Railroad Equipment Authority, memorandum to Chairman Eccles, FRB, Washington, December 2, 1938.

1939

Testimony, in U.S. Congress, Temporary National Economic Committee, *Investigation of Concentration of Economic Power,* Hearings, part 9, 76th Congress, 1st Session, 1939, pp. 3494–559.

Draft of the Works Financing Bill, U.S. Congress, Washington, July 1939.

RFC and the Budget, memoranda to President Roosevelt, November 15, December 11, 1939.

1940

Memorandum on Full Employment, memorandum to President Roosevelt, Official File 396, Washington, March 18, 1940, 18 pages.

Memorandum on Old-Age Pensions, memorandum to President Roosevelt, Washington, April 20, 1940.

Memorandum on Fiscal Policy, memorandum to President Roosevelt, Washington, June 4, 1940.

Memorandum on New Tax Legislation, memorandum to President Roosevelt, Washington, November 13, 1940.

Expansion Possibilities of Our System, memorandum to President Roosevelt, Washington, December 2, 1940.

1941

Notes on Conference with Chou En-lai at British Ambassador's Home, Chungking, February 14, 1941, 3 pages.

The Economic Problem, report to Generalissimo Chiang Kai-shek, Chungking, February 24, 1941, 12 pages.

Mission to China, January–February 1941, report to President Roosevelt, Washington, March 15, 1941, 34 pages.

Notes on Interviews with Chiang Kai-shek and Chou En-lai, memorandum to President Roosevelt, Washington, March 15, 1941, 44 pages.

Tax Program, memorandum to President Roosevelt, Washington, April 4, 1941.

Chinese Aircraft Requirements, Joint Board Paper 355, Washington, May 10, 1941.

1942

Mission to China, July–August 1942, report to President Roosevelt, Washington, August 24, 1942.

1943

Some Reflections on American Chinese Policy, memorandum to President Roosevelt, Washington, May 18, 1943, 5 pages.
Post-War Reparations; Discussion, reports of the Council of Foreign Relations, EA 39, 1943, p. 8.

1944

Testimony, Sub-Committee on Foreign Trade and Shipping, House Committee on Post-War Planning, Washington, September 28, 1944, 23 pages.

1945

The Foreign Economic Administration, report to President Roosevelt, Washington, January 17, 1945, 12 pages.
"Tumbling the Nazi Financial Redoubt," *New York Times,* April 29, 1945.
World Commerce: Free or Controlled? NBC radio discussion with Neil Jacoby and Nathaniel Pfeffer, pamphlet, University of Chicago, September 9, 1945.

1950

The Basis of a Development Program for Colombia, report of mission directed by Lauchlin Currie, Washington, International Bank for Reconstruction and Development, 1950, 615 pages (published in English and Spanish). Reprinted by the Departamento Nacional de Planeación, Bogotá, 1988.
"Some Prerequisites for Success in the Point Four Program," *Annals of the American Academy of Political and Social Sciences* 270, July 1950, pp. 102–9.

1951

Informe Final del Comité de Desarrollo Económico (Final Report of the Economic Development Committee), Bogotá, Banco de la República, 1951, 370 pages. Reprinted by the Departamento Nacional de Planeación, Bogotá, 1988.

1952

Reorganización de la Rama Ejecutiva del Gobierno de Colombia (Reorganization of the Executive Branch of the Colombian Government), report of the public administration mission directed by Lauchlin Currie, Bogotá, Banco de la República, 1952, 448 pages. Reprinted by the National Planning Department, Bogotá, 1988.

Programa Económico y Adminstrativo para el Departamento de Caldas, report of a mission directed by Lauchlin Currie, (Manizales: Imprenta Departamental, October 1952), 427 pages.

1953

Plan para Bogatá (Bogotá: Imprenta Municipal, 1953), 184 pages.

1954

Plan de Fomento para el Departamento del Atlántico (Barranquilla: Imprenta Departamental, 1954), 112 pages.

1959

Plan para la Reorganización del Ministerio de Fomento (Bogotá: Minsterio de Fomento), mimeo, 57 pages.

1960

Programa de Desarrollo Económico del Valle del Magdalena y Norte de Colombia, report of a mission directed by Lauchlin Currie (Bogotá: Impreso Arco, 1960), 379 pages.

Estudio sobre la Conexión del Ferrocarril del Atlántico con Barranquilla (Study on the Connection of the Atlantic Railroad with Barranquilla), Separata de la Memoria del Ministro de Obras Públicas, Virgilio Barco Vargas, a la Legislatura Ordinaria (Bogotá, 1960), 74 pages.

Las Posibilidades de Desecación y Aprovechamiento Económico de 135,000 Hectareas Adyacentes a la Ciénega Grande de Santa Marta (Possibilities of Draining and Economic Exploitation of 135,000 Hectares of the Ciénaga Grande of Santa Marta), Ministerio de Obras Públicas (Bogotá, 1960).

1961

Operación Colombia: Un Programa Nacional de Desarrollo Económico y Social (Barranquilla: Cámara Colombiana de la Construcción, 1961), 84 pages. Also published in *La Nueva Economia* 1:4, Bogotá, August 1961.

Algunas Consideraciones sobre la Industria de la Carne en Colombia (Some Considerations on the Meat Industry in Colombia; Bogotá: Ferrocarriles Nacionales de Colombia, 1961), 75 pages.

Informe sobre un Estudio Económico del Departamento del Meta (Bogotá: Departamento Administrativo de Planificación y Departamento del Meta, August, 1961), 272 pages.

1962

Estudio Agro-Económico de Recuperacion de Tierras en la Region del Río Zulia (Bogotá; Caja Agraria, February 1962), 81 pages.
La Industria Cafetera en la Agricultura Colombiana (Bogotá: Banco Cafetero, 1962), pp. xvi, 150.
Estudio Preliminar Agro-Económico de los Playones de Plato y Pinto (Bogotá: Fundación para el Progreso de Colombia, 1962), 62 pages.
Estudio AgroEconómico Preliminar del Valle Aluvial del Río Sinú (Bogotá: Fundación para el Progreso de Colombia, August 1962), pp. vi, 195.
Informe sobre un Estudio Económico del Departamento del Norte de Santader (Bogotá: Ministerio de Fomento, August 1962), 86 pages.
(With Hugo Belalcázar) *Proyecciones de la Demanda de Construcciones y Materiales de Construcción en Colombia para 1962–70* (Bogotá: CAMACOL, 1962), 174 pages.

1963

Ensayos sobre Planeación (A Collection of Essays on Planning; Bogotá: Ediciones Tercer Mundo, 1963), 222 pages. (Second edition, 1965).
Estudio sobre el Algodón (A Study of Cotton; Bogotá: Federación de Algodoneros, 1963), 174 pages.
"El Urbanismo y sus Perspectivas," in Plinio Mendoza Neira (ed.), *Colombia en Cifras* (Bogotá: Aedita Editores, 1963), pp. 523–28.

1964

Informe sobre la Escuela para Graduados (Report on the Graduate School), report for the University of the Andes, Bogotá, mimeo, April 5, 1964, 18 pages.

1965

El Manejo de Cuencas en Colombia (The Management of Watersheds in Colombia; Bogotá, Ediciones Tercer Mundo, 1965), 84 pages.
Un Plan Socio-Económico para Atlántico (Bogotá: Imprenta Nacional, 1965), 283 pages.
Una Política Urbana para los Países en Desarrollo (An Urban Policy for Developing Countries; Bogotá: Ediciones Tercer Mundo, 1965), 188 pages.
Enseñanza de la Economía en Colombia (The Teaching of Economics in Colombia; Bogotá: Ediciones Tercer Mundo, 1965), 61 pages.

1966

Accelerating Development: The Necessity and the Means (New York: McGraw-Hill, 1966), pp. ix, 255.
Algunas Barricadas en la Via del Desarrollo (Bogotá: Ediciones Tercer Mundo, 1966), 71 pages.

1967

"Economics and Population," *Population Bulletin* 23:2, April 1967, pp. 25–38.
"Planning in a Free Enterprise Economy," in Y. Larsson, P. de Wolff, and L. Currie, *Governmental Planning and Political Economy*, the Royer Lectures (Berkeley: University of California Press, 1967), pp. 53–88.
Obstacles to Development (East Lansing: Michigan University Press, 1967), 139 pages.
Enseñanza Universitaria en los Estudios Sociales (The University Teaching of Social Studies; Bogotá: Ediciones Tercer Mundo, 1967), 61 pages.
Notes on Material Prepared by David Wall and Harold Dunkerley on Coffee in Colombia, report for the Food and Agricultural Organization, Rome, July 29, 1967, 19 pages.

1968

"Marketing Organization of Underdeveloped Countries," in R. Moyer and S. Hollander (eds.), *Markets and Marketing in Developing Economies* (Homewood, Ill.: Richard D. Irwin, 1968), pp. 117–29.
The Supply and Control of Money in the United States (New York: Russell and Russell, 1968), reissue of 1934 book, with foreword by Karl Brunner.

1969

Alternativas para el Desarrollo Urbano de Bogotá, study directed by Lauchlin Currie (Bogotá: Centro de Investigaciones para el Desarrollo [CID], National University of Colombia, 1969), pp. xi, 231.
Review of Gunnar Myrdal's *Asian Drama*, in *Journal of Economic Issues* 3:2, June 1969, pp. 166–76.

1971

"The Exchange Constraint on Development: A Partial Solution to the Problem," *The Economic Journal*, 81. December 1971, pp. 886–903. Spanish version published as

"La Limitación de las Divisas al Desarrollo: Una Solución Parcial al Problema," *Revista de Planeación y Desarrollo* 3:3, 1971, pp. 3–24.
"Social Development and Economic Progress," J. G. Van Putten (ed.), *Local Government as Promoter of Economic and Social Development* (The Hague: International Union of Local Authorities, 1971), pp. 19–32.

1972

"The Keynesian Revolution and Its Pioneers: Discussion," *American Economic Review* 62, Papers and Proceedings, May 1972, pp. 139–41.
Guidelines for a New Strategy (Guias para una Nueva Estrategia; Bogotá: Departamento Nacional de Planeación, 1972), 159 pages. (Also known as *The Plan of the Four Strategies.*)
"Comentarios sobre las Criticas del Profesor Ranis al Plan de Desarrollo de Colombia"; also "Comentarios sobre el Trabajo de Miguel Urrutia," and "Comentarios sobre el Articulo del Doctor Guillermo Perry," in Miguel Urrutia (ed.), *Controversia sobre el Plan de Desarrollo* (Bogotá: CORP, 1972), pp. 71–98, 143–56, 243–52.
"El Papel de la Demanda en la Teoría del Desarrollo" (The Role of Demand in Development Theory), *Revista de Planeación y Desarrollo* 4:3, July–December 1972, pp. 63–70.

1973

"A Reply to Professor Ranis," *The Economic Journal* 83, March 1973, pp. 203–10.
What Colombia (and Other Developing Countries) May Learn from Singapore (New York: United Nations), ESA/HBP/AC 9/43, June 1973, 14 pages.
Urbanization Trends and Policies (New York: United Nations), ESA/HPB/AC 9/1, June 1973, 12 pages.
"La Política Monetaria y el Nivel de Precios," (Monetary Policy and the Price Level), *Revista de Planeación y Desarrollo* 5:2, April–June 1973, pp. 20–45.
Review of R. A. Solo and E. M. Rogers (eds.), *Inducing Technological Change for Economic Growth and Development,* in *The Economic Journal* 83, September 1973, pp. 965–67.

1974

"The Leading Sector Model of Growth in Developing Countries," *Journal of Economic Studies,* N.S. 1:1, May 1974, pp. 1–16.
"El Plan en Marcha," in Lauchlin Currie (ed.), *El Plan de Desarrollo Colombiano en Marcha* (Bogotá: Ediciones Tercer Mundo for the Departamento Nacional de Planeación, 1974), pp. 253–71.
Savings, Monetary Correction and Building: Essays on Interrelationships in Colombia, (Bogotá: National Planning Department, 1974), Spanish version: *Ahorro, Cor-*

rección Monetaria y Construcción (Bogotá: University of the Andes Press, 1974), 133 pages.

Ciudades Dentro de la Ciudad: La Política Urbana y el Plan de Desarrollo en Colombia (Cities-within-the-City; Bogotá: Departamento Nacional de Planeación, 1974), 121 pages.

"The Colombian Plan 1971–74: A Test of the Leading Sector Strategy," *World Development* 2:10–12, October–December 1974, pp. 69–72.

1975

"Wants, Needs, Well-being and Economic Growth," *Journal of Economic Studies,* 2:1, May 1975, pp. 47–59.

"The Interrelation of Urban and National Economic Planning," *Urban Studies* 12, 1975, pp. 37–46.

Criteria for Multinational Financial Assistance in Urban Development, report to United Nations Center for Housing Building and Planning, New York, 1975, 50 pages.

1976

Taming the Megalopolis: A Design for Urban Growth (Oxford: Pergamon Press, 1976), pp. ix, 127. Published in Spanish with a new introduction as *Urbanización y Desarrollo: Un Diseño para el Crecimiento Metropolitano* (Bogotá: CAMACOL, 1988), 249 pages.

"Controlling Land Use: The Key to Urbanization," *Ekistics* 244, March 1974, pp. 1937–43.

"Planeación Metropolitana: Moscu y Bogotá," *Revista de Planeación y Desarrollo* 8:3, September–December 1976, pp. 105–12.

"Indexación: Selectiva o General?" in James Hanson (ed.), *La Corrección Monetaria: Cuatro Estudios* (Santiago de Chile: United Nations, ILPES, 1976), pp. 171–83.

"A Reply to Professor Hanson," *Journal of Economic Studies,* N.S. 3:2, November 1976, pp. 164–69.

Review of Mancur Olson and Hans Landsberg (eds.), *The No-Growth Society,* in *Journal of Economic Studies,* 3:2, November 1976, pp. 83–86.

1977

"Urban Policy in the Context of Development," *Proceedings,* 5th Pacific Regional Science Conference, Vancouver, August 1977, pp. 287–99.

1978

"Factors Conditioning the International Financing of Scientific and Technical Research for Developing Countries," in Negoslav Ostojic (ed.), *The International Fi-*

nance of Economic Development (Belgrade: Republic of Serbia Government Press, 1978), pp. 317–28.

"The Objectives of Development," *World Development* 6:1, 1978, pp. 1–10.

"Comments and Observations" (on New Deal fiscal policy and the publication of two of Currie's Federal Reserve Board memoranda from the 1930s), *History of Political Economy* 10:4, Winter 1978, pp. 507–48.

1979

"Is There an Urban Bias? Critique of Michael Lipton's *Why Poor People Stay Poor,*" *Journal of Economic Studies,* N.S. 6:1, May 1979, pp. 86–105.

1980

"For Whom Should Housing Be Built?" *Habitat International* 4:3, 1980, pp. 291–97.

"The Role of Financing of the Transfer of Technology," paper presented to the Second World Scientific Banking Meeting, Dubrovnic, May 1980, mimeo, 12 pages.

"Causes of the Recession" (publication of 1938 paper, with foreword by Byrd L. Jones), *History of Political Economy* 12:3, 1980, pp. 303–35.

1981

"Allyn Young and the Development of Growth Theory," *Journal of Economic Studies* 8:1, 1981, pp. 52–60, Spanish version published in *Revista de Planeación y Desarrollo* 12:1–2, 1981.

Recursos para el Futuro: Colombia 1950–2000 (Bogotá, Banco Popular for the Instituto de Estudios Colombianos, 1981), 358 pages. (English version is on file in Resources for the Future, Inc., Washington, D.C.)

The Role of Economic Advisers in Developing Countries (Westport, Conn.: Greenwood Press, 1981, pp. xiv, 270. Spanish version: *Evaluación de la Asesoria Economica a los Países en Desarrollo* (Bogotá: Fondo Editorial CEREC, 1984).

Economics and Survival, convocation address, Simon Fraser University, Canada, mimeo, June 1981. Published in Spanish as "La Economia Politica y la Sobrevivencia," in L. Currie, *Politicas de Crecimiento y Desarrollo* (1982), pp. 223–43.

1982

Politicas de Crecimiento y Desarrollo (Collected Papers; Bogotá: Banco de la República, 1982), 243 pages.

"The Interplay of Specialization and Generalization in Economics." *Revista Javeriana* 3:3, December 1982, pp. 19–26.

"Is Small Beautiful?: A Retrospective Note," *Third World Planning Review* 4:3, August 1982, pp. 281–83.

1983

"The 'Multiplier' in Economic Literature," *Journal of Economic Studies* 10:3, 1983, pp. 42–48.

La Política Urbana en un Marco Macroeconómico (Collected Papers; Bogotá: Banco Central Hipotecario, 1983), 226 pages.

"Housing as an Instrument of Macroeconomic Policy," *Habitat International* 7:5–6, 1983, pp. 165–71. Spanish version published in *Desarrollo y Sociedad* 11 (Bogotá: CEDE, May 1983).

"La Unidad de Poder Adquisitivo Constante: Una Breve Historia de su Nacimiento" (The Unit of Constant Purchasing Power: A Brief History of Its Inception), *Desarrollo y Sociedad* 6, (Bogotá: CEDE, 1983), pp. 5–12.

"Neuvas Reflexiones sobre Oferta y Demanda de Vivienda" (New Thoughts on the Supply and Demand for Housing), in Fabio Giraldo Isaza (ed.), *Controversia sobre el Plan de Vivienda sin Cuota Inicial* (Bogotá: CAMACOL, 1983), pp. 57–69.

Moneda en Colombia: Comportamiento y Control (Money in Colombia: Behavior and Control; Bogotá: Fondo Cultural Cafetero, 1983), 17 pages. (Second edition published in 1988, 210 pages.)

1984

(With Alvaro Montenegro) *Crecimiento con Estabilidad: Un Modelo* (Bogotá: Fundación Simon Bolivar, 1984), 57 pages.

Proyecto Ciudadela Comunitaria del CAN, Study directed by Lauchlin Currie (Bogotá: FONADE-ICAVI, 1984).

1985

"Aspectos Macroeconomicos de la Politica Urbana," in Cristina de la Torre (ed.), *Modelos Economicos de Desarrollo Colombiano* (Bogotá: Editoriales Nikos y La Oveja Negra, 1985), pp. 103–20.

1986

"Sources of Growth, *World Development* 14:4, 1986, pp. 541–47.

"Crecimiento con Estabilidad" (Growth with Stability), and "La Tasa de Cambio: Una Etapa Intermediaria" (The Exchange Rate: An Intermediate Step), in Consejo de Asesores Economicos del Presidente Betancur, *Desarrollo Autosostenido de Colombia* (Bogotá: Presidencia de la República, 1986), pp. 37–53, 69–74.

The IMF and Growth with Stability, report for the Comision de Gastos, Bogotá, mimeo, June 1986, 55 pages. Published in Spanish as "Los Consejos del Fondo Monetario Internacional," in L. Currie, *Reactivación, Crecimiento y Estabilidad* (1988), pp. 127–52.

(With Luis Eduardo Rosas) *UPAC: A Theory Converted into Successful Reality* (Bogotá: Instituto Colombiano de Ahorro y Vivienda [ICAVI], 1986), 40 pages. Also published in Spanish.

Evolución de las Metas de la Política Macroeconómica, Contrato FNR 282, FONADE-CEDE (Bogotá: CEDE, November 1986), 156 pages.

"La Evolución de una Teoria General de Reactivación y Crecimiento" (Evolution of a General Theory of Reactivation and Growth), *Revista de Planeación y Desarrollo* 18:3–4, 1986, pp. 107–17.

1987

Some Aspects of Public Administration in Colombia, report commissioned by World Bank, Washington, mimeo, July 16, 1987, 170 pages.

The Mobilization of Savings for Housing, report for UN Habitat, Nairobi, Contract UNCHS-87-0097, mimeo, November 9, 1987, 29 pages.

Housing as an Instrument of Macroeconomic Policy, report for UN Habitat, Nairobi, mimeo, November 29, 1987, 31 pages.

1988

Housing Expenditures: Is There a Multiplier Effect? Report for UN Habitat, Nairobi, mimeo, January 20, 1988, 17 pages.

(Ed., with Luis Eduardo Rosas) *Sistema Colombiana de Ahorro y Vivienda: Memorias de los 15 Anos, 1972–1987* (Bogotá: ICAVI, 1988), 60 pages.

"La Naturaleza de la Banca" (The Nature of Banking), *Banca y Finanzas* (Bogotá) no. 1, January–February 1988, pp. 23–30.

The Nature of the Demand for Money: New Data and an Hypothesis (Bogotá: ICAVI), mimeo, January 14, 1988, 28 pages.

The National Accounts of Colombia and Housing, report for UN Habitat, Nairobi, mimeo, March 12, 1988, 17 pages.

"Quien Es lo Responsable de la Política Económica?" *Revista Javeriana* 56:543, April 1988, pp. 167–72.

A New Hypothesis on the Demand for Money: The "Accounting" Motive and Bank Costs, mimeo, June 2, 1988, 20 pages.

Reactivación, Crecimiento y Estabilidad (Collected Papers; Bogotá: Legis Editorial, 1988), 218 pages.

Administración Pública en Colombia (Bogotá: Contraloria General de la República, 1988), 161 pages.

1989

"Productividad, Crecimiento Económico y Distribución: Relaciones Conceptuales," *Desarrollo y Sociedad* 23, March 1989, pp. 13–23.

"Economic Advising in Colombia," in Joseph Pechman (ed.), *The Role of the Economist in Government: An International Perspective* (New York: Harvester Wheatsheaf, 1989), pp. 213–27.

1990

Growth: Classical and Neo-classical Theories (Bogotá: ICAVI), mimeo, January 2, 1990, 39 pages.

"Recollections of Allyn Young," preface to R. J. Sandilands (ed.), *Nicholas Kaldor's Notes on Allyn Young's LSE Lectures, 1927–29*, special issue of *Journal of Economic Studies* 17, 1990.

Index

About the Author

Roger Sandilands is Senior Lecturer in Economics at the University of Strathclyde, Glasgow, Scotland. He has been associated with Lauchlin Currie since 1967, when he was a graduate student in Canada. A specialist in international economics, Professor Sandilands has taught at universities in Britain, Canada, Sweden, Singapore, Colombia, and Peru. He is the author of numerous journal articles, a monograph on agriculture in Colombia (1974), and *Monetary Correction and Housing Finance in Colombia, Brazil, and Chile* (1980).

Library of Congress Cataloging-in-Publication Data

Sandilands, Roger J. (Roger James), 1945–

The life and political economy of Lauchlin Currie : New Dealer, presidential adviser, and development economist / Roger Sandilands.

p. cm.

"Bibliography of Currie's writings": p.

ISBN 0-8223-1030-9

1. Currie, Lauchlin Bernard. 2. Economists—United States—Biography. 3. United States—Economic policy—1933–45. 4. Colombia—Economic policy. 5. Economic development. I. Title.

HB119.C87S26 1990

338.9730092—dc20

[B] 89-71472

CIP